THE VIEW FROM LANGUAGE

THE VIEW FROM
LANGUAGE

SELECTED ESSAYS
1948–1974

by

C. F. HOCKETT

Goldwin Smith Professor of Linguistics and Anthropology
Cornell University

THE UNIVERSITY OF GEORGIA PRESS
ATHENS

Library of Congress Catalog Card Number: 75–3818
International Standard Book Number: 0–8203–0381–X

The University of Georgia Press, Athens 30602

Set in 10 on 12 pt. Mergenthaler Times Roman type
Printed in the United States of America

FOR
WILLIAM F. McDONALD
IN DEEPEST GRATITUDE

CONTENTS

PREFACE

These essays of an anthropological linguist have in common that none of them is a technical treatment of a technical linguistic topic. Instead, they look out from language at other things, or back at language in the light of other things.

The order in which the essays appear here is, as far as feasible, that in which they were written. Those which have been published before are reprinted unchanged except for minor emendations of style or wording; I have not updated the content. In some places, to be sure, it has been necessary to add a comment or correction from the perspective of the 1970s. Any such passage is preceded by the mark "∇" and is enclosed in brackets.

The introductory passage—with no "∇"—directly below the title of each essay includes relevant information about the circumstances under which the piece was written. Mention in these prefatory passages (not in the essays proper) of other writings of mine refer the reader to a complete bibliographical listing at the end of the volume. These scattered bits of connective tissue serve to tie the essays together, and thus obviate the need for any further remarks here.

C. F. Hockett

THE VIEW FROM LANGUAGE

H1. BIOPHYSICS, LINGUISTICS, AND THE UNITY OF SCIENCE

1948. Reprinted from *American Scientist* 36.558–572 (1948) with the permission of the Board of Editors.

My initial exposure to linguistics came early: in the spring of 1933, during my freshman year at Ohio State University, I registered for G. M. Bolling's only offering in general linguistics, and we used Bloomfield's *Language*, hot off the press. Somewhat later I took Ohio State's sole anthropology course (as of that era). Since there was no major in anthropology, I settled for what turned out to be a superb alternative: a combined Arts-Graduate major in Ancient History, with W. F. McDonald as tutor and mentor. My M.A. thesis in June 1936 was "A History of the Philosophical Use of the Greek Word *Logos* [through Plato!]"—perhaps classifiable as a variety of what later came to be known as "ethnolinguistics." It was unpublished and unpublishable (I didn't know Greek nearly well enough), but its introductory section, despite some weird uses of terms, clearly showed the Bloomfieldian impact: I had grasped the significance of analogy, and proposed analogically conditioned trial and error as the mechanism not only of speaking but of all human (or even all organic) action. I still do.

At Yale in 1936 I chose to major in anthropology, rather than in linguistics, because I was concerned with what language makes of our species, not just with the technical manipulation of data; but within anthropology I chose to concentrate on language because I wanted the linguistics I used to be professionally competent, not amateurish (as was that of so many anthropologists). The latter aim, plus wartime involvements and the exigencies of making a living, explain why my earliest publications were all either technical or pedagogical. But after coming to Cornell in 1946 and getting settled in, I was able to turn again to broader issues. This paper was the first result.

This paper was designed exactly for the audience before which its initial publication placed it: scientists, especially in fields remote from linguistics. Except in strategy of presentation, I sought no originality. I simply wanted to tell that audience what linguistics is and why it is scientifically important. Most of what I said had been said earlier by Bloomfield, and all of it had grown from the Bloomfieldian integration.

At the same time, partly because of its enforced brevity, the essay was programmatic. In §5 a whole series of topics are touched on, each in a sentence or so and each clearly demanding much more extended treatment. Thus it happens that this essay presents most (though not quite all) of the themes developed in the subsequent essays of this collection.

As in the original version, notes and references are given at the end (p. 17).

The purpose of this paper is to indicate certain parallels between the role of biophysics in biology and the function of an as yet unnamed specialty in the social sciences. If it turns out that the parallels are correctly delineated, then a clearer and deeper meaning can be ascribed to the expression "the unity of science," which often is little more than a catchphrase. The term "linguistics" appears in the title because the study of human speech has much to contribute to the "unnamed specialty in the social sciences" referred to above—more, perhaps, than any other discipline. The nature of this contribution will be discussed in due time, but, for clarity, it is advisable to begin with a brief summary of the method and content of science; the first three sections are devoted to that.

1. Scientific Statements. There is general agreement on the conditions under which a statement is acceptable as a hypothesis capable of scientific testing, and on the nature of that testing. We require of such a statement, first, that it be phrased—directly or recursively—in operationally defined terms; and, second, that it be capable of serving as the basis of predictions. When predictions based on such a statement do not come to pass, the statement is false, and is revised or rejected. Statements which do not meet our requirements, however, are neither true nor false, but meaningless; insofar as possible, we try to exclude meaningless statements from our discussions.

We may consider, for example, the statement: "The moon is 50,000 miles from the earth." This is built on operationally defined terms, involving the assumptions of Euclidean geometry and certain techniques of observation. It can be tested, not, it is true, with a yardstick or speedometer, but by predicting what readings certain instruments will show when certain operations are performed. Since the prediction is not verified, the statement is false.

The two requirements of operational definition and predictability are, of course, really just one requirement: predictions can be made only by specifying operations to be performed and stating what the results will be. This single requirement, with its obverse and reverse as described above, is sufficiently similar to many of our habits in everyday matters that some have been led to say "science is organized common sense." Like so many other well turned and oft repeated aphorisms, this says too much and too little: too much because what people call "common sense" often has a high assay of the meaningless and demonstrably false in it; too little because it hints at, without actually stating, the following important fact. Those engaged in any particular branch of science get much of their fundamental terminology—the "nontechnical" part—from everyday life, where words like *up*, *down*, *left*, *right*, *fast*, *slow*, *one*, *two*, *three* and the like are actually defined for us, as we grow up and learn to speak, by the operational process. Such common-vocabulary words cannot be eliminated from scientific discourse—a textbook on mathematical physics never consists *entirely* of equations—and if we remember that nontechnical terms, too, are ultimately operationally defined, we shall make no such foolish attempt. On the other hand, we must not fall into the error of taking common-vocabulary words for granted. Major revolutions in science have come about when someone decided not to take some nontechnical term or phrase for granted, but, instead, to examine critically its operationally acquired meaning: witness what happened when Einstein investigated what we mean when we say "What time is it?"

At any particular moment, the statements which pass our fundamental requirement, and which have not been proved false, constitute the working hypotheses of scientists. Within this group there is a somewhat smaller set of statements which have served as the basis for numerous predictions of a high degree of accuracy; this we may label the scientific knowledge of the moment. Between working hypotheses and scientific knowledge there is no sharp line of demarcation: a statement which up to a given time has always been involved only in predictions of a high degree of accuracy may at that time be invalidated by a new set of predictions which are not borne out. So scientific knowledge is relative, and is dated; one of the most important bits of information in any article on a scientific subject is its date of publication.

Sometimes one mentions additional criteria for the scientific acceptability of statements. There has been a hue and cry for the rejection of statements phrased teleologically. This seems hardly relevant; the terminologies of purpose, of causality, of probability, and of functional relationship are all available ways of talking about things, and we should be permitted to choose one or another of them, or invent a new one, on the basis of convenience, as long as we adhere to the fundamental requirement of operational definition and predictability. Of course, if one or another of the possible terminologies proves to be consistently confusing, in one phase of science or in all phases, then it is well that that terminology be abandoned; this may or may not be the factor responsible for the attempts to leave teleological wording behind.

It should also be obvious that only from within the framework of scientific method do we pass judgment on statements as meaningful or meaningless, as false or (for the time) true. There are other frames of reference than the scientific, involving other definitions of "meaningful" and "true." Since fruitful discussion is hardly possible unless the participants agree on a consistent usage of such terms as these, it is hard to see how an argument between a person who defends the scientific approach and a person who supports some other system can ever be settled. The scientist cannot profitably quarrel with the nonscientist.

2. Fields of Science. Our body of scientific knowledge is not spread evenly over all possible subject matter. People have been led to examine this or that facet of the universe for this or that reason; at any one moment there exist a variety of scientific statements, classed roughly under such rubrics as archaeology, psychology, botany, linguistics, embryology, and so forth. It is never completely clear, at a given moment, just what relations hold between the statements of these different fields, for the operational definitions of one differ more or less from the operational definitions of another.

If the expression "unity of science" is taken to imply something more than merely a methodological agreement between scientists in different fields, that something more is in the nature of a constant compulsion on scientists to understand the interrelationships among fields. We reverse the biblical injunction "Let not thy left hand know what thy right hand doeth"; we require, ideally, that the entire body of scientific statement be consistent. The statements of the chemist, for example, based on one approach, and those of the cytologist, based on another, should not contradict each other. The discovery of such contradiction serves, just as do inaccurate predictions, to stimulate reinvestigation and restatement.

In the course of this search for overall consistency, a significant fact appears; it is sometimes found, from a comparison of the operational definitions of terms in two different fields, that one field is markedly more *general* than the other. One of the statements of mechanics describes the motion of a falling body. The operational definitions underlying this law do not limit its application to inanimate bodies. The same law of motion covers the fall of a stone and of a cat. It is true that not all of the statements of mechanics have been tested with animate objects, but there is presumptive evidence that those statements, insofar as they hold at all, hold for all material bodies, regardless of those differentiae between stones and cats which the zoologist counts as important. The reverse is not true: the statements of the zoologist describe the behavior of animals, but not of stones. In this sense it seems legitimate to say that mechanics is a more general field than zoology.

Similarly, physics is more general than chemistry. Chemistry is concerned only with those properties of matter which depend on valence. The chemical properties of an element are definable as those which remain invariant under all purely nuclear transformations. Not all nuclear transformations are free from effects on the valence shell of electrons, so some physical changes are accompanied by chemical changes. But the chemist qua chemist is concerned in such a case only with the chemical results, not with the nuclear changes which accompany, or (if one prefers) which "cause" them.

Again, Newtonian mechanics, involving Euclidean geometry and Aristotelian logic, works out well for bodies of medium size moving at fairly slow velocities relative to the observer. It proves embarrassingly inaccurate for high velocities and for very small-scale phenomena. The problem therefore arises of constructing a mechanics which will account well for what is observed at high velocities and on a small scale, but which will contain within itself, as a special case applicable within certain limits, the earlier Newtonian mechanics. The new mechanics will then constitute a more general field than the old, in precisely our sense. Its geometry may be non-Euclidean, and yet operationally equivalent to Euclidean within certain bounds; its logic will perhaps be non-Aristotelian, and yet will contain Aristotelian logic as a special case.

3. The Reduction Theory. Although preliminary examination often leads us to suspect that one field is more general than another, that impression is not necessarily right. The crucial test is the possibility of what we will call reduction. Given chemistry, which involves the fundamental term "valence," and physics, which seems more general, can we, so to speak, "explain" the chemist's phenomenon of valence in the terms of the physicist? Can we translate the chemist's statements into a set of physical statements which do not involve the term "valence"?

The electronic theory of valence is an effort at such translation. We must distinguish between this particular theory and the more general theory of the reducibility of chemistry to physics. Each is a hypothesis, like any other scientific statement, but the failure of the former after prediction and experimentation would not perforce entail the rejection of the latter. The general theory could be disproved only by formulating, testing, and disproving every specific reduction theory logically possible. Such a program is not necessarily unending, for some of the specific theories would probably turn out to be testable in batches. Meanwhile the general theory of reducibility of chemistry to physics is fruitful, whereas its converse—that is, that there are chemical "ultimate simples"—is not. For this alternative hypothesis is not subject to any direct testing; it can be proved or disproved only as a result of the outcome of experimentation based on the theory of reducibility.

Economists build up a description of the economic behavior of individuals and groups within our own Western community, and are able to make some correct predictions on the basis of their theory. The attempt, often made, to "explain" their valid generalizations in terms of an assumed "economic man" is not an application of the reduction theory; for the "economic man" is not an inductive generalization, but rather simply part of the terminological apparatus economists use in describing and predicting. A reduction theory for the body of western economic doctrine would be an effort to translate the statements which constitute that doctrine into the more general terms of cultural anthropology, the statements of which are based on the observation of many different communities, not just of our own community of expanded Europe.

We must pause here to emphasize that the validity of that body of statement called chemistry, or economics—or, for that matter, hydrodynamics, linguistics, pomology, or any other field—depends in no way on the possibility of reduction to some apparently more general field. If, after all, there should prove to be chemical (or western economic, or hydrodynamic) "ultimate simples," then so be it; the irreducible field is still a branch of science, to the extent that its methods are those of operational definition and prediction.

Now when the reduction theory is presented in terms of chemistry and physics, few, if any, objections are raised. It seems a belaboring of the obvious. Not so, however, in the cases of two other pairs of fields which seem, at least superficially, to be related much as are chemistry and physics. One of these pairs is biology and physical science; the other is human sociology and biology. Certainly on first examination human sociology seems the least general of these three, and physical science the most general. Therefore one would assume that the reduction theory ought to apply here, as in other cases, as the working hypothesis in terms of which to test the validity of the impression.

In fact, however, only some of the workers in the fields concerned have made that assumption (under one label or another). Some social and biological scientists have not concerned themselves with the problem at all, and that is perfectly legitimate, since a particular investigator may simply say "I shall operate within such-and-such prescribed limits, and leave the problems of interconnections with other fields to other investigators." But when the reduction theory has been discussed, in each case there has been, and still is, a controversy between two opposing points of view. For biology and physical science the label *mechanist* has been applied to the point of view which assumes the reduction theory, and the label *vitalist* to the point of view which assumes the contrary. For social science and biology, the same label *mechanist*, significantly enough, applies to the approach which assumes the reduction theory, and the term *mentalist* is used for the converse approach.

We shall see shortly that the points of view of the vitalist and of the mentalist are quite similar. This does not imply any necessary identification of the two; that is, a vitalist may be, insofar as he concerns himself with the problem, either a mentalist or a nonmentalist, and a mentalist, when he feels entitled to take a stand on the biological problem, may be either a vitalist or a nonvitalist.

The claims of the vitalists, stated in the terminology of this paper, are more or less as follows: (1) It may be true that all of the generalizations of the physicist hold for living and nonliving matter alike. That has not yet been demonstrated; there is some reason to believe that living matter behaves in a manner contrary to some of the generalizations of physical science, based, as they have been, mainly on the observation of nonliving matter (e.g., do transformations in the cell nucleus really conform to the law of the conservation of energy?). (2) Even if the statements of the physical scientist prove to be general in their applicability, there nevertheless remains a core of operationally and predictably valid biological statement which cannot be translated into the terms of physical science, and which therefore requires the assumption of certain biological ultimates; we may use, for these, such terms as *life, élan vital, vital essence, entelechy*—the terms do not matter, as long as their status is clear.

The claims of the mentalists, similarly stated, are approximately these: (1) It may be true that all of the generalizations of the biologist (and of the physical scientist) hold for human beings and for other organisms alike. That has not yet been demonstrated; there is some reason to suspect that human beings behave in a manner contrary to some of the generalizations of the biologist, based largely on experimentation with other and simpler species. (2) Even if the biologist's statements prove to be general in their applicability, there nevertheless remains a core of operationally and predictably valid human-sociological statement which cannot be translated into the terms of biological (and physical) science, and which therefore requires the assumption of certain human-sociological ultimates. We may use, for these, such terms as *mind, spirit, soul, human nature*—the terms do not matter, as long as their status is clear.

Obviously either or both of these theories may eventually prove correct. Unfortunately, neither the vitalist nor the mentalist assumption tells us what experiments to perform, what observations to make, in order to test its validity. The situation is precisely analogous to that described for chemistry and physics. It is the theory of reduction, in its specific form of the two mechanistic assumptions, which here as with chemistry and physics tells us how to conduct our investigations. Here, as there, any ultimate proof of vitalism or mentalism can come only by default.

A slightly cynical cultural anthropologist might remark that the theory of reduction meets with greater difficulty in gaining acceptance for biology and for social science than it does for chemistry in relation to physics because of man's typical anthropocentrism—the common desire of human beings to mark themselves as something fundamentally different from the rest of the universe. This remark would really be irrelevant, since we are concerned here with methods and results, not with the motivations of scientists as human beings. But in the same vein it could be countered that for those scientists who, as human beings, dislike the "mysterious," the reduction theory strips the mystery from man, and from life itself; for those who, on the contrary, *like* the "mysterious," it may instead be regarded as adding the "mystery" of man to that of life, and the "mystery" of life to that of the rest of nature. Such matters are stylistic: neither Watson's matter-of-fact *Behaviorism* nor Sir James Jeans's lonely *Mysterious Universe* are properly to be judged in this light, but rather only in terms of whatever positive scientific content they may possess.

4. Biophysics and "Sociobiology." The problem of describing biological phenomena in the terminology of physical science is so intricate, and of such crucial importance, that activities directed toward its solution have received a name: *biophysics*. D'Arcy Wentworth Thompson, who is virtually the founding father of modern biophysics, sets forth the fundamental problem of the field in the introductory chapter of his remarkable book *On Growth and Form*, and states the point of view and the methodology in the following words: "We may readily admit . . . that besides phenomena which are obviously physical in their nature, there are actions visible as well as invisible taking place within living cells which our knowledge does not permit us to ascribe with certainty to any known physical force; and it may or may not be that these phenomena will yield in time to the methods of physical investigation. Whether or no, it is plain that we have no clear rule or guide as to what is 'vital' [i.e., irreducible] and what is not; the whole assemblage of so-called vital phenomena, or properties of the organism, cannot be clearly classified into those that are physical in origin and those that are *sui generis* and peculiar to living things. All we can do meanwhile is to analyze, bit by bit, those parts of the whole to which the ordinary laws of the physical forces more or less obviously and clearly and indubitably apply."

Even in 1917, when these words were published, Thompson was able to demonstrate the partial reducibility of a number of biological phenomena to physical terms: the similarities of behavior of a cell and an oil droplet, or of a quadruped backbone and a suspension bridge, or of walking legs and swinging pendulums, all afford clues; one can hardly assay the differences until such similarities are investigated. Since 1917 much more work has been done, and it may be there is a steady decline in the amount of biological statement which remains irreducible to physics; we need hardly be dismayed if the volume of such apparently irreducible biology still remains large.

The problem of describing human-sociological phenomena in the terminology of biological (and physical) science is as intricate and as important as the problem of biophysics, and much work has been done on it; but activities directed toward this have so far received no name—or, at least, no name on which there is general agreement. That need not hamper our discussion. Since there is no generally accepted word for just what we mean, we can, for the purposes of the present discussion, coin one. On the analogy of *biophysics*, we shall speak of *sociobiology*.

We can even define the problem of sociobiology by paraphrasing Thompson's words: "Besides phenomena which are obviously physical or biological in their nature, there are actions, visible as well as invisible, taking place within and between human beings which our knowledge does not permit us to ascribe with certainty to any known physical and biological forces; and it may or may not be that these phenomena will yield in time to the methods of physical and biological investigation. Whether or no, it is plain that we have no clear rule or guide as to what is 'mental' [i.e., irreducible] and what is not; the whole assemblage of so-called human phenomena, or properties of human beings and human groups, cannot clearly be classified into those that are physical and biological in origin and those that are sui generis and peculiar to human beings. All we can do meanwhile is to analyze, bit by bit, those parts of the whole to which the ordinary laws of physical and biological forces more or less clearly and obviously and indubitably apply."[1]

It is not surprising, all things considered, that no label generally agreed on has yet been assigned to the field of investigation here called sociobiology.

In the first place, it is obvious that the reduction theory cannot be applied in a field until there is a substantial body of scientific knowledge in

1. [∇ For a more recent and (I think) totally independent coinage of the term "sociobiology," in a sense very similar to that given the word in this essay, see E. O. Wilson, *Sociobiology: The New Synthesis* (Cambridge, 1975).]

that field itself. The status of our knowledge in social science is far from clear. That is partly because so much social study is still conducted within frames of reference other than that of science. It is partly because social scientists have until recently confined their attention almost exclusively to patterns within our own society, and so have not had an adequate basis for the extraction of the human common denominator, the patterns common to all human societies everywhere. But there is another factor, perhaps even more important. Contrary to the popular view, social science is not the easiest of the three main branches of scientific endeavor, but by far the most complex. One of the clearest bits of evidence for this is the great difficulty encountered in any effort to apply mathematical procedures in social science; the difficulty is less in biology, and least of all in physical science. Not unrelated, as evidence, is the historical sequence in which the three branches have been established; physical science first, then biology, then social science (and so one often hears that social science awaits its "Darwin," while biology awaits its "Einstein"). The complexity of social science also manifests itself in the intricate division of labor which now obtains, and perhaps must obtain: workers in different phases of social science have trouble enough trying to understand one another, without the superimposed problem of understanding biologists and physical scientists.

If such factors have prevented the emergence of sociobiology as a defined and ticketed discipline up to the present, it is nevertheless clear that the time must soon arrive for the overt establishment of that field. The relation between biology and biophysics has not been one-way; the relation between social science and sociobiology will not be one-way. Biophysics has served as a cogent stimulus for a wide variety of biological investigation, and has tended to unify and clarify biological science as a whole; a similar effect of sociobiology on social science would be eminently desirable.

5. Linguistics and Sociobiology. Our intention now is to state some of the specific lines along which that branch of social science called *linguistics* can contribute to the solution of the problem of sociobiology.

First we must indicate the position of linguistics among the social sciences. Linguistics is a subdivision of anthropology, which we may define quite specifically, in contrast to other social sciences, in terms of the fundamental problem of anthropology: what, precisely, are those patterns of behavior which are common to all human communities everywhere, but are not shared also by any nonhuman organisms? Within this framework, what are the ranges of variation? How, in history, were these specific patterns developed, in contrast to more general biological patterns? We may similarly state the fundamental problem of linguistics: of all that is generally but peculiarly human (as determined by anthropology), what specific portion is due to language, and in what way? Of the variations within this framework, which are due to linguistic differences, which are due to the nature of language in general, which are independent of language? How, in history, has language had the function it has? In this second set of questions there is but one common-vocabulary term which needs comment: by language the linguist means to include only speech, communication by sound, to the exclusion of gesture, writing, and other modes of behavior which are sometimes loosely called "language"; the first of these is known to be shared by all human communities which have been observed, whereas the others either are not known to be, or are known not to be.

Linguistics is only in its beginnings, and yet there is already a substantial body of achievement. These achievements, unfortunately, are almost totally unknown to the general educated public. When the subject is mentioned, most of us think first of all of the "grammar" we learned in high school; that bears about the same relation to scientific linguistics that the ancient Greek theory of the four "elements" bears to modern physics and chemistry. It would lead us too far astray to discuss this in detail; we shall have to assume a knowledge of the main tenets of modern linguistics just as we assumed familiarity with such matters as the electronic theory of valence earlier in our discussion.

Linguistics has, first of all, an indirect methodological contribution to make to sociobiology. We have said that social science is the most complex of the three major branches of science; of all the possible facets of human life on which one can focus, language, despite its enormous complexity, is one of the simplest. Consequently our methods in linguistics may be defined with relative ease and clarity, and there are already certain *general* results: once the necessary terms have been defined, one can speak without repetition for as long as fifteen or twenty minutes on those properties of human language common to all known human communities. There is serious question whether the list of generally valid statements about any other phase of human life would take that long to present.

But language is one part of culture—in the anthropologist's sense: patterns of behavior transmitted not through the germ plasm, but socially. Methods which have been worked out for the analysis of language ought to apply, at least in part, to the study of other phases of culture. One might propose a program in which the techniques of analysis which have been developed in linguistics would be extended, analogically, first to those human sign-systems, such as writing, which are historically and genetically derivative from language; then to whatever human sign-systems there may be (possibly facial gesture) which are not so related to language; and then to nonsymbolic phases of culture, if indeed there are any. Such an extension of linguistic methodology to other parts of cultural study, partly by those methods which have been called "ethnolinguistics," promises to be fruitful, and to the extent that it proves so, has an indirect bearing on sociobiology.

Beyond that, linguistics has also a much more direct and important bearing on sociobiology, because of the crucial position of language in human behavior. Language is the most typically human of all man's sign-systems, and unquestionably the most elaborate sign-system to be found, either among humans or elsewhere. On the biological and physical levels, it seems probable that to "explain" language, as well as any other human or nonhuman sign-system (here "explain" has the meaning given to it in the earlier discussion, page 5), just two things are needed. One is the biological mechanism known as the conditioned response. That is a complex matter, but we may regard the mechanism, for sociobiological purposes, as given; further analysis of conditioned responses is the business of biology, or perhaps of biophysics, but not of social science. The other requisite is a fuller knowledge of the structure of the human organism, particularly the central nervous system, as it bears on the process of speaking and hearing. This aspect of the matter has only recently begun to come under control; in a brilliant monograph Martin Joos outlines the nature of the problem and hints at what the answer may be.

Now let us direct our attention the other way, and examine some of the things that language accomplishes. Language is the fundamental mechanism of human collective behavior, functioning for human communities—as has been said again and again—much as the nervous system functions for the various organs of a single organism. This is more than an analogy. Because of language, a stimulus to one person (say the sight of an apple) may give rise to a response on the part of a different person (climbing a fence, picking the apple, and giving it to the first person); the most complex example of human collective behavior is but a more intricate manifestation of the same mechanism. The habits and apparatus with which human beings gather or produce their biological necessities constitute technology; the elaborateness of collective patterns among human beings in this regard is made possible by language so that it may quite literally be said that language is the most fundamental element of human technology.

Language channels those behavior patterns which underlie, or perhaps constitute, social structure. If we observe a community and chart the differences in speech-forms dependent on who is speaking, to whom, and about whom, and correlate this with nonspeech behavior patterns similarly organized, the resulting chart informs us completely as to the behavior of individuals in the community relative to one another. A newcomer to the community, e.g., a newborn child, assumes a position in the social structure, and changes that position from time to time; the pattern for such transformations of social position is socially inherited, and the main mechanism for the enculturation is language. This complex of more or less stable forms of speech and associated nonspeech behavior may be regarded either as a *representation* of social structure, or, with complete validity within our operational approach, as *constituting* social structure—just as a gravitational or electromagnetic field may be regarded either as a representation of how certain objects will behave under certain conditions, or else as an actual objective "reality."

In economic behavior, the role of language, and of secondary sign-systems derived from or made possible by language, is essential. Exchange of commodities is hardly a uniquely human matter; different species living in symbiosis manifest something more than vaguely similar. The special (though not universal) feature of commodity exchange among humans is the equating, for purposes of exchange, of varying quantities of different commodities, an operation possible in any elaborate form only because of language. In some societies, including our own, there is the further establishment of certain specialized commodities which have, in themselves, no or very little biological value, but which serve as a means for the equating of other commodities with one another. These special commodities (coins, currency, instruments of credit) are indubitably symbolic. The absence in them of any great immediate biological value is exactly the case of the lip-and-jaw motions or the sound waves which constitute speech, and their relation to items which do have immediate biological use is also exactly the case of language. Further, the historical process by which they came into being and acquired the semantics they have is a process which involves language at every step. Symbols may come to be manipulated without much regard for what they represent biologically; when this happens with the symbols which constitute language, one has metaphysics; when it happens with economic symbols, one has high finance. Either may have significant biological consequences.

Early in this paper we spoke of predictions. A prediction is a statement (an instance of language) about something that has not yet happened, about something in the future; every known language supplies its speakers with at least a dozen or so differentiated ways of speaking about future events. We shall see that predictions are of fundamental importance in various facets of human behavior, not only in science. A contract is a prediction; so is a law; so is a court decision. Difficulty over a contract arises when the terms used therein are not operationally defined, or when their operational definitions are different to the various parties, or when the provisions for various alternative possibilities are not elaborate enough, or when the contracting parties, one or more of them, behave as though one or another of these factors were involved—or, finally, when record of the contract (the written document which is commonly, though wrongly, termed a "contract") was either never made or has been lost, so that memories of the prediction may diverge. A law might be similarly characterized. A legal decision is a prediction; it is accurate if people have the habit of performing the operations which constitute punishment or corporation-dissolving or the like.

The nature of language and the particular quirks of specific languages shape our daydreaming and our philosophizing, and are instrumental in our errors and our neuroses. Bloomfield, describing the process by which the child acquires his speech habits, writes: "The [child's previously acquired] habit of saying *da* at sight of the doll gives rise to further habits. Suppose, for instance, that day after day the child is given his doll (and says *da*, *da*, *da*) immediately after his bath. He has now a habit of saying *da*, *da* after his bath; that is, if one day the mother forgets to give him the doll, he may nevertheless cry *da*, *da* after his bath. 'He is asking for his doll,' says the mother, and she is right, since doubtless an adult's 'asking for' or 'wanting' things is only a more complicated type of the same situation. The child has now embarked upon *abstract* or *displaced* speech: he names a thing even when that thing is not present." From "asking for" or "wanting" one passes on, with the great variety of terminological differentiation a language supplies, to more complicated emotional reactions; from naming things even when they are not present, one passes easily to naming things that cannot be present because they do not exist: hence the cultural channeling of emotion, institutionalization of error, the production of neurosis, daydreams, abstract philosophy.

In such matters, the differential effect of one language versus another is harder to pin down. The nineteenth-century philosophical-descriptive students of language, such as Humboldt, Steinthal, von der Gabelentz, Wundt, thought that they had discovered such differences, but much of what they had to say was based on an inadequate knowledge of the variety of language types to be found in the world, and, in addition, was based far

more on a-priori speculation than on induction. We are now past this stage
of easy generalization; yet there are clues. It has been proposed that the
structure of Aristotelian logic is what it is at least in part because of
the syntactic structure of the Greek language. It is equally possible that
the Chinese tradition of the "doctrine of the mean" is not unrelated to a
certain well defined set of grammatical patterns, found in most modern
Chinese dialects (though not in the artificial literary dialect), which may be
old enough and deep-seated enough to have shaped the emerging
philosophical doctrine some centuries ago. It has been demonstrated that
the language of the Hopi Indians is far better suited, in its essential
grammatical structure, to the discussion of vibratory phenomena of the
kind that concerns the modern physicist so much, than is English or any
other modern European language; yet it is our community that has developed harmonic analysis, not the Hopis. The followers of Alfred Korzybski emphasize this type of language influence; their control of the
accomplishments of linguistics is in general not sufficiently detailed, but
what they have said ought not to be written off on the grounds that they are
faddists. Benjamin Whorf, who made the Hopi demonstration, and who
was a well trained linguistic scientist, made some other extremely bold
statements along these lines during the thirties, and his work, even if of
doubtful validity in details, is of fundamental importance as a guidepost
pointing toward badly needed research.

Now it would be ridiculous to claim that in such phases of human life as
have been mentioned above, or others (political behavior, literature and
related fields of art, magic, religion, science), language was the *only* factor
making human behavior what it is. Our point is that the importance of this
factor is not to be underestimated; that in taking it into consideration one
cannot simply rest, as have many, upon acquiring a general notion of what
linguistics has accomplished, but must devote the necessary hard labor to
acquire the highly technical and precise procedures and terminology of
modern linguistics; and, above all, that since this is one aspect of human
behavior about which we do have some well established information,
linguistics affords an excellent point d'appui for the attack on the whole
field. To the extent that various phases of peculiarly human behavior, as
mentioned above, can be "explained" in terms of language, which in turn
is "explained" in terms of the conditioned response and the specific
structure of the human organism, a part of the problem of sociobiology
can be regarded as solved.

To emphasize the fact that linguistics is by no means a complete answer
to the problem of sociobiology, we may mention a few forms of human
behavior which are universal, or at least widespread, and which seem to

be quite unrelated to language. Unexpectedly, perhaps, one such institution is music: out of the same mouth come both song and speech, sometimes at the same time, yet our knowledge of the latter seems not to help us in understanding the mechanisms of the former (except perhaps methodologically). Other art forms—the dance, painting, sculpture, architecture—seem to be in the same position. It is only to the study of literature, and of the literary side of music or drama, that linguistics has any relevant contribution to make.

There are characteristically human ways of handling such general biological matters as reproduction, eating, elimination, walking, and the like, which may have no relation to the fact that man is the speaking animal. In every human community sex and reproduction are regulated, at least partly, by some more or less permanent form of family organization. Is there any correlation between man's language and his family structure, in contrast to the muteness and less permanent mating habits of the anthropoid apes? In most communities, though perhaps not in all, one eats *meals*: certain specific times are set aside for the intake of food, in contrast to the general anthropoid habit of eating whenever food is found, sometimes all day long. Was language a necessary antecedent to this? Bipedal ambulation is not exclusively human; but the precise manner of walking varies, from community to community and often from subgroup to subgroup or from individual to individual, in a way which is obviously partly culturally determined. In some communities women pointedly accentuate the breadth of the female pelvis in their gait, whereas in others women walk as much like men as is biologically possible (a contrast somewhat of this type is easily seen between female walking habits in most of Europe and in America).

Matters of this kind are just as important for anthropology and, by virtue of that, for sociobiology as are those where our understanding of language can help.

6. Conclusion. We return to our original concern: the implications of the expression *the unity of science*.

The first implication of this expression is an agreement in method, in point of view: any field of human endeavor in which those involved act in accordance with operational definition and predictability is a branch of science.

The second implication is somewhat deeper: we strive against any elementalistic acceptance of the various branches of science, or separate "sciences," as having no necessary relation to each other except that of agreement on method. In actuality, their various subject-matters overlap, so that we must search for overall consistency.

The third implication is our acceptance, as an overall fundamental working hypothesis, of the reduction theory, with physical science as most general, to which all others are reducible; with biological science less general; and with social science least general of all.

This third implication requires the recognition of two specific borderline fields with special tasks: biophysics, already well established, which deals with the reduction of biological knowledge to physical statement; and sociobiology, which treats of the translation of sociological knowledge into biological terms.

An endeavor has been made to show that sociobiology, although never before called that, already exists; that its problems, largely through what has been learned so far about the nature of human language, are already partway toward solution; that its further development is a prime desideratum for the demonstration of the fundamental unity of science.

NOTES AND REFERENCES

§1. Operationalism needs no comment; but on predictability see particularly Anatol Rapoport, "The Criterion of Predictability," *ETC.*, *A Review of General Semantics* 2.129–151 (1945). For scientific hypotheses as *statements* (and for many other remarks in this paper) see Leonard Bloomfield, "Linguistic Aspects of Science," *International Encyclopedia of Unified Science* 1:4 (Chicago, 1939).

Science as organized common sense: Thomas H. Huxley, *Collected Essays* 3.45. Operational definition of common-vocabulary terms: A. P. Weiss, *A Theoretical Basis of Human Behavior* (2nd ed., Columbus, 1929), pp. 21–23.

§2. On non-Aristotelian logic, see J. von Neumann and G. Birkhoff, "The Logic of Quantum Mechanics," *Annals of Mathematics* 37 (1936).

§3. For the anthropological frame of reference for economics, see the bibliography in chap. 6 of M. Jacobs and B. J. Stern, *Outline of Anthropology* (New York, 1947).

There is a pseudo-reduction theory which would forbid, for example, the discussion of the behavior of nations as wholes, because nations are "really" just agglomerations of individuals, and only individuals really "do" anything. This is well criticized by G. A. Lundberg, *Foundations of Sociology* (New York, 1939), pp. 163–172.

The mechanist-mentalist controversy is most apparent in linguistics and psychology; see the works of Weiss and Bloomfield cited above; also the latter's *Language* (New York, 1933), esp. pp. 31–33, and his "Language or Ideas?" in (the journal) *Language* 12.89–95 (1936). Other social scientists use terms such as *idea, mind, concept* as common-vocabulary words; the linguist must not, for part of his task is to investigate the operational definition of these terms and attempt their translation into more fundamental behavioristic language.

§4. D'Arcy W. Thompson, *On Growth and Form* (Cambridge, 1917), p. 14. In the present discussion biochemistry, which from its name sounds like a borderline field, is subsumed under the term "biophysics" insofar as its results are relevant.

§5. For the results of linguistics, see the works of Bloomfield already cited, especially his book *Language*. But the most penetrating discussion of modern structural linguistic method will be found in Zellig S. Harris, *Methods in Descriptive Linguistics* (Linguistic Society of America, 1948). [∇ When I wrote this paper I had read Harris's book in typescript, and the reference to it as just given was based on expectations. The book in fact did not appear until 1951, with the changed title *Methods in Structural Linguistics*, and with the University of Chicago Press as the publisher.]

The generic term *sign-system* is taken from Charles W. Morris, *Signs, Language, and Behavior* (New York, 1946).

"Ethnolinguistics": see C. F. Voegelin and Z. S. Harris, "Linguistics in Ethnology," *Southwestern Journal of Anthropology* 1.455–465 (1945), and their "The Scope of Linguistics," *American Anthropologist* 49.588–600 (1947).

The physiology of language: Martin Joos, *Acoustic Phonetics* (Linguistic Society of America, 1948).

Language as the nervous system of society (and the example): Bloomfield, *Language*, chap. 2; and his "Philosophical Aspects of Linguistics," *Studies in the History of Culture* (American Council of Learned Societies, 1942), pp. 173–177.

The passage from Bloomfield is from his *Language*, p. 30. The physiological components of "emotions" are probably not very highly differentiated; it is our large variety of emotion-words, classifying much the same physiological reactions in terms of various social situations, that makes for complexity.

Aristotelian logic and Greek grammar: passim in A. Korzybski, *Science and Sanity* (Lancaster, 1941). Hopi vibration terminology: B. L. Whorf, "The Punctual and Segmentative Aspects of Verbs in Hopi," *Language* 12.127–131 (1936).

H2. REVIEW OF SHANNON

1951–1952. Reprinted from *Language* 29.69–93 (1953) with the permission of the Linguistic Society of America.

In 1948, Norbert Wiener's "cybernetics" burst forth on the postwar intellectual scene, and Claude Shannon's information theory made its more subdued entrance. These struck me as genuinely new and as important. There had to be implications for linguistics and anthropology, and I set out to discover what they were. When I found enough to warrant writing this review, I wrote it. Subsequently I found more—indeed, the information-theoretical approach became part of my standard intellectual equipment, fitted neatly into the physicalist frame of reference announced in H1.

Section 2.1 of the review derives from M. Joos's *Acoustic Phonetics* (Linguistic Society of America, 1948), and from other of Joos's work, as much as from information theory; it is developed a bit further in chapter 4 of my *Manual of Phonology* (1955a). Failure to grasp the substance of this section has vitiated most of the research in acoustic phonetics done since. The frame of reference developed in this section is also necessary if one is to understand the mechanism by virtue of which sound shifts show the regularity noted by the neogrammarians a century ago; this side of the matter was developed in the relevant chapter of my *Course in Modern Linguistics* (1958a), then in "Sound Change" (1965a) and in chapter 4 of the otherwise futile "Language, Mathematics, and Linguistics" (1966b).

Section 2.4, on the other hand, incorporating as it does the post-Bloomfieldian notion of the atomic ("uncuttable") morpheme, instituted what was to be a fifteen-year wild-goose chase. The notion that a train of morphemes could be "transduced" within a speaker into phonemic material, and the latter in turn "retransduced" within a hearer into a train of morphemes, recurs in the introductory passages of the *Manual of Phonology*, in a partly concealed form in the *Course*, in full flower in "Linguistic Elements and their Relations" (1961a), and in riotous overgrowth in "Language, Mathematics, and Linguistics." As late as 1965, when I was preparing a biographical sketch of Leonard Bloomfield for the *International Encyclopedia of the Social Sciences* (1968b), I unfortunately let myself say that the only essential point on which Bloomfield's descriptive linguistics was out of date was his adherence to a "one-stratum" model instead of the newer "two-stratum" model. On the other hand, I expressed some discontent with the atomic morpheme as early as "Two Models of Grammatical Description" (1954b, but written about 1951), even more at the ends of "Linguistic Elements and their Relations" and "Grammar for the Hearer" (1960c), and finally abandoned the whole stratificational notion in the final section of "The Yawelmani Basic Verb" (1967c) and in my review of S. M. Lamb's *Outline* (1968g).

As for what replaced the atomic morpheme and the two-stratum model in my own thinking—see later prefatory passages in this volume.

The Mathematical Theory of Communication. By Claude L. Shannon and Warren Weaver. Pp. vii, 117. Urbana: University of Illinois Press, 1949.

Most of this book (pp. 1–91) consists of an article by Shannon, bearing the same title as the volume, which first appeared in the *Bell System Technical Journal* for July and October 1948. The remaining section, by Weaver, is entitled "Recent Contributions to the Mathematical Theory of Communication"; a more condensed version appeared in *Scientific American* for July 1949. Weaver's paper is less technical than Shannon's, and might well have been placed first in the book, as an introduction to Shannon's exposition. In this review explicit references to Weaver will be few, but that is deceptive: the reviewer found Weaver's more discursive treatment of great value in grasping Shannon's often highly technical presentation, and the reader who chooses to pursue the subject further will do well to read Weaver's paper before attempting Shannon's.

A number of other contributions to the theory of communication have appeared in recent years. Two by Robert M. Fano are worth mentioning here: "The transmission of information," Technical reports No. 65 (17 March 1949) and No. 149 (6 February 1950) of the Research Laboratory of Electronics, Massachusetts Institute of Technology. Fano's discussion is helpful because of a difference of approach, though his results are substantially the same as Shannon's.[1]

The appearance of the term "communication" or "information" in the title of an article or a book is naturally no guarantee that its contents are of any concern to linguists. Shannon's work stems in the first instance from

---

1. These and other contributions to information theory refer constantly to the work of Norbert Wiener: the famous *Cybernetics* (1948), and *The Extrapolation, Interpolation, and Smoothing of Stationary Time Series with Engineering Applications* (1949; earlier printed as an NDRC Report, MIT, 1942). *Cybernetics* consists of chapters of extremely difficult prose alternating with chapters of even more difficult mathematics; the other volume is reported to consist almost completely of the latter. The reviewer had managed to absorb some odd bits of the prose parts of the first of these before Shannon's articles appeared; the mathematical parts are beyond his capacity.

A fairly popular discussion of some aspects of information theory will be found in E. C. Berkeley, *Giant Brains* (1949), particularly the earlier chapters.

In June and July 1951, a grant from the Committee on the Language Program of the ACLS enabled the reviewer to attend the First Intensive Summer Course at MIT on Modern Communications; the various lectures and discussions in this course were of considerable help in following the work of Shannon and others in this field.

engineering considerations—telegraph, teletype, telephone, radio, television, radar, and the like—which would seem rather remote. But the theory is rendered so general in the course of mathematicizing that it may turn out to apply, in part or with some modifications, to communication via language; that, at least, is a possibility that must be investigated.[2]

We divide our review into three sections. In the first we outline what seem to be the key points in Shannon's theory. In the second we discuss linguistic applications. In the third we take up certain more general issues.

1. The Theory. "The fundamental problem of communication is that of reproducing at one point either exactly or approximately a message selected at another point. Frequently messages have *meaning*," but that is irrelevant for the communications engineer. "The significant aspect is that the actual message is one *selected from a set* of possible messages. The system must be designed to operate for each possible selection, not just the one which will actually be chosen since this is unknown at the time of design" (p. 3). Shannon's aim is to find some method for quantifying the commodity that is carried by a communications system, in order to establish a valid measure of the efficiency of such systems, and, primarily, to establish theoretical limits to this efficiency in terms of the known or determinable variables. The practical use of such theoretical limits is to channel design-research towards attainable aims. The commodity itself Shannon calls *information*.

The keynote of the quantification of information is the matter of choice of any message, for actual transmission at a given time, from a fixed repertory of possible messages. If you are constrained to answer every question I may put to you with a simple "yes," then there is no point in my asking any questions at all; I know in advance what the answer will be. If a telegraph key is tied down so that the receiver buzzes constantly, *energy* is being expended which would not be expended if the key were open for the same indefinitely long period, but no more *information* can pass from transmitter to receiver under the first condition than under the second. Somewhat more subtly, if the value of the mathematical constant pi is computed at one geographical point, and the result, to any desired number of decimals, is transmitted to another geographical point, no information has been sent: the value of pi is determinate, so that all one would have

2. References to information theory have already appeared in linguistic discussions: J. Whatmough, presidential address before the Linguistic Society, December 1951; C. F. Hockett, *Language* 27.337, 445 (1951); R. Jakobson, C. G. M. Fant, and M. Halle, *Preliminaries to Speech Analysis*, Technical Report No. 13 (January and May 1952) of the Acoustics Laboratory, MIT. It is not certain that all these references are based on adequate understanding of the theory.

to do at the second point would be to perform the computations independently; the answer would be the same (p. 31). Thus, if there is no indeterminacy, no element of choice, there can be no transmission of information.

If your answer to my questions, on the other hand, may be either a simple "yes" or a simple "no," with no further alternatives—as in the game Twenty Questions—then the system will transmit information from you to me, still provided that I do not know in advance which answer you will give to each question. If, in addition to "yes" and "no," there is some third alternative, say "maybe," it seems logical to say that the system can transmit more information per message, on the average, than with only two alternatives. That is, the larger the repertory of possible messages, the larger, in general, is the informational *capacity* of the system.

For various reasons the measure actually chosen is not the raw count of the number of messages in the repertory, but rather the logarithm of this number to the base 2—provided that the number of messages in the repertory is finite, and that they are all equally likely to be chosen. If either or both of these conditions is lacking, then the measure of amount of information becomes more intricate; but the more complicated formula reduces to the one described above when the conditions are met.[3]

The unit of information thus measured and quantified is called the *binary digit*, *bigit*, *binit*, or *bit*; the last term is currently the most favored. but we shall use *binit*.[4] A term is needed for the unit of capacity; we define one *shannon* as a capacity of one binit of information per second.

Thus, in the scheme outlined above, where I ask you questions which must be answered with "yes" or "no," and where those answers are equally probable, we have a system with a capacity of one binit per message. The fundamental assumption in the game Twenty Questions is that any animal, vegetable, or mineral can be specified unambiguously, on the average, by twenty successive dichotomizings of the appropriate kingdom; that is, that twenty binits of information will usually suffice for such specification. Skill at interrogation in this game consists in so phrasing one's questions that the region specified by the answers to all previous questions is divided into two essentially equiprobable subregions.

However, there is an important but peculiar restriction on the use of

3. Much of Fano's first report (see the first paragraph of this review) is devoted to a slow building up of this measure of capacity. He makes it eminently clear why one chooses the logarithm to the base 2.

4. —Because the assignment of a technical meaning to a word which is frequently used in our everyday vocabulary proves constantly embarrassing in more informal discussion. The replacement will be made even in (otherwise) direct quotations from Shannon's text. Similarly, "shannon" will usually thus replace "bit per second."

information-theoretical methods. They serve to measure the entropy of an information-source or the capacity of a channel (the terms will be defined in a moment), but they afford no means whereby we can state how much information is actually conveyed by the actual selection and transmission of any specific message. Your equiprobable yesses and noes transmit *on the average* one binit of information each but how much information is carried by any one specific yes or no is undefined.[5]

A concrete example will serve to introduce more of the necessary terms.

A general at a teleconference[6] writes out a message for transmission. In so doing he functions, from the viewpoint of communications, as a *source*. The *message* consists of a linear sequence of *symbols* (*message-units*), each one of which is selected from a repertory of 32 possible symbols: the 26 letters of the alphabet (with no distinction between capital and lower case) and six supplementary punctuation marks, one of which is a space.

At the keyboard of the teletype *transmitter*, an operator strikes keys in the order required by the message. This *transduces* the message (or *encodes* it) into a *signal*, in this case a set of electrical impulses which will travel along a wire until they reach the teletype receiver. The wire, or alternatively a bandwidth of frequencies of electrical impulse used on the wire, constitutes a *channel*. Teletypy operates in terms of a stock of 32 *signal-units* (or *symbols*)—different patterns of voltage variation—assigned in a one-to-one way to the 32 letters and punctuation marks allowable in messages to be so transmitted. These signal-units all require the same amount of transmission time. As far as teletypy itself is concerned, therefore, a transmission rate of n signal-units per second would imply the possible transmission of $5n$ binits of information per second, or a capacity of $5n$ shannons—since the logarithm of 32 to the base 2 is 5. For reasons which we shall examine shortly, teletypy never attains this maximum.

At the teletype *receiver*, the incoming signal is retransduced (or *decoded*), producing once again a message. This message will show nothing of the general's handwriting, of course, but normally it will be "literally" the same—that is, it will consist of the same letters and other symbols in

5. Wiener's approach is somewhat different, and specifies at least some circumstances under which we can state exactly how much information is conveyed in a given message. See his *Cybernetics*, chap. 3, esp. pp. 75–76. But it is not certain that Wiener is dealing with the same "information" as Shannon.

[∇ The remark in the text is wrong; see the Addendum (p. 50).]

6. A type of conference, common in military operations, in which participants at widely distant points communicate by teletype.

the same linear order—as the message produced by the general. The *recovered* message is then handed to a colonel, let us say, who from the viewpoint of information theory is a *destination* or *sink*.

In order for teletypy to operate at maximum capacity, it would be necessary for each one of the 32 signal-units to be equally probable at all times during the transmission, regardless of which signal-units had already been transmitted. Now as long as the 32 signal-units are assigned in a one-to-one fashion to English letters and punctuation marks, this condition cannot be met, since all the limitations on sequence of English spelling are directly carried over to the signal. Since the letter-sequences QL, TSR, SSS, and the like, never occur in English spelling, the corresponding sequences of signal-units will never leave the transmitter. Since #CHL (# = space) is relatively infrequent, while #CHE is rather more common, the same differences of frequency will appear in the utilization of the various signal-units. After the signal-unit assigned to T, the probability of the one assigned to H will be higher than that of the one assigned to C. All such deviations from constant equiprobability of the signal-units represent inefficiencies—the use of more transmission time than is necessary for the amount of information to be sent.

Greater efficiency can be attained by changing the code which assigns signal-units to message-units. A first step would be to use signal-units of varying durations (though with the same average duration as before), and to assign the shortest signal-units to the most frequent message-units, the longest to the least frequent. Or instead of considering the message-units one at a time, one could determine the relative frequency of all possible sequences of two message-units, and assign the shortest sequences of two signal-units to the sequences most frequently used. If one does not care how complicated the transmitter and receiver have to be—if that is a sufficiently trivial consideration relative to the cost of transmission of the signal from transmitter to receiver—then such change of code can be continued until the maximum capacity inherent in teletypy ($5n$ shannons) is approached. It is worth noting that more efficient coding of message into signal in general requires a delay at the transmitter, which must collect a number of successive message-units to be encoded all at once, and a similar delay at the receiver.

Most communicative systems involve at least some constraints on sequence; that is, some symbols are not followed by certain others, or are followed by various others with different relative frequencies. To handle this, "we imagine a number of possible states [of a source or a transmitter]. . . . For each state only certain symbols . . . can be transmitted (different subsets for different states). When one of these has been transmitted the state changes to a new state depending both on the old state and the particular symbol transmitted" (p. 8). The matter of relative frequency is easily added to this, by considering that each state is characterized by a set of relative probabilities as to which symbol will next be transmitted and, consequently, which new state will ensue.

We can illustrate with English phonemics. Having begun an utterance by pronouncing a /p/, a speaker of English is in a "post-/p/" state: he can choose any vowel, or /r, l, y, w/, as next "symbol," but not, for example, /t/ or /k/. The various possible choices have various relative probabilities. If he chooses /r/, he is then in a "post-/pr/" state, with new limitations and new probabilities: any vowel, but not, for example, another /r/ or /p/ or /l/. And so on. It is to be noted that the post-/pr/ state is not identical with the post-/r/ state, established when a speaker begins his utterance with /r/.

With this scheme, attention can focus on the whole set of possible interstitial states, instead of on the symbols; the latter can be regarded as elements "emitted" by the source (or transmitter) as it passes from one state to another. Mathematically the great advantage of this way of viewing the matter is that there is a well understood set of machinery at hand, the theory of Markoff chains, which is immediately applicable.[7] Any Markoff chain can be described by a square array of probabilities, the entry in a given row and column being the probability that the state corresponding to the row will be next followed by that corresponding to the column. To facilitate further inferences, some limitations have to be imposed on the variety of Markoff chains allowed; a very general limitation, which both renders further inference possible and also subsumes a wide variety of cases, is that the chain be *ergodic*: that is, the probabilities must be such that there is no state which can never recur.[8] This seems to me to correspond to the fundamental (and not always overtly expressed) assumption involved in synchronic linguistic analysis: the assumption that we as analysts, like the speakers of a language themselves, can ignore the short-term (hourly, daily, yearly) results of continual linguistic change, and still get valid results; the extent to which this assumption is false is a measure of the rate of linguistic change.

A source (or a transmitter) which emits its symbols with constant

7. A good new reference on this is W. Feller, *Introduction to Probability Theory and its Applications*, chaps. 14–17 (1950).

8. More strictly, there is no state which has probability zero of recurrence. Impossibility implies probability zero, but not conversely. Note that the term "ergodic" is currently used in a variety of more or less closely related senses, of which the present use is one of the simpler.

equiprobability is generating information at the maximum rate possible within the limits of the finite repertory of symbols it uses and of the rate at which those symbols are emitted. The actual rate at which a source generates information, on the average, is the *entropy* of the source; the ratio of this to the theoretical maximum is the *relative entropy*.[9] "One minus the relative entropy is the *redundancy*. The redundancy of ordinary English [writing], not considering statistical structure over greater distances than about eight letters, is roughly 50%. This means that when we write English half of what we write is determined by the structure of the language [i.e. of the language and of the writing system] and half is chosen freely. The figure 50% was found by several independent methods which all gave results in this neighborhood." One method "is to delete a certain fraction of the letters from a sample of English text and then let someone attempt to restore them. If they can be restored when 50% are deleted [at random] the redundancy must be greater than 50%" (pp. 25–26).[10]

Shannon's first major result (towards his aim, summarized in the first paragraph of this section) is the following "fundamental theorem for a noiseless channel" (p. 28):

> Let a source have entropy H [binits per symbol] and a channel have a capacity C [shannons]. Then it is possible to encode the output of the source in such a way as to transmit at the average rate $C/H - \varepsilon$ symbols per second over the channel where ε is arbitrarily small. It is not possible to transmit at an average rate greater than C/H.

The reader will recall our earlier discussion of the efficiency of teletypy and methods of increasing it by modification of code. The theorem establishes the outer limits within which such improvement can be brought about.

But there is a factor, not yet discussed, which sets narrower limits: *noise*. In engineering parlance, noise is anything which operates on the

9. Entropy can be measured in terms of time or in terms of symbols; the latter is useful in dealing with cases such as writing (or other forms of "information storage"), where the rate per unit time depends on the rate at which the written symbols are read. If the entropy in terms of symbols is H', and n symbols per second is the average rate of transmission, emission, or reading, then the entropy in terms of time is nH'.

10. Some of Shannon's discussion preparatory to this is fascinating, particularly on the subject of successive artificial (statistically controlled) approximations to written English (pp. 13–15), which underlie another method of determining the redundancy of written English. Those of us interested in such matters as literary style are particularly apt to enjoy the following paragraph (p. 26): "Two extremes of redundancy in English prose are represented by Basic English and by James Joyce's book *Finnegan's Wake*. The Basic English vocabulary is limited to 850 words and the redundancy is very high. This is reflected in the expansion that occurs when a passage is translated into Basic English. Joyce on the other hand enlarges the vocabulary and is alleged to achieve a compression of semantic content."

signal, as it travels along the channel, in such a way that the received signals are not always the same as the transmitted ones. To be noise, the effect must be random, and thus only statistically predictable. For if one knew in advance, for example, that precisely every fifth signal-unit would be distorted in the channel, then it would be easy simply to avoid those moments of distortion, and to transmit the entire message during the noiseless intervals.[11]

This recalls the necessary indeterminacy (for receiver and destination) in messages themselves, if any information is to be transmitted. If the receiver or destination knows in advance what message is going to be transmitted, its transmission conveys no information; if the receiver knows in advance what distortions are going to be imposed on the signal in the channel, those distortions are not noise and do not interfere with the transmission of the message. In fact, since noise is necessarily random, it is possible to characterize a "noise source" in precisely the same way that we characterize an information source: a noise source emits an undesired "message," with a statable entropy, and this undesired "message" interferes with the reception of the desired one. Put another way, if part of the capacity of a channel is used for the transmission of noise (undesired "message"), then just that much of the capacity is unavailable for the transmission of the desired message.

Occasional misprints in an article, or errors of transmission in a telegram, do not usually interfere with the intelligibility of the article or telegram for him who reads or receives it. Such misprints or errors of transmission are the result of noise (or, with a slight change of emphasis, can be said to *be* noise). The reason for usual intelligibility despite such noise is perfectly clear: the redundancy of written English. Here, then, is the importance of redundancy: channel noise is never completely eliminable, and redundancy is the weapon with which it can be combatted.

The capacity of a noisy channel is obviously not definable in the same way as that of a noiseless channel. If at the receiver the entropy of the incoming signal is actually equal to the capacity of the channel on the assumption of no noise, then a certain portion of that entropy is in fact due to noise, and only the remainder constitutes the effective maximum capacity of the channel—assuming that at the transmitter the message is being encoded into the signal in the optimum way. This defines the capacity C of a noisy channel (p. 38), and this definition proves to be a

11. On page 48 Shannon gives an example of noise which is indeterminate within certain precisely defined (determinate) limits, and of a method of counteracting its effect completely; this is, in a sense, only a more complex example of "determinate" distortion than that given here.

generalization of the earlier one for a noiseless channel, in that if zero be assigned to the noise factor in the new definition, the result is the old one.

It may seem surprising that we should define a definite capacity C for a noisy channel since we can never send certain information in such a case. It is clear, however, that by sending the information in a redundant form the probability of errors can be reduced. For example, by repeating the message many times and by a statistical study of the different received versions of the message the probability of errors could be made very small. One would expect, however, that to make this probability of errors approach zero, the redundancy of the encoding must increase indefinitely, and the rate of transmission therefore approach zero. This is by no means true. If it were, there would not be a very well defined capacity, but only a capacity for a given frequency of errors . . .; the capacity going down as the error requirements are made more stringent. Actually the capacity C . . . has a very definite significance. It is possible to send information at the rate C through the channel *with as small a frequency of errors . . . as desired* by proper encoding. This statement is not true for any rate greater than C. If an attempt is made to transmit at a higher rate than C, say $C + R_1$, then there will necessarily be an equivocation [an uncertainty at the receiver as to the correctness of any single received signal-unit] equal to or greater than the excess R_1. Nature takes payment by requiring just that much uncertainty, so that we are not actually getting any more than C through correctly. (P. 39)

These facts Shannon then rewords more formally as his "fundamental theorem for a discrete channel with noise." It turns out that noise can be effectively combatted only in sets of messages of relatively great length; that is, no matter what the coding, sufficiently short messages may always, with a probability greater than zero, be distorted irrecoverably.

We have now followed Shannon's discussion (with many omissions of detail) through the first two of his five numbered sections (through page 48). In the remaining three sections (pp. 49–81; 82–91 are appendices) there is a fundamental change of conditions. The systems dealt with so far have all involved sources which emit *discrete* sequences of message-units, transmitters which send and channels which carry *discrete* sequences of signal-units. An example is written English, a series of separate symbols, each of which is one or another letter of the alphabet (or punctuation mark). From this point onward Shannon's concern is with *continuous* transmission. An example is the speech signal—the train of sound waves produced by a speaking human being, which have measurable characteristics for any and every value of the continuous independent variable, time. Similarly, a speedometer needle delivers a continuous report on the linear velocity of the vehicle, and there is a continuous band of possible velocities.

From either the engineering or the mathematical point of view it is here that Shannon's argument becomes really interesting (and correspondingly difficult to follow). But for our purposes, we need follow no further. Suffice it to say that in the continuous case, as in the discrete, it proves possible to establish measures for the amount of information, the amount of noise, the entropy of a source, the capacity of a channel, relative entropy, and redundancy, all of which are in general analogous to the corresponding notions worked out for the discrete case.

2. Linguistic Applications. We discuss the linguistic applications of communication theory in six subsections.

2.1. Continuous and Discrete in Speech. The acoustician examines speech-signals and reports that they are continuous. The linguist examines them and reports that they are discrete. Each uses operationally valid methods, so that both reports must be accepted as valid within the limits defined by the operations used, and the apparent contradiction between the reports constitutes a real, not an imaginary, problem.

Neither the acoustician nor the linguist is able to examine the speech-signal directly, as sound-waves passing through the air. The acoustician currently makes use of oscillographs and spectrographs, both of which transduce the speech-signal into a visual report which can be examined at leisure. The transductions involved are quite complex, and do not always give facsimile-type accuracy; but whatever difficulties may be implied by that, at least one thing is certain: oscillographs and spectrographs do not impose a spurious appearance of continuity on a signal that is actually discrete.

The linguist, in phonemicizing, uses no hardware; but he, also, is unable to examine the speech-signal directly. The ear and the associated tracts of the central nervous system constitute a transducer of largely unknown characteristics; in what follows we shall attempt to infer at least a few of them.

A continuum can be transformed into a discrete sequence by any of various *quantizing* operations; the notion of quantizing is familiar enough to communications engineers, though the quantizing operations used in electronic communications are all quite arbitrary. Similarly, a discrete sequence can be transformed into a continuum by what might be called a *continuizing* operation. Now if the continuum-report of the acoustician and the discrete-report of the linguist are both correct, then there must be, for any given shared body of raw material, a quantizing operation which will convert the acoustician's description of the raw material into that of the linguist, and a continuizing operation which will do the reverse; the desired quantizing and continuizing operations must be inverses of each other.

Joos affords a point of departure for the search for these operations:[12] "Let us agree to neglect the least important features of speech sound [the speech-signal], so that at any moment we can describe it sufficiently well with n measurements, a point in n-dimensional continuous space, n being not only finite but a fairly small number, say six. . . . Now the quality of the sound becomes a point which moves continuously in this 6-space, sometimes faster and sometimes slower, so that it spends more or less time in different regions, or visits a certain region more or less often. In the long run, then, we get a probability-density for the presence of the moving point anywhere in the 6-space. This probability-density varies continuously all over the space. Now wherever [one] . . . finds a local maximum of probability density," there the linguist finds an allophone; and "there will be not only a finite but a fairly small number of such points, say less than a hundred."

By regarding the moving points as input, and adding certain further specifications, we shall convert Joos's description into that of a transducer. Forgetting for the moment about the probability-density, let us imagine, in the 6-space, a honeycomb of cells, with boundaries between them, such that every point in the space (save those on the boundaries) is in one or another cell. In each cell there is a trigger, which is activated whenever the moving point stays within the boundaries of that cell for a sufficiently long time. Each trigger, when activated, transmits a single output signal, so that the continuous operation of the transducer produces a discrete series of outputs. Finally, imagine that the boundaries are made of perfectly flexible rubber, so that the location of the different boundaries is not fixed; indeed, at a given time one cell may be enlarged so as to include almost the entire relevant volume of the 6-space, compressing the others to very small size. In a given short interval of time, the output of the system is a function of the input and of the location of the boundaries between the cells. Now we shall specify that the location of the cell boundaries, at any given moment, is a function of the immediately preced-

12. "Description of Language Design," *Journal of the Acoustical Society of America* 22.701 –708 (1950). Joos's number 6 is purely arbitrary; one might better replace it throughout by n.

ing succession of N output signals (*not* input), where N is some fairly
large number.

Such a system will indeed map a continuous input into a discrete output.
If the details of its construction are based on both the acoustic analysis
and the phonemic analysis of the speech-signal of a given language, then
the system will transduce the acoustician's description into the linguist's description, or, what amounts to the same thing, will transduce the
speech-signal in the physical sense into a linear sequence of allophones in
the linguist's sense.

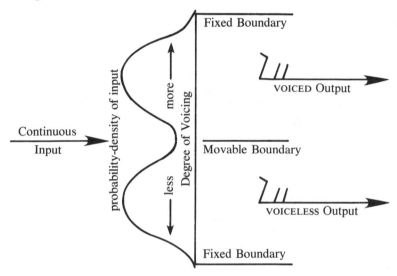

A one-dimensional reduction will serve as illustration. Suppose for a
moment that the only relevant feature of speech is voicing versus voicelessness. Even for just this one feature the acoustician tells us that the
voice-bar on a spectrogram may have virtually an infinity of degrees of
prominence (or could have on an ideal spectrogram), while the linguist
knows that, in French or English for example, there are two and only two
degrees of contrast along this particular scale. In the appended diagram
the continuous input arrives from the left. The curve represents the
probability-density along this one dimension; our reason for giving the
curve its particular shape will appear later. At the top and bottom of the
scale are two fixed boundaries. Between them is a movable boundary. If a
sufficiently long stretch of input falls above this movable boundary, the
top trigger is activated and the voiced output signal is transmitted; similarly below the movable boundary. At a given moment, if the probability

of voiced as the next signal is extremely high, then the movable boundary will slide very far down the scale, so that almost any next input-stretch will activate the voiced trigger rather than the voiceless trigger; and vice versa. The output will then be a discrete succession of signals, each of them either voiced or voiceless.

Let us return to the way in which the location of the movable boundaries is determined. It is determined, in the first instance, by the preceding N output signals. Since this preceding output depends, in turn, on input, one might suspect that the preceding N output signals, as a factor conditioning what happens to a given bit of input, could eventually be bypassed, as we consider the progressively earlier history of the transducer. But each of these preceding N output signals was also dependent, because of the principle which governs boundary locations, on the N output signals which preceded it, so that there can be no hope of bypassing the conditioning effect of "previous output" except by tracing the operation of the system back to some initial state, before any input at all. So far, such an initial state is undefined, but we will return to it in a moment. Examining the system in current operation, what the acoustician is able to do is to describe probability-densities. What the linguist can do is to state, on the one hand, the topological structure of the honeycomb of cells and, on the other, the contingent probabilities of each output signal after each sequence of N preceding output signals. Part of this is what the linguist currently does when he determines and describes phonemic structure; the remainder is what he could do with no further technique but some simple statistics. What the acoustician and the linguist working together can do is to determine the metric structure of the honeycomb under various conditions, including the relation of boundaries to local maxima of probability-density.

Our assumption is that, in a way, the above description of a transducer and a type of transduction applies to the processing to which the incoming speech-signal, after it impinges on the ear of a hearer, is subjected, within the central nervous system of the hearer. Because the linguist has such a transducer within himself, which operates on the speech-signal before he can begin to examine and analyze it, he cannot (using no hardware) perceive the continuous nature of the speech-signal, but necessarily interprets it as discrete.

It is known in information theory that if a continuous signal is quantized, no transduction is available which will recover the original continuous signal exactly.[13] Our assumption is that this is irrelevant, since the

13. Shannon's Theorem 13 (p. 53) does not contradict this assertion. It allows us to transduce a band-limited continuous signal into a discrete signal, but requires for complete

linguistic information carried by the speech signal accounts for only a small part of the total entropy thereof; the quantizing transduction performed within the hearer need only recover as much from the speech signal as was put into it by the speaker. The act of speaking is also a transduction; it converts an inner discrete flow of allophones, inside the speaker, into the continuous speech signal. The apparent discrepancy between the acoustician's report and that of the linguist is then due to the fact that they are tapping the same complex communications system at different points: the acoustician taps it in the external channel, where the information indeed flows in a continuous form; the linguist taps it after the quantizing transduction of hearing, or before the continuizing transduction of speaking, or both. Edward Sapir characterized these two transductions beautifully, though in a different terminology, when he wrote in 1921: "In watching my Nootka informant write his language, I often had the curious feeling that he was transcribing an ideal flow of phonetic elements which he heard, inadequately from a purely objective standpoint, as the intention of the actual rumble of speech."[14]

Since the linguist does not investigate these postulated "inner flows" with scalpel and electroencephalograph, it is proper to ask just what procedure he does use. To answer this we ask what might be meant by our earlier reference to an "initial state" of a quantizing transducer. If our requisite quantizing and continuizing transducers exist in human nervous systems, then the "initial state" of either is the state to be found in a child before he has begun to learn his native language. As he learns his native language, the child has access to only certain kinds of evidence to decide whether two stretches of incoming speech-signal are instances of "the same" signal (that is, are phonemically the same) or not: the physical properties of that speech-signal, insofar as human physiology can measure them, and the conditions under which the speech-signal arrives—in short, physical similarity and similarity of meaning. The building of the quantizing transducer in the child proceeds by trial and error, errors being corrected by failure to adapt appropriately, as with any learning process.

If the linguist cannot open up the transducers in the head of a native speaker of a language, he can do something just as effective: he can himself become as a little child (insofar as the specific language is concerned), and build within his own nervous system a reasonable facsimile of the transducer that the native speaker has. A reasonable facsimile is enough, for if a language is spoken by more than one person, the trans-

---

recoverability the use of an infinite repertory of discrete signal-units. All that can be done with a finite repertory is to approximate complete recoverability as closely as is desired.

14. *Language,* p. 58 fn. 16 (1921).

ducer inside any one person is no more than a reasonable facsimile of that inside another. That is what the linguist can do, and does. In addition, he does something that the child cannot do: he keeps an overt record of the structure of the system which is being built internally. This overt record in due time becomes his description of the phonemic system which has come to exist inside his own nervous system.

We can now see why local maxima of probability-density, determinable by acoustics without the help of the linguist, will show some correlation with the linguist's allophones. If there were no such correlation, the process of learning a language, and equally the linguist's problem of phonemicizing a language, would be impossible. That is why the curve of probability-density, in the simplified one-dimensional case of the diagram, was drawn with two local maxima.

The above considerations, if valid, define the problem of acoustic phonetics: accepting the phonemic findings of the linguist and the acoustical findings of spectrograms or oscillograms, it is the task of acoustic phonetics to determine and describe the very complicated nature of the two transductions which relate the two sets of findings.

2.2. Phonemicizing. When the communications engineer deals with telegraphy, teletypy, or the like, the signal-units which are involved are either presented to him as a fait accompli, or are invented by him, within certain constraints, to suit his own fancy. When the linguist begins to examine a language, the signal-units used in that language (speaking phonemically) are neither presented to him for effortless taking, nor can he invent them; he has to go through certain operations to *discover* them.

The nature of these operations was in part expounded in §2.1. Generally, however, the linguist does not stop with allophones; he proceeds to group allophones into phonemes. It is interesting to note that the criteria by which this is done, and the criteria which lead to the choice of one possible phonemicization over another, reflect a consideration which can be stated in terms of information theory; he prefers the phonemicization which yields maximum average entropy per signal-unit. The entropy of speech, in terms of whatever discrete signal-units may be discovered or set up by the analyst, is presumably invariant from one possible valid phonemicization to another, varying only with the rate of articulation. But the *entropy per signal-unit* is not thus invariant. For example, by identifying the unaspirated stops of English *spill*, *still*, *skill* with the aspirated stops of *pill*, *till*, *kill* (or, equally well in this connection, with the voiced stops of *bill*, *dill*, *gill*), we obtain a smaller repertory of signal-units with greater freedom of occurrence relative to one another, instead of a greater number with less freedom. This directly implies greater average entropy per signal-unit. Perhaps Harris has carried phonemic procedure further along this line than anyone else.[15]

Now a linguist, in the course of phonemicizing, manipulates his data not in the form of actual allophones, but in terms of graphic symbols in some way assigned to them. That is, of course, quite unavoidable; but it implies that a further transduction has been applied to the data before they are in manipulable form, and errors can always creep in during such a transduction. Furthermore, one of the chief practical aims of phonemic study is the devising of orthographies, at least as a basis for analysis of the language on other levels, if not for purposes of literacy. As a result, our current phonemic doctrines contain, to varying degrees, criteria based on orthographic rather than on purely linguistic considerations. This admixture is found in its most extreme form in Pike,[16] but is by no means absent elsewhere.

It is difficult to explain to a communications engineer what we mean by phonemicizing. The following explanation has worked in a few cases; it is also helpful because it shows more clearly how we can draw the line of demarcation between purely linguistic considerations and extraneous orthographic or notational considerations.

Suppose (goes the explanation) we devise a set of messages, each one of which consists of a sequence of ten digits, every digit being either "1" or "2," and all possible sequences of this kind being allowable in the system. Given equiprobability, the system is capable of transmitting on an average 10 binits of information per message. Call this binary code (a).

Now suppose that we decide, quite arbitrarily, to replace a random selection of the occurrences of the symbol "1" in these messages by the symbol "ɪ." The message which in code (a) would appear always as "1211212221" will now be transmitted in that same shape, or alternatively in the shape "ɪ211212221," "12ɪ1212221," "121121222ɪ," and so on. This modification gives us code (b). Nothing essential in code (a) has been changed; the entropy per message is the same as before; but we have a case of what the linguist calls "free alternation." That is, "1" and "ɪ" are physically distinct ("phonetically different," different "allophones"), but do not contrast. Yet if one began the study of a system which used code (b) by examining sample messages in it, one's first impression would be that the repertory contained three different symbols rather than two. Only statistical analysis would show that the code was essentially binary rather

15. *Methods in Structural Linguistics*, chaps. 1–11 passim (1951).

16. *Phonemics* (1947); "Grammatical Prerequisites to Phonemic Analysis," *Word* 3.155–172 (1947).

than ternary. The linguist would conclude, in due time, that "1" and "ı,"
though "phonetically" different, were "phonemically" the same: in free
alternation, and "phonetically similar" in that the shapes "1" and "ı"
resemble each other more than either of them resembles "2."

Code (b') is formed from code (b) by using the shape "3" instead of the
shape "ı"; the sample message given above might now be transmitted as
"3211232223," "1213212221," and so on, all equivalent. With respect to
information, this is still an inessential change, and the code is fundamentally binary. But the linguist at this point would balk at phonemically
identifying "1" and "3," despite the fact that they are in free alternation,
since the shapes "1" and "3" do not resemble each other any more than
either of them resembles the shape "2." The factor of "phonetic similarity" is lacking.

Next, suppose we keep three physically distinct symbols, "1," "2,"
and "ı" for code (c), "1," "2," and "3" for code (c'), but set up an
instance of complementary distribution instead of free alternation. Starting with the messages of code (a), we replace "1" respectively by "ı" and
"3" wherever in code (a) "1" is immediately followed by "2," but otherwise keep the symbol-shape "1." Once again, there is no essential change
in the code from an information point of view. But in code (c) the linguist
will note the complementary distribution and the phonetic similarity, and
will call "1" and "ı" allophones of a single phoneme; while in code (c') the
presence of the former and absence of the latter will lead him to set up
three phonemes, despite the lack of contrast between two of them.

Finally, we devise codes (d) and (d') by a rather different step, based on
messages as they appear in codes (c) and (c') respectively: we delete from
the messages all occurrences of "ı" or "3" which are immediately preceded by the shape "1," but retain those occurrences of "ı" or "3" which
are initial in a message or which are immediately preceded by "2." For
example:

code (a)	1221221112	1121211121
code (c)	1221221ı12	1ı21211ı21
code (c')	3223221132	1323211321
code (d)	122ı22112	12ı21121
code (d')	322322112	12321121

The messages of code (d) or (d') stand in one-to-one relation to those in
code (c) or (c'), and hence to those in code (a). The latter can be recovered
from those in (c) or (c') by operating on them as follows: wherever the
sequence "12" occurs, insert an "ı" (or a "3") between the "1" and the

"2"; then replace all instances of "ɪ" (or "3") by "1." In (d) and (d') the *entropy per message* is the same as in code (a).

However, neither the information theorist nor the linguist would claim that codes (d) and (d') are identifiable with code (a) in quite the same way as are codes (b) and (c).

In (d) and (d'), the *entropy per symbol* is different from that in (a); one has here a real ternary code, in which there are considerable restrictions in sequence, restrictions which reduce the overall entropy of the code to that of a binary code of type (a). From the linguistic point of view, "ɪ" and "1" are in contrast in (d), and "3" and "1" in (d'), because there are such initial sequences as 12... versus ɪ2... (or 32...), and such medial sequences as ...212... versus ...2ɪ2... (or ...232...).

Long before we get this far, the communications engineers will have asked us: Why bother to make such replacements and introduce such complications? Why not stick to just one shape for each symbol in the repertory? The answer to that is clear from the first paragraph of §2.2: such complications, arbitrary though they may be, are of the sort encountered by the linguist as he examines languages; they are not invented by him for the pleasure of complexity, but simply have to be accepted. When the linguist works with a language, what he finds accessible to study is in the first instance a body of messages exhibiting a large variety of such complications and limitations of sequence. His task, as phonemicist, is essentially to determine the precise nature of the allophonic units, the nature of the interrelations between them (free alternation, complementation, contrast, and the like), and in these terms to ascertain the various statistical restraints on sequence. So much, and only so much, is his *linguistic* task. He may do this in terms of allophones (cells in the 6-space described above), or he may break allophones down into simultaneous components and regard them as his fundamental units (equivalent to taking the coordinates of the local maxima of probability-density in the 6-space and handling those in each dimension as separate units).[17]

Essentially irrelevant orthographic considerations come in as soon as the linguist proceeds to the point of phonemic identification. When, in code (b) or (c), the linguist says that "1" and "ɪ" are "the same phoneme," he is simply summarizing the following facts: "1" and "ɪ" are, within the system, phonetically similar; they do not contrast; messages in

---

17. As described in the parenthesis, the result would be acoustical componential analysis. What we normally do is to change coordinates in such a way as to get articulatory components. The properties of the system are in theory invariant under any such change of coordinates, no matter how complex; if in practice they are not, it is because we do not yet understand well enough how to change the coordinates. That is part of the task of acoustic phonetics.

this code can therefore be transduced, in a manner that preserves the entropy, into a code with one fewer symbol; in devising a writing-system one can make use of this fact and eliminate a symbol needed earlier. When, for code (b′) or (c′), the linguist refuses to make a similar statement, he is reflecting an aspect of the meaning of the term "phoneme" which is irrelevant with respect to information—the requirement of phonetic similarity—and is therefore simply choosing a different terminology to report the remaining facts of the case. Some linguists would be tempted to "phonemicize" code (d) by saying that where overtly one has the allophonic sequence "12" there is "really" a variety—a zero alternant—of "1" between them; to base a writing-system on this consideration would clearly be feasible in an unambiguous way, but within phonemics such a step is not valid.

The communications engineer is right in not understanding fully what linguists mean by phonemics, for we linguists have been fairly muddy in our phonemic thinking. The establishment of phonemic units can be rendered relatively nonarbitrary by accepting the criteria of phonetic similarity and of contrast versus no contrast, and by preferring that otherwise valid phonemicization which maximizes average entropy per symbol. But the selection of these criteria is itself arbitrary. A redefinition of the aims and procedures of phonemic analysis along the lines suggested above, and a clearer segregation of purely orthographic considerations, is a desideratum.

2.3. The Entropy and Redundancy of Speech. Speech, examined linguistically, is discrete, but it is not necessarily linear. In telegraphy, which is linear, if two signal-units are to be transmitted, one of them can be sent either before or after the other, but there is no third alternative. In speech there is a third possibility: the signal-units may be simultaneous. That arrangement is possible, of course, only for certain phonemic units relative to certain others, not freely for all, even if we go to the extreme of componential analysis and say that at practically any time more than one phonemic component is being transmitted. Nevertheless, this greatly complicates the problem of measuring the entropy of speech. The mathematical frame of reference worked out by Shannon for such measurements can be applied only if we interpret all simultaneous bundles of components, or of short components and temporal segments of long components, as distinct phonological units, a procedure which does indeed portray speech, phonologically, as linear. In English, for example, /á/ (the vowel with loud stress), /â/, /à/, and /a/ would thus have to be interpreted as four distinct units, rather than as one vowel and four different accompanying and simultaneous stresses; and this set of four would have to be multiplied by four again to account for differences in phonemic tone. Such a procedure is obviously highly inefficient for most linguistic purposes.

An alternative is to modify Shannon's mathematical machinery so as to take care of a set of several linear sequences of symbols transmitted in parallel, where there are statistical constraints not only among those in the same linear sequence, but also between those in one linear sequence and those in others. I have no idea how complicated the necessary mathematical machinery might be, but I suspect that it would be very complicated indeed.

In the face of these difficulties, it may seem absurd to give any figure at all for the entropy of speech; we shall nevertheless state that the entropy of English, at normal conversational speed, seems to be very roughly in the neighborhood of 50 shannons. This figure may be off by as much as one hundred per cent, and is more likely to be an overestimate than an underestimate. For our immediate purpose that rather gross inaccuracy does not count for much, since we want to compare the entropy of speech, analyzed phonemically, with the capacity of the channel used by the speech signal. This channel is a bandwidth of acoustic frequencies; if fully used it could carry 50,000 shannons.[18]

The discrepancy is astonishing. Neglecting noise, it would imply a relative entropy of the source of only 0.1%, a redundancy of 99.9%. That would reveal human speech as one of the least efficient communicative systems in existence.

But there are other factors in the situation which render it a bit less striking. A speech signal carries more information than just that imposed on it by the phonological structure of what the speaker is saying. Some of this information serves to identify the speaker, since we do manage somehow to tell people apart by their voices. Some of it tells the hearer about the mood or state of health of the speaker—whether he is angry or contented, whether he has a spring cold.[19] Of course, linguistically relevant portions of the speech signal may also carry information, indirectly, about all of these matters, but that is part of the 0.1% and does not concern us. In the normal face-to-face situation of speech communication, there is

18. R. M. Fano, "The Information Theory Point of View in Speech Communication," *Jour. Acous. Soc. Am.* 22.691–696, esp. p. 694 (1950).

19. A certain proportion of the articulatory and auditory but nonlinguistic milieu of linguistic signaling is highly organized and culturally transmitted. This portion constitutes what G. L. Trager and H. L. Smith Jr. take as the object of *metalinguistic* study [∇ the term very shortly thereafter changed to *paralinguistic*]; see now Smith, *An Outline of Metalinguistic Analysis* (1952).

a good deal of interchange of information which is not carried by the speech-signals at all, but by the continuous train of socially conditioned bodily movement and gesture which both accompanies speech and goes on during silence.[20] If we could measure the capacity of this channel—for certainly it is one—and add that to the outside capacity of the channel of the speech signal, the relative figures would be even greater.

No one knows how much of the capacity of the speech signal is taken up by metalinguistic and speaker-identification information, but it may be a good deal. It is for all these reasons that the linguist has very little useful advice for telephone and radio engineers. Their job is to deliver the whole speech signal, with as high a fidelity as the public wants, or as high as is possible in terms of the cost the public will put up with. Measurement of fidelity has to be made psychoacoustically in terms of the whole speech-signal, not just in terms of its linguistic content; it may be important to be able to tell over the telephone that someone has a cold in the head.

Furthermore, language sometimes must operate under extremely noisy conditions. The high linguistically relevant redundancy of the speech signal can be interpreted not as a sign of low efficiency, but as an indication of tremendous flexibility of the system to accommodate to the widest imaginable variety of noise conditions. And here we mean not only "channel noise," which is noise in Shannon's sense, but "semantic noise," discrepancies between the codes used by transmitter and receiver, the kind of noise despite which we often understand someone with a speech-pattern widely different from our own.[21]

It is worth while also to consider the ratio of the amount of information which can be carried by any one phonemic contrast in a language, given the statistical structure of the whole phonemic system, to the total entropy of the phonemic system. Different contrasts obviously carry different amounts of "functional load"; just as obviously, no single contrast ever carries any very high proportion of the whole load. The redundancy of a phonemic system is so high that most of the time a hearer need receive accurately only a small percentage of the phonemic units transmitted by the speaker, in order to reconstruct the whole message. That bears on the

20. The significance of gesture has traditionally been underestimated, and its "naturalness"—the extent to which various cultures agree on gestures and their meanings—has been greatly overestimated. See R. L. Birdwhistell, *Introduction to Kinesics* (1952).

21. Semantic noise is discussed very briefly by Weaver towards the end of his paper in the volume under review. My paper "An Approach to the Quantification of Semantic Noise," *Philosophy of Science* 19.257–260 (1952), though set up in terms of a highly oversimplified model, perhaps shows how communication can take place despite failure to agree completely on code-conventions. [∇ "Semantic noise" turns out to be a poor term; it is better to speak of *code noise* alongside channel noise.]

problem of sound change. Any single contrast in a phonemic system can be lost, by sound change, without the speakers' being any the wiser. It also militates against Hoenigswald's theory that coalescence of phonemes can be brought about only by dialect borrowing.[22]

2.4. Phonology and Tactics. When the linguist goes beyond the phonological level to the tactical (or "grammatical" or "morphemic") level, he finds another way in which to regard utterances as discrete messages, the units in this case being not phonemes but morphemes. It is by no means certain that calculation of the entropy of speech in terms of morphemes will give the same results as calculation in terms of phonemes—though it is certain that the computation is vastly more difficult.

There is a way to approach the relationship between tactical pattern and phonemic pattern which may be physically and physiologically meaningless (though not necessarily so), but which nevertheless has some utility. This is to say that, just as the external speech-signal represents a continuizing transduction of an internal discrete phoneme flow, so this phoneme flow itself represents a transduction of an even deeper morpheme flow. The morphemes of a language, in this portrayal, cease to be *classes* of morphs, and become rather message-units on this deeper level which are *represented* by morphs on the phonemic level. The morphophonemics of a language is then a set of rules for transducing morpheme-sequences to phoneme-sequences. And in the hearer, after the more superficial quantizing of the arriving speech-signal into a discrete phoneme flow, the morphophonemic principles of the language are applied backwards to the phoneme flow to recover a morpheme flow.

To make this concrete, let us imagine a unit called a tactics box in the brain. This tactics box passes through a series of states. Each passage from one state to another is accompanied by the emission of a morpheme, and the new state depends both on the old state and on the morpheme emitted, as well as on two additional factors to be mentioned presently. When the box is in any given state, there are various probabilities that it will pass next to each of the various other states, and thus the same probabilities that it will emit next each of the various morphemes which constitute its repertory. Insofar as these probabilities are determined by previously emitted morphemes, they constitute the tactical structure of the language. The emitted stream of morphemes gets encoded into a stream of phonemes; there is delay at the transducer which does this, since the proper stream of phonemes for a given string of morphemes often depends

22. See, for example, his review of Hall's *Leave Your Language Alone*, in *Classical Weekly* 42.250 (1949).

on several successive morphemes, not just on one (*wife* is encoded into /wayv/ if the next morpheme is the noun-plural -*s*, and -*s* is encoded into /z/, rather than /s/, when the preceding morpheme is *wife*). The stream of phonemes is smeared by articulation into a speech signal; this, entering someone else's ear, is quantized again into a stream of phonemes, and then decoded into a stream of morphemes, which is fed into the tactics box of the hearer. For a tactics box is a combined source and sink; the impact of incoming morphemes is a third factor conditioning the sequence in which the box passes from one state to another. We can add the specification that on some occasions emitted morphemes are shunted directly back into the emitting box, or are converted into phonemes and then decoded back into morphemes in the same brain, instead of breaking all the way out in the form of overt speech; that is "thinking in words."

The last factor that conditions the probabilities of change of state in the tactics box is all that goes on in the rest of the central nervous system: the constant feeding in of a stream of perceptions, the retention of some of these, the reorganizing of others, the delaying of still others. We can say that the conditioning of the tactics box by this factor is the *semantics* of the language.

Since there is currently no way in which all this can be disproved, it does not qualify as a scientific hypothesis; it is merely a terminology. It should be apparent, however, that as a terminology it affords us a way to bring existing techniques in linguistics and existing methods in communication theory jointly to bear on the workings of language.

2.5. Immediate Constituents. Usually in tactical analysis (less often in phonological), linguists make use of the procedure of immediate constituents. Sometimes this is regarded merely as a way of attaining descriptive statements in economical form; sometimes it is regarded as an objective factor in linguistic structure which must be ascertained in the course of analysis. In either view, there would appear at first sight to be nothing in information theory to parallel it. As we shall show, however, there is.

At various points in an utterance in the course of transmission, say at the ends of successive morphemes, the degree of indeterminacy as to what may come next can in theory be computed. The indeterminacy is greater if the number of possible next morphemes is greater; with a given number, the indeterminacy is greater if the probabilities are nearly equal, less if they diverge widely from equality. Now generally in current practice, and universally in a theoretically possible optimum procedure, a linguist makes his primary cut of a composite form at that point where the indeterminacy is greatest. The form *red hats* (we ignore suprasegmental features) consists of three morphemes, with a cut between *red* and *hat* and another between *hat* and *-s*. It would seem that the indeterminacy after *red* is greater than that after *red hat*; certainly it is if we regard the singular form *hat* as involving a morpheme of zero shape "singular," since in that case there is only a small handful of morphemes which can immediately follow *red hat-*: this singular morpheme, or *-s*, or *-ed* (*red-hatted*); perhaps one or two others. Some forms, it may be, are not actually so cut, because the pressure of their similarity to large numbers of forms where the cutting is unambiguous may lead us to go counter to this first and fundamental criterion. Thus there is probably greater indeterminacy after the *hermetic-* of *hermetically sealed* than there is after the whole first word, but we would all choose to cut first between the words.

Shannon has conducted experiments in ordinary English orthography,[23] and the reviewer has conducted similar ones, with the proper audiences, in terms of phonemic notation, the results of which bear on the stated correlation between IC-analysis and information theory. One decides on a sentence which is totally unknown to the audience, and writes it down. Then one has the audience guess—without any hints—the first letter (or phonemic symbol) of the sentence, and records the number of guesses made, up to and including the right guess. Then the second letter (or phonemic symbol) is guessed, and the third; spaces in the orthographic form, and open junctures in transcription, count as symbols and have to be guessed along with the others. As might be imagined, the number of guesses necessary for each successive symbol varies considerably; this number decreases sharply within the body of a word or morpheme, and in general increases when any word boundary or morpheme boundary is reached. And one can discern some tendency for a larger number of guesses to be required at some cuts between morphemes or words than at others; the greater number usually correlates with a more elementary cut between ICs.

2.6. Writing. When one writes, one transduces a linguistic message into a different form; reading is the inverse transduction. In some writing systems (Chinese) the linguistic message is taken in morphemic shape for such transduction; in others (Finnish), it is taken in phonemic shape; in

23. Shannon, "Prediction and Entropy of Printed English," *Bell System Technical Journal* 30.50–65 (1951).

most—including actually both of the extremes named—both elements are involved in various proportions.[24]

Most traditional writing systems provide no machinery for the indication of certain relevant features of speech. In English writing, for example, there are no conventions for indicating stresses and intonations. The information carried in speech by stresses and intonations is therefore either lost in the transduction to writing, or is carried by the use of more morphemes of other types.

A short count seems to indicate that about one-sixth of the morphemes of English are lost in the act of writing in just this way. This was determined by counting the number of morphemes graphically indicated in several passages of written English, then counting the number which occurred when the same passages were read aloud. The specific morphemes added in reading aloud may not match the ones spoken by the writer preparatory to writing, but certainly the number of occurrences of such morphemes must be about the same.

The fact that written English is intelligible despite this loss, and that it can often be read aloud in a way which restores the lost morphemes with reasonable accuracy, implies, of course, a degree of redundancy in spoken English that we already know to be there. Nevertheless, not all passages of written English are intelligible. Given a writing-system which forces such loss, a good *writing style* is definable as one which compensates for the loss by the use of more segmental morphemes. All of us have seen, particularly in newspapers, passages which were not in good writing style.

The devising of utterances in a good writing style to be transduced into written form finds its analog in many other communicative situations. In preparing a written message for telegraphic transmission, for example, we refrain from any significant use of the contrast between lower-case and capital letters, since that distinction is not maintained in the transduction to telegraphic signal. The general at the teleconference of our first section imposed the same restraint on what he wrote, for the same reason. When it is necessary to transmit via telegraph or teletype a chemical formula or a mathematical equation, the task cannot be done by direct transduction; instead, we do the same thing that must be done in sending information about a building-plan or the like: we phrase and transmit a *description* of the formula, equation, or building-plan, on the basis of which the destination can construct a more or less reasonable facsimile. Compare with this

24. This is worked out in more detail in the reviewer's paper for the Third Annual Conference in Linguistics and Language Teaching (Georgetown University), to be published soon. [∇ "Speech and Writing," Georgetown University Institute of Language and Linguistics, Monograph Series 2.67–76 (1952).]

the difference between a dialog in a novel and on the stage: the novelist writes '*You can't do that!' he rasped*; the actor on the stage omits the last two words but rasps as he delivers the rest of it.

3. General Implications. We have demonstrated that a certain number of problems of concern to linguists can be phrased in the terminology of information theory. We have not proved that such rephrasing makes for added clarity, or leads to the posing of relevant new questions. It is always challenging to discover that a systematization will subsume a larger variety of phenomena than those for which it was in the first instance devised; the discussion in the last section implies not only that information theory is applicable to language, but also that linguistic theory is applicable, with certain restrictions or modifications, to other varieties of communicative behavior. But in our exhilaration we must always guard against misleading analogy and the invalid identification of meanings because the words for them are identical. Otherwise we may think we have obtained genuinely new knowledge when all we have done is to formulate old knowledge in a new terminology.

"Information" and "meaning" must not be confused. Meaning might be said, in a sense, to be what information is about. For the relatively simple communicative systems that Shannon handles, it is easy to introduce a realistic definition of the meaning of a signal or a portion of a signal: the meaning of a stretch of signal is the stretch of message which was transduced into it and into which, at the receiver (barring noise), it will be retransduced. In telegraphy the meaning of two dots is the letter I. The meaning of the English written word "man" is the spoken form *man*. The meaning of the speech-signal produced when someone says *man* is the sequence of phonemic units which compose that word linguistically. The meaning of the sequence of phonemic units is a certain morpheme. But if we inquire into the meaning of the morpheme, information theory cannot help us. Information theory does not deal with the way in which a source maps a noncommunicative stimulus into communicative output, nor with the way in which a sink maps communicative input into a noncommunicative response. Precisely this is the fundamental problem of semantics, and on this score the speculations of linguists such as Bloomfield or of psychologists such as Weiss have much more to tell us than information theory. It is possible that these speculations could afford the basis for an expansion of information theory in valuable directions.

There is a partial analogy between information and energy, which extends also, as a matter of fact, to money; the tendency is strong to make more of this analogy than is justified. Energy-flow is *power*; information-flow is *entropy*; money-flow (at least in one direction) is *income*. Energy is measured in ergs or watt-seconds or kilowatt-hours, power in watts or kilowatts; information is measured in binits, entropy in shannons; money is measured, say, in dollars, income in dollars-per-month. In all three cases it is, in a sense, the rate of flow that counts; energy, information, and money are substantialized (the last actually in the form of pieces of metal or paper, the other two only in words) primarily because we find it easier to think about problems in that way—perhaps because we think in languages of the type that Whorf called Standard Average European.

But there is a law of conservation of energy, while there is no law of conservation of information (I cannot speak for money). At this point the parallelism breaks down. Proof is easy. To supply one hundred-watt light bulb, a generator must transmit one hundred watts of power, plus a bit more to make up for line-loss. To supply ten such bulbs, the generator must transmit ten times as much power. If all the bulbs are turned off, the generator is forced to cease transmitting power—either it is turned off also, or it burns itself out. To supply a receiver with one hundred shannons, a source must transmit information at that rate, plus enough more to counteract noise. But to supply ten receivers with one hundred shannons each, the source need not increase its entropy at all (unless the hook-up produces more noise to counteract). The entire output, minus that lost through noise, reaches each receiver. And if all receivers are turned off, the source can continue to produce and transmit at the same rate. The information in this case does not dissipate (as energy might in the form of heat); it simply disappears. We have all had the experience of continuing to talk over the telephone after the person at the other end of the line has hung up.[25]

This defect in the analogy has proved uncomfortable for some investigators, who have also, perhaps, been misled by the homophony of "information" as a technical term and "information" in everyday speech. One writer tries to differentiate between *absolute information*, "which exists as soon as one person has it, and should be counted as the same given amount of information, whether it is known to one man or to millions," and *distributed information*, "defined as the product of the amount of absolute information and the number of people who share that information."[26] Whatever validity there may be in the distinction, neither of the items distinguished can be identified with Shannon's information,

25. The contrast between energy and information appears in biological study: the physiologist is concerned primarily with energy-flow, the psychologist (even the physiological psychologist) primarily with information-flow.

26. L. Brillouin, "Thermodynamics and Information Theory," *American Scientist* 38.594–599, esp. p. 595 (1950).

and Shannon's work affords no method for quantifying either. If it is necessary to maintain some analogy between an information-system and a power-system, then entropy can better be compared to voltage, since a single generator can supply current at a specified voltage to any number of outlets.

It helps in avoiding this particular error to note that a transducer is a kind of complicated trigger. When a marksman aims and fires a pistol, the energy that he must expend bears no necessary relation to the amount of energy produced by the burning powder in expelling the bullet. When the operator depresses a key on a teletype transmitter, the energy that he uses is not the energy which is transmitted along the wire, and bears no necessary quantitative relation to the latter. The human brain operates on a power-level of five watts; such a brain guides a derrick which lifts a stone weighing tons. In micrurgy, on the other hand, the operator expends much more energy on his apparatus than it expends on its object.

The distinction between trigger action and direct action is of fundamental importance at least in human life, possibly in the entire physical universe, and one line of argument implies that "communication" is ultimately definable only in terms of trigger action. In the world of man, the trigger effect of language is too obvious to need discussion. Human artifacts can be classed into tools, which involve no triggers or transducers, and machines, which do. Some artifacts are used for *sensory prosthesis*: telescopes and microscopes are tools for sensory prosthesis, while radar, electron-microscopes, Geiger counters, and the like are machines. Other artifacts are used for *motor prosthesis*: spades, shovels, wrenches, bows and arrows are all tools, while steam shovels, firearms, and draft animals are machines. Still other artifacts are used for *communicative prosthesis*: language itself (or rather, the vibrating air which is the artifaction produced by speech) is a tool, while writing, smoke-signals, and electronic apparatus of various kinds (including mechanical computers) are all machines. This ties in with White's notion of measuring human evolution in terms of the increasing amounts of energy controlled and utilized by human beings.[27] It is clear that human tools developed before human machines, and the simpler machines before the more complex. A very late development is the practice of coupling a device for sensory prosthesis, directly or through one for communicative prosthesis, to a device for motor prosthesis, so as to produce an apparatus which will perform as it is supposed to perform without human participation—e.g., an electric refrigerator or a radar-controlled antiaircraft battery. On the

27. L. A. White, "Energy and the Evolution of Culture," *American Anthropologist* 45.335–356 (1943). White gives credit in turn to Morgan.

level of human understanding, much of man's progress has consisted of a slow clarification as to what can be triggered, and by what means. If you can trigger a fire into cooking your meat, why can't you trigger the sky into giving you rain? The difference between the rites of a shaman and the seeding of clouds with dry ice is that the latter sometimes triggers a release of rain, whereas the former never does. All of this has an important inverse: a deeper understanding of man's role in the evolution of the universe.

The argument which attributes such cosmic significance to communication is based on an identification which may be as fallacious as that of Shannon's "information" and the common-vocabulary term "information." This is the assumption that the entropy of communication theory is physically the same thing as the entropy of thermodynamics. The latter is a measure of the degree of randomness of energy-distribution in a closed physical system; the second law of thermodynamics states than in any such system the entropy increases, by and large, until it is maximum. If information-theory entropy is actually the same thing, rather than something else which can be handled by the same mathematical machinery, then the transfer of information from a physical system represents a local decrease in entropy—an increase in orderliness and pattern.[28] Since the only completely closed physical system in the universe is the universe itself, local decreases in entropy do not controvert the second law of thermodynamics. It is nonetheless valuable to study the mechanisms by which local and temporary decreases are brought about. With Wiener's elegant discussion of this[29] we close our review:

> A very important idea in statistical mechanics is that of the Maxwell demon. Let us suppose a gas in which the particles are moving around with the distribution of velocities in statistical equilibrium for a given temperature. For a perfect gas, this is the Maxwell distribution. Let this gas be contained in a rigid container with a wall across it, containing an opening spanned by a small gate, operated by a gatekeeper, either an anthropomorphic demon or a minute mechanism. When a particle of more than average velocity approaches the gate from compartment A or a particle of less than average velocity approaches the gate from compartment B, the gatekeeper opens the gate, and the particle passes through; but when a particle of less than

28. [∇ No! I got my signs mixed here; the truth is the exact opposite. The transmission of information from a physical system entails an *increase* in the entropy of the system. The *storage* of information in a physical system involves (or consists in) a decrease in the entropy of the system.]

29. *Cybernetics*, pp. 71–73.

average velocity approaches from compartment A or a particle of greater than average velocity approaches from compartment B, the gate is closed. In this way, the concentration of particles of high velocity is increased in compartment B and is decreased in compartment A. This produces an apparent decrease in entropy; so that if the two compartments are now connected by a heat engine, we seem to obtain a perpetual-motion machine of the second kind.

It is simpler to repel the question posed by the Maxwell demon than to answer it. Nothing is easier than to deny the possibility of such beings or structures. We shall actually find that Maxwell demons in the strictest sense cannot exist in a system in equilibrium, but if we accept this from the beginning, we shall miss an admirable opportunity to learn something about entropy and about possible physical, chemical, and biological systems.

For a Maxwell demon to act, it must receive information from approaching particles, concerning their velocity and point of impact on the wall. Whether these impulses involve a transfer of energy or not, they must involve a coupling of the demon and the gas. Now, the law of the increase of entropy applies to a completely isolated system, but does not apply to a non-isolated part of such a system. Accordingly, the only entropy which concerns us is that of the system gas-demon, and not that of the gas alone. The gas entropy is merely one term in the total entropy of the larger system. Can we find terms involving the demon as well which contribute to this total entropy?

Most certainly we can. The demon can only act on information received, and this information . . . represents a negative entropy. The information must be carried by some physical process, say some form of radiation. It may very well be that this information is carried at a very low energy level, and that the transfer of energy between particle and demon is for a considerable time far less significant than the transfer of information. However, under the quantum mechanics, it is impossible to obtain any information giving the position or the momentum of a particle, much less the two together, without a positive effect on the energy of the particle examined, exceeding a minimum dependent on the frequency of the light used for examination. Thus all coupling is strictly a coupling involving energy; and a system in statistical equilibrium is in equilibrium both in matters concerning entropy and those concerning energy. In the long run, the Maxwell demon is itself subject to a random motion corresponding to the temperature of its environment, and as Leibnitz says of some of his monads, it receives a large number of small impressions, until it falls into "a certain vertigo," and is incapable of clear perceptions. In fact, it ceases to act as a Maxwell demon.

Nevertheless, there may be a quite appreciable interval of time before the demon is deconditioned, and this time may be so prolonged that we may speak of the active phase of the demon as metastable. There is no reason to suppose that metastable demons do not in fact exist; indeed, it may be that enzymes are metastable Maxwell demons, decreasing entropy, perhaps not by the separation between fast and slow particles, but by some other equivalent process. We may well regard living organisms, such as Man himself, in this light. Certainly the enzyme and the living organism are alike metastable: the stable state of an enzyme is to be deconditioned, and the stable state of a living organism is to be dead. All catalysts are ultimately poisoned: they change rates of reaction, but not true equilibrium. Nevertheless, catalysts and Man alike have sufficiently definite states of metastability to deserve the recognition of these states as relatively permanent conditions.

Addendum.[30] In the quantification of information there are two easy errors. One is the widespread fallacy that a less probable signal conveys more information than a more probable one.[31] In avoiding that, one can fall into the trap that caught me in §1 of this review (p. 23), where I blithely asserted that the amount of information carried by a channel can be defined *only* as an average. Not so. It is also possible in principle to define the amount of information actually carried by the transmission of a specific message on a specific occasion.

To do this we stand with a receiver, and have to assume that certain things are known at (or by) the receiver. Before a signal is received, there must be a known *a-priori uncertainty* U as to what signal will arrive. If the channel is noisy, then even after the signal has arrived the receiver may not be absolutely sure what signal it was; thus, there is also an *a-posteriori uncertainty* V, and this must also be known. The amount of information carried by the received signal is then $U - V$. If the channel is noiseless, then $V = 0$ and the amount of information carried by the received signal is just U.

Let the total repertory of possible signals of a system be $M_1, M_2, ...,$ M_n; at a given moment at a specific receiver, let p_i ($i = 1, 2, ..., n$) be

30. Written January 1974, drawing on several unpublished papers of the 1950s.
31. The fallacy is expressed, for example, by W. H. Goodenough in *Language* 33.426 (1957); by H. A. Gleason Jr. in *An Introduction to Descriptive Linguistics* (1955), p. 270, 2nd ed. (1961), p. 377; by Y. R. Chao in *Tsing Hua Journal* 2:2.1–17 (1961) (in Chinese); by J. Lyons in *Introduction to Theoretical Linguistics* (1968), pp. 84 ff.

the probability that the next signal actually received will be M_i. Thus, for all i, $0 \leq p_i \leq 1$, and $\sum_i p_i = 1$.

For any p we define the *informational component*

$$I(p) = -p \log_2 p \qquad \text{for } 0 < p \leq 1,$$
$$= 0 \qquad \text{for } p = 0.$$

Then, at the given moment for the given receiver, the a-priori uncertainty as to which signal will next arrive is (in binits)

$$U = \sum_{i=1}^{n} I(p_i).$$

U is always nonnegative. It equals 0 if and only if there is an i such that $p_i = 1$, $p_j = 0$ for $j \neq i$ (which says that the receiver knows in advance exactly what signal will arrive, so that there is no uncertainty and hence no transmission of information). For fixed n, U is maximum (and equal to $\log_2 n$) if $p_i = 1/n$ for all i; for p_i fixed at $1/n$ for all i, U increases with n.

Recalling Shannon's characterization of noise as "unwanted signal" (p. 27), we see that, for a system with a noisy channel, V can be defined and quantified just as U has been. However, in the examples that follow we shall for simplicity assume that V can be neglected.

Suppose we consider the simplest possible system: one with just two possible signals, M_1 and M_2 (for example, the "yes" and "no" of the game Twenty Questions).

If, at a given moment, the probabilities are equal, then $p_1 = p_2 = 0.5$, $I(p_1) = I(p_2) = 0.5$, and $U = 1$ binit. The arrival of either M_1 or M_2 conveys 1 binit of information.

If, at another moment (or in another system which is in all other respects like the preceding), M_1 is three times as probable as M_2, then $p_1 = 0.75$, $p_2 = 0.25$, $I(p_1) = 0.31228$, $I(p_2) = 0.50000$, and $U = 0.81228$. This is the type of situation in which, according to the common fallacy mentioned earlier, the actual arrival of M_2 would convey more information than that of M_1. But here, just as in the preceding case, the actual arrival of *either* signal removes all uncertainty; therefore the actual arrival of either signal conveys just 0.81228 binits of information.

To be sure, in this second case it does make a difference to the receiver which signal actually arrives. The difference is not in amount of information, however; it is in amount of *surprise*.[32] If we ask a question and have

---

32. The tie between probability and surprise is discussed in a stimulating fashion in W. Weaver, "Probability, Rarity, Interest, and Surprise," *Scientific Monthly* 670.390–392 (1948).

no more or less reason to expect a yes than a no, then neither answer surprises us. If we expect a yes and get it, we are not surprised. But if we expect a yes and get a no, we are surprised. Although all this could be formalized and quantified, I don't think any intuitively satisfying way of doing so would yield any simple relation between amount of surprise and amount of information; in any case, the two should not be confused.

H3. CHINESE VERSUS ENGLISH: AN EXPLORATION OF THE WHORFIAN THESES

1952–1953. Reprinted from H. Hoijer, ed., *Language in Culture* (Memoir 79 of the American Anthropological Association, supplement to *American Anthropologist* 56:6, 1954) 106–123, with the permission of the American Anthropological Association.

This paper was drafted in the autumn of 1952 for a conference held 23–27 March 1953 in Chicago, then modified slightly as a result of discussion at the conference. The examples presented in §2 had been accumulating during nearly ten years' work with Chinese (especially, I think, the research that went into the preparation of the *Dictionary of Spoken Chinese*, 1945b). The whole essay is clearly an expansion of remarks made in §5 of H1. There is no trace of information theory, perhaps because there was no place for it, perhaps because I had not yet learned how to work it in.

This paper consists of two parts. In the first, I attempt to classify the various points of contact between language and culture, linguistics and ethnography. The interrelations of the two disciplines, and of their subject-matters, are far more numerous than a narrow preoccupation with Whorf's writings would suggest. If we are to attempt verification or extension of his theories, we must first see them in proper perspective.

In the second part, we shall examine a number of points of difference between Chinese and English—with no effort to avoid the trivial—to see whether that particular pair of languages, contrastively examined, can shed any light on Whorf's theses.

1. Points of Contact of Linguistics and Ethnography. By "linguistics" we mean the study of human language (in the narrow sense accepted by most linguists; that is, excluding writing or other derivative communicative systems); by "ethnography" we mean the study of all of human culture. There is no need for us to dwell here on the long-standing and still unsettled terminological disputes about the precise coverage of the term "culture." I prefer a definition broad enough to guarantee that language is part of culture—broad enough, in fact, that the epithet "human" in the phrase "human culture" is not redundant. Such a definition seems logically and ontologically possible.

By virtue of these definitions, the relations between linguistics and ethnography are relations between a daughter discipline and a more inclusive parent discipline. The histories of the two fields, and the current organizational status of the two on university faculties and in learned societies, are of course other matters. The logical and the institutional interrelationships of the two fields should not be confused. An explorer from Mars might be justified in trying to infer the nature of the fields from the kinds of activities carried on by linguists and ethnographers. We who are actually in the fold cannot properly take any such circuitous approach; we must concern ourselves not only with what we have done and said heretofore, but also with what we ought to say and do in the future if the goals of our activity are to be approached.

The following is a possible outline of the points of contact with which we are concerned:

I. Existential:
  A. General—for the whole human species;
  B. Specific—to one or another community;
II. Methodological:
  A. Use of results attained in one field for purposes sought in the other;
  B. Development of methods for use in one field on the basis of methods already in use in the other.

By "existential" we mean the various relationships between language and any other phase of human culture, whatever the relationships may be, and whether anyone has noticed and reported on them or not. Existential problems are problems to be worked on with whatever methods can be devised; methodological problems start at the other end, and investigate how much and what kind of yield can be obtained with a stated method.

We shall discuss each of the four subdivisions briefly.

IA. Language is a human universal, but is also exclusively human. There are other exclusively human patterns and institutions, some of them universal, some of them merely widespread. In what ways does language interrelate, causally or otherwise, with these other phenomena? What does language do for humans which nothing does for our closest nonhuman cousins, the anthropoids? The behavior of humans is different from that of other so-called "social animals"; to what extent and in what ways is language responsible for the differences? Humans are domesticated animals, but human behavior differs in many ways from that of other domesticated animals, despite the similarities. To what extent and in what ways is language the responsible factor here? The search for answers to these questions requires the marshaling of evidence by various disciplines: the problems escape the bounds of ethnography, and stand as key puzzles in comparative zoology, in the determination of "man's place in nature."

These questions have also a historical phase. In the unfolding of human history, what role has language played in the emergence of distinctively human modes of behavior (other than, circularly, language itself)? What role has language played in the rise of other communicative systems? Are some communicative systems older than language—gesture systems, for example? If so, what role did these older systems play in the emergence of language? Of course, there are problems here which may never be solved, for lack of surviving evidence. Few of us, however, would be so narrowly operationalist as to assert that the absence of evidence renders the problems meaningless.

In the search for the human common denominator and its history, anthropologists still often lead themselves astray by the easy resort to mentalistic and finalistic terms such as "mind" or "idea." Under the tutelage of Leonard Bloomfield, linguists have for the most part learned to avoid pseudoexplanations cast in such phraseology. The lesson badly needs learning in anthropology as a whole. A pseudoexplanation, involving a parameter which is actually eliminable but not recognized as such, is worse than no explanation at all, since it puts a stop to further inquiry.

IB. When we examine different human communities (what many ethnographers call "different cultures"), either as they function at a given time or as they change their ways of life with the passage of time, we find both similarities and differences. Specific linguistic patterns vary from community to community along with almost everything else. Despite all the work of anthropologists for the past half century or so, we still have very few adequate yardsticks for the measurement of differences from community to community, and very few satisfactory rubrics for the typological classification either of whole "cultures" or of specific phases of culture. That is as true for languages as for religions, housing-habits, folklores, social organizations, or agricultural practices. We cannot blithely say, "Menomini is a language of type 1-A2-3X, whereas Mandarin is of type 2-A1-7Y," or anything remotely approaching this.

Therefore the search for correlations between patterns in speech and patterns in other aspects of behavior is largely impressionistic. Of course we all know of low-level correlations: the Eskimos have many terms for different kinds of snow (so do English-speaking ski addicts); Arabs do not talk about the weather (neither did Mark Twain in *The American Claimant*); some Australian aborigines cannot count higher than three or four (why should they bother?). The vocabulary of a people reflects their experiences and interests. It is here that we find the most reliable and the dullest correlations between the rest of culture and language. Whorf sought to dig deeper—to find correlations, not between the things and activities which environ a group and its lexicon, but rather between what we might now call the "themes" of a community's culture, on the one hand, and, on the other, the general grammatical and semantic tenor of the associated language. More specifically, he sought evidence for instances in which the state of affairs in a language was either (a) symptomatic of underlying cultural themes, or perhaps even (b) causally responsible for the choice of one course of action rather than another in given circumstances.

One technique which it would be well to use more extensively in this connection is to observe what difficulties a people encounters in trying to speak of new experiences. Settle a group of Arab families in central Minnesota, and see what they manage to do about speaking of the weather. Try to teach arithmetic and algebra to Australian aborigines in their own language. We know from many well attested instances that, given time enough, the linguistic pattern of a community adapts quite efficiently to new living requirements. But we do not know for sure how quick and easy the adaptation is; it may be that for a measurable period the inherited linguistic pattern is the dead hand of the past, delaying adaptation in specific ways which could be described. Whorf's example of the blower installed incorrectly in the fur-storage warehouse is an instance of this if his analysis is right: the installer thinks the task out at least partly in words, and the connotations of the word "blower" lead to the faulty performance.

IIA. The use of linguistic results for ethnographic purposes is too familiar to belabor: native language as a tool in field work, linguistic relationships as partial evidence for the reconstruction of aboriginal history, and so on. It is worth while to point out that excellent work of this kind was done long before terms such as "ethnolinguistics" or even "cultural anthropology" were invented: nineteenth-century classical philologists undertook to determine the whole pattern of ancient Roman and Greek life as attested by documentary evidence, and as an intermediate step the analysis and constant reanalysis of Latin and Greek were necessary. It is well recognized that linguistics has its historic roots in philology; it should be recognized that ethnography also has some roots there.

Similarly, the use of ethnographic results for linguistic purposes needs little detailing here. Whenever a linguist deals with the meanings of forms—and regardless of his theoretical stand on the matter he is constantly forced to do so—he is dealing with ethnographic information. The practical task of learning or teaching a foreign language cannot be successfully performed in an ethnographic vacuum. Without ethnographic (and historical) information, the Algonquian comparativist would be free to conclude that the pre-Columbian speakers of Proto Central Algonquian had guns and whiskey.

Some problems require such a close intermingling of linguistic and other techniques that they can hardly be classed as examples of the use of linguistic evidence for ethnographic purposes or vice versa; indeed, for the most part—despite the instances mentioned in the two preceding paragraphs—we ought not to raise the issue of scholarly hegemony. It does not matter whether we call the puzzle of the homeland of the speakers of Proto Indo-European a narrowly linguistic or a broadly ethnographic problem; it will be solved, if at all, only by taking all of the linguistic, cultural, historical, and archaeological evidence into account.

IIB. Of all the sister fields, named or nameless, which lie close compacted within ethnography, linguistics has without doubt attained, to date, the clearest methods and the most reliable results. Those who are aware of this fact are by and large hesitant to state it openly, for obvious reasons of professional politeness. But there is no reason for such hesitancy: if linguistics has progressed further, the chief reason is the relative simplicity of its subject-matter as compared with that of its sister disciplines or of ethnography as a whole. Language is complex enough, but its complexity is as nothing in comparison with that of the whole fabric of life of a community, of which language is but one part. Linguists deserve no special credit for having made more progress; rather, they would deserve censure if they had not.

However, this state of affairs suggests that linguistics may have methodological lessons for other phases of ethnography. In a few instances the analogical extension of methodology is fairly obvious: for example, in the study of writing-systems. It might seem much less likely that some phase of so-called "material culture," say house-building practices, could be studied more effectively by methods extrapolated from those of linguistics—but it would be wrong for us to jump to that conclusion. Theoretically we can divide the techniques of linguistics into two sets: those which work, in the analysis of language, because language is culture; and those which work because of the special characteristics which distinguish language from all other phases of culture. If we knew just which techniques belonged to each of these sets, then we could proceed to generalize those in the first set for use on other phases of culture. Actually, of course, only diligent trial and error will reveal the proper assignment of each individual procedure or approach.

As has already been indicated, the work of Whorf falls into our category IB. The extensive attention which has been devoted in recent years—primarily under Whorf's stimulus—to problems in this category is, positively speaking, highly commendable. Negatively, however, it has resulted in neglect of problems in the other three categories. We must not allow that neglect to continue. If work in the border area between linguistics and ethnography is to achieve such importance that a name for it, such as "ethnolinguistics," "metalinguistics," or "exolinguistics," is to become well established, then we must make sure that the term subsumes all of the types of problems which have been outlined above.

2. Chinese and English. In this part of our paper we take up a number of aspects of Chinese and English, beginning with those which are certainly most trivial. We are concerned largely with colloquial forms of the two languages, on the assumption that "thinking in words" is more apt to be colloquial than literary. Chinese is represented by the variety of northern Mandarin spoken by educated people in Peiping; citation is in Yale Romanization.

TRAINS. *Hwǒchē* '(railroad) train'; *hwǒ* 'fire'; *chē* 'car, cart, wheeled vehicle'. The tendency, in talking in English about the Chinese words just listed, is to say something like "Chinese *hwǒchē*, the word for 'train', means literally 'fire-cart'." Now, we can be sure of two things:

(1) When steam rail transportation was introduced into China, the term *hwǒchē* came into use because of the fire-spitting locomotive;

(2) The formal structure of *hwǒchē* is still validly to be described as a compound of *hwǒ* and *chē*, as listed and glossed above.

However, the remark given in double quotes above is misleading. Currently, *hwǒchē* means almost exactly what 'train' means—there is no necessary image of a fire-spitting locomotive inside the speaker's head when he uses or hears the word. Evidence for this is that 'electric train' (as on an electrified railroad) is *dyànlì-hwŏchē*, where *dyànlì* means 'electric power'; such a train does not have a fire-spitting locomotive.

This first example is given to illustrate the danger inherent in a study of this kind when the nonnative language is not thoroughly controlled—a danger not altogether avoided in the present study, though all points made have been carefully checked with native speakers of Chinese whose control of English is considerably better than my control of Chinese. What is apt to be called the "literal" meaning of a Chinese (or other) form in terms of English is very often the poorest possible basis for any judgment. No doubt the childish errors of nineteenth-century European students of comparative semantics stemmed from just such a basis: for example, the oft-repeated assertion that the Algonquians can say 'my father', 'thy father', or 'his father', but have no way of saying just 'a father', and hence "lack powers of abstraction."

CITIES AND WALLS. *Chyáng* 'wall (of a room, house, city)'; *chéng* 'city, city wall'; *chéngshr̀* 'city, municipality'; *chéngchyáng* 'city wall'; *dzài chénglì* 'be in the city'; *dzài chéngwài* 'be outside the city, be in the outskirts'; *cháng* 'long'; *wànlì* 'ten thousand Chinese miles'; *chángchéng* or *wànlì chángchéng* 'The Great Wall'. The form that is central to our interest is *chéng*. The range of meaning of this element cannot be understood in terms of Western culture, but is immediately obvious when we recall that Chinese cities (except Shanghai) are universally enclosed in a square wall. With the exception of Shanghai, a clustering of dwellings and other structures which is not so enclosed is not a *chéng*, but a *tswēndz*, which we can gloss as 'village' if we are willing to redefine the English word for the purpose.

Here is a correlation between a particular segment of Chinese culture other than language and certain semantic features of the language. The correlation is different from that found in the English-speaking community. We fully expect that any two languages, chosen at random, will display a welter of such low-level differences; indeed, an exact match is a rarity worthy of notice.

AGE. In stating a person's age in English we use a cardinal number, followed, if necessary for clarity, by 'years old' or 'years of age'. In Chinese one uses a cardinal number followed by the measure *swèi*. The possible matchings of English and Chinese expressions under various conditions can be shown as follows—where in English we assume that age is given to nearest birthday:

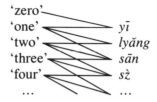

The absence of exact matching can be accounted for in terms of the meaning of the measure *swèi*. We can describe this as 'number of calendar years during all or part of which one has been alive'. In either language one can be much more precise in stating an age than these most customary expressions allow; in both languages the age of an infant is usually given in months, or months and days, rather than by any approximate formula. There are perhaps fewer occasions in Chinese culture in which such precision is called for than there are in English culture. To say 'so-many-years old' in Chinese, *swèi* in English, is possible but awkward. In ordinary usage one way of stating approximate age is as accurate, by and large, as the other.

Yet many Western scholars, approaching Chinese with too large a dose of glottocentrism, have passed snap judgment on the Chinese habit by saying something like, "In China [or: In Chinese] you are a year old when you are born."

FRUITS AND NUTS. If one has just eaten some strawberries, one can report the event in English by saying 'I just had some ———', filling the blank with 'strawberries', 'berries', 'fruit', or perhaps (this will not concern us) some even more generic term such as 'food'. A similar frame in Chinese, reporting the event, could be filled with *yángméi* or *tsăuméi*, with *shwĕigwŏ*, or with *gwŏ*. In both languages the terms listed are idiomatic, not nonce formations or especially coined descriptions. They line up as follows:

'strawberries'	*yángméi, tsăuméi*
'berries'	———
'fruit'	*shwĕigwŏ*
———	*gwŏ*

By this alignment we mean to indicate, for example, that 'berries' is a more inclusive term than *yángméi* or *tsăuméi*, but less inclusive than *shwĕigwŏ*.

Here there is close matching only at the most specific level. One can coin an expression in Chinese which will describe what 'berries' means in English; the expression is necessarily fairly long. Similarly, *gwŏ* can be paraphrased in English as 'fruits and/or nuts'. Neither the Chinese para-phrase for 'berries' nor the English paraphrase for *gwŏ* would ever naturally be used in the framework listed earlier. 'Strawberry' is a com-pound: it designates a kind of berry, and 'berry' is a single morpheme. *Yángméi* and *tsăuméi* are both compounds, designating (the same kind of) *méi*, but *méi* does not mean 'berry'. This particular morpheme *méi*, in fact, does not occur as a whole word; there is a homophonous morpheme *méi* which does occur alone and which means something like 'plum'.

Where English has a single morpheme 'fruit', Chinese uses a compound *shwĕigwŏ* 'moist or watery *gwŏ*'. *Gwŏ* which is not *shwĕigwŏ* is *gāngwŏ* 'dry *gwŏ*', but this does not match the English 'nuts', since *gāngwŏ* includes both nuts and dried fruits. Finally, there is no close match in Chinese for English 'nuts'.

The hierarchy of terms for specific items and various more inclusive classes of items, illustrated here in the field of fruits and nuts, is in any given language the product of a vast number of historical accidents; identical coverage of generic terms in two unrelated languages would be a second-order accident. There is a special idiom within the general frame-work of most Western languages in which the effect of these accidents is removed and categorization is based on actual structural similarities. This is the idiom of science—for fruits and nuts, the terminology of botanical taxonomy. Botanically speaking, the class of items which in everyday parlance are called 'berries' does not constitute a meaningful category. The idiom of science constantly replaces haphazard classifications by more objective ones. It is to be doubted whether any one language equips its speakers better than any other for the kind of semantic purification which the scientific approach necessitates. The Whorf approach suggests the value to an individual of learning a language of a type really alien to that of his own as a "second window" through which to view the universe. One may suspect that scientifically oriented study of the world about us is a more fruitful and enlightening experience of this sort than any study of a second language.

RANDOM HOLES IN PATTERNS. In any language we can expect to find points on which the grammatical pattern is such as to make speech awkward. In English it is difficult to ask an ordinary colloquial negative question with subject pronoun 'I' and verb 'be' in the present tense. In the past tense it is easy enough: 'Wasn't I with you at the time?' With a different pronoun it is easy enough: 'Aren't we all going together?' At a more elevated style level it is easy enough: 'Am I not going with you?' At a substandard style level it is easy enough: 'Ain't I going with you?' But at the precise place—stylistically, and with the stated subject, verb, and tense—described above, there is a hole in the pattern. There is no ordinary colloquial contraction of verb-form 'am' and negative element 'not'. The only one ever used besides 'ain't' is 'aren't', and 'Aren't I going with you?' is either pseudoelevated or vulgar, nor ordinary colloquial speech. The only thing for a speaker to do when the need to ask such a question arises is to ask some slightly different question instead: 'I thought I was going with you; isn't that right?'

One does not expect matching from language to language in this connection. It would be surprising if Chinese had this particular hole, or even grammatical patterns so similar that a closely comparable hole would be possible. But Chinese has its own holes. For example, it is difficult to distinguish between 'We all read those books' and 'We read all those books.' The 'all' is expressed with an adverb *dōu*, which grammatical habits require to be placed directly before the verb or separated therefrom only by one or more other adverbs. This adverb collectivizes a plurality itemized earlier in the sentence or in some previous utterance. 'I read all those books' is *nèisyē shū wǒ dōu nyàn le*, where *nèisyē shū* 'those books' comes at the beginning of the sentence and is collectivized by the *dōu*. 'We all read that book' is *nèibĕn shū wǒmen dōu nyàn le*, where *wǒmen* 'we' precedes and is collectivized by *dōu*. The sentence *nèisyē shū wǒmen dōu nyàn le*, where *dōu* is preceded by two substantive expressions which might be collectivized by it, means indifferently 'We all read those books', 'We read all those books', or even 'We all read all those books'.

Needless to say, fluent speakers of a language find their way around such holes without falling in. But even native speakers of a language can be inept, and a list of the pattern holes in a language is a good index of what specific ineptnesses will appear in the speech of a native speaker who has poor control of his language.

SUBJECT OF STUDY AND THE STUDY OF THE SUBJECT. Once I said to a chemist: "Ater all, all of chemistry can be regarded as a part of human history." His reply was "No; all of human history can be regarded as a part of chemistry." Both statements were true, since the word 'chemistry' was being used in two different senses. In the first statement, the word meant 'the study of a particular range of phenomena'; in the second, it meant 'a particular range of phenomena', whether studied or not.

In a few cases, including chemistry, this same ambiguity is possible in Chinese. In others, e.g., physics or geography, it is not: *wùlĭ* 'physics (as an object of study)': *wùlĭsywé* 'physics (as the study of an object)'; *dìlĭ* 'geography (as object)': *dìlǐsywé* 'geography (as study)'. The cases in which the ambiguity is possible are mainly new importations from the West: *hwàsywé* 'chemistry' (either sense); *shùsywé* 'mathematics' (either sense, for the modern Westernized field). In these cases, the importation of perhaps desirable features of Western culture into China has been accompanied by the importation of a kind of terminological confusion from which Chinese had theretofore been largely free.

INSTANCE AND VARIETY. In the discussion of codes and messages (including language) it is necessary to distinguish between an occurrence of an element (e.g., a signal, a phoneme) and a kind of element which can occur. This is sometimes confusing in English and other Western languages. The problem of "one phoneme or two" is thus two problems: single phoneme-occurrence versus cluster; two allophones of one phoneme versus two allophones of two different phonemes.

In his "The Non-Uniqueness of Phonemic Solutions of Phonetic Systems" (*Academia Sinica, Bulletin of the Institute of History and Philology* 4.363–397 [1933]), Yuenren Chao got around the difficulty by an importation from Chinese via "pidgin-Chinese": 'one-piece-sound' versus 'one-kind-sound'; in Chinese *yíge* 'one piece' versus *yìjǔng* 'one kind', with different measures. This particular stylistic difficulty is less apt to arise in Chinese than in English.

NUMBER. Most English substantives are subject to the obligatory distinction of singular versus plural; exceptions, such as 'sheep', 'deer', superficially resemble all Chinese nouns, for which there is no such obligatory category. Because of the prevalence of the contrast in English, such a sentence as 'If you take that road watch out for the deer' may leave us unsatisfied: does the speaker mean one deer or an unknown plurality? That dissatisfaction has even led some interpreters of English grammar to insist that 'deer' and 'sheep' have plurals just like other nouns, except that in these cases the plurals are made by "zero change"—an interpretation which renders the cited sentence grammatically ambiguous rather than just semantically so.

On this score English and Chinese do not differ as to what it is possible to specify, but as to what is relatively easy, or hard, to specify. To indicate a particular variety of substance or thing (for which a noun exists), without any implication whatsoever as to quantity, is easy in Chinese. In English it is accomplished in certain contexts with a generic singular ('Man wants but little here below'), in others by a generic plural ('Professors shouldn't do things like that'), but in still other contexts it is accomplished only quite awkwardly: 'That student or those students who arrives or arrive after the assigned time . . .'. Legal English shows many such awkwardnesses.

In English, on the other hand, it is easy to specify an indefinite plurality (that is, any number from two on up, but not just one). This is awkward in Chinese; expressions such as those equivalent vaguely to 'a few', 'many', and the like are of course otherwise matched in English, and cannot be counted as performing the specific semantic function of which we are speaking.

With its obligatory categories, certain nouns in English show fluctuation in the agreeing verb: 'My family is coming to see me'; 'Are your family all well?' The choice between agreement and nonagreement is semantically functional on the stylistic level; Chinese, lacking the number categories, is forced to make do with other devices, none of which exactly matches this one.

CHANNELS OF METONYMY FOR MOTION AND LOCUS. In English, and probably generally in Western languages, verbs of motion from one place to another are also freely used to express constant spatial locus of an object, or change of spatial relationship of parts of an object as in growth:

'fall':   'A man fell from the top of a building'; 'The land falls about ten feet behind the house'; 'The cake fell'.
'run':   'He ran around the lake'; 'The road runs around the lake'; 'They ran the road around the lake'.
'split': 'His lip (was) split in the fight'; 'The tree trunk splits into three large branches close to the ground'.

In Chinese, verbs which carry the central meaning of motion are not used in such extended senses. The few exceptions must be suspected of having developed under Western influence.

TAKING AND HOLDING. Here the situation seems to be reversed. In English, 'take', 'grab', 'snatch', 'pick (up)', 'lift', 'seize', and the like refer only to the event of passing from nonpossession to possession of an object, while other verbs, such as 'carry', 'hold', 'guard'—a smaller number, less highly differentiated—refer to the state of possession. 'Take' is marginal, verging on 'carry'. The progressive construction with 'keep' underscores the difference: 'He kept taking candy from the bowl' is a repetitive in meaning, whereas 'He kept (on) holding the spoon' is continuous.

In Chinese, on the other hand, there are a large number of verbs which denote, in themselves, simply the grasping or holding of an object in a particular way, with one or another body part or associated artefact: *nyē*: between the fleshy part behind the nails of thumb and forefinger; *jwā*: in fingers partly closed, palm downwards; and many others. Any of these can be used inceptively (*tā bǎ jēn nyēchilaile* 'He picked up the pin') or continuatively (*tā nyēje jēn jǎu syàn* 'Holding the pin between her fingers she looks for the thread'); the difference depends on other elements in the sentences.

BREAKING. We have many words in English for various kinds of breaking: 'shatter', 'crumble', 'tumble', 'crack', 'split', 'tear'. Many of these are used, however, mainly when especially called for, rather than whenever the opportunity presents itself. If a window has shattered to splinters, we will normally report—if the report is unemotional—simply 'The window broke' or 'The window was broken'. To say 'The window (was) shattered' either is more emotional or is in response to a request for further detail.

In Chinese the normal unemotional report of any such event will usually use a more specific verb, of the kind first listed above. Individually these do not exactly match the English words, as these examples show:

dwàn:	transverse breaking into segments of a long thin object, e.g., a pencil or tree branch;
lyè:	to split without coming apart, as of a pane of glass with one or two long cracks, or a board or a drying surface;
swèi:	to shatter into many small pieces, no longer in place relative to each other, as a pane of glass or a dish;
pwò:	to break into a number of relatively larger pieces, most of which still hang together, as a pane of glass through which a bullet has passed, taking one small piece of glass away and leaving radial cracks, or a skull which has received a hard blow;
tā:	to crumble down, collapse, implode, as an old wall or house;
jà:	to burst or explode outwards, as a bomb or balloon.

The word *hwài* is broader: 'to be or get out of order', as a watch or other mechanism, or an egg or piece of meat which is too old to eat, or a chair which still looks intact but which is apt to collapse (*tā*) if one sits on it. But *hwài* is not a generic for the specific terms listed above. When the window breaks, the normal Chinese report cannot be completely general; it will use *lyè*, *pwò*, *swèi*, or *jà* as the facts require.

In this and the two immediately preceding sections the examples seem to be more along the line of Whorf's interest than were those first given. We may perhaps call the example about cities and walls a "zero-order" difference: this is the kind we expect to find between any two languages. The fruits-and-nuts instance deserves then to be called a "first-order" difference: the point in this example is not that the semantic ranges of two relatively concrete nouns differ in the two languages (which would be a zero-order difference) but rather that there is divergence in the coverage of more inclusive generic terms. And if this is justified, then the motion-and-locus example deserves to be called a difference of even higher order. We have in it a situation in which not just one form from each language, but a whole semantically defined family of forms from each, have similar types of metaphorical or metonymic extension in English but not in Chinese. A higher-order difference, then, is establishable when a whole set of zero- or first-order differences seem to manifest parallelism. I do not wish, however, to push this sorting-out of orders of difference too far, nor for the reader to expect any great precision in it—I have no idea, for example, what the difference between a "second-order" difference and a "third-order" difference would be.

HANDLING TIME AND SPACE. Whorf made so much of the difference between Hopi and Standard Average European in this connection that it would be unfortunate not to examine other languages in the same connection. But I have only one comment to offer; the details need much more close analysis.

Whorf claims that we handle time like space, or like a thing, whereas the Hopi do not.

In a footnote in *Language* (24.160 [1948]), Fang-Kuei Li writes, "These two villages are only a few miles distant from each other, but there are already slight dialectal differences."

What concerns us is the use of the word 'already'. Conceivably this sentence was "thought out" purely in English, so that the 'already' introduces a real reference to time: the relevant connection is not the short spatial distance between the two villages, but an implied relatively short interval of time since all the speakers of both villages were in intimate contact. It seems more likely that 'already' is Chinese *yǐjing* or *jyòu*; that is, that 'already' was inserted in the English sentence because in many contexts it is equivalent to *yǐjing* or *jyòu*, though in this specific context it is not. In Chinese—if our exegesis is correct—the reference is not to time at all, but genuinely to space, to the relatively short spatial distance between the villages; but it is a reference to space *handled like time*.

Or, put a bit differently, one could say that here, as in some other contexts, the Chinese make use of the linguistic machinery which they have on hand primarily for discussing temporal sequence and separation, in extended senses which are alien to English. A Chinese will say *Jèijāng jwŏdz bǐ nèijāng cháng sāntswèn* 'This table than that long three-inches'—'This table is three inches longer than that'. On occasion one will hear *Jèijāng jwŏdz cháng sāntswèn le* 'This table long three-inches (particle for new state)'—'This table is three inches too long'. In the second one has, again, the use of a fundamentally temporal element (the particle *le*) in an extended sense. The most tempting explanation is to say that the speaker has been looking for a table of a certain length, and has been examining a series of tables to find an appropriate one, so that upon examining the particular one on which the sentence comments, there has actually been a temporal sequence of events: the *le* means not that the table under discussion has changed its length, but that we, in looking at successive ones, have now arrived at one which is three inches too long. But this explanation is English, not Chinese; I fear that it is not really relevant. The safest statement we can make would probably be that in Chinese there is machinery used with reference to a variety of sequences and processes, some of which coincide with what we take as temporal. When the specific reference is temporal, the usage strikes us as normal; when it is not, it strikes us as alien.

PIGEONHOLES AND SCALES. Chinese verbs include a subclass which are "stative" and "intransitive," which for simplicity we can call adjectives. Individually, Chinese adjectives have meanings much like those of English adjectives: big, small, tall, short, and so forth. Many, but not all, are paired: *dà* and *syǎu* 'large, small'; *gāu* and *ǎi* 'tall, short'; *gāu* and *dī* 'high, low'; *cháng* and *dwǎn* 'long, short'. This pairing is not just semantic; it is also shown structurally. In each pair, one member is the "major" member; this is shown by the selection of that member, rather than the other, in asking a colorless question about the degree of the particular quality. For example, just as in English, the normal question is 'How tall (*gāu*) is that building?—and such a question as 'How short (*ǎi*) is that building?' is most unusual.

Theoretically one can produce a grammatically complete sentence in Chinese by using a single substantive as subject and a bare adjective as predicate: *tā ǎi* 'He's short.' In practice such sentences occur only in response to questions of the form *tā ǎi buǎi?* 'Is he (relatively) short or not?' In making de novo statements, a predicate which includes a stative verb invariably also has modifiers—the negative modifier *bù* 'not', or some indication of degree like *hěn* 'quite', *dzwèi* 'very', *jēn* 'really'.

This last is the most frequent style of adjectival predicate. We may say that a pair of Chinese adjectives establishes a scale, and specifies one direction on that scale as "positive." The normal adjectival predicate then serves to locate the subject somewhere along that scale, but always more or less relatively to other items, never in an absolute way. That is, Chinese adjectives most normally handle qualities overtly as matters of degree of difference, rather than as matters of kind (pigeonhole).

A point of departure for the relative judgment of some given object can be supplied using the coverb *bǐ* 'as compared with': *Jèijāng jwōdz bǐ nèijāng cháng* 'This table is longer than that one'. The relative judgment can then be rendered quantitative by using, after the stative verb, a combination of numeral and measure: *Jèijāng jwōdz bǐ nèijāng cháng sāntswèn* 'This table is three inches longer than that one'. If the *bǐ* phrase is omitted, this becomes, as already stated in the preceding section, a judgment of amount of undesirable excess: 'This table is three inches too long'. A different pattern states the length (or other quality) of an object in terms of metric units, which are of course overtly relative: *Jèijāng jwōdz yǒu sānchǐ cháng* 'This table is three feet long'. These are the various possible modifications of the essentially relativistic use of stative verbs.

There is also a pigeonhole pattern; one adds *de* to the adjectival predicate, nominalizing it so that it names a class or pigeonhole, and the statement asserts the membership of the subject in that class: *Nèijāng jwōdz (shǐ) chángde* 'That table is one of the long ones' or '. . . is a long one'. Such a statement, with this particular adjective, is made only in a context where some preceding act or speech has set up the classifications in question.

A few Chinese adjectives are used, in the predicate, only in this pigeonholing manner: *nán* and *nyǔ* 'male, female' for humans; *gūng* and *mǔ* 'male, female' for animals. Thus 'male' and 'female' are never matters of degree or relativity in Chinese; they are absolute pigeonholes. A few other adjectives tend to be used in this pigeonholing way at least as often as they are used in the relativistic patterns, if not somewhat more often: the five adjectives for the five fundamental tastes 'sweet', 'bitter', 'salty', 'sour', and 'pepper-hot'; perhaps color adjectives. Except for 'male' and 'female', adjectives which are structurally paired are used normally in the relativistic patterns, in the pigeonholing pattern only when special contexts render such usage appropriate.

Now we may ask whether there is any attribute of Chinese culture with which this habitual relativism correlates. It will be recalled that the Chinese "philosophy of life," as often reported from observation and as codified in some of the Chinese philosophicoreligious systems, particularly Taoism, emphasizes a "doctrine of the mean": never get too happy, or you may also become too sad; moderation in all things. I do not know certainly that the speech habit outlined above is an old one; literary Chinese is so divergent that judgment would be precarious if built on it, and what is needed is extensive dialect comparison. If the speech habit is indeed old, then there may very well be a correlation between the speech habit and the "philosophy of life."

This suggestion is put forward with great hesitation. There are several crucial problems in addition to the one already mentioned. For one, if there is indeed a determinable correlation, then it would strike me that the direction of causality is in all probability from "philosophy of life" to language, rather than vice versa—though, of course, the linguistic habit might serve as one of the mechanisms by which the philosophical orientation maintains its existence down through the generations. Even more disturbing is the possibility that careful examination of the use of adjectives in English and other Western languages might reveal that we have much the same semantic pattern as has been described above for Chinese. If so, then what becomes of our pretty hypothesis? We would have a similar linguistic pattern in Chinese and in the West; in Chinese it would be hooked up with a philosophy of life, but in the West it obviously would not.

SUMMARY. From a tentative discussion one can draw only tentative conclusions. Yet the following three generalizations seem to be reasonably well supported in the specific case of Chinese versus English. I feel that they probably hold for languages in general, and they have been phrased accordingly:

(1) The most precisely definable differences between languages are also the most trivial from the Whorfian point of view. The more important an ostensible difference is from this point of view, the harder it is to pin down.

(2) Languages differ not so much as to what *can* be said in them, but rather as to what it is *relatively easy* to say. In this connection it is worthy of note that the history of Western logic and science, from Aristotle down, constitutes not so much the story of scholars hemmed in and misled by the nature of their specific languages as the story of a long and successful struggle against inherited linguistic limitations. From the time when science became observational and experimental that is easy to see: speech-habits were revised to fit observed facts, and where everyday language would not serve, special subsystems (mathematics) were devised. But even Aristotle's development of the syllogism represented a sort of semantic purification of everyday Greek.

(3) The impact of inherited linguistic pattern on activities is, in general, least important in the most practical contexts, and most important in such goings-on as story-telling, religion, and philosophizing—which consist largely or exclusively of talking anyway. Scientific discourse can be carried on in any language the speakers of which have become participants in the world of science, and other languages can become properly modified with little trouble; some types of literature, on the other hand, are largely impervious to translation.

H4. THE ANALYSIS OF COMMUNICATION

1953; never before published.

At the time, the Social Science Research Center of Cornell University was sponsoring a "Core Training Program": a group of investigators in various branches of social (or "behavioral") science held a series of sessions in which we tried to understand one another's approaches and to intercalibrate our diverse terminologies; then we designed and presented a "core course" intended to be of value to graduate students in any one of the participating disciplines.

As might be expected, one of the barriers to mutual understanding was the term "communication," which all of us used freely and with some reverence, but no two of us in quite the same sense. Hence this paper, distributed in dittoed form in October 1953. It was written hastily and badly, and may not have helped towards our common goal, but the circumstances did force me to concretize some vaguenesses and to pull together some scattered themes—including some aspects and implications of information theory. Some of the notions presented in this paper were the germs from which substantial portions of my subsequent research grew: for example, the remarks at the end of §11 about the necessary physical nature of information-storage (and on that see H14 in this volume). Other items, such as the relativity of report and command (§10), have so far lain dormant.

1. Astronomer and Economist. Suppose an astronomer offers to bet you ten dollars that at such-and-such an hour on such-and-such a night Sirius will be visible (barring clouds) at such-and-such a position in the heavens. Unless he is careless in his computations, that is practically a sure bet for him and a very bad one for you.

The astronomer's prediction, in which he expresses such confidence, is based on observation. We can base all sorts of predictions on observation. For example, suppose that I observe that my colleague John Doe often wears a white shirt, and that whenever he appears in a white shirt it is accompanied by a green tie. I can predict that the next time he wears a white shirt, it will be accompanied by a green tie. If I keep this prediction to myself, there is a good chance that it will be verified. However, suppose I bet you ten dollars that the predicted event will occur. That would be a very bad bet for me, and a very good one for you, since all you would have to do would be to speak to John about the matter and offer him a cut of your winnings. Of course, I could make him a similar offer, and before long the only possible winner would be John Doe himself.

What is the difference between the star Sirius and our friend John Doe? There are many differences, but only one that is relevant here: John Doe is equipped with apparatus for the reception and interpretation of *communications*, whereas the star Sirius is not. What you and I say about John Doe's behavior, past or future, may potentially play a part in conditioning his future behavior. What the astronomer and you say about the star Sirius's behavior cannot in any way serve causally to condition or change that behavior.

Whenever we try to observe, classify, and predict the behavior of entities which, like John Doe, are equipped with apparatus for the reception and interpretation of communications, we run into the same kind of difficulty we encountered in talking about his habits of dress. That means that every phase of social science is shot through with this difficulty; it is present, though to a much smaller extent, in biological science in general, apparently it is largely or totally absent in the physical sciences.

Here are some more examples:

(1) An economist observes the periodicity of pork production and prices. A farmers' organization reports his findings to hog-raisers, and advises them to try to make their hogs available during the slack periods, thus commanding better prices. In due time enough farmers adjust their schedules to change the periodicity, and the premium prices which they had sought become unavailable.

(2) A Plains Indian youth believes that he must go off alone and fast according to certain rituals, whereupon he will be visited by a spirit who will bestow on him certain powers. He behaves accordingly, and has the experience he expects.

(3) An ex-convict tries to settle down in a new community. The people about him find out that he has been in jail and predict that he will misbehave again. They treat him accordingly, and he does.

(4) A presidential poll shows that candidate A will probably gain the majority of the votes. On election day it is raining, and many people, having confidence in the poll, stay away from the voting-places. Candidate B wins.

(5) An ethnographer studies the ceremonies of a southwestern tribe. Thirty years later the members of the tribe find it advisable to perform a ceremony that has fallen into disuse—no one remembers the details. They obtain a copy of the ethnographer's monograph and perform the ceremony following his account of it.

(6) In the mid 1920s Joseph Stalin, on the basis of "Marxist analysis," predicts that the political forces of the world will polarize around an axis with the United States and the Soviet Union at its ends. Millions of

Russians behave accordingly, and so, in a sense, do millions of Americans and others. By the mid 1940s his prediction has brought itself about.

The expression "self-fulfilling prophecy" has been used for some matters of this kind, but it is too narrow, since some of our examples are rather of "self-defeating" prophecies. But there is apparently a realm in which wishing may make it so.

2. The Dilemma of Social Science. It is generally agreed that, in order to be scientific, a hypothesis must be (1) able to stand up when predictions are based on it, in that the predictions are verified, and (2) shared, or at least sharable, rather than the necessarily exclusive property of a single investigator or investigative group.

In our efforts towards the development of social science, we face a dilemma. We can guarantee the possibility of (1) only by sacrificing (2): if in our bet about John Doe we agree that we will keep it a secret from him, then he is in the status of Sirius. Contrariwise, we can guarantee the possibility of attaining (2) only by sacrificing (1).

There are certain narrow ranges of human activity in which the dilemma does not thrust itself upon us: types of activity which people don't care about, so that they are not influenced to any great extent by the making of predictions about their own behavior. A branch of social science such as linguistics, which is concerned primarily with such a range of behavior, can make (and has made) some progress.

But in order to deal with more "important" problems we must face up to the dilemma and learn to live with it. Perhaps we have to modify our theory of what kind of activity qualifies as scientific. Or perhaps we should not worry so much about the implications of the heavily loaded term "science."

3. The Importance of Communication. One thing we should do is to examine, in detail and with care, the machinery that gives rise to the dilemma: the nature and functioning of human communication and its position in the universe. The key importance of communication has been discerned again and again by social scientists in all sorts of special fields and with all sorts of special interests, but no concerted effort towards its analysis has ever been made. Specialists in "mass communications" make up their own terminology, which is not the same as that used by people doing "content analysis"; neither of these uses the general framework of communications theory as worked out by engineers concerned with electrical and electronic devices. All too often, an investigator who is led by the nature of his problem to the conviction that he must study communications starts out on his own, as though there were no backlog of accomplishment along this line by previous scholars. That controverts a third desirable characteristic of scientific work: that it should be cumulative.

Human society can be regarded as a tremendously complicated inter-locking, crisscrossing, and constantly changing web of communication channels. A very large portion of human behavior is important not as direct action but as communicative action (a distinction we shall clarify in a moment). There are few, if any, real problems in social science which are not either essentially problems in communications or else have a large and important communicative aspect.

We need a frame of reference for the handling of the communications aspects of all such problems—a frame of reference free from useless reification of processes, from mentalism, from eliminable parameters, from teleological notions, and from "explanations" of simple matters in terms of more complex ones. The beginnings of such a frame of reference are gradually becoming available, and this report is aimed at presenting what is available in brief outline.

4. Trigger Action and Direct Action. Suppose a book salesman comes into my office at a time when I do not wish to see him. I might attempt to get rid of him by picking him up and throwing him out. If we know his body mass and the distance he must be carried and thrown, we can compute roughly the amount of energy I must expend, from my own internal store, to accomplish that task. Or I might—much more likely—attempt to get rid of him by moving my lips, tongue, and jaw in such a way as to produce a certain train of sound. Let us assume that the latter procedure is success-ful. The amount of energy required to remove the salesman from the office remains much as before, but most of it supplied by the salesman himself, from his own internal store. I have only had to expend a trifling percentage of the total amount of energy involved. What I have done is to *trigger* the salesman into performing the rest of the task.

We call these two kinds of action "direct action" and "trigger action"; the latter term is apposite because the pulling of the trigger of a gun is another instance of the same phenomenon. If I shoot a deer with a spear, I must supply all the energy necessary both for aiming and for propelling the spear from my internal store. If I shoot a deer with a shotgun, I have to supply enough energy to aim and to pull the trigger, but the remainder of the required energy is supplied by the powder in the shell.

The distinction between direct and trigger action may be meaningless at the size-level of phenomena at which nuclear physicists work. But there is a size-level at and above which the distinction is meaningful. And that threshold size-level is fairly small, since a catalyst is a trigger; if current theories are right, a gene or a virus is a catalyst and thus a trigger. So we need not worry about the validity of the distinction at the size-levels at which occur phenomena of interest to us as social scientists.

Direct action conforms to the law of conservation of energy. The energetic input to a shotgun involves both the energy supplied by the marksman and that supplied by the powder, and regarded as an energetic system the law of conservation of energy is upheld. But in the typical case our interest in a triggering action lies only in the trigger-type input and the output, and in this there is no relationship which requires us to speak of the law of conservation of energy. The energy-level of input and of output can be widely at variance. A man expending ounces or pounds of force at the controls of a crane moves tons of freight. In micrurgy a man expending ounces or large fractions of ounces of force at the controls moves microscopically small objects in a very precise way. The physiologist in examining a human (or other animal) body is concerned with energy transformations. The psychologist—even the so-called physiological psychologist—is concerned rather with trains of trigger-action: with the flow of "information," as we shall see it can be called, rather than with the flow of energy.

Most of human life consists of people triggering one another or certain things in their environment, and of people being triggered by certain things in their environment in ways determined by their own momentary structure. The light which reaches the eyes of a military observer *is not* the energy involved in the message he sends over a wire to headquarters. The orders which go out from headquarters *are not* the energy which is expended by soldiers in the firing of weapons. The energy they expend in aiming and in pulling triggers *is not* the energy that propels the bullets, projectiles, bombs, and so forth. We find the most extreme cases of direct action by one individual on another in war and in the handling of criminals. But war is ninety percent triggering (not "nine-tenths waiting," unless that means the same thing), and even in a penitentiary it is only very rarely that guards actually move a prisoner bodily. We often hear someone say something like, "well, let's not just *talk* about this; let's *do* something." If the one who makes such a remark proposes a concrete program of "action," it usually turns out to be largely talking or other kinds of communicative behavior, not "doing" in the sense of direct action.

5. Transducers and Channels. A fancier word for a trigger is *transducer*. In a radio receiving set, the *energy* input is through the plug inserted into a light socket. That energy is *transformed* by the apparatus in the set, and a *wiring diagram* shows the energy flow. The *communicative* input is the very weak current induced in the antenna by radio waves—or, more accurately, is the modulation in those waves, imitated in the weak current. This input is *transduced* by the apparatus in the set into a message in the physical form of sound; a *control-flow chart* shows the flow of "information." The kind of transformation worked by a transducer is a *transduction*.

There are very simple transducers and very complicated ones. A microphone is a very simple one, which turns a continuous train of sound waves into a continuous train of voltage variations, the latter being, allowing for some distortion, a facsimile of the former. A loudspeaker does the inverse of that. It is possible to build extremely complicated transducers, such that two successive inputs of a given signal will not necessarily result in the same output: the output of the transducer in response to any given input signal depends not only on that signal but also on some definable past sequence of inputs or outputs or both. The encoding and decoding machines used to attain secrecy in military communications often show this kind of complexity.

A *channel* is a segment of a communications circuit where no transduction of the message takes place: anything that happens is energy-transformation—line-loss, random noise, and the like. In old-fashioned telegraphy a wire and the ground are the channel. In radio broadcasting, space (and the ground) form the channel. In speaking, the air is the channel. In writing, paper or some other flat surface is the channel.

6. Tools and Machines. Human beings surround themselves with physical objects on which human action has imparted certain characteristics: such objects are *artifacts*. Certain artifacts (or certain ones in certain functions) are devices of *motor prosthesis*: for example, a spear-thrower, with which a skilled operator can hurl a spear faster, and therefore farther, than he can with just his hand and arm. Certain other artifacts are devices for *sensory prosthesis*: spectacles, hearing aids. Still others are devices for *communicative prosthesis*.

Intersecting this three-way classification is one into *tools* and *machines*. In a machine, the supplying of energy and of guidance (information) are more or less clearly separated: they involve triggering, and thus are transducers. Tools do not involve triggering and are not transducers.

For example, a telescope is a tool for sensory prosthesis, whereas radar is a machine for the same purpose. A bow and arrow are tools for motor prosthesis; a shotgun is a machine. Domestic animals and plants are machines rather than tools: the energy invested by human beings in agriculture or animal husbandry is not the energy which the plants or animals supply when used as food, and, wherever farming has been economically worthwhile, the latter is greater than the former. A piano is a tool; an organ, supplied with power by plugging it into an electric outlet, is a machine. There are interesting borderline cases between tool and machine: an old-fashioned pump-organ, like an old-fashioned pedal sewing machine, is powered by the feet of the player and steered by his fingers; some organs of a half century ago were powered by a small boy working a pump; some organs in Germany in Bach's time were powered by a horse on a treadmill.

Writing is another sort of borderline case. The energy expended by a person speaking is just the energy that hits the ears of a hearer: speech is a tool, if we can regard the sound waves passing through the air as "artifact." But in writing the energy which puts marks on paper *is not* the energy that strikes the eyes of a reader: the marks on paper are triggers which shape light, from the sun or other source, into certain geometrical contours to strike the reader's eyes. So technically we must class writing as a machine rather than a tool. But it is a trivial machine, since the source of the energy that is triggered (sunlight, the sun) is free.

Speech and writing, of course, are communicative, which means that writing is a machine for communicative prosthesis. The classification of prosthetic devices as sensory, communicative, and motor depends on whether they stand between nonhuman sources of stimulus and a person, or between two people, or between a person and the object of his (direct) action.

7. Human Communication in the Narrow Sense. We have proceeded so far without any definition, even informal, of "communication"; but we have now laid the groundwork for at least a temporary definition.

By *human communication* we will mean the triggering of people by people, whether immediate or mediated by communicative artifacts in the sense expounded in §6. The definition is intended to include the case of an individual triggering himself.

As phrased, the definition may cover certain matters that we want to exclude or at least set aside. Since genes are triggering devices, perhaps one could insist that a sperm from a male triggers the sequence of events in a female which follows upon impregnation. I'd like to exclude that. It is possible that some gassy emanations from human beings have a direct effect of the enzyme type on other human beings. I'd like to exclude that. I think it will work if we limit ourselves to those instances in which the behavior of one person triggers a second—or himself—via the sensory receptors and the nervous system.

Another possible limitation is to say that we are concerned only with such triggerings as come about in a culturally determined way—where cultural heritage determines both the types of triggering behavior and the responses to having triggers pulled. Doubtless there are cases in which we are not sure whether culture plays a part or not; such cases are matters for future research.

Presumably almost any observable act of a human being may trigger responses in others. However, not all acts, or differences between acts, are noticed. The triggering effect of acts on others depends largely on the extent to which the acts in question form elements in a *triggering-system*, the elements contrasting with one another, having more or less clearly definable "meanings," and manifesting some stability as a system. The degree to which externally observable acts are systematized is greater than is often realized. Roughly, we can class human acts, and the triggering-systems in which they function, as follows:

(1) Prelinguistic systems (in the sense that they are probably older than human language, whatever impact the development of language may have had on them): bodily and facial gestures.

(2) Language.

(3) Systems *derivative from* language, involving artifacts, largely machines rather than tools: writing, and systems such as telegraphy that are based on writing.

(4) Systems *founded on* language, involving artifacts, but consisting of elements which do not in any sense "stand for" elements of language. Here belong all the nonce systems established for a specific purpose by talking matters over (one light versus two in the old church tower; "Pull the blind down when you want me to break in and take the pictures"), and also more permanent systems such as the international road-sign scheme used throughout Europe.

Modern electronic devices like the telephone, radio, and television occupy a peculiar position, in that their make-up permits them to transmit speech, or signals derived more or less immediately from speech, but also to transmit things which would not in the first instance be classed as communicative (that is, the *transmitting* is communicative, but the *item transmitted* in itself is not—as, for example, when a television camera picks up an actual landscape).

All sorts of features of human behavior which one would not be tempted to classify primarily as communicative nevertheless have a communicative aspect—usually belonging in category (4) above. Clothing is not communicative, but the selection of one type of garment or decoration rather than another may symbolize status, temporary state (black for mourning), provenience or personality (flashy striped suit), and the like. Similarly for architecture or anything else. Sometimes we look too hard for a symbolic (that is, communicative) justification when there is actually only a direct one. In parts of western Africa there is customarily a wall just inside the door of a house, about which one must walk to get to the major part of the interior. One ethnographer tried to elicit a symbolic explanation for that wall, in terms of spirits to be kept out or something like that. In point of fact, the wall is built to keep the strong prevailing winds in the territory from blowing out one's fire.

8. Simple Communicative Set-Ups. Entropy; Information. As in other fields of study, progress can be made in the analysis of communication only by concentrating (at least to start with) on systems which are artificial both in their great simplicity and in their relative isolation. The most fruitful work along this line in recent years has been done by engineers, who do not have to leave so much aside in achieving simple models, since their practical aims concern relatively simple systems (radio, radar, and television may not seem very simple, but certainly they are a great deal less complicated than are human beings).

The irreducible minimum of elements for any model are these:

(1) A *source*: for example, a person in New York who wishes to transmit certain information to someone in Chicago.

(2) A *message*: something produced or emitted by the source; let us say, a sequence of written words.

(3) A *transmitter*, which operates on the message to convert it into a form in which it can be sent via the available channel; in our example, a telegraph key, coupled to an operator.

(4) A *channel*: in our example, a wire running from New York to Chicago (plus the ground).

(5) A *signal*: that sent through the channel by the transmitter. In our example, a series of voltage pulses of varying durations.

(6) A *receiver*: the device which, driven by the received signal, produces a reasonable facsimile of the message that was fed to the transmitter.

(7) A *destination*: the person in Chicago who ultimately receives the information.

(8) A *code*: a set of conventions assigning elements in the message to elements in the signal. The transmitter operates according to this code; the receiver operates according to the inverse of the code.

(9) *Noise*: anything that interferes with the signal in such a way that the received signal is not always the same as the transmitted signal.

Engineers are concerned with problems of the following kinds: Given messages with certain known characteristics, what are the most efficient devices (measured in terms of energy or money) for their transmission? How can the effects of noise be minimized? Given a channel of known characteristics, as well as messages of known characteristics, what types of coding (and thus of transmitters and receivers) will guarantee the highest fidelity at the lowest cost?

In order to approach such problems certain engineers have first tried to decide what is the commodity which their communicative systems are supposed to handle, and have come out with the answer: *information*. They mean by this term something related to, but not identical with, the everyday sense of the word.

A communicative system must be built to accommodate not just a single message, but any of an ensemble of messages, since what specific message will be transmitted cannot be known at the time of design. If it were known, there would be no reason to build the apparatus. There is no point in building a communicative system, then, unless the source of messages will have at least a minimum of *choice*, unknown in advance, between alternative messages. The simplest range would be a binary choice, with the two messages equally likely. We can illustrate this with a sort of purified game of "twenty questions."

If I ask you a question knowing that no matter what I ask your answer will be "yes," then there is no point in asking the question. But if you may answer "yes" and may answer "no," and if I have no reason to expect one answer any more than the other, then the situation makes sense.

In our simplified "twenty questions," you decide first on an integer between 1 and 1,048,576 inclusive, using some device whereby all of these integers are equally likely to be chosen. I then proceed to ask you twenty questions, each one of which must be answerable by "yes" or "no," my aim being to ascertain the exact integer you selected without having to ask more than just those twenty permitted questions. I can achieve the result without fail as follows: I phrase each question in such a way that the alternatives not eliminated by all previous questions are exactly dichotomized, so that your answer "yes" will indicate the location of the target number in one half of the remaining set, and your answer "no" will locate it in the other half. Any procedure that guarantees such repeated dichotomizing will work without fail. Any deviation from such a procedure will enable me to get the answer in some playings of the game with fewer than twenty questions, but will make me pay for that by having to use more than twenty questions in just as many cases. The procedure first described will work because twenty successive equal divisions of 1,048,576 objects into smaller sets leaves just one object in each ultimate set. That is, $1,048,576 = 2^{20}$.

The *quantification of information* is based on the considerations just given. The simplest possible choice is an equally likely one between two and only two alternatives. The *amount of information* inherent in a situation so characterized is called *one binary digit* ($= bit$, *bigit*, or *binit*). If there are n equally likely alternatives, then the amount of information inherent in the situation is $\log_2 n$ binits. In the idealized twenty questions discussed above, any train of answers will convey 20 binits of information. That is, $\log_2 1,048,576 = 20$.

The *entropy* of a source is the average rate at which it can (or does) emit information. There are certain fixed relationships between entropy of source, amount of noise in a channel (also measurable in binits or in binits per second), and the maximum rate at which information from the source can be transmitted over the channel, regardless of how cleverly transmitter, receiver, and code are designed. By determining such constraints, engineers can prevent themselves from seeking unattainable goals in actual hardware design.

9. Limitations on the Quantification of Information. What we have covered in §8 omits a good many inherently fascinating and perhaps ultimately relevant features of the current engineering doctrine of information theory, but for the moment we have all we need.

One of the most challenging aspects of information theory is the actual achievement of a quantification of information. However, this is also a point on which there has been the greatest amount of speculative nonsense in the recent literature. So let us indicate immediately the sharp limitations within which the measurement of amount of information makes sense.

In the first place, . . . [1]

In the second place, quantification of information makes sense only with respect to a given closed system. "Amount of information" is not transferrable from one communicative system or network to another, as we can compare the amounts of energy in a storage battery and in a clock-weight suspended at a given height. There is no "law of conservation of information." To serve one 100-watt light bulb a generator must

1. [∇ At this point I proceeded to repeat the mistake of my review of Shannon (p. 23), corrected now by the Addendum to that review (p. 50).]

generate 100 watts of power. To serve ten 100-watt bulbs the generator must supply a kilowatt of power. If all the bulbs are unscrewed, the power sent out by the generator has to go somewhere: it leaks, or the generator blows out, or something equally drastic. To supply a telegraph receiver with 100 binits per minute a transmitter has to emit 100 binits per minute. To supply ten receivers each at the rate of 100 binits per minute, the transmitter still need only emit 100 binits per minute. If no one is receiving anywhere on the line, there is no "piling up" of information—it simply vanishes. It is exactly like pulling the trigger of an unloaded gun, or continuing to speak over a telephone after one's interlocutor has hung up.

In order to compare the capacity of two communicative networks it is necessary to couple them, and the coupling itself has to be informational rather than just energetic—via transducers, not via transformers. But that introduces new transducers into the scheme, and we cannot know whether different sets of introduced transducers would give the same results. This yields a rather puzzling indeterminacy.

We conclude that although the general approach of engineering information theory may be of value in our broader problems, the specific matter of quantifying information is of no great *practical* significance. New developments may in time change that.

10. Feedback; "Purposive" Behavior; Commands and Reports. Let us examine a system consisting of a set of observers, an officer in charge, and an antiaircraft gun crew. A target comes into view. The observers report its presence, location, and course to the officer in charge, who reports the same matters to the gun crew in the form of firing instructions. As the gun fires, the success or failure of the shells is observed by the observers, who send amended reports through to the gun crew and thus bring about adjustments in the aiming and firing.

The observers in this case are human beings working with certain apparatus of sensory prosthesis. The officer in charge is linked to the observers on the one hand and to the gun crew on the other via various types of communicative prosthesis; perhaps this involves some type of analog computing machine, which is a communicative machine in our terms. The gun itself is motor prosthesis.

In such a set-up the natural way of speaking is to say that the officer in charge, or alternatively all the humans who are participating, are behaving purposively: they have a purpose, namely, to bring down the target.

The human element can be eliminated. Observation instruments can be connected to a computer, the latter in turn to an automatically loaded and fired antiaircraft weapon. Then all human agency need do is turn the apparatus on: the target is tracked, the weapon aimed, the bursts of the shells are observed and the aim is corrected. In this case it is still natural to speak of the set-up as behaving purposively.

A simpler example of a "teleological mechanism" is a house-heating apparatus with thermostatic control. A small amount of the heat fed into the house by the furnace serves to operate the thermostat and turn the furnace off; as the house cools, the cooling thermostat eventually reaches a critical point and turns the furnace back on again. An electric re-frigerator works in just the reverse manner. The automatic furnace func-tions with a purpose: to keep the temperature in the house between certain limits.

The keynote in any such set-up is *feedback*. The thermostat sends signals (information) to the furnace, triggering it off and on. The result of the furnace's operation is observed by the thermostat and determines the instructions sent by it to the furnace.

We know from experimental evidence that certain varieties of control-feedback are involved in certain kinds of human behavior. In the articula-tory motions involved in speaking, for example, there are two types of feedback: kinesthetic (we feel the positions and motions of our speech organs) and auditory (we hear the sounds which we produce). Each of these can be interfered with experimentally, and the results show how important the feedback is. Kinesthetic feedback can be dulled by imbibing an amount of ethyl alcohol. The clarity of enunciation deteriorates unless the speaking process is slowed and is controlled more carefully via auditory feedback. Auditory feedback can be dulled by going deaf. Many a person who has become partly deaf but has not procured a hearing aid has been noticed by those about him to speak less clearly.

Some speculative investigators have been led to conclude that all instances of "purposive behavior" in human beings are examples of this mechanism. That is a very big jump, and cannot be accepted without a great deal of empirical investigation. In the meantime, however, we cloud our discussions if we speak in teleological terms about any phase of human or other animal behavior except just those phases for which control-feedback has been clearly demonstrated.

The military example with which this section began affords a point of departure for another interesting line of development. From the point of view of the officer in charge, information coming from his observers constitutes *reports*, whereas the information he sends to the gun crew constitutes *commands*. Let us remove the officer from the scene, and have the observers send the information they gather directly to the people and apparatus which aim and fire the gun. Now, looking from the gun to the observers, the information passing along the channel can validly be regarded as report; looking from the observers towards the gun, the very same information can with equal validity be regarded as command. Which is it? What is the essential difference between a report and a command? It does not lie in the information itself. It must then lie, as suggested, in the place within the communicative set-up at which we stand.

We tend to think of some communicating-and-acting systems as "nucleated": as having some sort of "integrating center." In the ordinary antiaircraft emplacement there is an officer in charge, and he is the nucleus: information flowing to him we call report, and information flowing from him we call command. But many systems are not nucleated in that way. Consider the terribly complex social unit called Cornell University. True enough, the "table of organization" of the university shows a titular head (Board of Trustees and President). If an outsider wants to "find" Cornell University in order to give the university a million dollars, he will have no trouble. But if an outsider wants to "find" the university in order to deliver a scolding for some actual or imaginary wrong, he may have a very hard time. Nothing as complex as a university actually has any single governing nucleus. A kindred error underlies the search for the "center" of this or that behavioral category in the human brain.

11. Types of Transmission. The transmitter and receiver mentioned in §8 are both transducers. Assuming that we have a flow of information (a "message") in some understood form reaching a certain point, there are certain different kinds of transmission to which it can be subjected.

One classification of types of transmission is into *tight-beam* and *broadcast*. Tight-beam transmission may be from a single transmitter to any number of appropriate receivers, but they are physically hooked together in such a way that only the receivers actually installed in the circuit can receive the transmitted signal. Telegraphy is a case. A letter, placed in a sealed envelope and mailed to a given recipient, is perhaps another case. Broadcast transmission is characterized by the fact that any appropriately designed receiver *within range* can receive and retransduce the signal; at a given moment there may in fact be only one such receiver, or even none at all. Speech is inherently broadcast transmission; we have to take special steps, such as whispering directly into someone's ear, to force it to be tight-beam. Any type of transmission which uses, as channel, a medium which constantly surrounds us all is fundamentally broadcast transmission. The types of "media" of concern in the study of "mass communications" are normally channels of this kind, thus involving broadcast transmission.

A special kind of broadcast transmission is the production of *records*. Records are a sort of temporal broadcasting: if a message in any form has been recorded, then it can be reconverted to its original form (more or less accurately) *at any later time*. Writing is recorded speech, with certain modifications and added features: you can read now, and again tomorrow, the note that you wrote to yourself this morning; archaeologists read now records carved in stone several thousand years ago.

Some information in transit takes the shape of a time-sequence of signals, and some takes the shape of a spatial array of marks. Records, whatever they may be a record *of*, necessarily take the latter physical shape. That is obviously the case of written records, or of the curves in the groove on a phonograph record; it is also true of the pulses in the mercury of a mercury delay tube, even though in this last case the whole packet of pulses is in motion, chasing its own tail round and round until it is drained off and erased.

12. The Communicative Hierarchy. If we tap a telegraph wire and observe the voltage pulses which are passing the tapped point, we can reasonably ask about the antecedents and consequences of those pulses.

The antecedents of the pulses are a spatial array of letters on paper: this spatial array was transduced, by the transmitting operator and his apparatus, into the pulses. The consequences are another spatial array of letters on paper, bearing some relation to the original array, into which the pulses will be transduced at the receiving end. It is natural to say: *original message*, converted by *step-up transduction* into *signal*, which is then reconverted by *step-down transduction* into *recovered message*, the latter being a reasonable facsimile (in some reasonable sense of "reasonable") of the original message.

If we are concerned only with telegraphy then this is all we need say. A particular code (Morse or Baudot) governs the assignment of letters to voltage pulses and vice versa.

But if we are concerned with the wider communicative framework within which the telegraphic episode occurs, then we must push farther, to investigate the antecedents of the original (written) message and the consequences of the recovered (written) message.

For it turns out that a piece of writing, though it serves as the original for telegraphy, is not itself directly related to noncommunicative matters. The piece of writing is itself a signal produced by a step-up transduction applied to a message in an even more elemental form: a stretch of speech. Likewise, at the receiving end the recovered written message is due to be retransduced by a step-down transduction into an even more elemental form: a stretch of speech.

The difficulty in this is that the transductions involved take place inside the skins of human beings. A small child in our culture may say words one by one to himself audibly, so that an observer can hear them, before he writes them out, and he may have to read something aloud in order to understand it. But adults are trained not to do that. How, then, can we be sure that a given individual, when he scribbles out a note or fills in a telegraph blank with no audible vocal noise, is actually saying to himself (perhaps entirely within his central nervous system) the oral message that the writing represents? The answer is that we cannot be absolutely sure, but that the weight of indirect evidence supports the proposal; this is not the place to survey that evidence.

We can then ask: is a message in spoken form really elemental? Or is it, in turn, a step-up transduction from something else? The former is apparently the correct answer: speech is *primary communication*. The antecedents of a stretch of speech consist of various triggering environmental forces operating on the speaker, processed by his internal structure as it is at the given moment (that structure being, in turn, the product of a long past history).[2] The antecedents of a stretch of speech are factors which are not themselves communicative.

Writing is then *secondary communication*, and telegraphy is *tertiary*; but for many purposes it is more convenient to group them together simply as *derived* communication, in contrast with primary, rather than to continue the sorting-out and numbering of derivative levels. Gestures are primary; language is primary; trigger-pulling physical contacts of various kinds, as when one touches a baby's shoulder and it turns over, or as during sexual activities, are all primary. Almost all other forms of communication used by humans are either derived strictly in the sense we have described, or else are subsidiary systems, even nonce-systems, involving conventions worked out by the use of primary systems.

13. Meaning and Meaning-Mechanisms. In telegraphy the *in-meaning* of a given stretch of signal is the letter or sequence of letters which was transduced into it, and the *out-meaning* is the letter or sequence into which it is retransduced at the receiver. Barring noise, in-meaning and

2. [∇ Statements of this sort never seem to make sufficient allowance for the remarkable and very important phenomenon of *displacement*: talking freely about things that are not present at the scene of the talking.]

out-meaning are the same, and we can speak simply of "meaning." The *semantic conventions* of telegraphy are Morse code, which assigns certain signals to certain letters: three dots are assigned to the letter S, and so on. If we did not know Morse code, but could tap a telegraph wire and could also know the input at the transmitter, observation of a sufficiently large sample would tell us what the conventions are.

In derived communication the problem of meaning is simple. In primary communication it is extremely difficult. The meanings of various linguistic forms (words, parts of words, phrases), for example, can be said to be the conventional associations between those forms and things or situations in the world about us by virtue of which speech takes the shape it does with the antecedents and consequences it has.

Given that there is such an associative bond between a thing-which-means and a thing-meant, there are two fundamentally distinct types of meaning-mechanisms or meaning-relationships: the *arbitrary* and the *iconic*. Both can be involved in the same system. For example, the assignment of three dots to the letter S in Morse code is entirely arbitrary; likewise the assignment of three dashes to the letter O. However, given these arbitrary assignments, it is iconic that the temporal sequence three dots, three dashes, and three more dots should represent the spatial sequence "SOS". That is, whenever there is some kind of *geometrical similarity* between that which means and that which is meant, there is an iconic element. It is typical of derived communicative systems that there is a small size-level where meanings are purely arbitrary, above which there is an increasing element of iconism.

But that is not the case with primary communication. The associative tie between the spoken word *man* and the entities or kinds of entities represented by that word is purely arbitrary. There is occasional slight iconism, as in onomatopoeia (*bow-wow* sounds only vaguely like the barking of a dog, but it sounds more like it than would, say, *Philadelphia*). Sometimes on very large size-levels, as in the minutes of a meeting, there is a trace of iconism in that the temporal sequence of topics discussed in successive sections of the orally given minutes matches the temporal sequence in which the things being reported on actually occurred. The great difficulty with any large iconic element in language is that the world about us is a many-dimensional continuum, whereas speech is linear.

14. Multiordinality. A particularly knotty difficulty in the analysis of the communicative aspect of human behavior appears in what I choose to call *multiordinality*.

In certain modern varieties of wire-transmission, as many as ten or twelve separate conversations can be carried simultaneously over a single channel. A small sample taken from the middle of such a transmission would contain features which were part of all or most of those separate messages.

Something partly similar occurs when we speak. A person in speaking transmits, as it were, two distinct *linguistic* messages. One consists of the sequence of words which he enunciates: this is the message that the conventions of our ordinary writing-system allow us to transduce into written records. The other consists of his intonation or speech-melody. The difference between this and multiple transmission of unrelated conversations over a single telephone wire is that in the case of speech the intonational message constitutes, as it were, a kind of running commentary on the word message. We are so accustomed to this that usually we do not even notice it. Yet anyone who has ever examined a stenotype transcript of speech delivered conversationally will immediately recognize how important the intonational commentary can be for the intelligibility of the word message. True to English writing habits, the transcript of what has been taken via stenotype transduces only the word message, leaving the intonational message out almost altogether. In more carefully planned writing, we provide for the necessary omission of intonation by so phrasing our word message that the loss does not make trouble.

But that is not the only communicatively significant thing that happens during speech. The word message and the intonational message are both part of what a linguist is required to study; they form subsidiary parts of language itself. In addition to that, there are various gradations of loudness, pitch, raspiness or smoothness of voice, definiteness or indefiniteness of pitch, and the like, which tell us something. These features have been collectively called *voice-qualifiers*. The difference between a heartfelt and a sarcastic *Thank you* can lie entirely in the voice-qualifiers, the two being linguistically identical—identical both in words and in intonation.

If we hear a voice from the next room, we can often tell, not only what words are being said and with what intonation, but also, via voice-qualifiers and the fundamental tone-quality of the voice, the mood of the speaker *and his identity*.

In other words, preoccupation with relatively simple highly derived communicative systems must not conceal from us that one of the chief complexities of primary communication is the customary simultaneous transmission of three or more simultaneous messages. To those which we have already mentioned, the continuous flow of gestures can be added. In actual interhuman activity all these different communicative media function simultaneously. It is not wrong to pull them out one by one for analysis, but it would be wrong if we did not restore them to their context in due time.

Let us imagine that a stenographer, a linguist interested in dialect differences, a police detective, and a psychiatrist are all listening to the statement being given by a suspect in a police station. (How the linguist gets there I don't know, unless he is also a suspect.) The suspect produces a unitary train of behavior, some of it overtly communicative, some of it apparently only fidgeting. Each member of the audience notices a different segment of the whole. The stenographer concentrates on the sequence of words, since that is what his training enables him to produce a record of. He may sometimes make unconscious use of intonation to help tell what word has been said, but the intonation itself does not go down in his notes. The linguist may hear other things, but his attention is caught primarily by certain key pronunciations of certain words and by certain vocabulary selections, on the basis of which he tries to decide where the suspect originally came from. The detective perhaps observes most fully: he is interested in whether what the suspect says is true or not, and he watches for intonations, quavers of the voice, or gestures which might give the lie to the pure word-message they accompany. He may not be able to give a very clear description of these behavioral clues, but if he is a good detective he makes use of them. The psychiatrist pays even more attention to all these minor and hard-to-observe "minimal clues"; like the detective, he may not be able to name all the behavioral features on which he bases his inferences, but he has been trained in the interpretation of them, and if he is a good psychiatrist he went into psychiatry in the first place because he was quick at drawing inferences from such clues.

Any information (or misinformation) which any of the four in the audience legitimately gets from his observations *is based on overt physical behavior* of the subject. There is very little (if any) of our overtly observable behavior which has not been culturally channeled into performing some communicative function. When the evidence is actual words, or the most easily described gestures, it is called "concrete." When it is more subtle deviations from unspoken "norms," or when it is perfectly obvious features of behavior which have never been analyzed and codified, the inferences are apt to be ascribed to "insight" or "intuition" or the like (in the extreme case, to "telepathy"). But *the fundamental mechanisms involved are the same for all.*

15. Unit-Recognition. If we knew nothing about telegraphy, but happened to tap a telegraph wire and record a stretch of signal for examination, we might be very hard put to it to figure out the inner structure of the signal—that is, to determine the recurrent unit signals of which it is composed. Suppose that someone "in the know" were to supply us with full information about the unit signals. We could then make a statistical analysis of a large sample of telegraph signal, which would tell us something about the *internal economy* or the *pure syntactics* of the system, but would tell us nothing at all about the *semantics* of the system—that is, we should still have no way of knowing which signal-units represent one thing and which represent another.

Telegraphy involves human beings, as parts of transmitters and receivers and as designers. Therefore it is easy for us to determine both the internal economy and the semantics of telegraph signal: we need only "ask a transducer," which in this case is capable of understanding our question and of supplying the answer. But in many communicative systems that is quite impossible.

For example, consider language. A speaker of any given language actually signals in terms of a small finite number of discrete points of reference (the "phonemes" of his language), at which he aims in his articulation, and to which he is trained to pay attention as a receiver of speech, the latter training involving also the ignoring of minor ("subphonemic") deviations. But this phonemic system was built into the speaker in his early childhood, by virtue of a very complicated sequence of experiences, and he cannot give reasonable and accurate answers to questions about it. He *controls* a phonemic system, but cannot *describe* it accurately.

The linguist is therefore forced to use indirect methods, somewhat resembling those of cryptanalysis, in order to determine even the very simple matter of the fundamental units of which utterances are built. The methods by which the linguist accomplishes that task need not be described here. Suffice it to say that, logically, there is only one way to accomplish the task: the *control* of the phonemic system and the *ability to analyze and describe* it have somehow to come to reside in a single individual. Theoretically there are two ways to achieve that: the linguist may teach phonemic theory to his informant, or he may learn the language from his informant. The latter does not necessarily mean acquiring all the complexity and fluency of control that the informant has, but it means acquiring certain habits of hearing and pronouncing which empirically match those of the informant, as shown by various tests. The second procedure is the one nearly always used.

An English-speaking linguist working with a Menomini informant will at the beginning hear Menomini speech in terms of the familiar phonemic pattern of English. In particular—for the sake of our example—he will hear both p-like sounds and b-like sounds. As native speakers of English we all know that the difference between a p-sound and a b-sound is relevant: the difference between these two, and only that difference, distinguishes such a pair of utterances as *They stored the cotton in pails* and *They stored the cotton in bales*. In working with Menomini, the English-speaking linguist in due time *unlearns* this contrast: he discovers that this difference never functions in Menomini, and that in detecting sometimes something more like a *p*, sometimes more like a *b*, he is overdifferentiating. On the other hand, certain types of difference which are quite irrelevant in English are relevant in Menomini, and the linguist in due time has to train himself to make and to recognize them systematically, not haphazardly.

The process by which the linguist comes to "feel" differences between speech sounds as his informant does, and to ignore differences that the informant ignores, has been called *empathy*.

When we work with any aspect of a culture radically different from our own, we either realize quickly that the organization of physically distinct experiences into "sames" and "differents" is different from our own, or else we get nowhere fast. When we operate within our own community, this absolute necessity of learning the codes and signals *used by those whom we are observing* is sometimes overlooked. A great many problems with which social scientists have dealt under the label "values" seem to belong here.

Let us take one radically different example. In an amusing piece on "Probability, Rarity, Interest, and Surprise," the mathematician Warren Weaver points out that, in terms of the probabilities of various different bridge hands, one has no right to be more surprised at a hand of thirteen spades than at, say, Spade 8-7-4-2, Heart J-9-6-3, Diamond A-10-5, and Club 8-6. The first hand, true enough, is very good, and the second one rather discouragingly bad. But the probability of receiving either of these hands is exactly the same. Not until well into his article does Weaver finally note—almost in passing—the really important factor. We distinguish sharply among different extremely good hands, less sharply among moderately good ones, and hardly at all among the great mass of poor hands. The second hand described above is one of a large set of equally poor hands, where the probability of receiving *some* one of this set (no matter *which* one) is relatively high. The first hand described is one of a very small set of remarkably good hands, and the probability of getting one *or another* of these very good hands is very small. We should be equally surprised, then, at getting any *specific* set of thirteen out of the fifty-two cards; but we have a perfect right to be more surprised at receiving *some* good hand than at getting *some* average-to-poor hand.

One of the most difficult aspects in the determination of the internal economy, as well as the semantic conventions, of a communicative system lies in the fact that equivalent physical units—two occurrences of one and the same signal-unit—need not necessarily have much in common physically. Or, put in another way, two manifestations of a single signal-unit of the repertory may be less similar physically than two manifestations of two distinct signal-units. What is equally confusing, two physically identical occurrences (physically identical as far as we can judge without measurements more careful than are usually made) may be instances of two distinct and contrasting signal-units. This we can illustrate. Here is part of a rapidly hand-lettered address on a letter:

Chicago, Illinois

This is perfectly legible. The postman knows what to do with it; he is not likely even to notice the point we are illustrating. Note that the second word begins with three roughly identical vertical strokes. No two of them, I believe, are more similar to each other than to the third. Yet the first counts as an occurrence of the letter "capital eye," whereas the other two are occurrences of the letter "lower-case ell." In physical shape, capital eyes vary around one norm, and lower-case ells about another: the norms are distinct. But the ranges of variation in physical shape of actual occurrences intersect or overlap.

When working with an unfamiliar communicative system this makes trouble. We have to find out what each signaling-unit in an actual message "really is"—that is, what it is taken to be by those who participate in the system, not merely in terms of its physical shape.

16. Possible Tasks. There is a degree of relativity in the valid use of the term "transducer." If we wish, we can regard a whole radio broadcasting set as a single complex transducer, the input to which is sound (impinging on the microphone), and the output from which is the radio signal which leaves the antenna. But for some purposes it is necessary to decompose this single transducer into a set of several transducers connected in tandem. A transduction takes place at the microphone: its input is sound, but its output is a modulated electric current. A transduction takes place within each step-up tube, since the modulated current from the previous tube (or from the microphone) *is not* the current which leaves that tube, although the *modulation* is essentially the same. And a transduction takes place at the antenna, since the input to it is a modulated electric current but its output is radio waves.

In the same way, there are some very simple circumstances in which we can choose to regard a human being as a unitary (though extremely complex) transducer; there are other circumstances in which it is relevant to speak as though a single human being contained a number of transducers hooked up in various ways. Sometimes this relevance is supported in the same way it is for the radio station: physiological psychologists actually observe, in a rough way, the gross structure of the nervous system and the general location of bundles of synapses. More often, however, it is an "as if" way of speaking, not supported by anatomical investigation, but nevertheless valid and fruitful if we remember that we are speaking in terms of control-flow charts, not in terms of wiring diagrams (§5).

In many a social-science enterprise, what we are confronted by is one or another type of partial observation of the actual operation of a communicative system, simple or complex; and what we seek is to draw inferences about aspects of the system not actually being observed. Now, in the simple case of electronic or other derivative communicative systems there are certain things that can be done along this line and certain things that cannot. Here are some of those that *can* be done:

(1) Given a transducer and a sufficiently large sample of input, one can analyze the structure of these two and predict the output, as well as determine the code. Analysis of input and transducer tells us the code because the code is physically embodied in the structure of the transducer—indeed, that is the only place and the only way in which a code "exists" as a physical reality.

(2) Given input and code (without transducer), one can predict output, and one can often describe a transducer which would operate on the input according to the code, though one cannot know that this describes the actual physical structure of the transducer in question.

(3) Given input and output in sufficiently large quantities, one can describe the code and (with the same limitations as for 2 above) the transducer.

(4) Given output and transducer, one can make an inverse prediction of input, and describe the code.

(5) Given output and code, one can make an inverse prediction of input and describe (in control-flow-chart terms) the transducer.

(6) Given a very large amount of output and general information about input, code, and transmitter, one can determine specific input. This is cryptanalysis.

It will be noted that in general two kinds of information are needed in order to draw any conclusions. A knowledge of input alone is obviously worthless—that would be like a psychologist trying test stimuli on a rat but not bothering to observe the rat's responses. A knowledge of output alone is similarly worthless: that is almost the state of affairs in the case of the Cretan inscriptions, and we have great difficulty even in the determination of the signal-units involved (are the first symbol in inscription 13 and the seventh from the right in inscription 92 instances of "the same" symbol, or of two different symbols? They look somewhat alike, but that is no guarantee either way). If we can acquire enough general information about the general pattern of life of the Minoans, we can put the problem of deciphering their inscriptions into category 3 of those listed above, and in due time perhaps succeed.[3]

In any situation in which we do not actually know the physical structure of the transducer (and we know it only in simple electronic cases or the like) there is another source of indeterminacy: the nature of the transducer, and hence of the code, may change as our observations are carried out. If the change is cyclical or otherwise determinate, as it is in even the most complicated electronic case, then in enough time the difficulty can be resolved. But in primary communication, change seems to be noncyclical and, if in fact determinate, so complex that the mathematics of probability is still the appropriate machinery with which to handle it. Even in the analysis of linguistic structure, our description of a language holds only in general and for a finite period of time: random individuals in the community say things that deviate from our description of the language of the community, and in the course of years the common pattern changes so that the description no longer fits.

17. Experimental Design and Bad Terminology. It is no part of the purpose of this report to try to relate any great number of social-science enterprises, which have been carried on within the framework of other terminologies, to the framework developed here. But let us take one sample case in "content analysis."

A social psychologist has certain individuals observe certain events and

---

3. [∇ I didn't know when I wrote this that Michael Ventris had already found the key for the decipherment of Linear B. Incidentally, he found it not by the laborious method proposed in the text but by serendipity (an unlikely guess that turned out to be right), which, whenever available, is much to be preferred.]

then produce brief written statements about what they have observed. He then attempts to analyze these written statements or "protocols." His aim is to try to differentiate between the writers of the protocols on the basis of what aspects of the observed events they have paid attention to and have bothered to mention.

In our terminology, the psychologist is trying to determine the characteristics, or some of the characteristics, of a number of very complex transducers, by controlling input and analyzing output. The case falls into category 3 of those listed in §16. The input in this case is not purely communicative, but a combination of communicative stimulus and "direct-action" stimulus. Only part of the total input is controlled, but the relativity of our use of terms permits us to regard anything else that goes on, say the nature and strength of hunger-pangs in the various subjects, as characteristics of the transducers rather than as additional, simultaneous, inputs.

The protocols in this case are messages directed from the subjects (as transmitters) to the psychologist (as receiver). In other instances of analysis of written documents, one must consider the documents as having been broadcast in one way or another, so that the analyst is only one of a family of potential receivers. In still other instances, what the analyst does is to tap a channel where presumably tight-beam transmission is occurring. In cases like these, the analyst does not control input, but must attempt to determine something about it from other sources.

The term "content" is a peculiarly bad one to use in connection with any enterprise of this kind. The "content" of something is, presumably, what is in it. The content or contents of a bucket of sand is the sand. But a stretch of message or signal has no content in this sense. The protocols produced by the subjects of the experiment outlined above are stretches of message; physically, they are marks on paper. They are written according to a coding-convention known to the psychologist, and represent transductions of speech forms also known to him: the subjects and the psychologist speak "the same" language and use "the same" writing system. The psychologist's interest is not in what lies *in* the messages—because *nothing* does. His interest is in what occurred *behind* them.

This same sort of mistake of reification often creeps into the terminology in which the psychologist describes his results. The psychologist is certainly not concerned with the physical structure of the transducers: his aim is not wiring diagrams, but only rough control-flow charts, or measures of certain kinds of difference between the control flow in the different transducers who were his subjects. Actually his best course is to do this in terms of apparent differences of codes, saying nothing at all even metaphorically about the physical structure of the transducers.

Our discussion of multiordinality (§14) implies that the experimenter must be careful to sort out the different types of evidence contained within the protocols. The subjects have different handwritings, and these differences constitute one kind of culturally conditioned evidence, a kind which must be "lifted off" before the experimenter proceeds to consider the rest. He may, of course, choose to ignore this particular part of the evidence. The subjects may vary in the accuracy with which they conform to the socially established norm of the writing system (in spelling and punctuation). This, in turn, must be taken as a separable layer of evidence. Only after that can the experimenter consider the string of speech-forms of which the written material is a transduction. But here, also, he can consider various things. He can make a close-grained grammatical analysis of each protocol, or he can make rather loose statistical determinations; or he can simply "receive" the protocol as a message in a code with which he is familiar, and draw his inferences from what is meant by the message rather than from the internal economy of the message itself.

In this last case, he is operating via a sort of empathy. In effect, he is saying to himself: "If I observed what this subject observed, and reported on it as he has, what would I be like?" We had better not jeer at this apparently misty approach—there is too much to do which can apparently only be done, if at all, via empathy. But we should be able to know when, and to what extent, this approach and procedure are being used.

∇ The references in the original of this paper were to Shannon's work and my review of it (see p. 96 in the present volume), to a paper by Brillouin (see p. 46 fn. 26 in the present volume), and to Weaver's paper (see p. 51 fn. 32).

H5. HOW TO LEARN MARTIAN

Late 1954. First printed in *Astounding Science Fiction* 55.97–106 (May 1955).
Popularization and teaching are akin: either, taken seriously, forces one to consider carefully what is important and what is not. The present piece deals only with the phonemic principle, but it points the way towards the ethnographic generalization of that principle carried out in later writings, especially in H6, H9, and Part One of *Man's Place in Nature* (1973a).

An agent of the Galactic Federation, sent to Earth to case the joint secretly for either friendly or inimical purposes, could do a good deal worse than to make a survey of the scientific terms that appear, quite casually, in contemporary science fiction. True enough, there would be some discrepancy between the state of scientific development suggested by such a survey and the actual state of development in laboratory and industry—atomic energy was spoken of quite freely in our type of fiction for decades before technology caught up with imagination—and, in reverse, real recent developments in some fields are only now beginning to find their way into science fiction. If the agent's sole aim were to measure our technological potential, science fiction would be of no great help. But if he also wanted to determine the *degree of general technological readiness* of the whole population—at least in so-called "civilized" parts of the world—then the suggested survey would be of considerable value.

One score on which, as a measure of real technological development, our agent's study of science fiction might badly mislead him, is in the matter of communication, particularly the basic form of human communication, *language*. An occasional term of modern linguistics turns up from time to time in science fiction: "phoneme," in particular, is a word to conjure with just as much as is "transistor" or "cybernetics." The effect sought by the use of such a word is spoiled if the story-writer pauses to explain: the use must be casual, implying that the reader knows all about such things. And, because many of our magazines regularly run factual articles or departments, and we addicts regularly read them, this assumption of the story-writer is very often true.

If we can pride ourselves on the number of modern developments which were anticipated by the lively imaginations of an earlier generation of authors, I think perhaps we should temper this pride with a bit of shame that we have been such Johnny-come-latelies about phonemes, morphemes, intonations, constructions, immediate constituents, the impact of language on culture, and the like.

Do you know when the fundamental principle of phonemics was first expounded? It was explained rather clearly—though of course without the word "phoneme"—by a twelfth-century Icelander who was annoyed by the inaccuracy with which his compatriots put down written marks to represent Icelandic speech. We can probably forgive ourselves for not having known about this particular early episode, especially since modern linguists had forgotten all about it and had to rediscover the principle for themselves. But even in modern times the phonemic principle was stated, in one way or another, as early as about 1910: the earliest mention I have been able to track down in science fiction postdates World War II.

Maybe we should catch up. If our authors would like to follow their usual custom of being ahead of the times instead of lagging behind, they must at least know what the times have to offer. If we readers insist that they should do this, they will.

We are going along on the first voyage to Mars, and very conveniently we shall find intelligent oxygen-breathing beings with respiratory and digestive tracts shaped very much like our own. (Later on we can point out why this last assumption is so convenient.) Our ship lands; we make the first hesitant contact with the Martians; and before long our xenologist, Ferdinand Edward Leonard, B.A., M.A., Ph.D., M.D., X.D.—who is about as chock full of modern anthropological, linguistic, communicative, engineering, psychiatric, and biologic training as one skin can be stuffed with—sits down with a Martian to try to find out something about the latter's language.[1] (Hidden assumption: Martians can sit down.) For short, we shall call these two "Ferdie" and "Marty"— the latter because even Ferdie won't be able to learn, or to pronounce, Marty's real name for quite a while. (Query: Do Martians have personal names?)

Ferdie points to the Martian's foot and says, of course in English, "What do you call that in your language?" Marty certainly does not understand, but at this moment he makes a bit of vocal sound, something like *GAHdjik*. Ferdie puts this down in his little notebook, and writes the English word "foot" by it. What Ferdie puts down to represent the

---

1. Roger Williams, of Rhode Island and Providence Plantations fame, wrote a little book called *Key Into the Language of America*—a grammar of a language spoken by a few hundred Indians in his vicinity, which was but one of *several hundred* distinct languages spoken in aboriginal North America. Some of our exploring science-fiction heroes fall into this same error. If there are millions of intelligent beings on Mars, there may be thousands of Martian languages.

Martian "word"—if it really is a word, and not just Marty clearing his throat in the typical Martian manner—doesn't look quite like what we have written above, because Ferdie has a special set of written marks which he can use more efficiently and accurately for the purpose (a "phonetic alphabet"); but we needn't bother with this, because it is merely a convenience, not an essential. Now Ferdie is not being a fool and jumping to conclusions when he makes his notebook entry. He knows perfectly well that the sound Marty has made may not only not mean "foot," but may not even be a word at all. Ferdie makes his entry only as a memory aid: it will be easy enough to scratch it out when and if necessary.

Ferdie also says *GAHdjik* himself—or tries to—and observes Marty's reaction. Just for fun, we shall pretend that Marty does not react, so that this time Ferdie has gained nothing.

Next Ferdie points to something else, gets another reaction from Marty which may be a "word," writes it down, and tries to imitate it. Then he points to a third thing. After a while, having elicited a number of such bits of what may be speech, Ferdie returns to Marty's foot. This time what Marty says doesn't sound like *GAHdjik*, but more like *KAHchuk*.

Right at this point, Ferdie comes face to face with the most ticklish and crucial problem which can be encountered by a xenologist or by an Earth linguist. (We except, of course, the task of working with the dragonlike inhabitants of Antares II, whose languages make use not of sound but of heat-waves.) Has friend Marty given two different "words" for two different meanings? Has he given two distinct "words" for a single meaning? Or has he simply said the same "word" twice, with slight differences in pronunciation which are clear to Ferdie but which would be entirely overlooked by Marty's fellows?

Since this problem lies at the very heart of phonemics, we had better return to Earth momentarily and look at some more homely examples of what is involved.

Suppose that your name is Paul Revere and that you want to arrange for me, over in Boston, to send you some sort of a signal across the Charles River so that you can know whether the British are coming by land or by sea. This is all you want to know—it is already clear that they are going to be coming one way or the other, but you need to know which way. What we have to do is to establish a code containing just two signals. One of the signals will mean "they're coming by land," and the other will mean "they're coming by sea." The physical circumstances have something to do with what kinds of signals we can choose. They must both be something that you, over on the Cambridge side of the river, can easily detect, so that a shout or halloo wouldn't do very well. Since it will be night, some sort of arrangement of lights—up in a high place—would be a good idea.

Another consideration is that there must be no possible danger of my sending one signal and you receiving what is apparently the other. That is, we want to keep the two signals physically distinct, so that there will be no danger of misunderstanding. Shall we use a red lantern for "by sea" and a green one for "by land"? No—green might not show up too well, and what's more, we haven't got a green lantern. But I know there are two lanterns over in the basement of the Old North Church: suppose I put just one of them up in the tower for one of the signals, but both of them, at opposite sides, for the other. "One, if by land, and two, if by sea?" Agreed! Good luck on your ride! Hope a fog doesn't come up.

People can make signals out of anything they can *control* and can *observe*, and they can make the signals mean anything they wish. We constantly establish little short-term signaling systems, use them, and then discard them. A wave of the hand, a drop of a handkerchief, a wink of the eye, the raising of a window blind, the toot of an auto horn—such events are assigned special meaning over and over again. Some signaling systems are a little more elaborate and a bit more enduring—for example, the pattern of lights, stable or winking, shown at night by a plane for takeoff, for landing, or during flight. The really elaborate systems are hardly "invented," but merely passed down from generation to generation, with gradual changes; among these, of course, belongs language itself. Now, however varied these different systems may be, they all conform to certain fundamental principles. One of these—the one with which we are concerned here—is that the users of the signals must be able to tell them apart. That sounds simple and obvious enough, but it has some pretty complicated results.

Paul Revere and his sidekick had no trouble on this score, because they needed only two signals—all Paul had to have was one item of information of the either-this-or-that sort. But suppose you had to work out a signaling-system which will include hundreds or thousands of distinct signals. Keeping them physically apart and easily distinguished is in this case much more difficult.

One technique that anybody confronted with such a design-problem is bound to hit on is to set up some fairly small repertory of basic elements, each of them quite different physically from any of the others, and then arrange for the actual signals to consist of some sort of arrangement or combination of the fundamental elements. Suppose Paul and his henchman had needed a couple of hundred different signals. They could have arranged, for example, for a row of five lights to be put up in the Old North Church tower, each light either red or green or amber: this yields two hundred and forty-three distinct combinations, yet calls for only fifteen lanterns to be available—one of each color for each of the five positions.

It is pretty obvious that this set of two hundred and forty-three signals would be much easier for Paul to read from across the river than, say, the same number of signals consisting each of a lantern of a different shade. The human eye, true enough, can distinguish several thousand shades of color, but finer distinctions are not easy to detect, and for rapid and efficient use ought not to be involved. Even as it is, if Paul's assistant is only able to find four really red lamps and has to fill in with one which is rather orange, there will be the possibility that the orange lamp, intended as functionally "red," will be interpreted by Paul as "amber." This danger can be avoided if Paul knows in advance that the "red" lamps will in actual transmission vary somewhat in precise shade, without making any significant difference in the signal.

That sort of thing has actually happened in every known case of a really complicated signaling system, including language.

When a linguist goes to work on a language he has never heard before, he can count on certain things along this line. The colored lanterns in this case are different motions of lips, tongue, throat, and lungs, which produce kinds of sound which can be heard, and told apart, by human ears. The investigator knows that the people who speak the language will make *distinctive* use only of certain differences of articulatory motion—that is, maybe they will use relatively red, relatively green, and relatively amber lanterns, but not also orange or blue. He knows that if an articulatory motion of an ambiguous sort occurs, it will count as a "mistake" and will be allowed for by the speakers of the language—since orange is not functional, the actual appearance of an orange lantern must be a mistake for red or for amber. But he does not know in advance just what differences of articulatory motion will be thus used.

After all, a lantern-code could make use of any number of different ranges of spectral colors, provided that no two of the significantly different shades were so close together as to give rise to serious danger of confusion. In just the same way, there are any number of ways in which a selection can be made, from the "spectrum" of all possible speech-sound, of shades to be used distinctively. The only way to find out what selection is actually made by the speakers of a given language is—but let's watch Ferdie and Marty again and see if we can find out.

We left Ferdie confronting the problem of *GAHdjik* and *KAHchuk*. Assuming that each of these is really speech, not just Martian throat-clearing, then there are three possibilities:

(1) They are two different words with two different meanings. If we were in the position of Marty, the first time a xenologist pointed to our ear we might say *ear*, and at a subsequent time we might think he was asking what the organ is used for, and say so say *hear*. *Ear* and *hear* are pretty similar: a Frenchman or Italian who knew no English might easily wonder whether they were two words or just one.

(2) They are two different words, but for essentially one and the same meaning. When we pronounce *room* with the vowel sound of *cooed* we are using one word; when we pronounce it with the vowel sound of *could* we are really using a different word. But it would be hard to find any difference in the meaning of the two.

(3) Marty has simply said the same word twice: the apparent variation in pronunciation would not be noticed by his fellow Martians. A speaker of Hindustani, hearing us say *pie* or *tie* or *cow* several times, might be convinced that we were pronouncing the initial *p-* (or *t-* or *k-*) now in one way, now in another, since Hindustani breaks up the "spectrum" of possible speech sound a little more finely in this particular region.

There are several things Ferdie can do to try to solve this problem. First, he points to Marty's foot again and says *KAHchuk*, to observe the response; a little while later, he makes the same gesture and says *GAHdjik*. For good measure, he also tries *GAHdjuk* and *KAHchik*, and even *gahDJIK* and *kahCHUK*, making the second syllable louder than the first. The hope is that he can manage to get something out of Marty's reactions which will indicate acceptance or rejection of the various pronunciations. If Marty accepts all the pronunciations except the last two, then Ferdie has fairly good indication that the answer is the second or third of the possibilities, rather than the first. Of course he can't yet be absolutely certain; perhaps Martians are too polite to criticize, or perhaps we simply haven't yet learned to read their gestures of acceptance and rejection.

Another procedure is available. Ferdie looks through his notebook and notices an entry *GOOpit*, apparently meaning "small tuft of green hair sprouting from the back of a Martian's neck," and an entry *KOOsahng*, which seems to refer to a low-growing yellowish shrub that is plentiful in the vicinity. This is what Ferdie does and how Marty reacts:

Ferdie (pointing to the tuft of hair): "*GOOpit*."

Marty (closing his middle eye—apparently the gesture of assent): "*FUM*."

Ferdie (pointing to the bush): "*KOOsahng.*"

Marty: "*FUM.*"

Ferdie (the tuft of hair): "*KOOpit.*"

Marty: "*FUM. NAHboo GOOpit.*"

Ferdie (the bush): "*GOOsahng.*"

Marty: "*FUM. NAHboo KOOsahng.*"

Ferdie (pointing to the spaceship in which we arrived): "*GOOpit.*"

Marty (popping all three eyes out on their stalks): "*HLA-HLA-HLA-HLA! EEkup SAHCH bah-KEENdut!*"

This last response, whatever it actually means, is certainly different enough from the others to be indicative. Ferdie concludes that he can probably work on the theory that the last response was rejection, the others all acceptance. But what does this tell him? It tells him the following:

(1) *GOOpit* (or *KOOpit*) does *not* mean "spaceship."

(2) The pronunciations *GOOpit* and *KOOpit* may sound different to us English-speaking Earthlings, but to Marty they are all the same.

(3) The pronunciations *KOOsahng* and *GOOsahng* are also all the same for Marty.

(4) The pronunciations *GAHdjik*, *GAHdjuk*, *KAHchik*, *KAHchuk* sound quite varied to us, with our English speaking habits, but the differences are irrelevant for Marty's language.

Or, in short, for the last three points, the difference between an initial *k*-sound and an initial *g*-sound, which is distinctive for us, is not functional in Marty's language. Ferdie has reached one conclusion about the phonemic system of Marty's language: in the region of the spectrum where English distinguishes between two phonemes, *k* and *g*, Marty's language has only one.

It is entertaining to follow the hard step-by-step field work of a xenologist or a linguist this far, but after this it quickly becomes boring, at least for everyone but the investigator himself—and, often enough, for him, too. Because what he has to do is simply more of the same—over and over and over again, eliciting, recording, checking, correcting, reaching an occasional tentative conclusion, finding out he was wrong and revising. It is a routine sort of task, before long, but unfortunately it is not one which can be assigned to any sort of machine. (At least, a machine that could perform the task would have to have all the logic *and illogic*, all the strengths *and weaknesses*, of human beings.)

Ferdie's aim can be stated rather easily. He wants to reach the point where he can supply an accurate description of all the *differences in pronunciation* which are *distinctive* in the linguistic signaling of Marty and his fellows. He wants to be able to state what shades of lanterns are used, in what sequences the different colors are allowed to occur, and just what range of spectral shades counts as an instance of each color. All of this constitutes the *phonemic system* of Marty's language.

Maybe you think it need not take Ferdie very long to achieve this aim. Well, if Earth languages are any guide, there is a good chance that our ship hasn't brought along enough food to supply Ferdie while he finishes the job; unless he can get along on Martian lizard-weed, the native staple, he is out of luck. In a day or so, a well-trained Earth linguist, working with a completely new language, can get the cultural wax out of his ears and begin to hear something that sounds like it might really be a language. Before that, everything is a mumbling buzz. In another ten or so days of hard work, the linguist can get perhaps ninety percent of what counts in the sound-making and sound-recognizing habits of the language, though his own hearing may not yet be too well trained for the new system. In another hundred days he can get perhaps ninety percent *of the remainder*. Sometimes it is years before he gets it all.

However, this rather long program shouldn't discourage us, since Ferdie can be making effective practical use of the local Martian dialect long before the full cycle is up. Ninety percent is actually pretty good, though as long as, in his own attempts at speaking Martian, Ferdie uses only ninety percent, he will impress Marty as having a pretty un-Martian accent.

Let us see what "ninety percent" means and why it is effective. The phonemic system of Marty's language—or of any other—is a set of distinctive *differences* between pronunciations. The units which we call "phonemes" are in themselves of no importance: it is the differences among them that count. A given phoneme, in terms of its use in communication, is nothing except something which is different from all the other phonemes in the system. In Morse code, a dot is a dot and a dash is a dash whether the former is a short voltage pulse and the latter a long one, or the former is a wave of a flag in one direction and the latter a wave in the other direction. This is why we will irritate Ferdie no end if we ask him after his first days work, "Well, do they have a phoneme *k*?" or "Well, is *k* a phoneme in Martian?" If you want to compare languages with one another, the sort of question that must be asked—the sort that will be meaningful to Ferdie even if he can't yet answer it—is "Does Marty have a phonemic contrast between *k* and *g*?"

The difference between *k* and *g* is distinctive in English, so that we have two phonemes rather than just one in this general region of the spectrum, because a great many pairs of words are kept apart by the difference and by nothing else: *good* : *could*, *gap* : *cap*, *glue* : *clue*, *bag* : *back*, *bigger* : *bicker*, and so on. In Marty's language there are no pairs of words kept apart in just this way. On the other hand, the difference between *EE* and *AH* is distinctive in Marty's language—as in ours—because *KEEtah* means "eyestalk" while *KAHtah* means "setting of Deimos."

The sole function of phonemes, then, is to be different from one another and, in being so, to keep words and utterances—whole signals—apart. But some differences between phonemes do a lot more of this work than do others. The difference between *k* and *g* in English carries, relatively speaking, a fairly large share of the total load, as you can easily see by looking for more pairs of words like those which we gave above—it is easy to list hundreds. The difference between the *sh*-sound of *she* or *hush* and the *zh*-sound in the middle of *pleasure* is also functional, but this distinction doesn't carry very much of the total load. If you look hard, you may be able to find three or four pairs of words in which this difference is the only one—one example is *measure* and *mesher*—but there are very few.

Actually, a technique deriving from information theory makes it theoretically possible to express the "functional load" of different phonemic contrasts in a language in quantitative terms, to any desired degree of accuracy. But the amount of counting and computing involved is enormous, and would hardly be undertaken without a properly designed computing machine—and then it costs lots of money instead of lots of time, which for linguists is even worse. But we don't need such figures here; the general principle is, we hope, clear enough.

It is because of this that Ferdie can begin making effective use of Martian long before he has ferreted out and pinned down every last vestige of distinctive difference in articulation of which the language makes some use. It is obvious on the face of it that the differences which he discovers first are bound to be, by and large, the differences of greatest functional importance. Working just with these in his own attempts to speak Martian, he will sometimes be misunderstood—but we misunderstand each other from time to time even under the best of circumstances. If you want further empirical evidence, you need only think of the German or the Frenchman who makes you understand him with imperfect English—or of you, yourself, managing to communicate in imperfect French or German.

If there *are* Martians, and they *are* intelligent and have a language, and if they *do* have upper respiratory and alimentary tracts shaped much like our own, and ears much like ours, and, finally, if they *do* make use of these organs in speech communication—given all these ifs, then the procedures of Ferdinand Edward Leonard will work, and he will be able to "break" the phonemic system of the language.

But suppose that the Martians fail on just one of the above ifs. Suppose that they have two tongues and no nose. How, then, is Ferdinand Edward Leonard to imitate and to learn to recognize their speech sounds?

Suppose something even more drastic. Suppose that the Martians communicate with a system just as complex as human language and with much the same essential structure, but that instead of modulating sound they modulate a carrier at frequencies above the reach of human ears—or radio waves, or a light beam, or odors, or electrical flows, or some kind of energy transmitted through the "subether." What kind of equipment and training shall we give our xenologists to handle situations of that sort? There are still certain fundamental design-features which any such languagelike communications system is bound to include, but the problem of observation and analysis is tremendously harder.

H6. ETHNOLINGUISTIC IMPLICATIONS OF RECENT STUDIES IN LINGUISTICS AND PSYCHIATRY

Early 1958. In W. M. Austin, ed., *Report of the Ninth Annual Round Table Meeting on Linguistics and Language Study* (Georgetown University Institute of Languages and Linguistics, Monograph Series number 11) 175–193. Meeting held and volume dated 1958; volume published and copyright 1960. Reprinted with the permission of the publications department, School of Languages and Linguistics, Georgetown University.

For its original appearance, the editor deleted the word "recent" from my title. The intended reference was in the first instance to the work I was engaged in at the time in collaboration with the psychiatrists Robert E. Pittenger and Jack J. Danehy of Syracuse, New York. The final report on that joint research was published (with Pittenger as senior author) as *The First Five Minutes* (1960a). But our research had in turn grown from earlier investigations carried on severally and in various overlapping groups by Gregory Bateson, Ray L. Birdwhistell, Henry W. Brosin, Frieda Fromm-Reichmann, Norman A. McQuown, Pittenger, Henry L. Smith Jr., George L. Trager, and me. My involvement had begun in earnest in the spring and summer of 1956, during the latter part of my year as a Fellow at the Center for Advanced Study in the Behavioral Sciences in Palo Alto, California.

It was Birdwhistell's kinesics, Smith and Trager's paralinguistics, and the psychiatric-interview context that gradually rendered me uncomfortable with post-Bloomfieldian "marble-slab" grammar with its atomic morphemes and that forced me to try to look at language in action. The results were slow in working out: they are really only anticipated in the present essay and in "Grammar for the Hearer" (1960c), but we will see more in H12 below.

In this paper I discuss ten things: *time*; *brevity*; *rapidity*; *developmental structure*; *size-level*; *contrast*; *local indeterminacy*; *feedback*; *editing*; and *ritual*.

The first part of the title is validated by the fact that I shall be talking about language and the rest of culture at the same time. The second part reflects the fact that the points I shall make were either learned, or reinforced, in the course of recent work in the application of linguistic (and related) techniques to the analysis of psychiatric interviews.

Time. Descriptive ethnology and descriptive (so-called "structural") linguistics have relegated time to the historians. That is a mistake. Historians are concerned with the macroscopic sort of time during which a system changes: Old English becomes Modern English; an American Indian tribe disintegrates under the impact of the West. There remains the everyday sort of time it takes to say or do something *within* a system. Utterances, and communicative acts in any other modality, require time. In an instantaneous cross-section they do not exist at all.

That truth has been concealed from us by our preoccupation with writing and other static records of activity. The novice linguist quickly learns that his knuckles will be rapped for the most obvious lay mistakes about language and writing. So he makes subtle mistakes instead—and continues to make them when his apprenticeship is over. In order to discuss the structure of an utterance, we find it convenient to set down some graphic representation of it. Then we forget that though, in dealing with the representation, we can look from left to right and back again, as an utterance actually occurs it is not only unidimensional but *unidirectional*. Time's arrow[1] applies to human behavior as it does to the rest of the universe. Only once in the plenum can we observe an act directly. Thereafter we can examine it only via hypostasis—memory inside, mnemonic devices outside.

Few contemporary cultural and linguistic theories have time in them; Pike's recent work is a noteworthy exception.[2] Many linguists—and I have at times been among them—have preferred to treat language as a sort of secretion of human life, analyzable without reference to its natural context. Examining speech only via written records on flat surfaces is something like trying to learn about the human body only by dissecting cadavers on marble slabs. Indeed, much of importance can be learned that way—but one also learns some things that aren't so. Eventually it is imperative to return from research *in vitro* to research *in vivo*. The rest of this paper deals with some of the implications of putting time back into the picture.

Brevity and Rapidity. The shortest event that is communicatively relevant for human beings is very short indeed. An English morpheme lasts, on the average, about one fifth of a second. Some paralinguistic and kinesic signals are even briefer.

1. See Adolf Grünbaum, "Time and Entropy," *American Scientist* 43.550–572 (1955); also chap. 1 of the work cited in fn. 10 below.

2. Kenneth L. Pike, *Language in Relation to a Unified Theory of the Structure of Human Behavior*; Preliminary Edition, Part I, Glendale (1954); Part II (1955); subsequent parts appearing. My vague impression, based on very desultory scanning of discussions of language by other than linguists, is that philosophers and logicians dealing with communication are most prone to ignore time, communications engineers most likely to take it into account.

Nor are these brief signals received one by one, spaced out in an embedding silence or darkness, as are successive tachistoscopic exposures in a perception experiment. The signals of a single communicative modality come in close-compacted sequence. Those in different modalities are overlapping or simultaneous.

Human communication is fast and complex. Yet that complexity is something with which we can and do cope, some psychologists to the contrary notwithstanding. The skill with which we receive and transmit messages in many channels at once suggests that we should think of a human being not as a monolith but as a colony. A respectable portion of the signals that come our way is registered in awareness. A much larger portion—the nine-tenths of the iceberg below the surface—is also registered and reacted to appropriately, but only out of awareness. A third portion, smaller than we usually think, is missed altogether. The fact that the greatest portion is registered out of awareness is due in part, perhaps, to repression in the psychoanalytic sense, but much more to *efficiency*—we all acquire "automatisms" and could hardly do what we do without them.

We can suspect this complexity, of which we are not usually aware, because we remember things that we didn't notice consciously when they happened; because other people tell us about things we missed; and because on some occasions we are aware of certain *kinds* of signals that must also have occurred—or have been conspicuous by their absence— on occasions when we didn't notice them. Moreover, under proper tutelage we can learn to pay conscious attention to types of phenomena earlier overlooked, and can then observe that these phenomena show just the regularity, partial predictability, and patternment that we find characteristic of all communicative behavior.

But the really convincing demonstration of complexity is made possible by tape and (though somewhat less satisfactorily) by film. Electrons are very much smaller and faster than human beings.[3] Electronic scanning can thus produce a truly "hi-fi" icon of behavior, in that nothing of conceivable human relevance need be left out. We can then expose ourselves over and over again to *exactly* the same train of communicative behavior, focusing now on one and now on another aspect.

Developmental Structure. Linguists speak of the *hierarchical* or *immediate constituent* structure of utterances. Thus *Poor John ran away* (to take a classic example), once we set intonation aside, has *poor John* and *ran away* as its immediate constituents; *poor John*, in turn, is composed of

3. See Erwin Schrödinger, *What is Life?*, Cambridge and New York (1947), pp. 4ff.

poor and *John*; *ran away* of *ran* and *away; ran* of *run* and past tense; *away* of *a-* and *way*. This is as far as we can go, because we have reached the *ultimate* constituents—the participating morphemes, than which nothing grammatical is smaller.

As far as I can see, all contemporary linguists acknowledge at least the utility, if not the "reality," of hierarchical structure, though terminologies and emphases differ and there are heated arguments about specific examples. Allowing for disagreement of this sort, we can observe the kinship of the linguist's notion of hierarchical structure to the practices of certain other specialists. Literary scholars describe the structure of a novel, short story, or poem, in terms of larger and smaller, more and less inclusive, parts. The application to music is obvious. Ethnographers resort (though less often and less fruitfully than they could) to the same whole-to-parts-to-smaller-parts procedure in describing the yearly cycle, or the daily routine, or a ceremony. It is patent to any psychiatrist that an interview, or a sequence of interviews with one patient, has a hierarchical organization. These similarities are not accidental. I believe that the recognition of hierarchical organization is necessary for the effective analysis and description of *every* phase of human culture.

The reintroduction of time into our efforts to understand culture means that the hierarchical structure of an utterance, or of a novel, or of a ceremony, is a structure in *time*—a *developmental structure*, in which the wholes and parts are *events*. Big events are built of smaller events in certain structural relationships to one another; these are composed of still smaller events; and so on until we reach the smallest events that are communicatively (and hence culturally) relevant.

In seeking to discover and describe the developmental structure of typical events in specific cultures, we should take a hint from the disagreements about details among linguists. Obviously there are conceivable criteria for structural analysis that would be totally irrelevant. One could regard a written English text as composed of a series of segments each of which (except perhaps the first) begins with the letter "a" and contains no further occurrences of that letter. There is no support for such a proposal: what the criterion yields correlates with nothing.[4] But when serious observers disagree, there is usually some justification for both or all points of view. We must doubtless recognize that one and the same composite event may have two or more *overlapping* developmental organizations, partially in disagreement, though involving the same ultimate constituents in the same temporal sequence.

4. Such bizarre criteria may well be functional in certain special experiences, such as crepuscular reverie or schizoid fantasy.

Size Level. In the light of the foregoing discussion, the meaning I wish to assign this term is probably obvious. Whenever a smaller event is a constituent (immediate or mediate) of a larger, the former is an event at a smaller size-level than the latter.

Size-level is not the same as size measured in some quasiphysical way. Suppose that a larger event A consists of B and C; B in turn of D and E; and C of F and G. Counting down from the whole event, it turns out that $D, E, F,$ and G are events of the same size-level. But F might be physically larger than G, or even than B, which is an event of a larger size-level.

There is no fixed number of size-levels between a composite event and its ultimate constituents. In *Poor John ran away,* we make only two jumps down the size scale to get from the whole to the ultimate constituent *poor,* while three are needed to get from the same whole to the ultimate constituent *a-* or *-way.*

For these reasons, it is often convenient to use the term "size-level" in a somewhat looser way: morphemes are on the average smaller (that is, at a lower size-level) than words; words than phrases; phrases than sentences; in writing, sentences than paragraphs, paragraphs than chapters, chapters than whole novels.

Using the term in this less precise way, we can note that one major difference between what linguists and nonlinguistic anthropologists have traditionally concerned themselves with is just a difference in size-level. Linguists have been chiefly concerned with very small events, from the size-level of the phoneme or the distinctive feature up to, but rarely beyond, the size-level of utterances. The latter is about the smallest size-level ever dealt with by the nonlinguistic anthropologist, say in field work and ethnographic reporting. This has left two large *terrae incognitae*: the finer-grained structure of nonlinguistic behavior, and the coarser-grained structure of speech.

Contrast. All of linguistics and anthropology—indeed, all of social science—rests on the acceptance of a simple but profoundly significant basic fact: in any culture, people class some events as *the same.*

To assert that two events are the same is not to assert that they are the same event. We can be confident that suitable measurements would demonstrate the falsity, in a physical frame of reference, of every such identification. If there are no other measurable differences between two events, at least their coordinates in the space-time continuum are different. Thus every identification is achieved by ignoring some differences. These ignored differences are called by various terms: linguists class them as *nondistinctive*; in information theory they are called *noise.*

Setting noise aside, we find it unavoidably convenient to break any event (elementary or composite) into two parts: a "spot" or *position*— that is, the location of the event in space-time, described either relatively or absolutely—and a "thing" or *element* that "occupies" that position. Identification of two events is then describable as identification of the elements, abstracted from the positions in which they occur, as mutual replicas or facsimiles. These elements are really not very "thing"-like. In general (technologically complex communicative systems, such as writing, afford partial exceptions), a member of a culture requires only energy in order to produce an indefinitely large number of replicas of any element. The production—or reception—of a replica is what we commonly call an *occurrence* of the element.

Culturally given identifications are not always absolute. Sometimes sameness is only relative to certain criteria, while by other criteria, also operative in the culture, there is difference. In such instances it is better to speak of *similarity*. But similarity seems always to reflect absolute sameness of certain parts or contours of two events, plus equally absolute difference or *contrast* of other ingredients.

Thus two composite events may be classed as similar because they are composed of the same number of immediate constituents in the same structural relationships. This is true of the sentences *Poor John ran away* and *The poor feeble old German tailor has a hard time threading his needles these days*. Each of these has two immediate constituents, a subject and a predicate, in that sequential order. Such parallelism of hierarchical (developmental) organization is what we mean by the term *pattern*.[5] The two sentences *conform to*, or *actualize*, or *manifest*, one and the same pattern. It is the pattern which is invariant between the two sentences; the immediate constituents themselves are quite different. If the corresponding immediate constituents of the two also conformed, in each case, to a single pattern (something not true of our two sample sentences), then the resemblance of the two wholes would be greater. And if this sort of identity of pattern applied all the way down the size scale to include an identity of corresponding ultimate constituents, we should say that the two events were the same: that is, that they were two occurrences of a single composite element—in short, two occurrences of the same sentence.

5. Note well the difference between structure and pattern. A composite event *has* a developmental structure; that structure *conforms to* a pattern. Two composite events cannot have the "same" developmental structure, since the latter, like the events, has spatiotemporal indices. But they may have structures that conform to the same pattern. We may then reify patterns and eviscerate events, ending with Plato; or we may insist that patterns "exist" only in their exemplifications. I prefer to speak in the latter way, but do not believe that there is much practical difference.

In other cases, two elements (minimal or composite) are classed as similar because they seem to have highly similar privileges of occurrence as constituents of larger elements. Within the economy of this essay, the English words *case* and *instance* are virtually interchangeable; if I were to replace some occurrences of each word by the other, everyone would agree that the revision was still the "same" essay. We say in any such case that the two elements have virtually the same *function*. [6]

Events at the lowest culturally relevant size-level, or the elements the occurrences of which constitute such minimal events, can be and are classed as to function. But this classification turns on the recognition of composite events as same, similar, or different. The latter classification, in its turn, rests in part on the identification as *absolutely* the same of some minimal events. This absolute identification cannot rest on similarity or identity of function without producing circularity. It cannot rest on identity of pattern, because minimal events have no developmental structure, which is why they are minimal. Identity within a culture of some minimal events has to be accepted as an axiom. Exegesis and deduction are quite useless. [7] All an investigator can do is to determine empirically, at best by participant-observation, which minimal events are actually treated as same and which as different by those who live in the culture. [8] We can believe that this is possible for the investigator if we believe that it is possible for an infant born into a community—who does seem, in due time, to come to make identifications and distinctions pretty much as others in the community do. Alternatively, we can decide that the task is impossible, but in this case we have to give up being scientists. Indeed, if we really took the second alternative seriously outside of office hours, we should soon be catatonic or dead. [9]

Contrast is the negation of sameness. At any size-level, the com-

6. If we are judging similarity and difference of function in terms of sufficiently large more inclusive events, and particularly if the more inclusive events involve elements in other communicative modalities, then we commonly speak of *meaning* rather than of function. There is no simple and sharp line of demarcation between "meaning" and "function" as those terms are commonly used. (*Denotation*, of course, is quite another matter: *boy*, *elephant*, and *unicorn* have denotations, while *and* and *if* and a half-laugh have none.)

7. I believe this is the upshot of Bertrand Russell's discussion in *An Inquiry into Meaning and Truth*, New York (1940), pp. 25–33 and passim.

8. This stricture applies equally to research in psychophysics—for example, in acoustic phonetics. The range of measurable nondistinctive variation for a phoneme (or a distinctive feature) can only be investigated with acoustic apparatus after the identification of various events as the same phoneme has been given. The only choice in psychophysics is between being systematic and being haphazard in the cultural identifications that serve as points of departure.

9. Francis S. Haserot, at the very beginning of his *Essays on the Logic of Being*, New York (1932), points out that if one's philosophy does not either assume or imply the possibility of communication one cannot communicate one's philosophy. This starting-point

municative significance of an element is totally a function of the occurrence of that particular element *rather than* any other element which might occur in the same immediate environment.

Nearly everyone has made this point. This is what Norbert Wiener means when he asserts that there is no information in the steady state: that is, for a signaling system to be workable, it has to involve a repertory of at least two possible signals, and the receiver cannot know in advance which is going to arrive.[10] It is what Hjelmslev means by "paradigmatic," as over against "syntagmatic."[11] It is what Pike means by "emic."[12] It is what Trager and Smith mean by "differential meaning"—a term which has produced an unconscionable amount of obfuscation and ought to be abandoned.[13]

The epithet "immediate" is important. The immediate environment of an event, or of the element the occurrence of which constitutes the event, consists of its partner or partners in the larger event of which it is an immediate constituent. In *Poor John ran away*, the immediate environment of *poor* is the following *John*. The uttering of *poor* in this immediate environment contrasts with a possible *rich*, *old*, *young*, and so on.

Sometimes a difference which is by definition contrastive in the immediate environment is damped out, as it were, as one mounts to higher size-levels. The interchange of *case* and *instance* throughout this essay, as already indicated, would make very little difference to the essay as a whole. I find that very little else in my day's activity seems to turn on whether I have toast or an English muffin as part of my breakfast.

In other cases (or instances!) a change at a small size-level has reverberations at much larger size-levels. In the sentence about the German tailor cited a number of paragraphs back, the immediate environment of *tailor* is the preceding word *German*. But if we replace *tailor* by *tailors*, the reverberations reach up through several size-levels to the whole subject and the whole sentence, then down through successive levels within the predicate, to require a corresponding replacement of *has* by *have* and of *his* by *their*. Quite similarly, I believe, the difference between a *yes* and a *no*—or between a willing and a hesitant *yes*—during a brief afternoon phone call can have ramifications lasting all evening.

is, I believe, equivalent to the axiom proposed in the above paragraph. Our conclusion is stronger: Haserot infers only that a noncommunicable philosophy is and remains solipsistic; we infer that a noncommunicable philosophy is and remains nonexistent.

10. Norbert Wiener, *Cybernetics*, New York (1948).

11. Louis Hjelmslev, *Prolegomena to a Theory of Language; Indiana University Publications in Anthropology and Linguistics* 7 (1953).

12. Op. cit. above in fn. 2.

13. See, for example, Henry L. Smith, Jr., *Linguistic Science and the Teaching of English*, Cambridge (1956), pp. 11–12; or *Language* 31.61 (1955).

That which is nondistinctive or noncontrastive within one frame of reference is very often distinctive in another. The choice between *case* and *instance* is only nondistinctive in certain larger contexts, not in others—and not, of course, in the *immediate* environment in which the choice is made. Sometimes the differing frames of reference are different communicative modalities, potentially functional for the same people. Snow on a television screen is "noise" for those who want to watch a program; but its precise configuration may be "signal" for a repairman, telling him which tube to test. A less and a more strongly aspirated *p* in English are the same phoneme, but the stronger aspiration may be a simultaneous half-laugh, indicative of something about the speaker's mood. If a Fox Indian says *yōhi* 'over there' with the *ō* strongly rounded and lips protruded, these unusual features of the *ō* are not part of the phoneme, but a simultaneous *pointing*—the Fox point with their lips, not a finger. In a crowded room, Mr. Jones's speech is noise if you are trying to hear Mr. Smith, but if you switch your attention to Mr. Jones then Mr. Smith's speech becomes noise. The information theoreticians were wiser than they realized when they demonstrated that noise can be treated mathematically as *unwanted* signal.[14] Perhaps somewhere in the web of human communicative behavior there is a residuum of "pure" noise—activity of no communicative relevance at all—but one putative example after another seems to vanish upon sufficiently close scrutiny. The fruitful working assumption is that any act of one human being which can be detected by the senses of any other—or by those of the actor himself—is communicative.

In language, sameness of minimal elements is absolute, and contrast is absolute and discrete. "Is same as" is here a transitive relation: if *A* is same as *B* and *B* is same as *C*, then *A* is same as *C*. That may hold in most human communicative systems. But there are probably some instances, outside of language, in which contrasting alternatives constitute what has been loosely and inaccurately called a *continuous* rather than a discrete array. For these, "same as" is nontransitive: from the facts that *A* is the same as *B* and that *B* is the same as *C* it does not necessarily follow that *A* is the same as *C*.[15] That may be so, for example, for degrees of loudness of speech. We might agree that a speaker's second phrase is spoken at the

---

14. Claude E. Shannon, in Shannon and Weaver, *The Mathematical Theory of Communication*, Urbana (1949), pp. 34ff. The point is also made by Wiener, op. cit. above in fn. 10.

15. This way of defining what we have loosely been calling "continuous"—and, of course, we have the right to define the term "continuous" this way if we want to, even if this definition differs from the mathematician's—was the brilliant insight of Noam Chomsky: see *International Journal of American Linguistics* 23.232–233 (1957).

same volume as his first, and his third at the same volume as the second; yet, if confronted with a spliced tape in which the second phrase was omitted, we might also agree that the third is louder than the first. Such "gradient" or "clinal" ranges of contrast promise to make a great deal of wholesome trouble for us in the epoch of research which we are now entering.

Local Indeterminacy. At any interstice between successive events, the colony which is a human being, or a group of human beings functioning together vis-à-vis the rest of the world, has a set of *expectancies* as to what is going to happen next. Rarely, if ever, do we know *exactly* what is next in store for us; rarely, if ever, are we at a complete loss. Our momentary set of expectancies is the product of immediately preceding events and of their similarities to and differences from earlier past experiences. The expectancies are conditioned by identity and patterning, which afford us only limited possibilities of classification and interpretation of whatever actually does happen next.

I call this momentary indeterminacy "local" because it is a function of the obvious fact that no human being or group occupies the entire universe. Whether the physical world is absolutely or only stochastically determinate, what is to happen here next is in part a function of what is happening elsewhere now. We cannot know what is happening elsewhere now except by receiving signals from elsewhere. The arrival of the signals is part of what happens here next. It has been said that to know all is to predict the future without residue; morally, it has been claimed that to know all is to forgive all. The second may be healthy advice, but the underlying requirement is only asymptotically related to human capacities. Omniscience requires omnipresence.

Indeterminacy about the future and indeterminacy about elsewhere are thus, in a rather deep sense, equivalent. The extent to which the next signal actually received resolves our uncertainty is the measure of the "information" in the message. That can be measured only in terms of the a-priori and a-posteriori *local* uncertainty, not in any absolute or "objective" terms.[16]

Exact quantification of local indeterminacy is possible if we focus attention on specified narrow channels of communication, setting aside a

16. This view is apparently not very popular among statisticians and probability theoreticians; but it is espoused by Leonard J. Savage (who calls it "personal probability") and made the cornerstone of his *The Foundations of Statistics*, New York (1954). What Savage does not discuss—and there is no reason why he should, since it can be left to others—is the lines of causality which lead an individual to make the assumptions of probability that he does make.

vast amount of activity as, for the nonce, nondistinctive. But loose quantification is attainable without this artificial narrowing, and shows an important rough correlation with transition-points in developmental structure. A boundary between larger events is generally characterized by greater indeterminacy than a boundary between smaller events. When you have heard *Poor John ran*—, the possible next elements are certainly numerous, but they are not so varied as they are when you have heard *Poor John ran away*. After the first course of a banquet you at least assume that there will be another course; when the eating is over, there may be a toast or a speech or you may go home.

It is not often that we are both highly uncertain and also highly *anxious* about what is going to happen during the next second or so. If we drive over a hilltop and see a truck approaching in our lane, we may have only a split second to survey the probabilities and to decide what to do. Ordinarily, however, there is greater predictability or less concern, or both. That part of the future about which we are certain or undisturbed is what Sullivan calls the *neighboring future*.[17] Together with the past of immediate retention (as over against recall), it constitutes what has been called the *specious present*.[18] The scope of the specious present varies from moment to moment. For human beings, the true measure of duration is not given by clocks or by the absolute velocity of light, but by the varying scope of the specious present.[19]

Feedback. Part of our uncertainty at a given moment concerns what we ourselves are going to do next. Relative to our shell of sensory equipment, through which incoming messages must pass, our own motor equipment is "elsewhere"—even if not very far away. We can know what messages we are transmitting only because we ourselves receive them, via *feedback*.

As a man observes his own behavior via feedback, he interprets and classifies it in terms of the same identifications and distinctions which apply in his interpretation of the behavior of others. There is one impor-

17. Harry Stack Sullivan, *The Interpersonal Theory of Psychiatry*, New York (1953).
18. Wiener speaks of this in op. cit. above, fn. 10; he gives credit for the term to William James, who in turn, I am informed, ascribed it to E. R. Clay.
19. J. B. S. Haldane, *American Scientist* 33.130 (1945), points out that we can use any measure of time we want to. The physicist uses clocks rather than, say, a heart-beat, only because it renders mathematical treatment much easier. From another point of view, the clock time and other highly neat, presumably "etic," units of physical investigation are really a special brand of "emic" units (as all "etic" units are), evolved in a certain subculture of Western Society for certain special purposes. For those purposes, they have tremendous power. For our purposes in the study of human behavior, they have a subsidiary though useful role; but we have to remember that one man's "emic" is another man's "etic," and we have to ride the clocks, not let them ride us.

tant difference: transmission can be at such a low power level that the messages do not reach anyone else. They may not even be routed outside the central nervous system of the transmitter, and hence may remain totally indetectable to others. That is what is often called "thinking." The categories basically involved in "thinking," however, are just the categories involved in communication between different people. They are built into the life of an individual by his participation in society. It is very misleading to "define" communication as the transmission of information from one mind to another.[20] Instead of this, we must conceive of "thinking" as a calque on communication.

All this applies to such matters as emotions or feelings as well as to so-called "intellectual" communication and thinking. To experience an emotion is to receive, via feedback, the socially established signals of that emotion which one is transmitting, at however low a power level.

We thus establish a priority of reception over transmission. Reception is a larger category than transmission, since one receives all of one's own transmission plus some of the transmissions of others. That is important for cultural and linguistic analysis. In studying the grammar of a language, we should examine speech in that language from the hearer's point of view, not from the speaker's. This is why it is so important to reintroduce time into linguistics: even if sometimes a speaker plans a lengthy discourse in advance and then simply recites it, for his hearers the discourse unfolds bit by bit.

Editing. In a great many situations, we are granted the opportunity to look before we leap, to try out various alternatives in a tentative way before the final "go for broke" choice. The process of trying-out may be called *editing*, though there are other appropriate terms: planning, rehearsal, revising, trial and error. Often the editing takes place at a low power level, the "real" choice at a higher one. This sort of relatively implicit trial and error is another type of activity to which the term "thinking" has been applied.

Editing occurs at many size-levels. Stuttering is a sort of editing at the level of phonemes or syllables. False starts in speech, hesitation-forms, and the like are indicative of editing at a somewhat higher size-level. Small-scale editing can occur in the framework of larger-scale editing, within a whole that even after reworking is discarded in favor of a differently built one. In football (or other sports), a play in which there has

20. As is done by most laymen and most philosophers—for example, by Warren Weaver on p. 95 of op. cit. above in fn. 14, or by Haserot in op. cit. above in fn. 9.

been an action contrary to the official rules is formally erased—provided it is observed—and then, except for the penalty, things proceed as though the misplay had never occurred. Sometimes the final version towards which editing is aimed never materalizes. Sometimes what everyone thinks of as a final version later becomes a prefinal one. Sometimes it is the editing activity itself that really counts—there is nothing as dead as a completed crossword puzzle.

Editing goes on constantly in ordinary conversational give-and-take. Much of it passes unnoticed. We seem to have a good stock of socially established "cancel" signals, whereby when a speaker chooses to discard something actually spoken as not really what he meant to say, his hearers also ignore and forget the discarded bit. We can get the general impression that a speaker is hemming and hawing a lot, but it is much harder to remember just exactly where the hems and haws occurred. Often, a seemingly fluent speaker does just as much editing as the halting one, but fills the hesitations in deceptively with selections from a repertory of apparently meaningful phrases instead of with hems and haws. When discourse is to be transduced into written form, editing becomes extreme. Our preoccupation, even in linguistics, with written records has led us to base our understanding of language largely on such highly normalized speech. In this lies one of the most startling revelations in store for anyone who seriously works with ordinary speech via tape recordings.

In editing, cultural conditioning (that is, the monitoring of production via feedback, so that what is overtly transmitted conforms to pattern) enters in two ways. In the first instance, it enters in the editing process itself: each segment actually produced, at any size level, whether ultimately retained or discarded, is shaped *entirely and absolutely* by the particular individual's internalized share of the culture.[21] In the second instance, it enters in the form of the larger pattern towards the filling-out of which the editing process is aimed. This can be illustrated by the process of composing a poem, or equally well by the process of working out a proof of a mathematical theorem. The poet works from the outset with a more or less precise pattern into which words and phonemes must fit in order to qualify as a poem of the particular variety he wishes to write. The mathematician knows in advance the pattern in which words must be arranged in order to count as a logically valid proof. Each proceeds by trial and error until the pattern is satisfactorily filled, or until he gives up and does something else instead.

21. Which is, of course, never more than an "excerpt" from the culture of the community—a point emphasized by Sullivan, op cit. above in fn. 17, p. 169.

In one brief episode—about three seconds long—in a taped psychiatric interview which I have been studying, the patient goes through an observable process of emotional editing. She manifests, in turn, the signs of three different namable emotional reactions to what has gone before. The only way I can understand this episode is to assume that the patient cannot know what emotion she "feels"—that is, which emotion is culturally appropriate to the setting—without trying a bit of each and judging it by feedback. The manifestation is at a low power level, giving the impression of a sort of pastelle kaleidoscope of emotionality; but the power level is not so low as to render the sequence indetectable.

What we may perhaps call "Whorfian determinism" tends to be concealed by editing. The impact of language habits on "thought" and behavior with which Whorf was concerned is chiefly an impact at a small size-level. When small elements have been tried and discarded and rechosen until they fit satisfactorily into a larger-scale pattern, this small-size-level impact has often been edited out. But if one listens carefully to the editing behavior itself, one discovers innumerable examples of just what Whorf was talking about. When action is at its fastest and editing is forced to a minimum, Whorfian determinism increases in importance.

We live in, and are part of, a physically determinate world. But by virtue of local indeterminacy, editing, and the transmission to us via society of a multiplicity of patterns which function as the goals in editing—all three of these explainable, I believe, only on the assumption of physical causality—we have *free will*.[22] I do not for a moment believe that this exegesis of free will is tantamount to a denial of it, or to a proof that it is "illusory." Free will is a basic reality of our postinfancy lives, susceptible to explanation but not to be explained away. Students just embarking on the study of anthropology, particularly of linguistics, often develop a strong distaste for the subject and abandon it, for many proffered reasons; the real reason is in many cases that the study proves threatening to their egos—that is, to their free wills and to their belief therein. It is this threat that is illusory. The only genuine freedom is that founded on reality. The charting of a constraint is the first step towards bulldozing it away.

Ritual. From time to time, probably in every human community, people embark on a relatively lengthy and complex episode within which uncertainty is reduced almost to zero.

As an example, consider the music lover who is extremely fond of a

---

22. I believe this account is more satisfactory than that given by Schrödinger in op. cit. above in fn. 3, pp. 87–91.

certain orchestral composition, has a hi-fi record of it, and has heard the record dozens of times so that he knows it by heart, On a particular evening, alone in his room, he puts the record on his machine and sits quietly and listens to it. He has no particular expectation that there will be an external interruption, say a visitor or a power failure, although such intrusion is always possible. Within the train of music itself there is no unpredictability. No punches are telegraphed and then not delivered. He can anticipate every climax, every modulation, every changing nuance of harmony and tone color, because he is thoroughly familiar not just with the composition but with the particular rendition of it on his record. Since there is no uncertainty, it follows that the experience is devoid of information. Yet this is a kind of experience that the music lover repeatedly seeks; and those who do not care for music seek and find logically comparable experiences in other genres.

I think it is appropriate to use the term *ritual* for episodes of this sort. It is not particularly important to spell out just how far uncertainty has to be reduced, or for how long a time, for an episode to be a ritual, except that there is not much value in the special term unless we constrain its application to episodes that are relatively unusual on both counts. Thus the fact that most written English sentences have subject-predicate structure, or that every sonnet has fourteen lines with a fixed rhythm and rhyme scheme, does not lead us to class "the English sentence" or "the sonnet" as a ritual: they are just patterns, of relatively small size-levels, and allowing great diversity from one instance to another. A firmly entrenched custom of greeting a new acquaintance with *how do you do* would not be a ritual, despite the lack of diversity, because the size-level is too small. Football is not a ritual because even though a game is an event of relatively large size-level, only certain general patterns are prescribed in advance; within those, as within the subject-predicate pattern, there is room for tremendous diversity.

A game of football is a large enough event to afford us an instructive contrast with the kind of episode I have chosen to call ritual. Without the general patterns prescribed in advance, and understood by all participants (players and onlookers), there could be no game. A foreigner watching a football game for the first time sees and feels nothing—just as we Americans are unmoved by cricket, and do not understand things said in Russian or Chinese unless we have learned those languages. But the essence of football as a *kind of game*, rather than as a ritual—and this is the source of motivation for playing or watching the play—is the unpredictability of detail. We know in advance what kind of event will constitute a climax: a long run, a successful pass, a touchdown (particularly a sudden or hard-fought one), a fumble and recovery. But we do not know just when these climaxes will come, or if they will come at all. The action on every successive down is packed with information, whether it is surprising or dull, pleasing (because favorable to our side) or distressing, because on every successive down the general conventions, plus the specific situations, allow a large array of possibilities.

Although football can hardly be enjoyed except as a game, it is not the case that music can be enjoyed only as ritual. Some people seek the game element—the element of unpredictability—in music; we may suspect that they seek ritual in other contexts. Thus Eric Simon, an oboist, argues against the use of phonograph records for two reasons, the second of which he states as follows:[23]

> *Complete predictability* is one of the most deadening aspects of the phonograph record. If, for example, we go to hear Serkin play the *Emperor Concerto* with the New York Philharmonic-Symphony Orchestra, and if he happens to play the same piece with the same organization one year later, we can ask ourselves "How is he going to play it now?" This anticipation is essential for the enjoyment of music, and is lacking in a record, where each performance is identical.

Mr. Simon's attitude is doubtless related to the fact that he is a professional musician. Perhaps it is unlikely, in our culture, that one's source of ritual satisfaction will be found in one's area of professional concern.

The distinction between ritual and nonritual experience makes possible a comparable distinction between two varieties of editing. The editing required in preparation for a nonritual event, such as playing or watching football, or carrying on conversation, or taking an examination, or improvising at the piano, can be called *practice*. That required in preparation for ritual participation can be called *rehearsal*. In the latter connection we must note that the orchestral players are not the only ones who have to rehearse a symphony: if the symphony becomes a ritual for a particular music-lover, it is by dint of repeated hearings.

Ritual participation takes many forms: literature, folk-tales, religious ceremonies, rites of passage, music, and so on. An extreme form is the contemplation of graphic art products—paintings, sculpture, and the like. In fact, I suspect that the only reason such unmoving forms of art have for existence is their utility, for properly rehearsed people, in ritual participa-

23. Eric Simon, "In Praise of 'Live' Listening," *Music Clubs Magazine* 37:1.7 (September 1957).

tion. To me this is what T. S. Eliot is saying in the following passage from *Burnt Norton*—and, indeed, it is this passage that finally explained the graphic arts to me after I had been baffled by them for many blind years:

> Words move, music moves
> Only in time; but that which is only living
> Can only die. Words, after speech, reach
> Into the silence. Only by the form, the pattern,
> Can words or music reach
> The stillness, as a Chinese jar still
> Moves perpetually in its stillness.

The universality in human society of ritual participation is something for which I can offer no explanation—unless Eliot's lines offer one—but which must be very important. It is particularly intriguing that people in all cultures find satisfaction in two logically antithetical varieties of experience: ritual and game, the temporary suspension of unpredictability on the one hand, the heightening and highlighting of uncertainty on the other. The latter seems more closely allied to the everyday routine of living. Perhaps the former represents a sort of necessary rest, a recurrent withdrawal from indeterminacy—something like sleep. Perhaps we can say—though perhaps this is mere metaphor—that ritual participation rotates an unusually large segment of time at right angles to itself, to yield an unusually ample specious present within which decisions do not have to be made and anxiety is impossible.

H7. LOGICAL CONSIDERATIONS IN THE STUDY OF ANIMAL COMMUNICATION

1958–1959. Reprinted from W. E. Lanyon and W. N. Tavolga, eds., *Animal Sounds and Communication* (Washington, D.C.: American Institute of Biological Sciences, Symposium Series number 7, 1960) 392–430, with the permission of the American Institute of Biological Sciences.

The other line of investigation I got started on at the Center for Advanced Study in the Behavioral Sciences in 1955–1956 (see the prefatory note to the preceding essay, p. 107), foreshadowed only vaguely in §5 of H1 and in §1 of H3, was the reopening of serious investigation of the origins of language. With stimulation and guidance from Alfred L. Kroeber, James N. Spuhler, and Eckhard Hess, all three Fellows at the Center the same year, I read in general biology, in organic evolution, and in (nonhuman) animal behavior, and began to formulate what later came to be known as the "design-feature" approach in the comparative study of animal (including human) communication. I wrote a review of several relevant books (published in *Language* as 1956c), and drafted a paper on language origins intended for inclusion in an issue of *Language* to be dedicated to Kroeber, but had to withdraw the latter before publication because it had been done too hastily. That was as far as it went in Palo Alto, because I turned to other matters; but when I returned to Ithaca in September 1956 I took seven design features with me.

Those seven were featured in the first publication that emerged from this line of research: "Animal 'Languages' and Human Language" (1959a), prepared at Spuhler's urging. The same seven were presented, in much the same way, in the final chapter of my *Course in Modern Linguistics* (1958a).

The paper written for Spuhler came to W. E. Lanyon's attention, and thus led to the more extended treatment reprinted here. The volume *Animal Sounds and Communication* grew from a one-afternoon session on the same topic held on 27 August 1958 at the annual meeting of the American Institute of Biological Sciences in Bloomington, Indiana. Lanyon had invited me to participate. After the meeting, the participants were given the chance to revise and enlarge their contributions to the proportions they individually deemed appropriate, and copies of all the other papers, as revised, were made available to me so that I could draw on them for examples in my own much more general treatment. Some of the flavor of symposium-participation remains in the essay as reprinted here.

In this essay the list of design features is increased to thirteen, found also in the popularized rewrite for *Scientific American* ("The Origin of Speech," 1960e). In H8 the design features are dealt with only in passing, but the number grows to sixteen.

Meanwhile, the primatologist Stuart A. Altmann had been independently elaborating something very much like the design-feature approach. When we learned of each other's work we began to put it together. We were both participants in a Wenner-Gren Symposium on Animal Communication organized by Thomas A. Sebeok and held at Burg-Wartenstein in 1965, and for that we prepared the joint paper "A Note on Design Features" (1968d). That is, as far as I know, the most recent and most mature treatment of the issue, but it needs some of the earlier treatments for full intelligibility.

In another direction, this essay led to "The Human Revolution" (1964c), written in collaboration with Robert Ascher, later revised and updated to appear as appropriately placed chapters in *Man's Place in Nature* (1973a).

The ancient Greek maxim, "man is the measure of all things," is poor advice for the zoologist, who learns as much by comparing snails and birds as by comparing either of those with *Homo sapiens*. Yet that does not preclude the occasional use of our own species as a point of departure. The comparative study of human and animal communication bears on the problem of man's place in nature. Also, this study may yield viewpoints of value to the zoologist who is investigating the communicative and social behavior of some other species in its own right.

Some five or six thousand human languages are spoken in the world today. Each is a communicative system the conventions of which are shared more or less precisely by a group of human beings. The small number of languages on which we have fairly adequate information show wide variation in many respects, and as reports on other languages become available the range of known variation increases. Yet, in the face of the variety, we are confident that all languages share certain basic design-features.

Our confidence stems partly from the reasonably random nature of the sample of languages about which more is known, and partly from definition. If a community were discovered, in some hidden corner of the world, in which there was no communicative system characterized by these basic features, we should conclude that the community had no language, and might even refuse to call the individuals in it human beings. (Needless to say, no such revolutionary discovery is anticipated.) Contrariwise, if some species of animal is discovered on the deep sea bottoms, or on Mars or 61-Cygni-C, that uses a communicative system with all the basic design-features of human language, we shall have to recognize that system as genuinely, rather than merely metaphorically, a language, even if not a human one. Pending such discovery, the epithet "human" before the word "language" is tautologous, and will be omitted in the rest of this paper.

Below we shall discuss in turn thirteen design features of language that seem to be most crucial. They are not all of equal importance, and they vary a good deal as to the extent to which they can be characterized in purely abstract terms. There are probably other design features waiting to be singled out and described—the list given here has grown from seven during a single year's part-time research (Hockett 1959). In connection with the discussion of each feature, we list animal communicative systems (if any are known) that seem to have the feature and others that do not, drawing insofar as possible from the other articles in this volume.[1]

1. The Vocal-Auditory Channel. The signals used in any language consist, without residue, of patterns of sound, produced by motions of the respiratory and upper alimentary tracts. No concomitant activity of a speaker, even if it produces sound, is part of his language. The signals are received through the ears, though on occasion the sight of the speaker's articulatory motions helps a hearer to understand signals that might otherwise be distorted beyond recognition by ambient noise.

Not all the sounds and features of sound produced by articulatory motions are part of language. The activity of speaking produces also a variety of sound-effects, "vocal gestures" and the like, that are not part of language and that are classed together under the term *paralinguistic phenomena*. The systematic analysis of these has recently begun; the most complete treatment so far is Trager (1958). The distinction between language and paralinguistic phenomena is not arbitrary. It turns, however, on some of the criteria that will be discussed below; therefore the reader is asked to accept the distinction for the present without further discussion.

As pointed out by Alexander (1960) in his summary, apparently only vertebrates and arthropods have developed systems of sound communication, but in those two phyla such systems are widespread. Our internal ear is an early vertebrate development. The external ear is part of our amphibian heritage, adapted to the exigencies of hearing in air rather than water. Breathing with thoracic muscles rather than by swallowing is necessary for the production of speech sounds as humans produce them; that is common to the reptiles and their descendants (Romer 1959 for the last three points). Almost all mammals (the giraffe is an exception) produce vocal sounds. In a general way, then, the vocal-auditory channel used by language, as opposed to other varieties of channels involving sound, is a common mammalian trait. The mechanisms of sound-

---

1. [∇ That is, in the volume in which this article first appeared (see introductory note on p. 124).]

production and -detection among birds are so similar that one might wish to subsume bird song also under the term "vocal-auditory."

Anthropologists have always been somewhat hesitant about referring to the human organs of speech as "organs of speech." Sapir (1921) humorously pointed out that this is something like calling the hands organs of piano-playing or the knees organs of prayer, and others (Bloomfield 1933; Hockett 1958) have accepted that view. On the other hand, to reject the designation or to insist that it is purely metaphorical might be something like insisting, on evolutionary grounds, that a swimming bladder is "really" a lung or that external ears are "really" gills. There is a difference: swimming bladders and external ears perform no respiratory function, whereas the organs of speech all still perform the functions they had before the development of language—the lungs breathe, the tongue manipulates, the teeth tear and masticate, and so on. Yet the human speech apparatus is structurally different in a number of ways from the homologous organs even in other Primates, and language (or its immediate functional precursors) may be old enough to have conditioned the anatomical changes that have occurred. In other Primates (Spuhler 1959; DuBrul 1958) the larynx is very close to the soft palate, or even touches it; the human larynx is further down the throat, and the root of the tongue can be bulged backward into the space in the lower pharyngeal cavity thus supplied. The human soft palate is freely moved back and upwards to close off the nasal passages from the nasal pharynx; other Primates cannot do that with ease. To a considerable extent, these and other alterations are doubtless tied in with the development of upright posture and the migration of the face from the end to the ventral side of the head, placing the oral and nasal cavities approximately at right angles to the pharynx instead of in line therewith, but there is every reason to believe that these grosser modifications, also, have constantly conditioned and been conditioned by communicative and social behavior.

VOWEL COLOR. In speech, air passing (usually but not always outwards) through the larynx sometimes sets the vocal cords into vibration and sometimes does not. The air stream is largely controlled by the lungs, operated by the diaphragm and the interior and exterior intercostal muscles; this sublaryngeal apparatus must not be dismissed as a "mere bellows," since it is involved in subtle variations of rhythm and volume that are relevant in most languages, probably in all (for instance, in English, compare the noun *PERmit*, with the first syllable louder, with the verb *perMIT*, with the second syllable louder). The sound produced by the vibration of the vocal cords, or by cavity friction when they are quiescent, is distinctively modulated by motions and positions of the movable parts of the throat and mouth. In addition to the brief silences, mufflings, and hissings produced by the motions, they yield a constantly changing acoustic effect called *vowel color*, which is known to do much of the work of carrying information from speaker to hearer (Hockett 1955 and literature cited).

Borror (1960) describes sound spectrography. Spectrograms of human speech look somewhat different from those of animal sounds; for examples see Joos (1948). Voicing—the vibration of the vocal cords—appears as a dark trace near the bottom of the spectrogram, representing the fundamental, with a number of spaced-out lighter traces above and roughly parallel to it, representing the harmonics. The intensity of the harmonics varies, because of the changing shape of the supraglottal cavities, in such a way that one can discern darker bands sometimes coinciding with a bundle of adjacent harmonic traces and sometimes cutting across them. These darker bands represent *formants*: resonant reinforcements of the energy at certain absolute frequencies, regardless of the pitch of the fundamental. Combinations of formants at specified frequencies constitute vowel colors. Thus the formants for the English vowel *a* (as in *father*) are essentially the same for a male and a female voice, despite the differences in pitch of fundamental and in tone quality.

There is considerable doubt whether any animal vocal-auditory system makes distinctive use of vowel color. There is even doubt that such a domesticated animal as a dog, in responding to human vocal signals, pays any attention to differences of vowel color. The repertory of human commands to which a trained dog reacts is usually rather small, so that in general any two commands are differentiated not only in vowel color but also in many other ways—rhythm, volume, voice quality, even accompanying body motions and, for all we know, subtle differences of odor that humans ignore but dogs do not. Experimental testing of this is a desideratum.

CORTICAL CONTROL.   It is abundantly clear that speaking is a cortically governed function. Spuhler (1959) writes as follows: "Consider the muscles used in speaking. Most of our coordinated muscular movement involves corrections and adjustments from proprioceptors. But the laryngeal muscles lack proprioceptors, and feedback control of speech comes by way of the ear and the 8th cranial nerve. When we talk, the voice box, tongue, and lips must work together smoothly and precisely. The 10th nerve controls the adjustment of the vocal cords and the 5th nerve the movement of the lips. Both of these involve branchial muscle while the

12th nerve moves the tongue with somato-motor muscle." We may add that the diaphragm and intercostal muscles, whose cooperation is crucial, are controlled by a whole series of spinal nerves. "The neurological basis of speech is not clear, but it is clear that the only place where the motor organs and steering apparatus of speech are wired together is in the cerebral cortex."

The importance of mouth and ear in human life is reflected in the large cortical representation of those two regions: both sensory and motor for the mouth, and sensory for the ear. This is shown by the two "homunculi" presented by Penfield and Rasmussen (1950), summarizing extensive studies of cortical representation via pinpoint electrode stimulation. Washburn (1959) reproduces Penfield and Rasmussen's motor homunculus alongside a similar homunculus for a monkey of unidentified species. The differences in proportional representation are enormous.

HAND, EYE, MOUTH, AND EAR.   It is not particularly surprising—hindsight being of the keenest—that our prehuman ancestors should have "selected" the vocal-auditory channel for the development of a truly flexible and fluent system of communication. Primates have hands, which, under the feedback control of the excellent primate eye, perform a great deal of the manipulation of objects that many other animals perform with the mouth. The cooperation of hand and eye is most highly developed in the hominid line, where bipedal locomotion frees the forelimbs completely from participation in walking. It has been guessed (Spuhler 1959; Washburn 1959) that the advantages of hand-eye cooperation set the stage for increased complexity of cortical control in general; it could also be guessed that the same advantages promote the development of upright posture and bipedal locomotion. These various functional shifts free the mouth from some of its classical burden, so that it can perform new duties. At the same time, flexibility in a vocal-auditory communicative system as opposed, say, to a gestural system, leaves hand and eye free for other activities. Several individuals, using their hands and eyes at some joint task, can coordinate their actions with a vocal-auditory system without having to interrupt their task in order to communicate about it. That is a meaningful convenience as soon as cooperative environmental manipulations (as over against the interactions of sex, infant-care, and fighting) are undertaken; the beginnings of such cooperation, to judge from its absence among contemporary nonhuman primates (Sahlins 1959), must have taken place somewhere in the hominid line between *Proconsul* and modern man (Spuhler 1959). True, a vocal-auditory system has also at least one major disadvantage, but that is better discussed in the next section.

INTERSPECIES COMMUNICATION. Differences in the structure of sound-producing and sound-detecting mechanisms have an important bearing on interspecies communication, including the variety thereof involved when human zoologists study the sounds of other animals. As a point of departure for our discussion of this, let us consider first what happens when a speaker of one language is exposed to speech in another. Suppose an American who knows no German hears a German say *Buch* 'book'. It is probable that he will hear this word as though it began with a consonant like the English *b* of *book*, continued with a vowel like the English *oo* of *moon*, and ended with a consonant like the English *k* of *book*. If the American repeats the German word, he will probably use these English sounds in the sequence indicated. But if he does, he will be saying a different German word, *buk* 'baked'. The point is that although all human beings speak with the same anatomical apparatus, different languages make use of different articulatory motions. We hear speech in another language, at first, either as an impossible jumble or in terms of the articulatory-acoustic patterns of our own language, and only in time adapt to the different articulatory-acoustic patterns of the other language. That the adaptation is rarely complete is attested by the prevalence of people who speak one or more nonnative languages with a "foreign accent."

In the case of the human naturalist attempting to imitate and to describe the sounds of another species, say bird songs, the situation is a good deal more complicated. Many ornithologists have attempted to describe bird calls in English orthographic form: *tsee-tsee-tsee*, *kuk-kuk-kuk-kuk*, and so on. It is not enough merely to say, as every naturalist knows, that such renderings are impressionistic. We must come to grips with the transductions actually involved. A bird does not have the same structures above the syrinx that a human has above the glottis—and a syrinx is not a glottis. Though birds do modulate their syrinx tone (or tones) with suprasyringeal, and in some cases with subsyringeal, motions, the modulations cannot possibly be congruent with those produced in human speaking. What happens, then, is that as the bird call enters the naturalist's ears it is processed *as though* it had been produced by human speech organs. Certain effects of pitch and tone quality are interpreted as vowel colors, and certain percussive effects as consonants. The data are then further processed according to the complex correlations of English speech sounds and English spelling to yield an orthographic representation. The first part of this process is probably a very old human habit, since many bird-names in many languages (*cuckoo*, *bob-white*; Potawatomi *kokkok'o* 'owl') have been shaped in this way. But the transductions cannot be reversed. The experienced naturalist, who remembers what the bird call really sounds like, may ignore the orthographic form and imitate the call from memory—sometimes well enough to fool the birds. But if anyone else, not familiar with the particular call through direct experience, tries to produce it by following the orthographic representation, he fails miserably.

Such considerations as the foregoing have been partly responsible for the resort to devices like the oscillograph and spectrograph for the study of animal sounds. Clearly that is desirable, but there are important things that spectrographs and oscillographs cannot find out for us. The spectrograph does not hear sound as the human ear and brain do, nor as a bluebird ear and brain do. A spectrogram can show in fine physical detail what sounds have been produced, but cannot show which features of the sound are communicatively significant for the species or for the particular animal community. In working with a hitherto undescribed language, linguists know fairly well how to find out what articulations and sounds are relevant for that language and which are not. In essence, the method turns on the fact that the observer has the same basic equipment and capacities as the observed: the linguist learns the new language and observes his own articulatory motions. This technique is not in general feasible in the study of animal communication. The development of methods by which one can determine, for example, which features of bluebird song are communicatively functional *for bluebirds* is probably the knottiest problem in the whole field of animal communication.

2. Broadcast Transmission and Directional Reception. Unless guided, as in a stethoscope tube, sound, like light, moves in all directions from its source through any uniform medium, its intensity diminishing according to the familiar inverse square law. Unlike light, sound waves pass through or around certain types of obstacles: we can hear someone speaking around a corner where we cannot see him.

In any communicative system that uses a sound channel (vocal-auditory or other), transmission is therefore basically of the broadcast type: any receiver within range will detect the signal. A message transmitted to friends can also be received by predators and by prey. The situation is like that in bidding at bridge, where any information sent to one's partner is also (barring resort to unannounced conventions, which is cheating) transmitted to opponents. There must be many ecological conditions in which this public nature of sound communication is potentially contrasurvival. That is the disadvantage of the vocal-auditory channel mentioned, but not described, earlier.

The complement to broadcast transmission is that hearing is reasonably directional under many circumstances. The parallax of binaural hearing can always be supplemented by motions of the ears or of the whole body. Consequently, the sound signals transmitted by an animal do not usually need to include specification of where the animal is: this information is conveyed by the physical structure of the channel itself—and is, indeed, difficult to withhold. A gibbon, finding food, emits the food call (Carpenter 1940), which is distinctively different from the danger call and certain others. But the acoustic properties of the food call do not tell where the food is; only the location of the source of the call tells that. In somewhat the same way (or for the same ultimate reason), all languages have words like *here* and *I*, the denotations of which have to be inferred from our observation of where and who the speaker is as the words are spoken.

Privacy in communication can be achieved in several ways:

(1) Under some momentary conditions, by transmitting at a power level that will allow the signal to reach the intended destination but become unintelligible or inaudible at greater distances: for example, whispering. (In line with this is the fact that those animal cries indicative of the most imminent danger tend to be the loudest—there is little hope left for the yelping victim, so that a loud cry loses him nothing, while others of his band are more likely to be saved by a loud cry than by a quiet one. Human vocal signals do not always conform to this tendency.)

(2) By using a channel for which undesired receivers have no sensory organs: for example, walkie-talkies in a man-hunt. The use of sounds of very high frequencies by some birds and insects (Collias 1960) might well exemplify this, in that some of their natural enemies may have only lower ranges of hearing.

(3) By so encoding the information that undesired receivers cannot decode it, so that, at most, they can observe that transmission is occurring and the location of the transmitter. Speech during a hunt for animal prey would illustrate this. Birds that mock the calls of other birds perhaps imitate accurately enough to fool enemies, and yet retain characteristic features by virtue of which others of their own species can distinguish between the mocking call and the mocked one. If so, then this illustrates also a further measure for privacy: concealment of the very fact that certain information is being transmitted. Human spies or military agents sometimes attempt this: see Pratt (1939).

(4) With a tight beam. Although familiar enough in recent human history, otherwise this technique is apparently very rare. But there is one sure nonhuman example: the interconnecting nerve net of a coelenterate colony, which, according to some, was the precursor of the nervous system of the individual chordate.

3. Rapid Fading. The physical nature of sound yields another design-feature in any communicative system that uses a sound channel: a signal has to be received just at the right time or it is irrecoverably gone. The sound waves keep traveling, and continue to attenuate until any communicatively distinctive contours are totally masked by thermal noise.

In time, of course, any message encoded in any way is subject to fading. That is a simple corollary of the second law of thermodynamics. A cuneiform inscription six thousand years old may still be legible today, but eventually it will be worn smooth or disintegrated. Yet, relative to the time scale of individual animal lives, we can usefully distinguish between *nonrecording* and *recording* communicative systems. A signal transmitted in a system of the former kind has to be received just at the right moment or it is gone. A signal transmitted in a recording system can be received thereafter at the convenience of the receiver, in some cases repeatedly. Recording systems are required for what has come to be called *information storage*. Information originally encoded with a nonrecording system can be stored by transducing it into storable form, as when a stenographer takes dictation or a microphone and stylus transduce sound into a wiggly groove on a wax disc.

There is a rather obvious axiom about information storage that will be important to us later in this paper: the storage of information requires the construction of an internally stable and enduring spatial array. Thus the sheet of paper that bears the printer's ink that forms the words that the reader is now perusing can be moved from one place to another as a whole; also, the molecules that compose it are jiggling around; but within these boundaries of size-level the array of paper and ink is stable. Even circulating storage in some computing machines, where a train of signals traverses a column of mercury and then is fed electronically back to the starting end of the column, conforms to this axiom: the whole array is moving, but its internal organization is reasonably invariant. Similarly, we do not try to make yardsticks out of water or air. Whether stored information can be "read" or not depends on the availability of equipment to perform a transduction the inverse of that by which the information was stored. Subject to this limitation, the axiom can be turned hind end to: any internally stable array is stored information about past events. This is the assumption on which geology, palaeontology, archaeology, and all other historical sciences are founded.

A widespread characteristic of animal sounds is that a particular call is repeated as long as the condition for which it is appropriate continues. If a single signal could hang in the air, at least for a while, and be received repeatedly at leisure, there would be no need for more than the one transmission. This latter is what happens in the case of trails and spoors. As an animal moves about it leaves a spoor, which may vary somewhat in chemical structure depending on what the animal is doing and what is happening to it. A spoor is not permanent, nor are broken twigs and bent grass, but under most conditions these signs of passage fade much more slowly than does a sound signal. Thus there is an interval of time during which other animals, encountering the spoor, can react to it after their own fashion. Olfactory signals have the advantage (or at least the property) of slow fading, but also the disadvantage of slow diffusion, so that an urgent signal cannot be transmitted over any great distance rapidly enough to be of use. Sound signals have the advantage of rapid transit, but the disadvantage of virtually instantaneous fading, a disadvantage overcome by repetitive transmission.

Human sound communication also shows this characteristic of repetitive transmission. A man in difficulties may call repeatedly for help, even after he has seen his rescuers approaching. A mother croons to her infant until she gets tired or the infant goes to sleep. Lovers may talk about a huge variety of things, but they use appropriate tones of voice, that alter only when a quarrel develops or there is some sort of intrusion. However, these features of continuity or repetition are manifested more in the aura of paralinguistic signals accompanying speech than in linguistic material proper.

The nonrecording nature of language has been compensated for in recent human history by the development of various derivative recording systems, of which writing, only a few thousand years old, was clearly the first. The information stored by a writing system is first coded into linguistic form, and then transduced into marks on a flat surface. Writing seems to have no analog anywhere else in the animal kingdom.

4. Interchangeability. Alexander (1960) mentions certain insects (Gryllidae and Tettigoniidae) for which there is a sharp sex difference in communicative use of sound: the males emit certain calls to which females and other males react, but which females do not produce. In some species, at least, the females do produce sounds, but of a different type from those produced by males.

Again, in the courtship behavior of sticklebacks (*Gasterosteus aculeatus*; Tinbergen 1953) each participant assumes an appearance and moves in contours that, together, serve as adequate stimulus for the partner. But neither participant could transmit the signals characteristic of the other—the roles are not interchangeable.

Bee dancing (von Frisch 1950) shows interchangeability among the workers, in that any worker may dance and any may heed the instructions danced by another. From this interchangeability queens and drones are excluded.

Any speaker of a human language is capable, in theory, of saying anything he can understand when someone else says it. For language, humans are what engineers call "transceivers": units freely usable for either transmission or reception.

To be sure, there are certain apparent, or real but marginal, exceptions to this interchangeability among humans. A pathological exception is the mute who understands what others say but does not speak himself, whether this be due to injury to the speech organs, brain lesion, or socially induced neurosis; or, conversely, the totally deaf person who can still talk intelligibly. An interesting apparent exception is found in certain communities where men and women use markedly different vocabulary, even to different sets of inflectional endings (Bloomfield 1933). In such a community, no male would ordinarily use women's speech forms, or vice versa—at first sight, there seems to be a sort of sexual dimorphism in speech behavior. But if a member of either sex happens to be telling a story in which some of the characters are of the other sex, the narrator does not hesitate to use the appropriate vocabulary in direct quotations from the characters. The seeming lack of interchangeability thus does not cut very deep. A third kind of exception, obviously marginal, is the virtuoso speech performance of certain people who have worked hard to acquire the special skills involved: few of us could even recite a Gilbert and Sullivan patter song as rapidly as the D'Oyly Carte specialist sings it. Finally, it is obviously true that interchangeability does not extend to young humans who have not yet acquired the language habits of their community.

With similar apparent or marginal exceptions, interchangeability seems to be the rule for a great many mammalian and avian systems of vocal-auditory communication.

5. Total Feedback. In the courtship behavior of sticklebacks, mentioned above in §4, one of the necessary visual stimuli to the male is the appearance of the female's abdomen, distended with roe; among the necessary cues to the female are the seasonal colors of the male's eyes and belly. Neither can see its own belly, nor can the male see his own eyes. Each participant transmits crucial signals that he cannot receive. The only feedback to, say, the male, is of an indirect and transformed sort: if the courted female responds properly, the male has transmitted the proper signals.

In normal circumstances (that is, barring deafness and perhaps sleep-talking), a speaker of a human language hears everything he says as he says it. Auditory feedback is supplemented by kinesthetic and proprioceptive feedback from the speech organs, except that there is no proprioceptive feedback from the laryngeal muscles (§1 above, quoting Spuhler 1959). Informal experiment and observation show that both sorts of feedback are important for intelligible speech. The clarity of articulation tends to deteriorate with deafness, though this leaves kinesthetic and proprioceptive feedback unimpaired; it also deteriorates under the influence of ethyl alcohol, which apparently affects the latter before it disturbs hearing.

It is true that one's voice does not sound the same to oneself as it does to others. That can be shown by recording one's voice and listening to it. The difference lies in the bone conduction of sound, operative between a speaker's vocal organs and his own ears but obviously not between the former and the ear of others (or a microphone). However, this auditory difference has to do with the basic voice quality, not with the superimposed modulations that constitute the signaling units of a language. The latter are transmitted equally well with or without bone conduction.

It seems likely that every vocal-auditory communicative system—perhaps, indeed, every sound system, vocal-auditory or other—shares this property of total feedback. There may be exceptions of a trivial sort in cross-species communication: one species might react to frequencies in the sound signals of another species to which the hearing organs of the latter cannot respond. A bat might be flushed by a dog making no sound audible to canine (or human) ears.

The significance of total feedback is twofold.

In the first place, for any animal that typically emits whole trains of sound signals, whether relatively repetitious (as for many insects) or varying (as for some birds and mammals), one must consider the possibility that the feedback reception of each emitted signal forms part of the stimulus conditioning the emission and nature of the next. Wherever this is discovered to be so, there is the further possibility that the feedback serves as the basis for adjustments in the train of signals, towards some norm the image of which is stored within the central nervous system of the animal. From information currently available, we should expect these mechanisms to be most important for communicative systems that are not fully participated in by the newly born or hatched young, and the acquisition of which seems in the ordinary course of events to involve, if not to require, appropriate stimuli at appropriate times from surrounding adults (see §13, below). Thus Lanyon (1960) cites instances in which passerine birds, deafened at an early age, have failed to develop the full panoply of song normal for their respective species. Apparently it is not the facts but their interpretation that is still in doubt here. In seeking the correct interpretation, we should remember (as Lanyon points out) that a deafened animal suffers a major loss of feedback, as well as of stimuli from other animals. One the other hand, a bird raised in acoustic isolation in a soundproof chamber is cut off from stimuli from adults but loses no feedback. A comparison of the results of experiments of these two types should thus shed much light on the mechanisms described above.

The second implication of total feedback rests not alone thereon, but on the joint presence of total feedback and of interchangeability. This is the possibility of "short-circuiting." A sequence of signals normally, or originally, passed around among several members of a group of animals, each signal serving at once as part of the response to the preceding signal and as part of the stimulus for the following, may come to be acted out entirely by a single animal playing all the "roles" involved. It may be that this does not happen anywhere in the animal kingdom except among humans. But it is clear that it cannot happen in a communicative system not characterized by interchangeability and total feedback, and it is also clear that much of the power of language lies in such short-circuiting. A group of humans, facing a practical problem, typically talks the situation over before arriving at a program for action. Any single human, once he has participated in such consultations, can hold a conference with himself about a problem he encounters when alone, thus indirectly bringing to bear on the problem some of the experience and tradition of the whole group. A further short-circuiting also seems to take place, at least for our own species: the single human being holding his lone conference comes to transmit signals at such a low power level—perhaps confining them entirely to his own central nervous system—that others cannot receive them, so that the only immediate consequences of the signals are the internal ones via feedback. This is one version of the behaviorist theory of "thinking." It may be quite erroneous, but as a hypothesis it has the advantage of underscoring realistically the lines of connection and the direction of causality between the social and the "mental."

6. Specialization. A husband may be cued to wash his hands and come to dinner by the sight and sound of his wife setting the table. Or he may be brought to the table when his wife announces that dinner is ready. There is a clear difference between these two situations. The difference is easily described if we are willing to speak teleologically: when the wife announces that dinner is ready the obvious purpose of her act of speech is to bring the husband to the table; whereas when she sets the table the obvious purpose is to get the table set, and any influence on her husband's behavior is, so to speak, a side-effect. For reasons too numerous and well known to require itemization here, this simple explanation, even if in some sense true, cannot serve us. But a nonteleological paraphrase requires some preliminary discussion of seemingly unrelated matters.

Joe Snakebite hurls a spear at an elk; Peter Jones uses a shotgun. Joe must supply from within himself all the energy necessary for both aim and propulsion. Peter supplies personally only the energy for aiming and for pulling the trigger; the powder in the shell supplies the rest. If we take a line of sight through Joe and the spear trajectory, or through the powder in the shell and the shot trajectory, we see only direct (energetic) action. That is the orientation constantly sought by the physicist, who consequently discovers such generalizations as the conservation of energy. If, instead, we sight through each hunter's behavior and its consequences, we see direct action in the first case, but trigger action in the second. Both hunters succeed, we shall say, in bagging their quarry, but by significantly different operations. In trigger sequences there is no principle of conservation, of energy or of any other definable commodity.

It is tempting to draw a comparison between the simple paradigm of triggering just given and certain phenomena that have not customarily been discussed in quite these terms. Thus a virus or a gene, in the proper medium, might be said to trigger the synthesis of replicas of itself. The genetic pattern of a fertilized ovum supplies neither the material substance nor the energy for maturation, but guides the development of the new individual in a way that might well be called triggering. When a catalyst speeds up the rate of a chemical reaction by lowering the free energy of activation, something similar to triggering seems to be taking place. A neutron striking an atomic nucleus may trigger the release of much more energy than it carries. Lotka (1925) reflects the classical dichotomy of physical science when he uses the terms *stoichiometry* and *energetics* for the analysis of the migrations and transformations respectively of matter and of energy. But these are only two of a triad of angles of approach to a wide variety of phenomena; the third, whatever term we might choose for it (perhaps "cybernetics," following Wiener 1948), has to do with triggering sequences. At the smallest size-levels of concern in physics, the distinctions among these three angles of approach may break down, as witness the replacement in recent decades of the two traditional laws of conservation by a single law of conservation of matter-and-energy. But in such fields as ecology, animal or human sociology, or human behavioral science, the distinctions work quite well and all three approaches are fruitful.

Whether or not the notion of triggering has the far-reaching ramifications just suggested, and without attempting to foist a formal definition of "communication" on anyone who prefers some other approach, it seems fair to assert that when we study communicative behavior we are focusing our attention on the ways in which organisms (or, sometimes, machines or parts of organisms) trigger one another. That is very broad, but does not subsume everything. For example, suppose a man sees the sun going down, and prepares for bed: that is not communicative, because the sun is not an organism. Or suppose a bartender's bouncer throws a drunk out bodily: that is not essentially communicative, because the action is direct (it doubtless has communicative side-effects—the drunk's attitude towards the bouncer may be very different upon their next encounter). But if a man prepares for bed when someone tells him the sun is going down, or the bartender gets rid of the drunk with a threatening gesture, we have triggering between organisms, and hence communication.

Now we are ready to return to our original examples, of the husband being brought to the dinner table in either of two ways. Both ways are communicative—direct action would require that the wife deposit the husband at the table just as she puts the plates and silver there, and that is not often done. The difference can be gotten at if we remember that any act of an organism, including an act that transmits what some other organism takes as a signal, involves the expenditure of energy and therefore has direct energetic consequences. When the wife sets the table, the direct consequences of her actions are that the silver, plates, and food are in place; in the lifeways of our own society, these direct consequences are intimately tied up with the biological function of alimentation. When the wife calls out "Dinner's ready," it is only the trigger consequences that have any biological relevance. The direct consequences are a flurry of sound waves in the air, damping out with a slight rise in temperature of air and walls, all of which would seem to be quite trivial in terms of biological functions.

We shall say that a communicative act, or a whole communicative system, is *specialized* to the extent that its direct energetic consequences are biologically *irrelevant*. Obviously language is a specialized communicative system; so, also, are most varieties of animal communication to which our attention is normally apt to be drawn, since we are perhaps not inclined to think of communication as *systematic* and worthy of careful study unless it has this property. Some investigators, indeed, may

prefer so to constrain the term "communication" that unspecialized triggering side-effects of functional behavior are excluded. Terminology is of
no great importance, but it is important to recognize that what we would
call unspecialized communication is extremely widespread and that,
phylogenetically, it was probably the matrix within which and from which
specialized communicative systems developed.

Thus the panting of a dog with tongue hanging out provides for cooling
through evaporation, and constitutes part of the animal's machinery for
thermostatic control. The panting produces characteristic sound, that can
inform other dogs (and people) about the location and state of the panting
animal and perhaps even identify him to them. The communication is
unspecialized.

Again, the roe in a female stickleback during the breeding season is
ultimately deposited in the nest in which the male then deposits his milt.
Meanwhile, however, the roe distends the female's belly, and this altered
bodily appearance is crucial in courtship, since a male will not court a
female whose belly is not properly distended. This feature, at least, of
stickleback courtship signaling is unspecialized.

The seasonal coloration of the male stickleback, like that of a great
many animals of both sexes, is doubtless biochemically tied up in a very
intimate way with the gonadal changes that prepare for reproduction. The
basic metabolizing substances in both plants and animals, such as the
chlorophylls and hemoglobins, are pigments: tetrapyrrole ring compounds
closely akin to others that supply coloration without functioning intimately in metabolism (Blum 1955). A particular seasonal coloration can
thus be a phylogenetically "accidental" by-product of a mutated pattern
of metabolism, surviving only because it functions triggerwise to identify
the animal and the animal's state to others. In this sense, the male
stickleback's characteristically red belly and blue eyes during the breeding season can be regarded as communicatively specialized. However,
that inference may stem from ignorance. Conceivably—though im-
probably—the color differential between belly and eyes plays a part in
some internal energy-flow of key importance in sperm production. Similarly, the conversion of chemical into acoustic energy by the crepitation of
a male cricket, or the bathing of the cricket's body in the sound waves thus
produced, might possibly play some direct role in adjusting its body
chemistry for reproduction, in addition to triggering females into approaching. The point of these rather dubious examples is that it is not
necessarily easy to be sure whether communicative behavior is
specialized or not. That is perhaps a good reason why we should not tip

the scales in advance by choosing an overly narrow definition of the term "communication."

7. Semanticity. The following example is from Hockett (1958). Let us picture two men seated side by side at a lunch counter. John has a cup of coffee for which he wants some sugar, but the sugar bowl is out of reach beyond Bill. John says, "Please pass the sugar." Bill passes it. This reveals, in bare outline form, the behavioral antecedents and consequences in which the act of speech is embedded. These antecedents and consequences are different for John and for Bill: John wants the sugar and gets it; Bill merely passes it. The same utterance could occur under other conditions: for example, Bill might have the coffee and ask John for the sugar. In the original situation, some of the behavioral consequences are not due to anything about the structure of the speech signal, but to concomitant circumstances. Bill passes the sugar to John rather than to Carl because it is John, not Carl, who produces the speech signal. But the way in which the act of speech serves to bridge between the antecedents and the consequences also depends on the fact that John and Bill share certain *semantic conventions* about constituent signals of English. Thus there is an associative tie between the word *sugar* and a certain familiar substance: Bill does not pass the salt. There is a tie between *pass* and a familiar action: Bill does not throw the sugar bowl to the floor. There is a shared understanding that *please*, with certain word order and intonation, is a polite request: Bill is not insulted or annoyed. Without these shared conventions, John would have had to get up and fetch the sugar himself, or else go without.

When the elements of a communicative system have such associative ties with things and situations, or types of things and situations, in the environment of its users, and when the functioning of the system rests on such ties, we say that the system is *semantic* or is characterized by *semanticity*. Human languages are semantic, despite the fact that every language includes a minority of forms that lack any obvious semantic tie—e.g., English *unicorn* or *and*. The possibility of such peculiar forms seems to rest on certain design features yet to be discussed (§10 and 11, below).

Some anthropological theorists have tended to imply, perhaps unintentionally, that only human communicative systems are semantic (e.g., White 1959 and earlier works cited). Under our definition that is clearly not so. A hungry gibbon reacts to the sight or smell of food by approaching the food, by emitting the food call, and, presumably, by salivation and other familiar anticipatory behavior. A hungry gibbon reacts to the sound of the food call by this same concatenation of behavior: motion in the direction of the source of the call, repetition of the call, and doubtless the other food-anticipating reactions. That does not mean that the gibbon "identifies" food and the food call, any more than John would try to sweeten his coffee with the word *sugar*. But it certainly implies that there is some sort of associative tie between food and the food call, whereby either food or the food call elicits a pattern of reactions different from that elicited by, say, danger or the danger call. That is all the evidence we need to class gibbon calls as a semantic system.

Again, bee dancing is semantic, since the dance denotes a location in terms of direction and distance from the hive or swarm. The reaction of the observing workers is to proceed to the location denoted.

On the other hand, if we consider once again the courtship signaling of sticklebacks, there seems to be no semantics. The reaction of the male to the appearance of the female is not like his reaction to anything else, but merely a contour of behavior that in turn triggers the female into her next step in the courtship dance. A word is, as we say, a symbol for something. A gibbon call is a symbol for something. A rate or direction of a bee dance is a symbol for something. The darting dance of the male stickleback is an effective triggering, but is not a symbol for anything outside itself.

In judging semanticity it is important to distinguish between the communicative behavior proper and the attendant circumstances. The fact that Bill passes the sugar to John rather than to someone else is not due to anything in the semantics of the English phrase "Please pass the sugar," but to the attendant circumstance that it is John who utters the phrase. The fact that a gibbon, hearing the food call, moves to the northwest rather than in some other direction is not due to anything in the semantics of the food call, but to the attendant circumstance that the call he hears comes from that direction (compare §2 above). The location denoted by a bee dance is sometimes the location of a source of nectar, sometimes that of a possible hive site. But the dance itself does not make this distinction. If the bees are swarming, the location is that of a possible hive site. If they are in or at a hive, the location is that of a source of nectar.

8. Arbitrariness. In a semantic communicative system, the associative ties between meaningful elements and their meanings can be of either of two types, or can have features of both. A symbol means what it does *iconically* to the extent that it resembles its meaning in physical contours, or to the extent that the whole repertory of symbols in the system shows a geometrical similarity to the whole repertory of meanings. To the extent that a symbol or system is not iconic, it is *arbitrary*. The signals of a nonsemantic system, be it noted, cannot be classed as either iconic or arbitrary, since they have no meanings.

A road map involves a blend of these two types of semantic relation. The iconic element is obvious: the dots and lines that represent towns, hills, rivers, and roads are arranged on the map roughly the same way the actual towns, hills, rivers, and roads are arranged on the surface of the earth, with a specified reduction of scale. But the width of a line representing a road or a river is not indicative of the width of the actual road or river. The color of the line representing a road is not iconic: we do not find in our peregrinations that main paved roads are red, minor ones black, and unpaved roads checkered. Arbitrary features are sometimes mistakenly taken as iconic. In *Tom Sawyer Abroad,* Huck Finn looked out of the balloon in which he and Tom were traveling and insisted that they must not yet have left Illinois, since the ground was still green: in his geography book, Illinois was printed in green, Indiana in some other color.

The iconic-arbitrary classification of symbols and signals is by no means simple. It is tied up with many complex problems of the psychology of perception and cognition, as well as with physics and geometry (Gibson 1954). It is doubtless safe to say that no semantic relationship is completely iconic, since for a symbol of anything to be completely iconic it would have to be indistinguishable from the original, and would thus *be* the original. But degrees, and perhaps kinds, of arbitrariness vary. A stereoscopic and stereophonic moving picture of a President of the United States is less arbitrary than a fine-grained still photograph, but the latter is less arbitrary than a cartoon caricature, and the latter less so than the phrase "President of the United States."

The basic semantic relations in a language are extremely arbitrary. There is no similarity between the sound of the word *dog* (or French *chien*, or German *Hund*, and so on) and the sight, sound, or smell of a dog. Nor is the difference between the sounds of the words *dog* and *cat* in any way parallel to the difference between the sight, sound, or smell of a dog and that of a cat. Big words can name small things and small words big things: *microorganism, whale*. There are probably faint traces of iconicity in so-called "onomatopoetic" forms, such as English *ding-dong, bow-wow, bob-white*, but any cross-language study shows that words like these also involve a large arbitrary element (Hockett 1958, chap. 35; Brown 1959, chap. 4; and literature cited). A clearer element of iconicity appears when we use the sound of a form as a name for the form, as in speaking of "the word *dog*" or "the suffix *-ing.*" A narration may be iconic in that events are described in the sequence in which they actually happened, but that is not an invariable rule.

In the paralinguistic accompaniments of language there may be instances of a kind of iconicity. In our culture, a speaker often increases his volume with anger, and there is perhaps some rough correlation between the degree of anger and the degree of increased volume. Degrees of anger are meanings and degrees of volume are the signals that carry the meanings, so that the continuous mapping of the former into the latter is iconic. Beyond that the situation is not clear. It is possible that the mapping of anger into increased volume rather than, say, into diminished volume or lowered pitch or something else, is arbitrary. More probably, however, increase in volume is one part of the whole behavioral gestalt known to us as anger. In that case, increase of volume is what Langer (1942) calls a *symptom,* and the semantic relation can hardly be regarded as arbitrary.

Insofar as mammalian and avian vocal-auditory systems are semantic, they seem also to be basically arbitrary. So, certainly, for gibbon calls, though the call system seems to be embedded in a framework of continuous variables just as language is embedded in a paralinguistic matrix, and in this framework there may be iconic features. The general intensity with which a gibbon emits the danger call may be a direct function of the imminence or seriousness of the danger. The association between danger and the characteristic danger call is then arbitrary, but the correlation of imminence and intensity is iconic.

Bee dancing is largely iconic. The rate of the dance is inversely proportional to the distance to the target location; the angle of the dance from the vertical is equal to the angle between the line of sight to the sun and the direction towards the target location. Presumably one could invent an organism (or a machine) that would transmit the same information with other underlying associations, say mapping distance into an angle and direction into a rate. That the bee dance gives the polar coordinates of the target location with rate and angle is therefore arbitrary, but within this arbitrary framework the further details of the system are iconic.

A degree of arbitrariness has a certain advantage, in that there are all sorts of things and situations about which communication may be important but which can be represented iconically only with great awkwardness. The Laputans, encountered by Gulliver in one of his later travels, carried a veritable hardware store about with them in order to communicate with iconic examples rather than arbitrary words. It is interesting to note the difference in utility between analog (iconic) and digital (arbitrary) computers. An analog computer can often be extremely well adapted to a narrow operation defined clearly in advance. A digital computer is much more flexible, since it can be reprogrammed for an endless variety of operations. On the other hand, the very term "arbitrary" implies that the orginal development of an arbitrary system, by evolution or construction, is problematic, since the necessary circuitry seems so senseless.

9. Discreteness. When asked where something is, we often respond by *pointing*. The orientation of the pointing finger can be to any of a non-denumerable infinity of directions, restricted only by degree of accuracy. But the relative positioning of hand and finger that constitutes pointing, as a signal, is an all-or-none matter. The gesture either occurs or it does not occur. Physically, of course, hand and finger can be placed in any of an infinity of contours, just as the finger can be turned to any of an infinity of directions. But we do not make communicative use of this whole infinity. One continuous subrange within the total range of possible hand and finger positions is classed together as "pointing," and the remaining continuous subrange as "nonpointing." The pointer directs his behavior roughly into one subrange or the other, and the observer pays attention only to the difference between the two subranges. That sort of segregation of regions out of a physical continuum of possibilities is *quantizing*: it yields a repertory of all-or-none *discrete* signals. If a continuum of possibilities is not thus quantized, then the repertory of signals is, of course *continuous*. Pointing, as we have seen, involves both: the discrete contrast between nonpointing and pointing, and, within the latter, the continuous array of possible directions.

In semantic communicative systems there is one restriction between the matters discussed in the preceding section and those under discussion here: a continuous repertory implies iconicity. Rigorous proof of this is perhaps not possible, but the following considerations render it highly plausible. Given a continuous repertory, and iconicity, a slight error in a signal tends to yield only an equally slight error of interpretation, which under most conditions can be compensated for. If the dance of a bee is somewhat inaccurate, or if the bee that reads the dance does not fly in precisely the indicated direction, when the target comes into sight the course can be corrected. If, on the other hand, the signals of a continuous repertory were assigned arbitrary meanings, then any one signal would be surrounded by others indefinitely similar to it in physical contours but with totally dissimilar meanings. The slightest error of transmission or reception could then yield indefinitely large or serious misinterpretation. But errors—"noise" in the communication engineer's sense—are at bottom ineradicable (Shannon 1947). One way to combat noise is to assign a continuous array of possible signals to a continuous array of meanings—yielding iconicity. Another way is to quantize the continuous array; meanings can then be either iconic or arbitrary. Quantization of a continuum leaves fuzzy boundaries between the adjacent communicatively distinct subregions, so that ambiguous signals can still occur. However, the size of each quantized region, within which differences are communicatively irrelevant, reduces the frequency of occurrence of ambiguous signals, and when one does occur it is ambiguous only among two or a few alternatives, whereas without quantization it would be ambiguous for a nondenumerable infinity of alternatives.[2]

We can now briefly pass in review the sample systems discussed in the preceding section. An analog computer is iconic and continuous. The iconic features of bee dancing are continuous. Gibbon calls are discretely different from one another; the range of variation in intensity (i.e., in volume, register, duration, or amount of repetition) for each call is perhaps continuous and, if so, also iconic. For many mammalian and avian systems we do not know the answers, partly because the relevant questions have not yet been put experimentally. An ornithologist's classification of the observed and recorded songs of a particular species or variety of birds may reflect a functional discreteness for the birds, but it may also—though this seems unlikely—be an artifact of the sampling and of our human tendency to pigeonhole rather than to scale.

That human tendency is a real one. In the nineteenth century it rendered a whole generation of European mathematicians unhappy about scales and continuities, until they worked out a way of "generating" the continuum from the discrete integers as raw-material (Dedekind, Cantor, and others; see, for example, Huntington 1917). Possibly the source of this tendency inheres in the fact that our most typically human communicative system, language, is wholly founded on discreteness.

Any utterance in any language consists of an arrangement of certain basic signaling units called *phonemes*, of which a given language has a definite and finite stock. Phonemes are not sounds, but *ranges* of sound quarried by quantization out of the whole multidimensional continuum of physiologically possible vocal sound. In different languages this quarrying yields different sets of phonemes—a difference of sound that is functional in one language may or may not be in another. We can illustrate both the quantizing and the ways in which languages differ by considering just one physiologically given dimension: voicing, the vibration of the vocal cords.

2. Mathematical note: The term "continuous" is used loosely here. The argument actually turns only on denseness, and, if it proves anything, proves only that a dense repertory of signals is incompatible with arbitrariness.

In English the scale of degrees of strength of voicing is quantized into two subregions. Thus the initial consonants of the words *pat* and *bat* differ only as to voicing: the *p* is most typically voiceless, the *b* most typically voiced. Yet some occurrences of *p* are slightly voiced, and in some occurrences of *b* the voicing is very weak. But if a hearer hears something that is not clearly marked as a *p* or as a *b*, it is only this two-way ambiguity that he has to try to resolve. There is no further alternative, except to leave the ambiguity unresolved—and that is not an alternative within the system, but a breakdown of the system. In some other languages, such as Menomini, the scale of degrees of strength of voicing is not quantized into smaller contrasting regions at all: a speaker of Menomini does not at first hear any difference between English *pat* and *bat*. In still other languages, such as Hindi, degree of strength of voicing is quantized into two regions, and exact timing of onset of voicing is likewise quantized into two, to yield four contrasting units where English has two and Menomini only one.

We do not yet know whether the paralinguistic accompaniments of language are continuous or discrete. At least some of them are certainly continuous (compare the discussion in §8 above). If any are discrete, then there would seem to be something of a problem in demonstrating that they are properly classed as paralinguistic rather than as part of the language; but it may be that other criteria (such as that discussed in §12 below) resolve the dilemma.

10. Displacement. A few semantic communicative systems, including language and its derivatives, have the property that what is being communicated about can be removed, in time or space or both, from the setting in which the communication takes place. This property, *displacement* (Bloomfield 1933), is apparently quite rare; outside of human behavior, the only really well-attested instance is in bee dancing, where the context is quite different. Even as to displacement itself, there is the difference that bee dancing is always and necessarily displaced, whereas language sometimes is and sometimes is not.

The survival value of displacement has never been described better than by V. Gordon Childe, but it should be noted that what he says, quoted just below, turns also on certain other design-features of language, especially that dealt with in §13 below. Once children have acquired the language of their community, says Childe (1936), "parents can, with the aid of language, instruct their offspring how to deal with situations which cannot conveniently be illustrated by actual concrete examples. The child need not wait till a bear attacks the family to learn how to avoid it. Instruction by example alone in such a case is liable to be fatal to some of the pupils. Language, however, enables the elders to forewarn the young of the danger while it is absent, and then demonstrate the appropriate course of action."

Gibbon calls are normally not displaced. A gibbon, finding food, does not return to the rest of the band to report it, but shouts his "Eureka!" as he proceeds to eat. That accords with the general rule for most mammals: out of sight, out of mind. However, if a gibbon encounters danger he does not stay still as he announces it, but flees—if he can. The direction of flight no doubt sometimes brings him closer to other members of the band, as though he were coming to warn them. Such an incident bears the outward guise of displacement. Similar incidents among our speechless hominoid ancestors may have been crucial forerunners of the displacement that subsequently developed in language. We can imagine an early hominoid wandering away from his band and catching sight of a predator, without being detected thereby. If for any reason, say through fright, he did not immediately burst out with his danger call, but first sneaked silently away towards the remainder of his band, that would afford the whole band a head start in escaping the predator. The delaying of the call would thus have survival value, and would promote the selection of those factors, whatever they may be, that allow delay and point towards more extensive displacement.

Displacement implies, or consists of, the ability to discuss today what happened yesterday or what may come to pass tomorrow. A commoner way to talk about such abilities is to say that they rest on "retention" and "foresight." Upon closer scrutiny, this common phrasing develops the flavor of tautology or even of inverted definition, rather than of explanation. What could we possibly mean by "foresight," for example, except the ability to discuss now (in a group or with oneself; cf. §5 above) what may happen later?

Well, "foresight" might also refer to certain other typically and exclusively human phenomena, outstandingly the carrying and making of tools (Spuhler 1959). A tool is a piece of the physicogeographical environment used by an animal in manipulating other parts of the physicogeographical environment, including other animals, but otherwise of no direct biological relevance. This definition is somehow supposed to exclude birds' nests and beavers' dams and houses, as well as the separate raw materials from which such structures are assembled. The difference between a tool and such behavioral products as those just named is perhaps reminiscent of the difference between specialized and unspecialized communicative behavior (above, §6). The mere *use* of an unshaped stick or stone as a tool is not unknown among nonhuman hominoids, at least in captivity; but only human beings seem to be willing to lug an awkward implement around because an occasion may arise in which it will be convenient to have it at hand, and only human beings spend time and energy manufacturing tools.

Since tool-carrying and displaced communication are both almost exclusively human (we can forget about the bees here, since they are phylogenetically so remote), it is difficult or impossible to tell which came first. The best guess is probably that neither really came first; each developed in small increments furthered by the already-achieved increments of itself and of the other, as a man can shinny up inside a chimney by moving his shoulders up one wall and his feet up the opposite one. Yet perhaps some slight edge of priority goes to tool-carrying: our hominid ancestors achieved an essentially modern conformation of limbs long before the brain, skull, and teeth became as they are now (Le Gros Clark 1959).

It is at this point that we evoke the axiom about information storage presented above in §3. If an animal participates in any sort of communicative system, then the conventions of that system must somehow be stored within the animal. This is a very general kind of storage. In a sense, it implies and is implied by the metastability of structure of any living matter, in which, over sizable periods of time, tiny constituent parts are replaced without disturbing the pattern of the whole. This is to assert that, by our axiom, an organism *is* a record, just as is a book, a spoor, or a fossil. But displacement implies the superimposition of the capacity for a further sort of information storage. Any delay between the reception of a stimulus and the appearance of the response means that the former has been coded into a stable spatial array, which endures at least until it is read off in the response. Action at a distance is impossible. The fact that our thoughts can turn in a twinkling from Andromeda to Arcturus does not mean that "thought travels faster than light"; the only "traveling" is the replacement of one symbol by another in ourselves or our immediate neighborhood.

During her return flight from target to hive or swarm, a worker bee somehow records within herself the relative location of target and home-base; the "reading-off" of this record is her dance. In one important sense, we have not the faintest idea how this is accomplished. That is, we do not know what internal circuitry is involved, nor just where nor how the record is laid down. In another sense we know rather more. It would not be too difficult to build a mechanical bee (it might be rather large) which, having been moved from home-base to a target and back, would display the polar coordinates of the target. That implies a kind of black-box knowledge about real bees that should not be underestimated. The "wiring diagrams" of the real bee and the mechanical one would doubtless be enormously different; but the "control-flow chart" of the mechanical bee would have some validity for the real one (Wiener 1948).

The information storage required for displacement need not always be entirely within the organism. Our imagined hominoid ancestor, fleeing a predator silently until the latter is out of range and only then emitting the danger call, has to retain the fact that danger, not something else, is to be reported. But perhaps he does not outrun the odor of his own fear, which clings about him and serves as a mnemonic device. In the case of tool-carrying, the tool is itself stored information. In the case of tool-making, frequently an earlier exemplar of the same kind of tool is at hand to serve as a model.

Nevertheless, an increasing capacity for internal storage clearly has to accompany any radical increase in displacement, and it is not surprising that the development of language, from the proto-hominoids to ourselves, has been paced by increase in size and complexity of the brain. For, whatever other functions the human brain may perform, it unquestionably supplies tremendous room for information storage. Recent experimentation has even begun to suggest what portions of the cortex may be primarily involved (Penfield and Roberts 1959, especially pp. 45f).

11. Productivity. It is a commonplace that a human being may say something that he has never before said nor heard, and be perfectly understood, without either speaker or audience being in the slightest aware of the novelty (Wells 1949, referring to Bertrand Russell).

A communicative system in which new messages can be coined and understood is *open* or *productive*. Bee dancing is open, since a worker may report a location which has never been reported before by either her or her coworkers. Some bird-song systems may be open, at least in that each individual bird works out elaborations on the basic repertory of his community, rendering his song characteristic of himself as well as of his community or species (Lanyon 1960; Marler 1960). In contrast, gibbon calls are effectively closed. The bands observed by Carpenter (1940) had a total repertory of some ten or a dozen distinct calls. No matter how novel may be the circumstances encountered by a gibbon, he is constrained to respond vocally with one or another of this small finite number of calls, or to remain silent. There is seemingly no mechanism for the coinage—and understanding—of a new call.

A continuous semantic (and therefore iconic) communicative system is necessarily also productive. A discrete system is not; and the mechanisms which render language productive are very different from those responsible for openness in bee dancing. Any language provides a large number of elementary signaling units that have meanings. Roughly, though not exactly, these are the units traditionally called "words"; the current technical term for them is *morphemes*. The language also provides certain patterns by which these elementary significant units can be combined into larger sequences, and conventions governing what sorts of meanings emerge from the arrangements. These patterns and conventions are the *grammar* of the language. A new message is built with familiar elements, put together by familiar patterns, but yielding a composite total that has not occurred before. The hearer understands the new message—usually, though of course not always—because the parts and patterns are familiar to him as they are to the speaker. Confronting a novel situation, a human being is not constrained to react to it exactly as he has reacted to one or another earlier experience, but can, and often does, coin a new utterance, drawing on the partial similarities between the new situation and many diverse earlier experiences. Indeed, even when a speaker produces a complex utterance exactly like one he has heard or said before, he is often coining it anew anyway.

There is a distinction in principle between an open and a closed discrete semantic system, even if the latter has an enormous number of messages. For if a discrete system is closed, then although it may provide a very large number of messages, that number is necessarily finite. Openness, on the other hand, involves only a finite number of elementary signaling units (morphemes) and of patterns, but allows the generation of a transfinite, though countable, number of distinct whole messages. There is also a clear difference in efficiency. For the control of a single message of a closed system, let us posit that it requires on the average k "storage units"—whatever those may be: genes, weakened synapses, "punched molecules," reverberating neural circuits, relays, flip-flop tubes, or what have you. Then if an organism is to participate in a closed system with, say, 10,000 distinct messages, $10,000k$ storage units must be assigned to this task. Perhaps the control of a single elementary signaling unit or a single pattern of an open system requires ten or one hundred times as many storage units. Then, with just $10,000k$ such units, only 1000 or only 100 different signaling units and patterns could be provided for, but that would still generate an infinite number of distinct whole messages, to yield an infinitely large net gain in efficiency.

The great advantage of openness of the sort language has, coupled with displacement, is that one can say things that are not necessarily so. That underlies lying, fictions (*unicorn*), and errors and superstition; but it also underlies the making of hypotheses. With displacement but without productivity, a child can be taught in relative safety how to deal with bears and other dangers, but openness is necessary if a community is to work out *better* ways to deal with such dangers. We cannot, of course, be sure, but it is at least reasonable to guess that the development of openness in language was the first step towards the ultimate growth of man's fantastic powers of imagination, which now greatly exceed the bounds of what can comfortably be dealt with purely in terms of verbal symbols. If so, then the development of openness was also the Fall of Man, the Eating of the Fruit of the Tree of Knowledge, the Origin of Sin: it is man's imagination that exposes him to delusions of persecution or power, to feelings of guilt or anxiety—the whole sad panoply of neuroses and psychoses to which seemingly only our own species is significantly susceptible.

12. Duality. Suppose that Paul Revere and his confederate had needed a total repertory of several hundred messages, instead of just two. It would have been inconvenient to have had several hundred lanterns on hand in the church tower. But it could have been agreed that each message would take the form of a row of five lights, each one either red, or yellow, or green. Then only fifteen lanterns would have been needed—one of each color for each position—but the system would have provided for a total of $3^5 = 243$ different messages. We assume that meanings would have been assigned only to the whole messages, so that, for example, "red light in first position" would not have had any separate meaning of its own, but would merely have served to distinguish certain messages from certain others. This expanded Paul Revere system would then show what we mean by *duality of patterning*: a set of conventions in terms of *smallest meaningful elements* (here the whole messages), and also a set of conventions in terms of *minimum meaningless but differentiating ingredients* (the three colors and five positions).

Another example of duality is found in commercial cable codes. Important words and phrases, apt to be needed repeatedly in transmitting information of commercial importance, are assigned as the meanings of arbitrary sequences of five letters. The smallest meaningful elements are then these five-letter sequences. The minimum meaningless but differentiating ingredients are the individual letters. Thus ADBQR might mean 'credit rating' and ADBQS 'yours received': the partial shared by these two, ADBQ, obviously does not correlate with any shared feature of the meanings of the two whole sequences, nor can any meaning be described for "R" or for "S" in fifth position.

Still another example appears in the Morse code as used for old-fashioned telegraphy and pre-voice radio (or, with differences of detail, in the Baudot code now used for cabling). Here the *cenemes*—the "minimum meaningless but differentiating ingredients"—are short voltage pulses (dots), longer voltage pulses (dashes), and pauses of several lengths. The *pleremes*— the "smallest meaningful elements"—are the arrangements of those cenemes to which meanings have been assigned: a single dot means the letter "E", two dots the letter "I", and so on.

For the users of most semantic communicative systems, the problem of transmission has two phases, *encoding* and *emission*, and the problem of reception has a converse two, *detection* and *decoding*. Longfellow's Paul Revere had to look sharp to tell whether one or two lights were on display across the river (detection), and he had to remember which signal had been assigned which meaning (decoding). His nameless confederate had to remember the assignment (encoding) in order to know how many lights to hang out (emission). Failure either in emission and detection or in encoding and decoding would have destroyed the functioning of the whole system. Channel noise (mist rising from the river) could have interfered with emission and detection; code noise (discrepant memory between Paul and his confederate) could have interfered with encoding and decoding.

In a system with duality of patterning, the problems of emission and detection are to some extent separated from those of encoding and decoding. Emission and detection have to do with cenemes; encoding and decoding have to do with pleremes. The principle of duality is, in one way, a source of efficiency and economy for any communicative system for which a large number of different meaningful signals is desired. A small handful of cenemes, chosen so as to be easily emitted and so as to be easily distinguished by the sensory receptors or hardware receivers involved, can be ordered into a large number of brief groupings, and the meanings can be assigned to the latter. In this way emission and detection can be kept relatively simple despite complexities of encoding and decoding. As if by way of compensation for this gain in simplicity, the total amount of machinery required at transmitter and at receiver is increased, since, in addition to the rules of encoding and decoding, that machinery must provide for the transduction from pleremes to cenemes at the transmitting end and from cenemes to pleremes at the receiving end. Duality for telegraphy is economical because the end-point complexities can be handled by stationary machinery or by trained humans, at a cost less than the amount saved by using a very simple channel. The failure of chimpanzees or gibbons to talk—that is, to use a vocal-auditory system like human language—is not to be ascribed to their mouths or ears, but to their cortexes (Spuhler 1959; Gerard 1959; despite Kelemen 1948).

It is implied by the above discussion that some communicative systems are not marked by duality. The original Paul Revere system was not. True, one could analyze the system and discover its cenemes: one light and two lights; and one could analyze from a different angle and discover its pleremes: one light and two lights. But if the cenemes and the pleremes are the same, then there is no point in speaking of duality. Again, one could undertake to determine the smaller graphic elements out of which the letters of the English alphabet are built, on the tentative assumption that the whole letters are the pleremes of the English writing system. In some type-faces,

p   q
b   d

constitute a small subset of letters built out of a vertical line and a flattened circle, in differing arrangements. But if one carries this through for the whole writing system, it turns out that there is a much larger stock of ostensible "meaningless but differentiating ingredients" than of different letters—even allowing for capital versus lower case and the like.

Significant duality, we can say, is found when a system not only has both cenemes and pleremes but also uses a relatively small stock of the former to build a relatively larger stock of the latter. Morse and Baudot codes build about thirty-two pleremes out of about five cenemes. A commercial cable code uses twenty-six cenemes to yield thousands of pleremes.

Languages have duality of patterning. The cenemes of a language are its phonemes (§9 above); the pleremes are its morphemes (§11). The number of phonemes in a language ranges from a dozen or so up to about one hundred. The number of morphemes runs to the thousands or tens of thousands. Phonemes do nothing but keep morphemes (and sequences of morphemes) apart. Thus, in English, the phoneme /b/ at the beginning of a word has no meaning of its own, but merely serves to distinguish *beat* from *meat, bat* from *pat, bet* from *debt, bill* from *ill,* and so on. The parallel with the other dual systems discussed in this section is complete.

Paralinguistic phenomena, on the other hand, do not have duality. That is probably true by definition, in that any portion of human vocal-auditory communication characterized by duality and by discreteness cannot be operationally distinguished from the portion we traditionally call language, and hence must be part thereof (compare the discussion in §9 above).

More generally, it can probably be proved (the reasoning is not entirely clear) that continuity and duality are incompatible, just as are continuity and arbitrariness (§9 above).

There are no clearly attested instances of significant duality in animal communicative systems. Alexander (1960) adopts the linguistic terms "phoneme" and "morpheme" for the description of certain types of insect communication, but since the system he describes has but one "phoneme" and two "morphemes" there is at least an enormous difference of degree between the duality of such a system and that of the human systems we have described in this section. Yet it would be premature to conclude that significant duality is an exclusively human prerogative. The complex song systems of some passerine birds—Western Meadowlark, Song Sparrow (Lanyon 1960)—need further study with special attention to openness and duality. The songs of some of these species consist of different arrangements of a basic stock of motifs. New whole songs sometimes occur (or are sometimes observed for the first time), but built out of the same old motifs. If these systems are semantic, then there are several possibilities. Perhaps the motifs are cenemes and the whole songs pleremes: that would be duality without openness. Perhaps the motifs are pleremes and the whole songs are like the composite grammatically-structured sentences of a language: that would be openness, though doubtless with a much lower rate of incidence of newly coined "sentences" than holds for language. In the second case, it could still be that the motifs were functionally indivisible, so that the openness would be unaccompanied by duality, or it might be that the motifs are built out of a limited stock of even smaller figures, functionally comparable to the phonemes of a language.

13. Cultural or Traditional Transmission. In a period of time the length of which depends on the species—from five to ten decades for human beings—the membership of any metazoan community is totally replaced. Yet the new members go about their affairs in pretty much the same way as did their predecessors. Ways of life change for all animals, but for the most part at a much more leisurely rate than that of births and deaths. This basic continuity of behavior patterns is due to a number of biological *mechanisms of continuity*. One of these is the generally noncatastrophic development of the physicochemical environment: the sun continues to supply the earth with energy; the earth's gravity field hardly varies; available chemical raw-materials in any single ecological niche usually change but slowly. Another is the genetic mechanism, seemingly as widespread as life itself. A third, perhaps not so widespread but nonetheless important, is the mechanism that some anthropologists call *cultural transmission* and some ornithologists *tradition* (Hochbaum 1955). As Dobzhansky has so beautifully pointed out (1956), it is not fruitful to approach the lifeways of any one species of animal with the notion of sorting out those that are genetically transmitted and those that are transmitted by some other mechanism. One does not hope to say "this is cultural," "that is genetic." The habits manifested by any single animal represent the blended result of the various contributing mechanisms of continuity. The analytical problem is to sort out and describe the specific nature of the blend in any one case.

A human being speaks no language at birth. The language that he later comes to speak is the one used by those about him, whether or not that is the language of his biological forebears—and, if it is not, that makes not the slightest difference in the degree of skill he achieves in his language nor in the time it takes him to achieve it. If, as occasionally happens, an infant is raised in extreme isolation or by animals, he learns no language at all (Brown 1958). If, on the other hand, an infant is raised in society and is biologically normal save for such a peripheral deficiency as deafness or blindness, it is noteworthy that such handicaps are frequently overcome. The sensory details of a deaf person's participation in language are necessarily different from those of normal people: where the normal person relies on stored motor-acoustic images, the deaf person must rely instead on stored images of finger or lip motions or the like. But some kind of special "switching code" is worked out, whereby the bulk of the deaf person's language habits are effectively isomorphic to the language habits of those with whom he lives. Finally, various efforts have been made to teach a language to a member of some other species (reviewed in Brown 1958); they fail.

The inferences to be drawn from the above are clear. Human genes are not specific to the idiosyncrasies of any one language, but permissive for any and all. Human genes are a necessary but not a sufficient condition for acquiring a language. The role of genetics is not, however, purely and passively permissive. The human phenotype includes a strong positive drive towards participation in the communicative interchange of society, a drive that can be frustrated only by the most radical isolation (Lenneberg unpublished MS).[3]

So much for the role of genetics in language. The rest of the continuity of language habits from generation to generation is provided by the mechanism that we shall here call "tradition"—respecting the preference of some anthropologists for reserving the term "culture" for something a little more specific (see below).

All traditional behavior is learned, but not all learned behavior is traditional. Let us take maze-running as a paradigm for all learning. If

3. [∇ Now Lennenberg 1967.]

members of one species (say human beings) place a member of another species (say a rat) in a maze, the latter may acquire the learned skill of running the maze; but that learned skill is not traditional, because the rat's teachers—those who build the maze and put him it it—are members of a different species. If the members of a species place another member of the same species in a maze and the pupil learns to run the maze, the acquired skill may still not be traditional. Whether it is depends on the nature of the teaching behavior. If the teaching behavior is itself purely or largely genetically determined, then the phenomenon is a sort of maternal effect. But if the teaching behavior is itself learned from still other teachers, then the acquired skill is traditional.

So defined, tradition is clearly not a human prerogative. Some short-lived traditions have been observed among chimpanzees in captivity (*fide* Spuhler). The kinds of observations that have led Hochbaum (1955) to posit the existence of traditional behavior among waterfowl might well, if carried out on a sufficient scale, lead us to conclude that tradition is widespread among birds and mammals, though it must be conceded that expert opinion is not unanimously in agreement with Hochbaum even for the several species that he has studied. The extent to which tradition supplements genetics in the transmission of bird songs from one generation to the next, or gibbon calls, or the vocal patterns of various other species—including the waterfowl that Hochbaum discusses—is still an open question; several articles in this volume report experiments and observations that bear on its ultimate solution.

In this connection something must be said of *imprinting* (Hess 1959). The facts seem to be that the young of many species, in the course of maturation, pass through a stage, often very brief, during which certain experiences with the environment will "take": if exposure is too early or too late, the habit is not acquired, and in some instances that can lead to fatal results. We do not in general know whether the habits acquired during imprinting stages are traditional. But the existence of special imprinting stages could well have been of vital importance in evolution, in that it set a stage for the development of tradition. The very long period of pliability in the fetalized human life cycle (see the comparative developmental charts in Spuhler 1959), during which each child acquires his language and his culture, could be thought of as a remarkably extended imprinting stage. It will be fascinating to find out, if we ever can, whether there is any similarity between the neurological and biochemical bases of imprinting stages in other species and of childhood plasticity in our own.

Tradition becomes transformed into cultural transmission (in the sense favored by many anthropologists, especially White 1959) when the passing down of traditional habits is mediated in large part by the use of symbols, in the manner of Childe's fable about bear-handling. First the young begin to acquire the communicative system of their community. As soon as a little of it had been learned, further learning, both of the communicative system and of all manner of other lifeways, is carried on in terms of the communicative system as well as via direct demonstration and experience. For a communicative system to function efficiently in this way it must certainly have the properties of semanticity, arbitrariness (and hence discreteness), displacement, and productivity, and probably that of transmission via tradition. That combination of design features apparently yields symbols in the sense described by White and by Langer (1942).

Cultural transmission has an obvious survival value in that it allows a species to learn through experience, and to adapt to new living conditions, at a rate much greater than is possible purely with the genetic mechanism. That is a truism if we compare human history during the past few millennia with, say, what we know of hymenopteran history since the Tertiary. But we must posit an early stage in hominid, hominoid, or primate history when the capacity for tradition was but feebly developed, so that adaptation via genetic selection and via changing tradition were about equally powerful. Possibly some animal species living today have this same delicate balance. In our own ancestry, the balance was tipped in favor of a strengthening and deepening of the capacity for tradition. We do not know the attendant circumstances. We can guess, however, that at first the survival value of increased capacity for tradition was conservative rather than innovating: it made for greater efficiency in the acquisition by the young of the time-tested lifeways of their predecessors—just as the original importance of strong limbs among the crossopterygians who evolved into amphibians was not that they could live on land, but that they could get back to the water when the occasion arose (Romer 1959).

It should be noticed that our definition of cultural transmission, and of the design features of a communicative system that can make cultural transmission possible, is tantamount to an assertion that, as far as we know, only *Homo sapiens* has culture. We must not let that conclusion prejudice us against future empirical discoveries to the contrary (cf. Vercors 1953). Yet one can argue that it would be highly improbable for two disparate species to develop the language-and-culture lifeway characteristic of ourselves unless they were, for a very long time, out of touch with each other. The ecological niche of a species that develops language and culture sooner or later expands into the whole world. If two different species started in this direction, they would eventually come into contact and one—perhaps both—would probably be eliminated. At least, the history of interspecies relations, and of relations between separate cultural strains of the only animal known to us that has culture, renders such an inference plausible. Furthermore, one such instance may be a matter of record. *Homo neanderthalensis*, with as big and as convoluted a brain as our own (Le Gros Clark 1955), disappeared from Europe and the world in the late Pleistocene.[4] Some believe that he was caught by the last glaciation, while *Homo sapiens* was carrying on in more favorable climes; but it is also possible (Le Gros Clark 1959) that he was wiped out by invading groups of our ancestors. Perhaps we can discern, not in language and culture themselves, but in our modern struggle to analyze and understand those phenomena, the seeds of a kind of "maturity" that may in time put an end to our intraspecies quarreling and may better equip us for eventual contact—however improbable this may be—with intelligent extraterrestrial life.

Summary. The essence of our summary is presented in the table. The eighth column has been added for purposes of comparison: the reference is to our own Western tradition, say from Bach to the present. A question mark means that the answer is doubtful, or not known, or not known to the writer. A dash means that the particular design-feature cannot be determined because some other is lacking or indeterminate: e.g., arbitrariness and iconicity can be judged only for a system characterized by semanticity.

The reader's attention is called to the last part of Hockett (1959), in which there is a survey of the possible course of phylogenetic development of language from the early hominoids to the present. Some of the more obvious errors and gaps in that survey are corrected by the phylogenetic asides in the present paper.

---

4. [∇ The Neanderthals are no longer accorded status as a separate species of *Homo*; they were either a late strain of *H. erectus* or else just a local subtype of *H. sapiens*. But this change in official terminology does not much affect what is said in the text.]

TABLE

	1 Some Gryllidae and Tettigoniidae	2 Bee dancing	3 Stickleback courtship	4 Western Meadowlark song	5 Gibbon calls	6 Paralinguistic phenomena	7 Language	8 Instrumental music
1. Vocal-auditory	auditory, not vocal	no	no	yes	yes	yes	yes	auditory not vocal
2. Broadcast	yes	yes	yes	yes	yes	yes	yes	yes
3. Rapid fading	yes (repeated)	?	?	yes	yes (rep.)	yes	yes	yes
4. Interchangeability	limited	limited	no	?	yes	yes (largely)	yes	?
5. Total feedback	yes	?	no	yes	yes	yes	yes	yes
6. Specialization	yes?	?	in part	yes?	yes	yes?	yes	yes
7. Semanticity	no?	yes	no	?partly?	yes	yes?	yes	no (in general)
8. Arbitrariness	?	no	—	if semantic, yes	yes	in part	yes	—
9. Discreteness	yes?	no	?	?	yes	largely no	yes	partly
10. Displacement	—	yes, always	—	?	no	in part	yes, often	—
11. Productivity	no	yes	no	one or both, } yes	no	yes	yes	yes
12. Duality	? (trivial)	no	—	}	no	no	yes	—
13. Tradition	no?	probably not	no?	?	?	yes	yes	yes

LITERATURE CITED

Alexander, R. D. 1960. "Sound Communication in Orthoptera and Cicadidae." In Lanyon and Tavolga, eds., 1960, pp. 38–92.

Bloomfield, L. 1933. *Language*. New York: Holt.

Blum, H. F. 1955. *Time's Arrow and Evolution*. 2d ed. Princeton: Princeton University Press. [∇ 3rd ed., 1968.]

Borror, D. J. 1960. "The Analysis of Animal Sounds." In Lanyon and Tavolga, eds., 1960, pp. 26–37.

Brown, R. 1958. *Words and Things*. Glencoe, Ill.: Free Press.

Carpenter, C. R. 1940. "A Field Study of the Behavior and Social Relations of the Gibbon." *Comparative Psychology Monographs* 16:5.

Childe, V. G. 1936. *Man Makes Himself*. London: C. A. Watts.

Collias, N. E. 1960. "An Ecological and Functional Classification of Animal Sounds." In Lanyon and Tavolga, eds., 1960, pp. 368–391.

Dobzhansky, T. 1956. *The Biological Basis of Human Freedom*. New York: Columbia University Press.

DuBrul, E. L. 1958. *Evolution of the Speech Apparatus*. Springfield, Ill.: Thomas.

Frisch, K. von. 1950. *Bees: Their Vision, Chemical Senses, and Language*. Ithaca, N.Y.: Cornell University Press.

Gerard, R. W. 1959. "Brains and Behavior." in Spuhler, ed., 1959, pp. 14–20.

Gibson, J. J. 1954. "A Theory of Pictorial Perception." *Audio-Visual Communication Review* 1.3–23.

Hess, E. H. 1959. "Imprinting." *Science* 130.133–141.

Hochbaum, H. A. 1955. *Travels and Traditions of Waterfowl*. Minneapolis: University of Minnesota Press.

Hockett, C. F. 1955. *A Manual of Phonology*. Indiana University Publications in Anthropology and Linguistics No. 11.

———. 1958. *A Course in Modern Linguistics*. New York: Macmillan.

———. 1959. "Animal 'Languages' and Human Language." In Spuhler, ed., 1959, pp. 32–39.

Huntington, E. V. 1917. *The Continuum and Other Types of Serial Order*. Cambridge, Mass.: Harvard University Press.

Joos, M. 1948. *Acoustic Phonetics*. Baltimore: Linguistic Society of America.

Kelemen, G. 1948. "The Anatomical Basis of Phonation in the Chimpanzee." *Journal of Morphology* 82.229–246.

Langer, S. K. 1942. *Philosophy in a New Key*. Cambridge, Mass.: Harvard University Press.

Lanyon, W. E. 1960. "The Ontogeny of Vocalizations in Birds." In Lanyon and Tavolga, eds., 1960, pp. 321–347.

Lanyon, W. E., and W. N. Tavolga, eds., 1960. *Animal Sounds and Communication*. Washington, D.C.: American Institute of Biological Sciences, publication no. 7.

Le Gros Clark, W. E. 1955. *The Fossil Evidence for Human Evolution*. Chicago: University of Chicago Press.

————. 1959. "The Crucial Evidence for Human Evolution." *American Scientist* 47.299–313.

Lenneberg, E. H. 1967. *Biological Foundations of Language*. New York: Wiley.

Lotka, A. J. 1925. *Elements of Physical Biology*. Baltimore: Williams and Wilkins. [∇ Paperback reprint under the title *Elements of Mathematical Biology*, New York: Dover (1954).]

Marler, P. 1960. "Bird Songs and Mate Selection." In Lanyon and Tavolga, eds., 1960, pp. 348–367.

Penfield, W., and L. Roberts. 1959. *Speech and Brain-Mechanisms*. Princeton: Princeton University Press.

Penfield, W., and T. Rasmussen. 1950. *The Cerebral Cortex of Man*. New York: Macmillan.

Pratt, F. 1939. *Secret and Urgent*. Indianapolis: Bobbs-Merrill.

Romer, A. S. 1959. *The Vertebrate Story*. Chicago: University of Chicago Press.

Sahlins, M. D. 1959. "The Social Life of Monkeys, Apes, and Primitive Man." In Spuhler, ed., 1959, pp. 54–73.

Sapir, E. 1921. *Language*. New York: Harcourt, Brace.

Shannon, C. E. 1947. "The Mathematical Theory of Communication." *Bell System Technical Journal*, July and October. Reprinted in Shannon and Weaver [same title] Urbana, Ill.: University of Illinois Press (1949).

Spuhler, J. N. 1959. "Somatic Paths to Culture." In Spuhler, ed., 1959, pp. 1–13.

————, ed. 1959. *The Evolution of Man's Capacity for Culture*. Detroit: Wayne State University Press.

Tinbergen, N. 1953. *Social Behaviour in Animals*. London: Methuen; and New York: Wiley.

Trager, G. L. 1958. "Paralanguage: A First Approximation." *Studies in Linguistics* 13.1–12.

Vercors [pseudonym for Jean Bruller]. 1953. *You Shall Know Them*. Translated from the French by Rita Barisse. Boston: Little, Brown.

Washburn, S. L. 1959. "Speculations on the Interrelations of the History of Tools and Biological Evolution." In Spuhler, ed., 1959, pp. 21–31.

Wells, R. S. 1949. [Book review]. *Language* 25.322–325.

White, L. A. 1959. "Summary Review." In Spuhler, ed., 1959, pp. 74–79.

Wiener, N. 1948. *Cybernetics*. New York: Technology Press.

H8. THE PROBLEM OF
UNIVERSALS IN LANGUAGE

Early 1961. Reprinted from J. H. Greenberg, ed., *Universals of Language* (Cambridge, Mass.: The M.I.T. Press, 1963) 1–22 (second edition, 1966, pp. 1–29) with the permission of the M.I.T. Press.

This paper was prepared in the early months of 1961 for a conference on language universals (which I was not able to attend in person) held under Greenberg's leadership in Dobbs Ferry, New York, 13–15 April.

1. Introduction. A language universal is a feature or property shared by all languages, or by all language. The assertion of a (putative) language universal is a generalization about language.

"The only useful generalizations about language are inductive generalizations" (Bloomfield 1933, p. 20). This admonition is clearly important, in the sense that we do not want to invent language universals, but to discover them. *How* to discover them is not so obvious. It would be fair to claim that the search is coterminous with the whole enterprise of linguistics in at least two ways. The first way in which this claim is true is heuristic: we can never be sure, in any sort of linguistic study, that it will not reveal something of importance for the search. The second way in which the claim is plausible, if not automatically true, appears when we entertain one of the various possible definitions of linguistics as a branch of science: that branch devoted to the discovery of the place of human language in the universe. This definition leaves the field vague to the extent that the problem of linguistics remains unsolved. Only if, as is highly improbable, the problem were completely answered should we know exactly what linguistics is—and at the same millennial moment there would cease to be any justification for the field. It is hard to discern any clear difference between "the search for language universals" and "the discovery of the place of human language in the universe." They seem rather to be, respectively, a new-fangled and old-fashioned way of describing the same thing.

But, however described, the problem is important; and it is fitting that from time to time we set aside our sundry narrower professional concerns and take stock. What are we really sure of for all languages? What are the oustanding gaps? Can we point to specific investigations of probably crucial importance? What are the most important differences of expert opinion, and how are they to be resolved?

In the present essay the writer will touch on five matters. The balance of §1 sets forth a number of assumptions, warnings, and pitfalls; these might be regarded as an expansion, perhaps even as a clarification, of Bloomfield's terse remark quoted earlier. §2 summarizes some features found (if the writer is right) in all human languages but lacking in one or another system of nonhuman animal communication. §3 proposes a set of features as criterial for language; that is, if a communicative system has all the features of the set, it is proposed that we call it a language. §§4 and 5 list a very few properties, respectively grammatical and phonological, that seem to be shared by all human languages but that are not obviously necessitated by the presence of the features of the criterial set.

1.1. *The assertion of a language universal must be founded on extrapolation as well as on empirical evidence.*

Of course this is true in the trivial sense that we do not want to delay generalizing until we have full information on all the languages of the world. We should rather formulate generalizations as hypotheses, to be tested as new empirical information becomes available. But there is a deeper implication. If we had full information on all languages now spoken, there would remain languages recently extinct on which the information was inadequate. There is no point in imagining that we have adequate information also on the extinct languages, because that would be imagining the impossible. The universe seems to be so constructed that complete factual information is unattainable, at least in the sense that there are past events that have left only incomplete records. Surely we seek constantly to widen the empirical base for our generalizations; equally surely, we always want our generalizations to subsume some of the unobserved, and even some of the unobservable, along with all of the observed.

1.2. *The assertion of language universals is a matter of definition as well as of empirical evidence and of extrapolation.*

If the next "language" on which information becomes available were to lack some feature we have believed universal, we could deny that it was a language and thus save the generalization (cf. Kemeny 1959, pp. 97–98). Triviality from this source can be avoided by various procedures, but they all involve making decisions in advance—and such decisions are definitions. We can decide that any system manifesting a certain explicitly listed set of features (the *defining set*) is to be called a language. The universality of the particular features we have chosen is then tautologous. Of course, the list itself can be revised, for each successive round of the search for universals.

1.3. *A feature can be widespread or even universal without being important.*

This is most easily shown by a trick. Suppose that all the languages of the world except English were to become extinct. Thereafter, any assertion true of English would also assert a (synchronic) language universal. Since languages no longer spoken may have lacked features we believe universal or widespread among those now spoken, mere frequency can hardly be a measure of importance.

1.4. *The distinction between the universal and the merely widespread is not necessarily relevant.*

The reasoning is as for 1.3. Probably we all feel that the universality of certain features might be characterized as "accidental"—they might just as well have turned out to be merely widespread. This does not tell us how to distinguish between the "accidentally" and the "essentially" universal. On the other hand, that which is empirically known to be merely widespread is thereby disqualified as an "essential" universal—though careful study may show that it is symptomatic of one.

1.5. *The search for universals cannot be usefully separated from the search for a meaningful taxonomy of languages.*

(Here "taxonomy" refers to what might also be called "typology," not to genetic classification.) Suppose that some feature, believed to be important and universal, turns out to be lacking in a newly discovered language. The feature may still be important. To the extent that it is, its absence in the new language is a typological fact of importance about the language.

Conversely, if some feature is indeed universal, then it is taxonomically irrelevant.

Here is an example that illustrates both 1.4 and 1.5. It was at one time assumed that all languages distinguish between nouns and verbs—by some suitable and sufficiently formal definition of those terms. One form of this assumption is that all languages have two distinct types of stems (in addition, possibly, to various other types), which by virtue of their behavior in inflection (if any) and in syntax can appropriately be labeled nouns and verbs. In this form, the generalization is rendered invalid by

Nootka, where all inflectable stems have the same set of inflectional possibilities. The distinction between noun and verb at the level of stems is sufficiently widespread that its absence in Nootka is certainly worthy of typological note (1.5). But it turns out that even in Nootka something very much like the noun-verb contrast appears at the level of whole inflected words. Therefore, although Nootka forces the abandonment of the generalization in one form, it may still be that a modified form can be retained (1.4).

The Port Royal Grammar constituted both a putative description of language universals and the basis of a taxonomy. The underlying assumption was that every language must provide, by one means or another, for all points in the grammaticological scheme described in the Grammar. Latin, of course, stood at the origin in this particular coordinate system. Any other language could be characterized typologically by listing the ways in which its machinery for satisfying the universal scheme deviated from that of Latin. This classical view in general grammar and in taxonomy has been set aside not because it is false in some logical sense but because it has proved clumsy for many languages: it tends to conceal differences that we have come to believe are important, and to reveal some that we now think are trivial.

1.6. *Widespread (or universal) features are most apt to be important if they recur against a background of diversity.*

1.7. *Widespread (or universal) features are the more apt to be important the less readily they diffuse from one language to another.*

Given a taxonomy, if we find that languages of the most diverse types nonetheless manifest some feature in common, that feature may be important. It is not apt to be, however, if it is an easily diffusible item. Thus the fact that many languages all over the world have phonetically similar words for 'mama' is more significant than a similarly widespread general phonetic shape for 'tea'. (On the former, see now Jakobson 1961.)

In allowing for diffusion, we must also take into consideration that even features that do not diffuse readily may spread from one language to others when the speakers of the languages go through a long period of intimate contact. This fact, if no other, would seem to render suspect any generalizations based solely on the languages of Western Europe. And it is true that some such generalizations are refuted by the merest glance at an appropriate non-European language. But contrastive study based exclusively on European languages also has a merit: our knowledge of those languages is currently deeper and more detailed than our knowledge of languages elsewhere, so that generalizing hypotheses can also be deeper.

They may be due for a longer wait before an appropriately broad survey can confirm or confute them, but they are valuable nonetheless.

1.8. *Universal features are important if their presence in a system can be shown not to be entailed by the presence of features of the "defining set," or if they are entailed thereby but not obviously so.*

The notion of a "defining set" was introduced in 1.2. For examples illustrating the present point, see 5.7 and 5.6.

The second part of the point may need some justification. Mapmakers have found empirically that they never need more than four colors in order to guarantee that any two continuous regions that share a boundary (not merely a point) shall be assigned different colors. This is presumably a topological property of planes and of spherical surfaces, yet it follows so unobviously from the mathematical definitions of those surfaces that no mathematician has yet succeeded in proving the implication formally. If a proof—or, indeed, a demonstration that five colors are needed rather than four—is attained, the glory of the achievement will not be diminished in the slightest by the fact that the conclusion is implied by the premises.

1.9. *A universal feature is more apt to be important if there are communicative systems, especially nonhuman ones, that do not share it.*

It may seem peculiar at first to propose that we can learn more about human language by studying the communicative systems of other animals; but a moment's reflection is enough to show that we can only know what a thing is by also knowing what it is not. As long as we confine our investigations to human language, we constantly run the risk of mistaking an "accidental" universal for an "essential" one—and we bypass the task of clearly defining the universe within which our generalizations are intended to apply. Suppose, on the other hand, that after discovering that a particular feature recurs in every language on which we have information, we find it lacking in some animal communicative system. In some cases, this might lead us to add the feature to our defining set for language. In any case, this seems to be one way of trying to avoid triviality in the assembling of our defining set.

The point just proposed threatens a very lengthy program of investigation of the communicative behavior of other animals, since zoologists recognize approximately one million living species and one can never be sure just where in this vast collection some relevant property (or its notable absence) may appear. Who would have thought, fifteen years ago, that we would learn something crucial in linguistics from bees!

It might be suggested that we bypass the whole task by an appropriate definition. We could simply assert that a communicative system is not a language unless it is manifested by human beings. Good enough; but we must now ask our confreres in anthropology and biology to identify for us the class of human beings. A serious reply is apt to include the remark "human beings are hominoids that talk"—and the circle has been closed and nothing achieved. We had better define language without reference to human beings. Then, if it appears that—on our planet—only human beings talk, that becomes a significant empirical generalization.

The comparison with nonhuman communication can be revealing in another way. We have already noted that many languages have a nursery word like *mama*. If we ask whether the gibbon-call system has this feature, we find it embarrassing merely to give the technically correct negative answer. The question has been put badly. One hesitates to speak of "words" in discussing gibbon calls. Thus we are led to examine more closely what we mean in speaking of "words" in various languages, and just why we are uncomfortable using the word "word" for gibbon calls; and such lines of inquiry may yield a more meaningful comparative question and a significant generalization about language.

1.10. *The problem of language universals is not independent of our choice of assumptions and methodology in analyzing single languages.*

This is a terribly unstartling proposal, yet important. We must generalize from our information about specific languages; we must collect information about a specific language in terms of some general frame of reference. The latter includes notions as to what language must be as well as points of methodology. The study of individual languages and the search for universals thus stand in a dialectic complementation that can equally well propagate error or truth.

To force such a system of investigation toward truth, the point of entry is our way of manipulating data on specific languages; and the procedure is the familiar one of contrapositive assumption. Whatever one's favorite notion about language design, one asks "if I assume that this particular language does *not* conform to my pet scheme, can I describe it satisfactorily?" A single success refutes or requires the revision of one's pet hypothesis. A failure, on the other hand, merely means that the hypothesis is still *tentatively* usable. Hypotheses, about language universals or anything else, are by definition proposals to be knocked down, not beliefs to be defended.

2. The Search for Universals through Comparison with Animal Systems.
The design features listed below are found in every language on which we
have reliable information, and each seems to be lacking in at least one
known animal communicative system (cf. 1.9). They are not all logically
independent, and do not necessarily all belong to our defining list for
language—that is a point to be taken up separately, in §3.

All but the last three of these features have been presented in detail
elsewhere (Hockett 1960). Exact repetition would be inappropriate here,
and the writer shrinks from the task of replacing the earlier treatment by a
newly formulated one of comparable detail. Therefore the reader is re-
quested to accept the present listing as the briefest sort of synopsis, and to
turn to the reference just given for fuller information.

2.1. *Vocal-Auditory Channel. The channel for all linguistic communication is vocal-auditory.*

Some animals have communication that is auditory but not vocal (e.g.,
crickets); some have systems with totally different channels (bee-dancing
is kinetic-tactile-chemical).

The phrasing of this first design-feature excludes written languages
from the category "human language" just as it excludes African drum
signals. The exclusion is intentional; the grounds for it will be discussed
later (§3).

2.2. *Broadcast Transmission and Directional Reception. All linguistic signals are transmitted broadcast and are received direc-
tionally.*

These properties are the consequences of the nature of sound, of
binaural hearing, and of motility, and are thus implied by 2.1. "Tight-
beam" transmission is rare in the animal world, but occurs in the nerve-
nets of coelenterate colonies. Directional reception is the general rule,
barring occasional masking. An example of the latter is that in a field full of
crickets locating any one cricket from its call is difficult, even for another
cricket.

2.3. *Rapid Fading. All linguistic signals are evanescent.*

To hear what someone says, one must be within earshot at the right
time. Spoors and trails fade more slowly. The property of fading is also a
consequence of 2.1.

2.4. *Interchangeability. Adult members of any speech community
are interchangeably transmitters and receivers of linguistic signals.*

Among some species of crickets, only the males chirp, though both males and females respond to the chirping of others.

2.5. *Complete Feedback. The transmitter of a linguistic signal himself receives the message.*

There are pathological exceptions (as, also, to 2.4). In certain varieties of kinetic-visual communication, as in the courtship dance of sticklebacks, the transmitter cannot always perceive some of the crucial features of the signal being emitted.

2.6. *Specialization. The direct-energetic consequences of linguistic signals are usually biologically trivial; only the triggering effects are important.*

Even the sound of a heated conversation does not raise the temperature of a room enough to benefit those in it. A male stickleback will not court a female unless her abdomen is distended with roe; the distension is thus an essential part of her signal to the male; the direct consequences of the distension are of obvious biological relevance.

2.7. *Semanticity. Linguistic signals function in correlating and organizing the life of a community because there are associative ties between signal elements and features in the world; in short, some linguistic forms have denotations.*

The distension by roe of the belly of the female stickleback is part of an effective signal, but does not "stand for" something else.

2.8. *Arbitrariness. The relation between a meaningful element in language and its denotation is independent of any physical or geometrical resemblance between the two.*

Or, as we say, the semantic relation is *arbitrary* rather than *iconic*. There are marginal exceptions, including traces of onomatopoeia. In bee-dancing, the way in which the direction toward the target site is mapped into a direction of dancing is iconic. The relation between a landscape painting and a landscape is iconic; the relation between the word *landscape* and a landscape is arbitrary.

2.9. *Discreteness. The possible messages in any language constitute a discrete repertory rather than a continuous one.*

Any utterance in a language must differ from any other utterance of the same length by at least a whole phonological feature. Utterances cannot be indefinitely similar to one another. Bee dances can be: the repertory of possible dances constitutes a twofold continuum.

In a continuous semantic system (one with property 2.7 but with the converse of 2.9), the semantics must be iconic rather than arbitrary. But in a discrete semantic system there is no necessary implication as to iconicity or arbitrariness; therefore, for language, 2.8 is independent of 2.7 and 2.9.

2.10. *Displacement. Linguistic messages may refer to things remote in time or space, or both, from the site of the communication.*

"Remote" means out of the perceptual field of the communicators. Gibbon calls are never displaced. Bee dances always are. Utterances in a language are freely displaced or not.

2.11. *Openness. New linguistic messages are coined freely and easily.*

We can transmit messages (produce utterances) that have never been transmitted before, and be understood. Bees do this; gibbons do not.

Actually, this property reflects two partially separate facts about language that deserve individual mention:

2.11.1. *In a language, new messages are freely coined by blending, analogizing from, or transforming old ones.*

This says that every language has *grammatical patterning.*

2.11.2. *In a language, either new or old elements are freely assigned new semantic loads by circumstances and context.*

This says that in every language *new idioms* constantly come into existence.

The openness of bee-dancing might be described as due to a very special sort of "grammatical patterning"; surely there is no evidence that bees create new idioms.

2.12. *Tradition. The conventions of a language are passed down by teaching and learning, not through the germ plasm.*

Genes supply potentiality and probably a generalized drive, since nonhuman animals cannot learn a (human) language and humans can hardly be prevented from acquiring one. Bee-dancing is probably genetic.

2.13. *Duality (of Patterning). Every language has both a cenematic subsystem and a plerematic subsystem.*

More commonly, we speak rather of the phonological and grammatical (or grammaticolexical) subsystems of a language. The unusual terms, borrowed from Hjelmslev, are more appropriate for the discussion of communication in general, since they circumvent the unwanted connotation that the physical channel of a system with duality must necessarily be sound waves.

By virtue of duality of patterning, an enormous number of minimum semantically functional elements (pleremes, morphemes) can be and are mapped into arrangements of a conveniently small number of minimum meaningless but message-differentiating elements (cenemes, phonological components). No animal system known to the writer shows a significant duality.

Some contemporary investigators strongly suspect that a human language involves not just two, but at least three, major subsystems: for example, "phonemic," "morphemic," and "sememic."[1] For our present purposes this possibility can be set aside with the remark that a system with "triality" of patterning would a fortiori have our property of "duality." The essential contrast is between one and more than one subsystem.[2]

2.14. Prevarication. Linguistic messages can be false, and they can be meaningless in the logician's sense.

I can assert that it is ten miles from the earth to the moon, or that the interior of all opaque solids is green until exposed to light. Lying seems extremely rare among animals.

This feature is not independent. It would seem to rest on semanticity (2.7), displacement (2.10), and openness (2.11). Without semanticity, a message cannot be tested for meaningfulness and validity. Without displacement, the situation referred to by a message must always be the immediate context, so that a lie is instantly given away. Without openness, meaningless messages can hardly be generated, though false ones

1. G. L. Trager and S. M. Lamb have been exploring the "triality" notion (or even more complex proposals), as yet without published accounts to which reference can be made. My most thoroughgoing discussion of duality is Hockett 1961.

2. [∇ In this paragraph and fn. 1 I made the mistake of letting politeness (and laziness) overrule scholarly honesty. In fact, I believed in 1961 and still believe now that insistence on a basic triality or multiplicity is a sign of having missed the point—of having overlooked the absolutely crucial nature of *duality* of patterning. This criticism applies to Trager's views (1963, 1972); it applies to W. H. Goodenough's remarks in Goodenough 1971 (pp. 5–6).

[Another way to lose sight of the importance of duality is to confuse it with the notion of stratification. That is what I had done in the 1961 paper to which I referred in fn. 1. It was Lamb's (1966) elaboration of stratification that finally showed me this error; see Hockett 1968.]

can: a gibbon could, in theory, emit the food call when no food had been discovered. Perhaps, however, one can imagine a system with these three underlying properties used by a species (or a collection of machines) that never lied.

It ought to be noted that without the property here labeled "prevarication" the formulation of hypotheses is impossible.

2.15. *Reflexiveness. In a language, one can communicate about communication.*

Bees dance about sites, but they cannot dance about dancing. This property, also, is presumably derivative, resting largely on 2.11.2.

A tempting alternative to this property is "universality": in a language one can communicate about anything. Reflexiveness would obviously follow from universality. The difficulty is an empirical one: if there are indeed things that we cannot communicate about, the fact that we cannot communicate about them may prevent us from recognizing that they exist. Anyway, the idiom-forming mechanism of openness (2.11.2) guarantees that we can come to communicate via language about anything that we are capable of experiencing.

2.16. *Learnability. A speaker of a language can learn another language.*

In a science-fiction story (wisely rejected by all editors), the writer once invented a nonterrestrial species that had a communicative system like human language in all respects except that its conventions were transmitted almost entirely through the germ plasm. The members of this species could learn a new language, but only with terrible effort. On earth, at least, it seems likely that the relative ease with which humans can learn other languages rests on design feature 2.12.

There is probably more of this sort of flexibility of readaptation among animals than we give them credit for; but some systems, at least, lack the feature altogether (bee-dancing, stickleback courtship).

3. Definition and Basic Hypotheses. The design features just presented are admittedly diverse. The list was originally assembled not in a search for language universals, but rather through a series of comparisons of human speech with the communicative behavior of certain other animals. It includes any point that such a comparison suggested. Thus it comes about that some of the points apply directly to a language as an "abstract" system (though "abstract" means different things to different investigators); others rather to the organisms that use the system; still others to how the organisms use or acquire the system. That is also why some of the points mention physics or biology (a most un-"abstract" policy), while others do not.

In reweighing the sixteen design features for our present purposes, the first decision we must make concerns writing. Shall we attempt a defining set of properties that subsumes writing systems, or some of them, as well as "spoken languages"? Or shall we class writing systems with drum signals and other clearly secondary and derivative phenomena, as something apart from "language"?

Either choice can be justified. In the long run we should probably do both. But in this paper I shall exclude writing. The reasons are as follows:

(1) Spoken language is part of the "common denominator of cultures," and its antiquity is undisputed. Any generalization about spoken language is also a hypothesis about human cultural universals (Murdock 1945). Writing is a recent invention, and has not yet spread to all human communities. Although this in itself does not preclude an attempt to determine what all spoken and all written languages have in common, it seems reasonable to break the total task up in a way that correlates with cultural universality and its absence.

(2) One crucial design feature of writing systems is relative permanence, the exact opposite of the rapid fading (2.3) characteristic of spoken language. If we try to characterize spoken and written language at the same time we have to omit both rapid fading and relative permanence. But the relative permanence of writing is an important source of its enormous power; and the rapid fading of speech (and of its prehuman precursors) was a crucial factor conditioning the evolution of human communication of all varieties. The joint consideration of spoken and written language can thus best follow the detailed consideration of the two taken separately.

(3) Writing systems are quite varied in their designs, so that it is difficult to be sure just what features are common to all. Do writing systems have duality (2.13)? In one view, only a few do. The Ogam script, for example, had cenemes consisting of certain elementary strokes, and pleremes represented by certain arrangements of those strokes; the denotations of the pleremes were the phonemes of Old Irish. In this view, English writing does not have duality of patterning, because our pleremes (letters) are not built out of a small stock of simpler cenemes. If we shift ground and say that a writing system has duality in that it shares (essentially) a plerematic subsystem with the correlated spoken language, manifested cenematically in "phonic substance" in speech but in "graphic substance" in writing, then how do we distinguish between the Ogam script and contemporary English writing, or between the latter and Chinese?

Clearly, these questions can all be answered. The writer claims the privilege of not attempting the answers here.

Having made this decision, we can consider the following defining set for language: openness (2.11), displacement (2.10), duality (2.13), arbitrariness (2.8), discreteness (2.9), interchangeability (2.4), complete feedback (2.5), specialization (2.6), rapid fading (2.3), and broadcast transmission with directional reception (2.2). Any system that has these ten properties will here be called a language; any language manifested by our own species will be called a human language. Every language also has semanticity (2.7), since the contrast between arbitrariness (2.8, included in the defining set) and iconicity is meaningless without it. Presumably, but not so clearly, every language has prevarication (2.14) and reflexiveness (2.15); at least, every human language does.

To show the importance of the features of the defining set, we can think of human language as we know it and consider the consequences of suppressing, in turn, each feature.

A language deprived of openness would generate only a finite number of whole messages. Lying might be possible, but hypothesis-formation would not.

A language deprived of displacement would not allow its users to communicate about the past or the future. Planning would be impossible. Fictions—hence speculation, literature, science—would be precluded.

A language deprived of duality would be extremely cumbersome, since each plereme would have to differ holistically from all others. It is hard to imagine any species remotely like our own being able to handle—or, at least, to evolve—such a system. However, perhaps duality is simply the mammalian way of achieving a system with all other relevant properties. Some extraterrestrial species might do differently.[3]

A system without arbitrariness either lacks semanticity altogether or else has iconic semantics. The former possibility is most unlike language. A system with iconic semantics is constrained to use about things and situations that can be imitated, pictured, or diagrammed. Swift's account of Gulliver's encounter with the Laputans should be enough to show the crucial importance of arbitrariness.

The alternative to discreteness is continuous repertories of signals, as

3. [∇ It was not long after 1961 that I reached a modified view on this point. To be sure, a languagelike system without duality would be cumbersome. Even so, the development of duality may well have been one of the last steps in the emergence of language among our ancestors (Hockett and Ascher 1964); moreover, that decisive final step may have been as recent as about fifty thousand years ago (Hockett 1973 chap. 27).]

among the bees. But a continuous semantic system necessarily has iconic semantics.

It is interchangeability that enables a human to "internalize" the roles of others and to carry on conversations with himself, thus carrying over to the situations in which he is temporarily alone the problem-solving powers of language.

Complete feedback also seems essential to the use of language just described.

Specialization is such a general property of communicative systems (human and animal) that some investigators hesitate to use either the term "system" or the term "communication" of types of behavior from which it is absent. In any case, specialization renders possible communication at a power-level (in the literal physical sense) that is convenient for the species involved. One does not have to increase the power-level to communicate about large-scale matters, or to reduce it when concerned with minutiae.

Rapid fading means, positively, that messages already transmitted do not clutter up the channel and impede the transmission of new ones (as happens sometimes when one has a blackboard but no eraser). Thus, emergency signals can get through. On the other hand, it implies that the import of a message has to be stored internally in the receiver if it is to be stored anywhere at all. The "attention span" required of human hearers to take in a long and involved sentence is considerable, when measured on the general animal scale. The evolution of the capacity for such an attention span has surely been conditioned by the rapid-fading property of vocal-auditory communication, and is related to the development of displacement, as well as to such nonlinguistic matters as tool-carrying and tool-making. Rapid fading is not an "incidental" property of human language. When its undesirable implications were overcome, by the development of writing, a major revolution had occurred.

Broadcast transmission and directional reception also carry both advantages and disadvantages. A warning cry may tell all one's fellows something of the location of the danger, but also, if the danger is a predator, it tells the predator where one is.

If we think only of the modern "civilized" world, in times of peace, rapid fading, broadcast transmission, and directional reception may seem relatively unimportant. But if we think of the living conditions prevalent during the bulk of human history, we see that these properties are not lightly to be regarded as secondary. They are part of our heritage from prehuman times; they have conditioned our own evolution and that of language; and they are still with us, their potentially deleterious effects canceled out only under special technological circumstances.

There is, nonetheless, a sense in which openness, displacement, and duality (together with traditional transmission, which does not appear on the defining list) can be regarded as the crucial or nuclear or central properties of human language. From an examination of what is known of the vocal-auditory communicative systems of contemporary nonhuman hominoids, it seems that the vocal-auditory system of the proto hominoids must, at least, have lacked these three or four features. These three or four, then, are human or hominid innovations. Otherwise, human language is not truly distinguishable from hominoid communication in general.

Now we are ready for some generalizations that go beyond the defining set.

3.1. *Every human community has a language.*

Surely no one will counter with the instance of a Trappist monastery: there would be no need for a rule against talking if talking were not a possibility.

3.2. *No species except our own has a language.*

This may be disproved at any time by new zoological discoveries. No guess either way is implied about extinct species and genera of the hominids (*Homo erectus, Australopithecus*).

3.3. *Every human communicative system usually called a (spoken) language is a language in our sense.*

The writer is disturbed by the possibility that a few human systems not ordinarily called "spoken language," and that we do not wish to include, may also fit the definition; for example, Mazateco whistle-talk (Cowan 1948). The derivative status of such a system is obvious, but it is not clear just how to provide formally for its exclusion.

3.4. *Every human language has the vocal-auditory channel (2.1).*

This feature was excluded from the defining list because it seems that its implications (broadcast transmission, directional reception, rapid fading) are structurally more important, and one can imagine other channels— say light, or heat-waves—that would yield the same implications. Therefore this assertion is not trivial.

3.5. *Every human language has tradition (2.12).*

If we design and build a collection of machines that communicate among themselves with a language, this property will be lacking.

3.6. *Every human language has learnability* (2.16).

Probably this is a corollary of the preceding.

3.7. *Every human language has both an intonational system and a nonintonational system; this dichotomy cuts across that into cenematics and plerematics.*

English, for example, has segmental (nonintonational) morphemes that are mapped into segmental phonological features, and intonational morphemes that are mapped into intonational phonological features. A speaker transmits, simultaneously, a nonintonational and an intonational message. The hypothesis is a guess that this basic organization is true in all human languages. It does not imply that the phonic "raw material" for intonation is invariably the pitch of the glottal tone, as it is, in large part, for English.

If true, this generalization is striking, since there seems (at the moment) absolutely no reason why an otherwise languagelike system should have this property. Most writing systems do not carry it over.

Another generalization about intonation is tempting, on the basis of very limited observation, but the evidence is scarcely strong enough to present it as a numbered point: Many highly diverse languages (English, other languages of Europe, Chinese, Japanese, Samoan, Fijian) share a "most colorless" intonation for flat statements, in the face of (1) different phonemic structures for the intonation (which is *phonetically* similar from one language to another) and (2) wide disparity in the remainder of the intonational system.

3.8. *In every human language, plerematic patterning and cenematic patterning are both (independently) hierarchical.*

Grammatically, an utterance consists (let us say) of clauses, a clause of phrases, a phrase of words, a word of morphemes. Phonologically, an utterance consists of macrosegments, a macrosegment of microsegments, a microsegment of syllables, a syllable of phonemes, and a phoneme of phonological components. (Except for morpheme, phonological component, and perhaps utterance, the terms used for this explanation are not part of the generalization.)

3.9. *Human languages differ more widely in cenematics than in plerematics.*

3.10. *Human languages differ more widely, at least in their plerematic subsystems, at small size-levels than at large.*

These two assertions are not of universals, but perhaps point toward some. For example, 3.10 suggests that all languages share certain large-scale syntactical patterns, however varied may be the smaller-scale patterns by which the constituents for the larger patterns are built up. Point 3.9 can be challenged on the grounds that we have no reliable way of measuring and comparing the differences referred to. At present that is doubtless true; but the assertion seems impressionistically valid to me, and formal ways to confirm the impression (or to disprove it) may be found.

4. Grammatical Universals. The generalizations of the preceding section mention grammar (or plerematic design), but do not belong in a set of generalizations about grammar proper because they involve the relationship of grammar to other aspects of language design. From what has already been said, we know (or assume) that every language has a grammatical system, and that grammatical patterning is hierarchical. In addition, we can with reasonable confidence propose the following points:

4.1. *Every human language has a stock of elements that shift their denotations depending on elementary features of the speech situation.*

That is, every language has deictic elements ("substitutes," in Bloomfield's terminology): in English, the personal pronouns, demonstrative pronouns and proadverbs, and so on.

4.2. *Among the deictic elements of every human language is one that denotes the speaker and one that denotes the addressee.*

First and second person singular pronouns are universal. There seems to be no reason internal to our definition of language why this should be so; yet, if we try to imagine a system that lacks them, the results seem quite alien.

4.3. *Every human language has some elements that denote nothing but that make a difference in the denotation of the composite forms in which they occur.*

Such elements are *markers*, for example English *and*. *Match and book* denotes something different from *match or book* or *match book*, but *and* denotes nothing. The assumption that such elements must denote something just as do *man, sky, honor,* or *unicorn* has generated much bad mentalistic philosophizing, populating the universe with abstract entities or the human mind with concepts, both of which are as superfluous as the luminiferous ether.

There are also *impure markers*, for example English *in, on,* that have some denotation as well as a marking function. It may be that we should go only so far as to assert the universal presence of markers (pure or impure).

4.4. *Every human language has proper names.*

A proper name is a form that denotes just what it denotes. If it denotes more than one thing in different occurrences, the class of things that it can denote has no criterial property in common other than the (extrinsic) property of being denoted by the proper name. All Americans named *Richard* are probably males, but many males are not called *Richard*, and when one meets someone for the first time, it is in no way possible to examine his properties and infer that his name must be *Richard*.

A form may be a proper name and also something else: *Robin/robin, John/john, Brown/brown.* The generalization does not deny this.

4.5. *Every language has grammatical elements that belong to none of the three special categories just itemized.*

Comparatively, it is worthy of note that all signals in bee dancing are deictic elements, and that no gibbon calls are of any of the three special types.

4.6. *In every human language there are at least two basic orders of magnitude in grammatical patterning.*

Where there are just two, the traditional terms "morphology" and "syntax" do very well. When the morphology-syntax boundary appears fuzzy, closer scrutiny often reveals a separate order of magnitude of grammatical patterning sandwiched between. As familiar a language as Spanish offers an example. The internal organization of *dando, me,* and *lo* is morphology; the participation of *dándomelo* in larger forms is syntax; the patterns by which *dando, me,* and *lo* are conjoined to yield *dándomelo* are not conveniently classed as either.

However, 4.6 is shaky in another direction: a deeper understanding of languages of the Chinese type may yet show that they are best described without either the two-way morphology-syntax dichotomy or a more complex three-way layering.

In many languages in which the morphology-syntax dichotomy is clear-cut, phonological patterning correlates: that is, grammatical words are also, for the most part, phonological units of a distinctive sort. But there are many exceptions, so that this points toward morphophonemic taxonomy rather than toward universals.

> 4.7. *Apart from the three special categories of elements already mentioned (deictic elements, markers, and proper names), no human language has a grammatically homogeneous vocabulary.*

There are always forms with different ranges of privileges of occurrence, so that one can always validly speak of form classes.

> 4.8. *A major form-class distinction reminiscent of "noun" versus "verb" is universal, though not always at the same size-level.*

This was discussed in connection with 1.5.

> 4.9. *Every human language has a common clause type with bipartite structure in which the constituents can reasonably be termed "topic" and "comment."*

The order of the constituents varies. Typically in Chinese, Japanese, Korean, English, and many other languages, one first mentions something that one is going to talk about, and then says something about it. In other languages, the most typical arrangement is for the comment, or part of it, to precede the topic. Of course, the generalization refers only to a "common clause type." Every language seems to have clauses of other types as well.

> 4.10. *Every language has a distinction between one-referent and two-referent predicators.*

In *Mary is singing*, the predicator *is singing* is of the one-referent sort (and *Mary* is the referent); in *John struck Bill*, the predicator is of the two-referent sort.

Both 4.9 and 4.10 are shaky in a special way. Although we tend to find these patterns in language after language, it is entirely possible that we find them because we expect them, and that we expect them because of some deep-seated properties of the languages most familiar to us. For some languages, some scheme that is far less obvious to us might actually fit the facts better. Although this is true of all proposed generalizations, it nevertheless seems especially true of these two.

5. Phonological Universals. From what has already been said, we know (or assume) that every human language has a phonological system, and that phonological patterning is always hierarchical. Purely phonological generalizations are then to be considered within that tentatively established framework.

5.1. *In every human language, redundancy, measured in phonological terms, hovers near 50 percent.*

The notion is that if redundancy tends to increase much above this figure, communication becomes inefficient, and people speak faster or more sloppily, while decrease much below the figure leads to misunderstanding, and people slow down or articulate more clearly.

It may be that the redundancy figure would be about the same were it measured in grammaticolexical terms; and it may be that this approximate figure is the rule for a wide variety of communicative systems, at least among human beings. Printed English yields the same figure (Shannon 1951), in terms of letters.

5.2. *Phonemes are not fruitful universals.* .

We can, indeed, speak quite validly of phonemes in the discussion of any one language, but their status in the hierarchy of phonological units varies from one language to another, and also, to some extent, through varying preference or prejudice of analysts. The status of phonological components, on the other hand, is fixed once and for all by definition— phonological components are the minimum (not further divisible) units of a phonological system. Given that all phonological patterning is hierarchical, the exact organization of the hierarchy, varying from one language to another, becomes a taxonomic consideration of importance, but not the basis of a generalization in the present context.

There are certain languages of the Caucasus (Kuipers 1960) where one can, if one wishes, describe the phonological system in terms of perhaps a dozen phonological features organized into some seventy or eighty phonemes, which in turn occur in about twice that many syllables. Each syllable consists of one of the seventy-odd consonant phonemes, followed by one of the two vowel phonemes. It seems clear in such a case that the vowel "phonemes" are better regarded simply as two additional phonological features, so that a unit such as /ka/ is just a phoneme—or, alternatively, that the term "phoneme" be discarded and one discuss the participation of features directly in syllables. Either way, one does not need both the term "phoneme" and the term "syllable." The case may be extreme, but it is real, and underscores the importance of the "antiuniversal" given as 5.2.

5.3. *Every language makes use of distinctions of vowel color.*

Vowel color is defined as combination of formants. Acoustically, it is known that for languages like English differences of vowel color do much of the work of keeping consonants apart, as well as distinguishing vowel phonemes.

5.4. *A historical tendency toward phonological symmetry is universal.*

Jakobson has offered a number of synchronic generalizations about phonological systems, to some of which there seem to be a few marginal exceptions. One, for example, is the assertion that a language does not have a spirant of the type [θ] unless it has both a [t] and an [s], nor an affricate like [č] unless it has both a [t] and an [š]. However, Kickapoo has [t] and [θ] but no [s]. Another is that a language does not have nasal continuants at more contrasting positions of articulation than it has stops of some one manner of articulation. It is possible to analyze certain varieties of Brazilian Portuguese so as to violate this generalization. A third is that a language does not contrast unaspirated and aspirated stops unless it has a separated phoneme /h/. Mandarin Chinese is almost an exception, in that the nearest thing to an /h/ is normally a dorsovelar spirant.

Yet these generalizations seem far too widely borne out merely to be thrown into the scrap heap by virtue of a handful of exceptions. When facts invalidate a hypothesis, one tries modifying the hypothesis before one discards it altogether. In each of the cases given, we seem to have an indication of a historical tendency toward some sort of symmetry. The tendency can be disrupted, so that not every system viewed in synchronic cross section will conform to the rule; but diachronically the tendency is real.

5.5. *There are gaps, asymmetries, or "configurational pressures" in every phonological system, no matter when examined.*

Most systems, by virtue of a sort of semimagical logistics of maneuvering on the part of analysts, can be forced to appear neat and symmetrical. The maneuvering is always worth undertaking, not in order to force symmetry where there is lack of it, but because it is heuristically valuable—it helps to show relationships within a system that might otherwise be missed. But the asymmetries, however pushed about, remain in the system.

5.6. *Sound change is a universal. It is entailed by the basic design features of language, particularly by duality of patterning.*

By "sound change" is meant a mechanism of linguistic change that is not reducible to other mechanisms (see, e.g., Hockett 1958, chaps. 52–54). When a system has duality of patterning, the basic role of its cenematic system is to identify messages and keep them apart. Usually an utterance produced in given circumstances is far more than minimally different from any other utterance that might be produced in the same language in the same circumstances. Thus there is room for much nondistinctive variation in details of articulation and even more in the shape of the speech signal by the time it reaches the ears of the hearer. Therefore there will be sound change. The implications of sound change for the phonological and grammatical systems of a language are another matter. (See the reference given earlier.)

5.7. *Every phonological system contrasts phonemes that are typically stops with phonemes that are never stops.*

Stops are sounds produced with complete oral closure and complete velic closure. By "phonemes that are typically stops" we mean phonemes that are stops in slow careful speech or in key environments, though they may be weakened or spirantized in some environments or in faster speech. The contrasting nonstops vary widely from one language to another. In a few languages of New Guinea, the nearest nonstops are nasal continuants. More commonly they are spirants.

5.8 *No phonological system has fewer than two contrasting positions of articulation for stops.*

The only attested cases with only two are Hawaiian and fast colloquial Samoan, with labial versus lingual (formal Samoan has three). [∇ Add Tahitian, with labial versus apical.]

5.9. *If a language has a vowel system, it has contrasts of tongue height in that system.*

5.10. *If we define a "vowel system" to include all the segmental phonemes that occur as syllable peaks, then every language has a vowel system.*

For 5.10, clearly some adjustment is required in order to subsume the languages of the Caucasus referred to earlier. If we define a "vowel system" to include all the segmental phonemes that occur *only* as syllable peaks, then at least one language, Wishram, apparently has a vowel system of one element, which is only trivially a "system." With these adjustments, 5.9 becomes a true universal, applying to all human languages.

Another way to express 5.9 is to say that if a language has vowel contrasts other than those of tongue height, it also has those of tongue height, but not necessarily vice versa.

Further generalizations along the line of the last three mentioned can probably be formulated, although all of them are subject to modification at any time by empirical information on some as-yet-unanalyzed language. As a set, however, they point toward something rather puzzling. It would seem easy enough to devise a phonemic system that would have no stops at all, or no vowels at all, or the like. The phonological systems of the world, despite their great variety, all seem to have more in common than is strictly "necessary." That is, the degree of resemblance strikes one as greater than is required merely by the defining features of language and the known cultural and biological properties of our species. Granting that the variety may actually be somewhat greater than we currently realize, there is still a problem in this degree of similarity. Are there constraints imposed by as-yet-unrealized properties of the organs of speech and of human hearing? Is the resemblance due to a common origin, in relatively recent times—say forty or fifty thousand years ago—of all human languages on which we have any direct evidence or can obtain any? (The latter hypothesis does not, of course, propose that human language is only that old, merely that all other older strains have died out.)[4] These questions are open; the answers may actually lie in some totally different direction.

ACKNOWLEDGMENTS

The author is indebted to Sidney Lamb for detailed criticisms and suggestions. He also wishes to thank Fred Householder and Joseph H. Greenberg for comments on certain aspects of the present paper.

REFERENCES

Bloomfield, L. 1933. *Language*. New York: Holt.
Cowan, G. M. 1948. "Mazateco Whistle Speech." *Language* 24.280–286.
Goodenough, W. H. 1971. "Culture, Language, and Society." An Addison-Wesley Module. Reading, Mass.: Addison-Wesley.
Hockett, C. F. 1958. *A Course in Modern Linguistics*. New York: Macmillan.
———. 1960. "Logical Considerations in the Study of Animal Communication." (In this volume, pp. 124–162.)
———. 1961. "Linguistic Elements and their Relations." *Language* 37.29–53.

4. [∇ As indicated in fn. 3, I now believe that "true" language—language with all the design-features declared crucial in this article—may actually be only about fifty thousand years old. If so, then the answer just hinted at in this paragraph may actually be the right one.]

————. 1968. Review of Lamb 1966. *International Journal of American Linguistics* 34.145–153.

————. 1973. *Man's Place in Nature.* New York: McGraw-Hill.

Hockett, C. F., and R. Ascher. 1964. "The Human Revolution." *Current Anthropology* 5.135–168.

Jakobson, R. 1961. "Why 'Mama' and 'Papa'?" *Perspectives in Psychological Theory*, pp. 124–134.

Kemeny, J. G. 1959. *A Philosopher Looks at Science.* Princeton, N. J.: Princeton University Press.

Kuipers, A. H. 1960. *Phoneme and Morpheme in Kabardian.* The Hague: Mouton.

Lamb, S. M. 1966. *Outline of Stratificational Grammar.* Washington, D.C.: Georgetown University Press.

Murdock, G. P. 1945. "The Common Denominator of Cultures." In R. Linton, ed., *The Science of Man in the World Crisis* (New York: Columbia University Press), pp. 123–142.

Shannon, C. 1951. "Prediction and Entropy of Printed English." *Bell System Technical Journal* 30.50–65.

Trager, G. L. 1963. *Linguistics is Linguistics.* Buffalo (*Studies in Linguistics, Occasional Papers* 10).

————. 1972. *Language and Languages.* San Francisco: Chandler.

H9. SCHEDULING

Spring 1962. Reprinted from F. S. C. Northrop and H. H. Livingston, eds., *Cross-Cultural Understanding: Epistemology in Anthropology* (New York: Harper & Row, 1964; copyright © 1964 by the Wenner-Gren Foundation for Anthropological Research, Incorporated) 125–144, with the permission of Harper & Row, Publishers, and of the Wenner-Gren Foundation.

The volume just named resulted from a symposium of the Wenner-Gren Foundation held at Burg Wartenstein bei Gloggnitz, Austria, 16–26 September 1962, under the leadership of F. S. C. Northrop. The original title of the symposium was "The Determination of the Philosophy of a Culture." All papers for the meeting were prepared and distributed in advance, so that the actual meeting-time could be devoted to discussion.

The key notion I chose to elaborate for my contribution to the symposium had been simmering on the back burner since my student days at Yale (1936–1939): I remember sitting in the anthropology reading room of the library with an array of books on Algonquian ethnography before me, and asking myself "how can we organize this confused mass of material so as to make some sort of sense out of it?"; and I remember tentatively answering "maybe it would help if we indexed each type of act or event in terms of *when* and *where* it is expected to happen." But I couldn't have elaborated the notion successfully any earlier than I did. The bare notion of scheduling was not enough; it needed the support of the ethnographic generalization of the phonemic principle (yielding what in the essay I call the "inside view"), and it needed the state-parameters, foreshadowed in H6 (and elaborated further in *Man's Place in Nature*, 1973a). With those ingredients at hand, I think I managed in this essay to get about where Edward Sapir had been thirty years earlier—but on a less purely intuitive, more formalized (and thoroughly physicalistic) foundation.

This paper extends to ethnography certain assumptions and procedures of linguistics.

1

An observation is a function of two variables, the observed and the observer. In physics, the theory of relativity seeks to lay bare those properties of the observed that are invariant from one observer (actual or imaginable) to another, and only such properties are ascribed to physical reality. In ethnography, a similar search yields different results, for we find two equally objective views that can be taken towards the life of any human community.

One is the outside view, whose frame of reference is that of physics. An ethnographer speaks from this view when he locates a tribe by latitude and longitude, or estimates its population, or describes its habitat. A linguist speaks from this view when he describes the speech sounds of a language in terms of articulatory motions. In aim, if not always in actuality, any properly trained observer—including one who belongs to the community under examination—would agree with such reports.

The other is the inside view. This does not arise in physics because stars and electrons are not observers. The members of a community are, and they perceive and react to things in certain ways. An ethnographer speaks from this view when he locates a tribe in a valley at the center of the world, surrounded successively by mountains, a river, and a sea of fire. A linguist speaks from this view when he describes a phonemic system. The inside view is subjective for the members of the community, but for the investigator it is just as objective as the outside view.

Both of these views are necessary for ethnography. Conjointly, they are sufficient. Other approaches are approximations or mistakes. Such terms as "religion," "property," or "schizophrenia" are only dubiously to be ascribed to the frame of reference for the outside view, and until a particular community has been studied one cannot know if they are relevant for the inside view of that community. Hence, a proposal to investigate the religion of some largely unstudied community constitutes a projection from one inside view—that of Western culture—into another. Such cross-cultural projections are inevitable as an ethnographer begins his work; the work is not complete until they have been eliminated.

For the outside view, the ethnographer can solicit help from a vast array of fellow scientists. For the inside view, he stands alone, except, of course, for the members of the community he is studying, and he must often extrapolate from what they teach him in ways in which they would not. (For example, people speak within a phonemic system they cannot ordinarily describe.) The inside view is thus the special province of the ethnographer, and is our concern in this paper.

2

The ethnographer's task is to discover and describe the ways of life of a human community. The discovery is achieved at best by participant-observation, though no technique is taboo unless it is inhumane. Up to a point, what the ethnographer does as a participant-observer parallels what a member of the community does by growing up within it. One obvious difference is that the ethnographer is pledged to report what he learns, while the community member is not. This suggests an approach to ethnographic theory. We ask: How can an ethnographer, back from the field, process his findings to yield a report of maximum accuracy and clarity? Is there an optimal format into which he can cast his data? If so, can advance knowledge of the format guide him in the field and obviate some gaps and uncertainties in the ultimate report?

Such questions emphasize the role of the ethnographer as a link between the community he studies and the anthropological profession. Accuracy and clarity are not independent. The most accurate understanding of a community might be achieved by an ethnographer who went native and published nothing. The clearest exposition could perhaps be written by an imaginative novelist who did no field work. But private accuracy is abortive, and factitious clarity is fraudulent.

The linguist in the field is an ethnographer with a restricted assignment: just the language of the community, not its whole way of life. (It is almost certain that "language" is a valid term in the outside view, so that the restricted assignment is legitimate.) There is an established format for the linguist's report. It will appear as a grammar and dictionary.

A dictionary is a serial list of linguistic elements of a certain sort. Such elements *occur* from time to time as the language is spoken. There are constraints on the circumstances in which each element is apt to occur. The constraints are of two kinds, grammatical and semantic. The former are limitations on the ways in which linguistic elements combine with one another; thus, in English, we do not commonly say *the men is*. The dictionary subsumes constraints of this sort by cross-reference to the grammar. Semantic constraints have to do with the nonspeech context of speech. These are described in the dictionary itself.

A grammar covers three matters. It sets forth the grammatical constraints on the elements listed in the dictionary. It describes the phonemic system of the language. And it specifies the habits by which lexical elements—the dictionary entries—are mapped into sequences of phonemes.

A form that recurs, or may recur, as a language is spoken does not necessarily belong in the dictionary. It must be listed only if its occurrence and the circumstances attendant thereon cannot be inferred from the rest of the information in the dictionary and grammar. Thus, English *boy* requires listing; *boys and girls* does not; *time heals all wounds* does.

A language is an open system: its speakers often say things that have not been said before, usually with no disruption of communication. This property of a language is matched by the linguist's report in the following way. To the extent that a dictionary and grammar are complete, one can interpret a newly observed utterance in the language. If the whole utterance is not in the dictionary, then its parts are, and the patterns by which the parts have been put together are in the grammar. To the extent that the dictionary and grammar are accurate, one can draw information from them and generate a new utterance that will pass the test of casual acceptance by the speakers of the language. Thus the linguist's report parallels the language skills that the speakers carry inside their heads. There is, of course, neither need nor reason to assume that the spatial organization of these skills in a speaker's central nervous system conforms to the distribution of data that the linguist finds convenient in his report.

A language is also a changing system. The mechanism of change that works most rapidly is that forms are spoken in circumstances that are in one way or another unusual, thus giving rise to new lexical items. A fixed dictionary and grammar cannot reflect this property of a language. It is possible, however, to observe the patterns that are most favored in the formation of new lexical items and to report this in the grammar. It would also be possible to prepare a dictionary and grammar in loose-leaf form and revise as the language changes, but the result would not be what is usually wanted, which is a portrayal of the workings of the language as of a specified date.

There is another sort of variation in language habits, however, that an account must cover. No community is homogeneous. Different members and subgroups behave in different ways, in speech as in other respects. The active vocabulary of a fisherman is not that of a woodworker. A chief may be permitted turns of phrase forbidden to a commoner. Such differences reflect, and constitute part of, the social structure of the community. It would be incorrect, not merely uneconomical, to prepare a separate grammar and dictionary for each social dialect, since this would obscure the extent of their overlap. The fisherman can learn the technical terms of woodworking; the commoner can understand, if he may not imitate, the chief. The proper description presents the common core of all dialects and then describes the departures from it.

3

We now introduce the terminology of scheduling.

We recall a point made above: that a linguistic element is something that *occurs* from time to time in the speech behavior of the community. From the outside view, a word exists as, and only as, it is occurring. Between occurrences it does not exist, though records of it exist in the central nervous systems of the speakers (if nowhere else). These internal records are such that the word is recognized when it does occur, and also such that the word is expected to occur under certain conditions and not, or only with lower probability, under others. We paraphrase by saying that in the expectations of the speakers the word is *scheduled* to occur under certain conditions. The grammar and dictionary prepared by a linguist are a statement of such schedulings.

To say that a word is recognized when it occurs is to say that, when a word occurs, users of the language can tell what word it is. Recognizability is not absolute but differential. It turns on the contrast between, first, a word and a nonword and, second, one word and any other word. If the users of a language can identify an event as an occurrence of a certain word rather than of any other word or of any nonword, it is because they are attuned to certain sensable physical properties of the word, or of its immediate setting, that differ from those of any other word or of any nonword. These are the *distinctive* properties of the word. An occurrence of a word typically has also sensable properties that are not distinctive: e.g., English words sound different from male and from female speakers, but are the same words none the less. What has just been said is the principle of *contrast*. It lies at the heart of ethnography. To realize its importance one need only imagine trying to play bridge with a blank deck.

All that is said above about a word applies without modification to such a social phenomenon as, say, American presidential inauguration. This is scheduled to occur every four years, on a certain day, at a certain place, with certain participants identified by role, and with a prescribed sequence of constituent actions. Some variation is permissible, but there is a distinctive core that cannot be violated: if the departures are too great, the event is not recognized, and not accepted, as a presidential inauguration. The ceremony exists only as it is held. Between occurrences, all that exists is records. The records constitute the scheduling of the phenomenon and are the basis of the recognizability of the ceremony when it does occur.

I shall use the term *trait* for any lexical element in a language and for any such social phenomenon as American presidential inauguration. A trait, then, is a thing that recurs, or may recur, in the life of a community; that exists only as it occurs; the occurrences of which are scheduled in one way or another in the expectations of the members of the community; and an occurrence of which is recognizable by them by virtue of specifiable distinctive properties. As with language, so also in the general case, a potentially recurrent phenomenon is not a trait if it is built out of smaller elements, and if its occurrence and the attendant circumstances are subsumed by an adequate description of the latter and their schedulings. *Boys and girls* is not a lexical unit, hence not a trait; a dinner of several courses in a customary sequence is not a trait. *Boy* and a soup course are traits. *Time heals all wounds* and American presidential inauguration are traits despite their internal complexity; that is, although they include smaller traits, they are not, as wholes, predictable purely in terms of those smaller traits and their schedulings.

Some schedulings are tighter than others, but all are contingent and probabilistic rather than absolute or determinate. A linguist cannot predict the exact time and place of a use by a speaker of English of the word *are*, nor can the speaker predict this with certainty even of his own speech. Both know, however, that if a sentence begins with *the boys* (contingency), the next word is more likely to be *are* than *is* (probability). We are most apt to hear *Good morning!* in the morning. An American dinner could start with pie and end with soup, but this would clearly be deviant.

4

I propose the following answer to the questions about ethnographic theory posed at the beginning of §2. The ethnographer's report of the inside view should appear as a tabulation of the traits of the community, of the distinctive properties of each, and of their schedulings. There is nothing to be said of a community's way of life that cannot be said in this fashion, and no format can yield greater accuracy and clarity.

These assertions constitute the theory of scheduling. Certain kinds of ethnographic data fit the specified format almost effortlessly, and we shall discuss these first. But ethnographers also indulge in generalizations that are perhaps true and profound but that would seem to be more resistant to the scheduling format. Resistant they may be—the claim of accuracy and clarity does not imply ease of application.[1] I shall try to show that the theory allows for such more profound inferences provided they are meaningful.

The theory of scheduling is not supposed to apply to the outside view. Yet that view is indispensable for the application of the theory, in that it must be evoked in describing the distinctive properties of traits. The

---

1. In any case, this article is not concerned with practical difficulties. Note that all the strictures of §2, as to what a description of a language can and cannot do, apply equally to the whole of culture and its description.

vowel system of a language is an inside-view matter; its description requires reference to tongue and lip positions, which is outside view. Similarly, the preferential manufacture of axe handles from the wood of a certain tree is inside view; the taxonomic identification of the tree is outside view.

For the inside view, it is not at all the ethnographer's responsibility to report his observations, though there are two good reasons why he may. One is to afford concrete examples of how schedulings "actualize" in behavior in the community. The other is that the reader may check on the ethnographer's inferences and perhaps add his own. When a linguist appends a sample text to a grammar, the purposes are these. Neither purpose justifies the presentation of raw data as a substitute for the description of inferred patterns.

5

Many traits in any community have an obvious scheduling in terms of natural cycles: the year, the (lunar) month, the day, the life cycle, the menstrual cycle, the recurrent increase and release of pressure in the seminal vesicles, and others. These natural cycles are given by the outside view. They vary with geography and, to some extent, with genetic constitution. Many communities have also man-made periods such as the week. All scheduling relative to such natural and pseudonatural cycles will be called *calendrical*.

It is standing practice to report really tight calendrical schedulings. No account of a Cree band would ignore the seasonal cycle of dispersion in small hunting groups for part of the year and collection at a central point for the rest. If a ceremony is performed with the first spring thunderstorm, or before sunrise each day, or when a boy reaches puberty, this is mentioned.

In fact, however, every trait is scheduled calendrically. The correlation between the occurrences of a certain trait and, say, time of year may be zero. But zero correlation must be distinguished from the case in which the investigator does not discover what the correlation is.

The scheduled activities of a community move its members about along scheduled routes. What they see as they move depends on what they are trained to look for and on the physicogeographical environment, including in the latter the modifications, such as houses, trails, and garbage dumps, that they have imposed on it. This spatial aspect of scheduling is the *dwelling pattern*. Farmers who live on the land they work have very different dwelling patterns from those who live clustered in villages and travel out to their land. All traits work into the dwelling pattern of a community, in the same sense in which all have some kind of calendrical scheduling.

Differences of scheduled activities from one individual or subgroup of a community to another generate a pseudospatial distribution of people commonly called social structure. The outside view affords two dimensions of social structure, sex and age, the former inoperative only in a monastic community, the latter universal. Every community elaborates these two in its own way (American society has "sex-grading" as well as age-grading) and adds others. If any of these others is universal, that is a fact awaiting empirical proof. Every trait is scheduled relative to social structure.

Personality and social structure are conjugate variables. Personality is the idiosyncratic way in which a particular individual plays his roles in the community. But an individual's roles are just his position in social structure. To change the way in which roles are played is to change the roles, hence also the social structure. It is a mere matter of convenience that we use both concepts. The facts to be described can be subsumed wholly under either.[2]

Artifacts are modified parts of the physicogeographical environment. They are not traits, but their manufacture, manipulation, and ultimate disposal are scheduled activities composed of traits. But an artifact is also a record. Some of the skill necessary for the use of a hammer is stored in the user; some is stored in the hammer. If this were not so, archaeology would be futile.

6

Calendrical scheduling and the dwelling pattern are *external* constraints on the occurrences of traits; the schedulings of traits relative to other traits are *internal* constraints. A set of traits constitutes a *cultural system* (or just a *system*) if the constraints on their occurrences require to be sorted out in this binary way. The aggregate of all traits of a community is thus a system. Language is a system: the semantic constraints are external (even

2. [∇ But this overlooks a very important point. As from the inside view of a particular community, both social structure and personality may be quantized, but not necessarily in parallel ways. A chief may be viewed (because of his personality) as "good"; his successor may be thought of as "bad"; and yet both have been recognized within the community as chiefs—both have occupied the same "point" or "cell" in the social structure of the community. We have to say that a role imposes certain constraints on the personality of him who plays it, but that within the constraints there can be personality variations that do not change social structure. Only when an individual actor is too much of a maverick is there a (social) restructuring.]

when they are internal to the whole culture), the grammatical ones internal.

One cultural system may be wholly included in another; we may then say that the first is a system of a lower "level" than the second. The language of a community is part of its total way of life; the language consists, in turn, of two nonoverlapping smaller systems, the grammaticolexical and the phonemic. (Two systems are nonoverlapping if no trait belongs to both.) Hunting, house-building, courting, and many other activities for which English supplies labels are doubtless systems in various communities, but the ways in which these overlap with, include, and are included in others vary and are difficult to discover. In general, it is easier to demonstrate that traits belong to the same or to different systems at some level than it is to discern the exact total arrangement of systems. It is easy to list traits that certainly do not belong to the same low-level system: e.g., the word *boy*, trumping one's partner's ace, and striking a nail with a hammer. More important is a basic test: if two traits can be acted out by the same person at the same time, they must belong, at some level, to different systems. We intone as we utter English words: intonation and words belong to different subsystems, though both are included within the language. We can clap our hands and shout *Encore!* simultaneously: the former is gestural, the latter linguistic, and these do not overlap each other, though both overlap with concert-going.

Time heals all wounds and American presidential inauguration are both *complex* traits, in that they incorporate smaller traits but cannot be wholly accounted for in terms of the latter. Every trait, simple or complex, belongs to at least one system. *Time heals all wounds* belongs to a system to which its smaller included traits also belong: the language. American presidential inauguration, on the other hand, involves smaller traits of many different systems, of which perhaps none is a system to which the complex trait itself belongs. We must thus distinguish between *one-system* and *cross-system* complex traits.

In language, a form larger than any one lexical element (simple or complex) is *composite*. Composite forms are built from lexical units by grammatical patterns called *constructions*. By eliminating the specific reference to language, we can use these terms for any cultural system.

The structure of a composite form is typically hierarchical. That is, the whole form consists of smaller forms some of which are also composite; those in turn of still smaller forms some of which may be composite; and so on until one reaches the ultimate constituent traits. *The books on the bottom shelf are all blue* consists of the immediate constituents *the books on the bottom shelf* and *are all blue*, put together by a construction called predication. The same construction appears in *psycholinguistics appears to be a strange field*, though with different constituents. *The books on the bottom shelf* consists, in turn, of *the books* and *on the bottom shelf* involving another construction; the second of these consists of *on* and *the bottom shelf*, with still another construction; and so on. Similarly, the eating of a dinner has, as its immediate constituents, the eating of each successive course; the eating of a single course consists, perhaps, of the successive bites and sips. The particular set of constructions that are manifested in *the books on the bottom shelf are all blue* are manifested also in an indefinite number of other sentences; in the same way, if one starts with chopped liver instead of herring, and continues with noodle soup instead of consomme, lamb instead of beef, apple strudel instead of seven-layer cake, tea instead of coffee, the result is still the eating of a dinner. A construction is a frame into each slot of which any of a set of interchangeable forms (simple or composite) can be inserted. The forms also fit various slots in other frames; two composite forms can share no trait and yet involve the same frame.

A complex trait typically consists of simple traits put together by familiar constructions. This is the case with *time heals all wounds*, which has subject *time* and predicate *heals all wounds*. It is a complex trait, rather than merely a composite form, because it is remembered as a whole and recited from memory rather than being built anew upon each occurrence. Similarly, if a family forms the habit of a fixed menu for Sunday dinner, then Sunday dinner is a complex trait despite the fact that it consists of compatible courses as does any other dinner. A description of dinners in general, no matter how detailed, could not subsume the Sunday fixation, just as a description of English predication, no matter how accurate, could not subsume the idiomatic quality of *time heals all wounds*.

Composite forms, like complex traits, can be one-system or cross-system. This means that there are cross-system constructions as well as intrasystem constructions. Various styles of nodding the head and various intonations are compatible with each other and with saying *yes*, but some gestures are not: shaking the head while saying *yes* is an incongruity in our culture just as is saying *the men is*.

Activities conducted simultaneously need not stand in clear-cut cross-system constructions to build complex traits or composite forms of some more inclusive cultural system. Sometimes they are merely compatible. One can carry on a conversation while driving a car, or eat a sandwich while watching television, or plait sennet while gossiping. Yet mere compatibility is itself a fact of scheduling, and the absence of any cross-system connection should not be hastily inferred. Samoan men commonly plait sennet as they sit and rest after a meal, a time also appropriate for gossip.

There is no outer limit to the length of a composite form or the complexity of the constructions by which it is built. A lecture is typically much longer than a single sentence, but it has a hierarchical structure. The annual cycle is a construction for the whole way of life of a community. The life cycle is a construction for any one individual. Even the great ground swells of growth and decline over many generations, suspected by some scholars, may conform to constructions, though in this case the constructions probably escape the inside view of any single community (except via hindsight).

There are traits that cannot be acted out by a single individual. We take these to be complex by definition. The contributory actions of any one participant stand in *cross-personal* constructions with those of the others. Cross-personal constructions also generate multipersonal composite forms of varying degrees of complexity—in the end, the whole history of the community.[3] Differences of expected role in multipersonal activities yield social structure, which we have already discussed.

7

Apart from the cultural systems to which they individually belong, constructions fall into a number of types based on formal properties.

A construction is *centered* to the extent that the choice of one constituent imposes more widely ranging contraints on surrounding choices (within the same system) than does the choice of the other or others.[4] In *the books on the bottom shelf*, the center or "nucleus" is *the books* and *on the bottom shelf* is a "satellite"; in *the books*, the nucleus is *books*. Thus, if we replace *books* by *book*, the predicate given earlier (*are all blue*) is rendered insuitable; *are* must at the same time be replaced by *is*. If *the* is replaced by *these* or *those*, there are no such reverberations, nor are there if we replace *on the bottom shelf* by *in my study* or *that he has written so far*. A housewife planning the menu for a dinner party usually settles on the pièce de résistance first and then decides what other courses are suitable; that suggests that the pièce de résistance of a dinner is the nucleus. The intonations we use while speaking seem in general to constitute running commentaries on, and hence satellites to, the words.

3. Except that traits and schedulings change.
4. [∇ The standard traditional terms in linguistics are *endocentric* and *exocentric* (thus, for example, in my *Course in Modern Linguistics*, 1958). But *centered* and *uncentered* are really more apt. I have been using them since about 1962.]

Not all constructions are centered in this simple sense. Some seem to have two or more *coordinate* centers: the phrase *men and women* is not built about *men* as center any more than it is about *women*; in ballet, one could argue whether the music accompanies the dancing or vice versa, which probably means that they are coordinate. Some seem rather to be *uncentered:* the subject and predicate of *the books on the bottom shelf are all blue* show some congruences but are forms of diverse sorts, whereas *men* and *women* in *men and women* are highly similar forms. There are problems here that have not been solved even for the simple case of language. Whether the coordinate and the uncentered types can be distinguished outside of language is not clear.

Experiencing a long composite form, in any cultural system, is something like crossing over a range of mountains. Insofar as the form is built by centered constructions, the successive nuclei are like the successive ridges, some higher than others. The intervening valleys find their analog too, and the point at which successive constituents abut is often signaled by a trait specialized for that function. In English phonemics, there are as many intonation phrases in an utterance as there are primary stresses, and between any two successive primary stresses there is one and only one terminal contour. English primary stress, or any other trait the occurrences of which mark nuclei or climaxes, is a *culminator.* An English terminal contour, or any other trait that marks the boundary between successive constituents of some larger form, is a *demarcator.*[5] At the end of an interview with a student, the professor's voice increases slightly in volume: this is a demarcator. In music, the pauses between the movements of a symphony are demarcators; cadences within a movement are demarcators of a lower order. Beethoven used dissonance for culminative effect against a backdrop of consonance; Hindemith reversed this. Not all peaks and boundaries are marked by culminators and demarcators, but it is important that some traits are specialized for these functions.

8

We view an individual, or a group engaged in a multipersonal activity during which they are validly to be segregated from the rest of the community, at the momentary interstice between successive acts of a single cultural system. The individual or group is the *actor*. The actor is in a *state*.

5. The terms are adapted from Trubetzkoy.

Suppose someone has just said *That man over there is my* ———; at this point we stop the camera to survey the possibilities. With only this much information, about all we can say relates to the grammatical constraints of English. The next word may be a noun such as *father*, *son*, *friend*, or an adjective like *good*, *worst* (due to be followed in turn by some noun), and so on. The linguistic possibilities for the next word are finite because there are only a finite number of words in the language. There might not be any next word—the speaker might stop, or be shot—but this we treat linguistically as a single additional possibility. If we know more of the attendant circumstances, we shall be able to narrow our prediction. Let the speaker be young and the man pointed to old. We shall not then expect the next word to be *son*.

The more we know, the more precisely we can predict. Does this mean that, at the limit, to know all the attendant circumstances (from the outside view as well as the inside) would enable us to predict exactly what the next act will be? The question is meaningless because it is impossible to reach the limit. From any vantage point, including that of the actor, only some of the contributing factors can be discerned. This yields a range of indeterminacy.

We wish to characterize the actor's state from the vantage point of the actor himself, not from that of any outside-view observer. States differ from one another at least in these four ways: (1) predictability; (2) freedom of choice; (3) urgency; (4) anxiety.[6]

The predictability from a state varies inversely with the indeterminacy of the state; the latter is a function of the number of alternatives available for the next act and of the relative probabilities of each. We shall speak of the *alternative array*. The actor need not be consciously aware of all the alternatives actually available.

There is some correlation between the degree of indeterminacy of a state and the point the actor has reached in the hierarchical structure of a composite form. Indeterminacy is higher (and predictability lower) at the end of some large form than at the end of its constituents: higher at the end of a sentence than at the end of its subject; higher at the end of a dinner than after a nonfinal course; higher as one is about to graduate from college than when one has just completed the junior year and is planning the senior year's work. It is lower in the middle of what may become a complex trait than in the middle of an equally complicated composite form: after *Hell hath no fury like a woman* —— we are quite surprised to

6. [∇ I am glad I said "at least" here. The count is now up to six: uncertainty (better than its converse, predictability), freedom of choice, urgency, pleasantness, anxiety, and seriosity. See my *Man's Place in Nature* (New York: McGraw-Hill, 1973), pp. 230–232.]

hear anything but *scorned*, but after *I went to town yesterday afternoon and bought* —— there are any number of unsurprising possibilities.

In principle, indeterminacy can be precisely quantified.[7]

Freedom of choice and predictability are independent. Suppose we observe that a certain man invariably wears a blue necktie, and infer that his state each morning, as he selects his necktie, has high predictability. Discreet detective work then reveals that he has ties of many colors in his wardrobe and that, in his own opinion, he freely chooses the color he prefers each time. This does not materially alter our estimate of the predictability. The information bears on a different parameter: an actor has as much freedom of choice, in any state, as he believes he has.

A person is an actor as he speaks, and also as he listens to someone else speak. In the former case, predictability and freedom of choice are often both high; in the latter, both are often low. However, predictability is high and freedom of choice low for a ceremonial participant; predictability is low and freedom of choice high for the contemporary painter who applies pigment to canvas with anything from a blue necktie to a shotgun.

The urgency of a state is the inverse of the amount of time available for the selection of the next act. Whenever urgency is sufficiently low, there is time for tentative trial-and-error "editing" (itself scheduled) before the definitive selection of the next act is made.[8] A young man drafting a sonnet for his beloved experiences no great urgency, though if there is a deadline the urgency may increase as it is approached. When urgency is high, the actor must exercise his freedom of choice quickly or outside factors change the state. Waiting for the doctor to choose between whole blood and plasma, the patient dies.

Urgency is obviously quantifiable.

Anxiety has to do with the actor's concern about the consequences of the next act: what new state it will establish, what subsequent acts and states it will render more or less probable. An actual experience can be painful. Anxiety is not pain but the expectation of probabilistically scheduled pain.

A state can be characterized by a profile of four numbers, of which the first relates to predictability, the second to freedom of choice, the third to urgency, and the fourth to anxiety. Using "H" for relatively high numeri-

---

7. [∇ In the original there is here a cross-reference to an appendix, in which the formal quantification is given, complete with some mathematical errors. The essence of the matter is that we treat the things that might happen next as though they were the signals of a communicative system. The measure of indeterminacy is then just the measure U of a-priori uncertainty defined in the Addendum to the Review of Shannon (this volume, p. 50).]

8. Editing is discussed more fully in my "Ethnolinguistic Implications . . . " (this volume, p. 107).

cal values, "M" for intermediate ones, "L" for relatively low ones, and "V" for variable, indeterminate, or irrelevant, we can describe the typical states encountered in certain familiar cultural systems:

sitting in the dentist's chair:	HLHH
sitting in the barber's chair:	HLHL
watching a football game:	MLVV
playing in a football game:	MMVM (or MMVH)
listening to a favorite familiar piece of music:	HLHL
encountering a truck in one's lane as one reaches the top of a hill:	MLHH
selecting proper therapy for a slow but deadly disease:	MMLH
selecting proper emergency treatment for a bad accident case:	MMHH
sleeping:	HLLL.

A ritual is a scheduled sequence of events during which the states are predominantly of type HLVL. This does not exclude the case in which a designated participant (say, one due to go under the sacrifical knife) experiences states HLVH. Games are characterized by MMVL: for onlookers the second index is lower, and for active players the fourth may be higher, but if anxiety is too high the activity loses its game character. Adventure is LHVL; an exciting episode in an adventure is LMHM.

9

The ethnographer's initial contact with a community, like that of any other outsider, is characterized by the presence of two different sets of expectations: those of the community and his own. The extent of the difference between the expectations of any two individuals or groups defines the amount of *code noise* that characterizes their joint activities. We cannot expect code noise to be completely absent in any transaction between humans or human groups, even when they belong to the same community. The noisiness of cross-personal activities tends to diminish as the activities are repeated (if they are), since the expectations of each participant are modified by the actual behavior of the others. For example, tribelets that speak mutually unintelligible languages often conduct their wars according to shared conventions that have arisen through past contact. Clearly, code noise plays a vital role in culture change.

The term "community," accepted uncritically so far in this essay, need not remain undefined. A community is any cluster of people in social structure—that is, any group whose activities are tied together by cross-personal constructions and thus marked by some degree of freedom from noise. We may at will apply the term "community" either to a village, or to a single family within a village, or to a functioning group of villages. This freedom of scope is not license: we cannot dissect entirely to suit our own fancy, but must follow the joints.

10

When an ethnographer speaks of the themes of a culture, or of its values, or of national character, modal personality, or philosophy, he is attempting to pass beyond detail and to achieve some simpler, broader, and deeper characterization of a way of life. The generalization need not be one which the members of the community would themselves overtly make, but it is supposed to be empirical, in the sense that it is distilled from ethnographic detail, and operational, in that it can yield predictions of behavior subject to observational check.

Generalizations of this sort find their place within the scheduling framework. We shall see that it is no accident that terms used in portraying "national character" or "philosophy" tend to be those used in describing the character or personality of individuals.

Suppose a culture repeatedly subjects participants to states in which freedom of choice is low and anxiety high. The participant learns this pattern, and comes to interpret all sorts of states as though they involved little freedom and much anxiety. This is a change of personality; hence, because of the conjugate nature of personality and social structure, it is also a change in social structure. The habits acquired by a newcomer to the community depend on where in social structure he enters the community. Newcomers (children) can be exposed in increasing numbers to the VLVH pattern. In due time the whole community may be marked by fatalism and anxiety. Alternatively, such a combination as fatalism and anxiety might become widespread for certain cultural systems only, other systems having different properties.

The degree of ritualization of a way of life is the extent to which states in various cultural systems are characterized by the HLVL pattern. It has been suggested that if a way of life involves great anxiety in certain contexts, it compensates for this by ritualization in others. The Japanese live on seismically unstable islands, where a major disaster may come at any moment without warning. The Japanese play baseball by American rules, but with differences of style: if a Japanese batter is called out, he bows politely to the umpire and returns to the dugout.[9] Ritualization reduces noise, but it also cuts down on the rate at which information flows. It is not surprising that the uncertainty and anxiety of dealings between nations should be accompanied by a high degree of ritualization of diplomatic transactions.

Shame and guilt are different properties of cross-personal constructions, reflected in the relation of predictability to freedom of choice and to anxiety.

Hostility, tolerance, and love have to do with scheduled ways of dealing with noise in cross-personal and cross-group transactions.

9. The suggestion and illustration were proposed by W. F. Twaddell.

H10. NOTES ON THE CREATIVE PROCESS

March 1965; never before published.

In 1964–1965 and 1965–1966, a Seminar on the Creative Process was hosted by the Wenner-Gren Foundation for Anthropological Research, with the historian Edward Lurie as prime mover and with diverse scientists, humanists, and artists as participants. The two-part paper partly reproduced here was written for the final session of the first season, held in New York 13–14 May.

I was participating in the seminar not only as anthropologist-linguist but also as composer. It happened that I had maintained rather full records—and memories—of the sequence of actions that had constituted my composing of a certain piece of music ("The Quest for the Waters of Lethe," for English Horn and Piano, completed November 1962). Part One of my seminar paper was a description of that *composing* sequence, presented in detail to show how radically it differed from the ultimate *performing* sequence—that is, the temporal order in which the music is revealed to the listening audience. My purpose was to demonstrate that what we were honoring by the elegant term "creative process" was not necessarily anything more than one sort of analogically conditioned trial and error—one kind of *editing*, as I had been calling it for a number of years (see H6).

That first and longer part of the paper is omitted here, because it is not intelligible unless accompanied by the musical score, and to print the latter would be too costly.

Anyway, a demonstration of the trial-and-error nature of composing, however convincing, would not in itself be of much value, since a host of other human activities are also trial and error. The second part of the paper, reproduced below, was an attempt to set forth the context in which composing takes place and which makes composing different from other sorts of editing.

The composer is a musical person, though not all musical persons are composers (many who could be don't try). Inside the head of a musical person there is a never-interrupted stream of music, sometimes at the focus of awareness, sometimes receding far into the background, but always present as a running contrapuntal commentary on everything the musical person experiences and does, day and night, awake and asleep, as far back as he can remember and presumably to be ended only by death.[1]

1. [∇ Since this was written I have learned that the stream of music vanishes under general anaesthesia—but so does everything else.]

When the musical person listens to music, at a concert or from records, the musical input from outside takes over and controls the development of the internal musical stream, often completely, sometimes only in part. The great musical experiences are episodes in this continuum in which, for a time—perhaps an hour or so, perhaps only a minute—the developmental structure is sharp, coherent, and artistically patterned. For almost all musical people almost all the time, these great experiences are wholly induced by input from outside.

For the musical person, a distinction between the internal musical continuum and the sequence of emotional or feeling states (I see no way to distinguish between these latter) is practically impossible to make. Ontogenetically, perhaps the musical continuum derives from emotions elicited in early life by all sorts of other things and slowly attached to bits of music; but the music in time proliferates far beyond the repertory of "ordinary" emotions, in variety and in depth. I used to say that I have a repertory of emotions that are elicited by nothing in life except music; the question is whether one can distinguish between the music itself and these added emotions. Recently I was rereading an old science fiction story by Robert A. Heinlein—one of his para-utopia variety, in which all sorts of dreams such as telepathy, teleportation, immortality become realities. One of the adepts of a marvelously "advanced" secret community is described as "possibly our most able and talented artist"; it turns out that the medium of her art is emotion: "She composes moods—arranges emotional patterns in harmonic sequences. It's our most advanced and our most completely human form of art. . . ." Setting the fantasy aside, this is indeed exactly what the composer attempts to do.

That is a slight oversimplification, since the composer may aim his work at either of two audiences: the performing audience or the sitting audience. Music aimed primarily or exclusively at the former is *Gebrauchsmusik*. It is not to be sneered at. It is in some cases very dull to listen to, but it is often a lot of fun to play. One joy of being able to play an instrument, even badly, is that it opens up to the musical person an enormous wealth of music of this kind much of which he could never really enjoy merely as part of a sitting audience. But in this discussion I am concerned with music that is aimed, at least equally, at the sitting audience.

The composer's aim is so to organize a musical input (to other musical people, and to himself) that the result will be a significant episode in the musical continuum inside their heads—a period of a minute, five minutes, or an hour, in which that continuum will be dominated from outside. Remember that to talk about the musical continuum inside the head of the musical person is to talk, at exactly the same time, about his moods, emotions, and feelings.

The composer's materials are, on the one hand, *motifs* and *themes*, on the other hand *developmental structure* (or *architecture*). Motifs and themes—brief snatches or passages several measures long—come easily and constantly. They emerge in the course of the inner continuum of music. Sometimes one catches them and jots them down, but almost any composer is apt to say to his audience, like a fisherman bringing home his catch, "you should have seen the ones that got away." Many of the raw-materials that emerge this way prove to be quite unusable. Often enough, there was something in the original inner context in which they occurred that rendered them striking; but the context is forgotten, and the theme, when reexamined, is now trivial.

I do not know the psychological or physiological (or cultural) mechanism for the inner musical stream in which thematic material is born. I doubt if anyone does. The analogy of the random generator and the screen may be right, and may be more than an analogy.[2] On the other hand, let us notice that human language, an institution shared by no other species, has the very striking property of being *open*: speakers of any language freely and frequently coin utterances they have never heard nor said before, and are usually understood. Psychologists who are experts in learning theory have told me that their theories can account for the acquisition of the conventions of a *closed* signaling system, but not for an open system. Nineteenth-century linguists called the mechanism of open-ness of language *analogy*. Perhaps that is a label, not an explanation. Whichever it may be, I am reasonably certain that the driving mechanism for the inner stream of music is the same kind of thing—except that for language it is a human universal, for music a special development (almost a new mutation) within our western culture.

Thematic material is useless in isolated bits. It is merely the raw-material for a developmental structure, as various sizes and shapes of bricks are the raw-materials for architecture. Certain themes may suggest certain architecture, and certain architectural plans may suggest certain kinds of themes. There is a dialectical relation between the two. Any one theme used in a composition must be *distinctive*, and at best is also *beautiful*. If one attempts a composition with half a dozen themes that all sound alike, then no architecture is achievable. For architecture is not observable by the audience except by virtue of *recurrence* of themes, and

2. [∇ The reference is to a mechanical model for the creative process proposed by one of the seminar participants: a generator that emits a sequence of random signals, and a screen that passes only those that meet certain criteria, rejecting all others.]

one cannot recognize that a particular theme is recurring unless it is sufficiently distinct from the other themes used in the same piece. It is much less important if a theme happens to resemble some theme of a different composition. Brahms was properly undisturbed by the resemblance of one part of the theme of the last movement of his first symphony to a passage in the last movement of Beethoven's ninth. Many contemporary composers waste far too much time and energy seeking thematic originality. The architecture is a great deal more important.

There is also a question as to how long a theme can be. It must be short enough that it can be grasped as a whole—short enough that "immediate recall" (as over against "remembering") holds the beginning of it in awareness as the end is heard. Or this can be put in terms of the "specious present": the whole theme must exist simultaneously in the "specious present" for the audience, even though physically it is a time-series. Both of these characterizations use terms of which present-day psychologists are highly suspicious: I am talking about experiential realities which are answers for us, problems and questions for the psychologist. Some of the most wonderful themes in music stretch the audience's powers of immediate retention to the limit: for example, the first theme of the first movement of Brahms's second string sextet (Op. 36). Most musical people are especially enchanted by this when it is done effectively. The more popular absorption, of relatively nonmusical people, in the rhythmic and structural simplicities of Rock and Roll and its predecessors and successors is a dislike for that kind of complexity, an urge towards the unchallenging.

There are many familiar and recurrent architectural forms: the sonata-allegro, the rondo, and so forth. Actually, these are cover terms, and two sonata-allegros (even two classical ones) can be somewhat more different than, say, two sonnets. It is not surprising that the sonata-allegro is so prominent. It is, in essence, the temporal sequence of thesis, antithesis, and synthesis, presented in philosophical guise by Hegel; there are endless varieties of experience in our culture which follow this temporal pattern, hence endless mood-sequences that we have all passed through that conform to the same pattern—hence ample reason for the use of this pattern in music. But there are others. The simple expanded two-part song form with trio (without return to the first part), developed with striking materials for a total duration of just two or three minutes, presents itself in the musically masterful and powerful marches of John Philip Sousa and in a number of wonderful marches by others. And there is no prohibition against experimentation with any number of new architectural forms. Interestingly, most new forms turn out to be minor variations on older ones. My "Quest" can be treated as a modified sonata-allegro, in which the third cycle is the development section and the fourth cycle the recapitulation and coda bound together, or as a rondo, or as a theme and variations. Architecture is in the first instance specific to specific pieces of music; the terms we have mentioned in this paragraph were invented by musical theorists to account for what composers were doing.

When a theme or motif (the only difference here is that a motif is shorter than a theme) reaches the audience embedded in various places in a composition, it is of course greatly conditioned by the context in which it is heard. There are composers who have been able to build magnificent structures with motifs that, taken out of context, are utterly trivial. Beethoven often did this—in my opinion, for example, in the first movement of his fifth symphony. We see that it is dangerous to judge a motif in the abstract. Yet it is just this that the composer is forced to do, since typically that is the way his themes and motifs come to him. We see here another case of "random" generator and screen. The thematic material that occurs to a composer has to pass the test of architectural usability. That is why a composer jots down themes and motifs in notebooks for future reference, if he is not able to use them right away. A subsequent frame of mind, brought about by everything he has experienced in the interim, may render a theme usable that is not usable when it first appears.

The essential difference between the composer and the musical person who does not try to compose is not, I believe, a difference in ability, but merely of drive. Perhaps the composer is the musical person with a power drive. That would be a cynical view, but it may be reasonably close to the truth. However, many a composer continues to compose long after it is obvious that he will never have much audience to dominate; he continues because he cannot do otherwise. He seeks the machinery for an emotional experience that will transcend, in one way or another, any he has had in his exposure to the music of others. He seeks the Grail; some composers, such as Brahms, have caught glimpses; yet every composer is trying to achieve something that he is convinced has not yet been achieved by anyone. He keeps on trying even if he in time becomes intellectually convinced that the goal is in fact not achievable by himself or anyone else—like Heaven, it is a direction, not a place.

At the same time, the most wonderful benefit of being a composer is the deepened appreciation it makes possible for the music of other composers. When one has tried oneself, one stands in awe repeatedly at the ingenuity, the determination, the genius, the glimpses of the Grail (however fleeting) of the greatest of one's predecessors. This reaction is superimposed on the music-emotion tie (or identity) already there. I think any really serious would-be composer must love Brahms, not only for his degree of success, which is tremendous, but because on close listening one can also detect the striving, the desire and the frustration, the all-too-human musicianship—through the performing sequence, as heard, one can detect something of the composing sequence. In this way, the musical experience for a musical person who tries to compose is different from, and deeper than, that of the musical person who does not try.

H 11. CAUCHEMAR ON CREATIVITY

1966; never before published. Prepared for the 15 April 1966 session of the Wenner-Gren Seminar on the Creative Process (see the prefatory remarks to H10, p. 204).

Casimir Cauchemar's birth (somewhat like that of Athene) took place as his parent was strolling across the Cornell campus on a pleasant autumn day in 1965. This paper was his first substantial contribution. In April 1968 he hosted a party in Ithaca in honor of the hundred millionth birthday of the placental mammals. By the autumn of that year he had acquired a fairly full biography, included as a preface in the first edition of his slim volume of verse, *Rugged Nuggets* (Cayuga Depths, N.Y.: The Humanist Backlash Press, 1968; second edition, revised and belittled, 1971). I haven't heard much of him since then; he seems to be fading back into the woodwork.

I met the author of the following in the summer of 1964, at a symposium on Animal Misbehavior and Human Evolution held at Burg Wartenstein bei Gloggnitz, Austria, under the auspices of the Wenner-Gren Foundation for Anthropological Research. He gave me the paper in the form of a tattered offprint from *The Harvard Journal of Teleology and Cornucopia* 19:6.1–96 (1961). It says so well what I would have wanted to say about the nature and structure of innovating acts that I reproduce it intact (except for the vast critical apparatus of the original) instead of trying to paraphrase.—C.F.H.

INNOVATION AND CREATIVITY

by
Casimir Cauchemar
Adjunct Professor of Etruscan Rhetoric
The University of Pschonsch

1. Once upon a time, as it were, somewhere in the arctic or subarctic lands of northwestern North America or northeastern Asia, there was a hunter whose bow was wearing out, so that he needed to make a new one. He searched in vain for a bow-tree, whose wood his tribe had used from time immemorial for making bows. For he was one of the small band that had wandered off from its ancestral home, into new territory in which game was plentiful but trees of any kind were scarce and stunted. Back home there were plenty of fine bow-trees; here there were none, and the road home was long.

Finding no proper wood for a new bow, he sought to repair the old one. There was an impending longitudinal crack in it, which might break through at the very next draw and leave the bow in two pieces. He looked for anything at all, even a very thin piece of flexible wood which he could bind to the bow with sinew, so that it would bend without breaking for a while longer. Finding none, in desperation he took a thick strand of sinew and tied it as tightly as he could to the bow, as a makeshift until he could repair it properly or replace it. He was afraid that it would not hold. To his amazement, it pulled harder, straightened with more zing, and propelled his arrows faster and more accurately than ever before.

His friends laughed when he first drew the awkward thing in their presence, but their laughter turned to awe when they saw his arrow fly straight and true to the heart of an elk. The shaman, whose responsibility it was to render understandable anything that actually happened, quickly explained that the sinew, itself taken from an elk, had a sympathetic attachment to its own kind, transferred to the arrow so that the latter sought its target. For game other than elk, the new bow would have no special power, though in the hands of such a skilled hunter it might work fairly well. Our hero kept silent, despite his personal notion that maybe the bow worked well because the sinew was strong and springy.

In any case, tying sinew to a wooden bow became the Thing To Do, and the custom slowly spread to other bands. Even those who had ready access to good bow wood came to do it. In due time someone tried gluing the sinew to the wood; later, a groove was carved in the wood first and then the strip of sinew was glued into it. There came to be dozens of minor variations. The shaman's explanation, also, was variously modified, forgotten, and reinvented. By the time Europeans finally got around to discovering America, the sinew-backed bow was known deep into Asia and, in the New World, as far south as California.

2. Beauty and the Beast. Once upon a time there was a small business man[1] who had three daughters, because three is a magic number, of whom only the third will concern us very much. She was generally conceded to be slightly more attractive than her older sisters, whereupon, in accordance with the then prevailing principles of verbal thaumaturgy, her name was called "Beauty." So was she (a typical case of careless medieval metonymy).

1. 5'2".

It came to pass that the father was compelled by economic factors beyond his control to make an overland trip to the Capital. He took with him the only Beast of Burden at his command, a feeble jenny-hinny, to carry the goods which he hoped to acquire at the Capital; and a haunch of venison, and Beauty, to gather faggots each dusk and roast the meat for him and her to eat.

The path led them by the edge of a thick wood, and as they neared this point on their journey a violent storm arose and they lost their way. For some hours they wandered in misery through the wood, the sky ever darker and the rain ever heavier. Then they chanced upon the gate of a chateau, and immediately fell upon it to rouse the inhabitants and ask for succor. The gate was in due course thrown open, by a gigantic hairy figure of a man with a limp in his left foot and a withered right arm, who glared at them from under bushy brows and then said, in a humble quiet voice,

"I see you have lost your way and are wet and cold and miserable. Please to enter. I am called Jacques Pataud. We will quarter your jenny-hinny with my jack-ass for the night; and the two of you shall become warm and comfortable again as guests in my abode."

The Great Hall of the chateau was lighted by numerous flambeaux placed in brackets affixed to the walls, and at one end an enormous fireplace held a roaring log big enough to have supplied the lumber for half a dozen ranch-type houses. Before the dancing flames they were allowed to warm and dry themselves, after which they were fed hot tea and sweet gâteaux and conducted to bedchambers for the night.

Contrary to their expectations, both father and daughter slept well, and in the morning, by the light of day—the storm having spent its fury and gone its way—over a sumptuous breakfast, they soon discovered why. Though their host was of fearsome aspect, his actions clumsy, his voice at certain points quite harsh and creaky, there was withal an ineffable aura of grace and kindness which shone constantly through, and his vocabulary and intonations were of the sort that both father and daughter would have expected to find in the King's Court (which neither had ever visited). Given the blanket of dark superstition under which everyone then lived, nothing was more natural than for father and daughter to suspect that they were face to face with some Prince, forced to LIVE and convey his true personality through a VEIL of EVIL enchantment cast upon him out of spite by some VILE witch.

As they broke their fast, and during the desultory conversation that ensued, the gaze of the Beast who was their host fell again and again on Beauty. When it was time for the travelers to depart and complete their journey to the Capital, he begged the father to leave her as a guest at the chateau until he would reclaim her on his homeward way.

"We are lonely, my jack-ass and I," he said. "I assure you no harm will befall her under my care. Between here and the Capital you must descend a winding rocky trail from this plateau, and coming back you must ascend it again. Let her rest, and keep us company."

"But," said the father, "in that case I would have no way to transport the wares I shall be procuring in the Capital."

"Excuse me," said the Beast, "but I was not referring to your jenny-hinny, as attractive as she is. I was speaking of your comely daughter."

After this clarification the father thought for a moment, but finally refused, though without explaining how much he hated to gather faggots and to roast haunches of venison. However, he did in the end agree that they would revisit the chateau on their homeward trip, and suggested that mayhap at that time he would allow his daughter to tarry.

And so it was.

Several weeks later, the father trudged on homewards alone, and Beauty began what was intended to be a fortnight's stay at the chateau of the Beast.

We need hardly dwell in detail on the couse of events of that fortnight, nor of the next—for, inevitably, the visit was extended. Suffice it to say in the most delicate of terms that the Beast was ever more enamored of her grace; while she, for her part, though more and more discerning his fine qualities of Mind and Heart, continued in a not unnatural ambivalence, for a man is more than Mind and Heart. Yet when, in due course, he at last gave full voice to his affection for her and expressed his willingness—nay, eagerness—to preface the desired ultimate consummation by the imprimaturs of Church and State, she said "Maybe," and forthwith her family was sent for and the necessary clerks and clerics were assembled for the Rite of Passage.

Thereafter they retired together to what was thenceforth to be their chamber. The Beast knelt on an escabeau, and gave his bride a beautiful cadeau, then said in tones so low, speaking to her as he had not spoken before:

"Beauty, my love, I am sad at heart that I cannot strip off this ugly husk and emerge in the manly shape a maiden so rightly desires in her husband. Alas! I cannot; for thus was I born. I can only strive to compensate in tenderness and adoration for what I cannot supply in the way of the culturally preferred secondary sexual characteristics."

She smiled and kissed him tenderly and said, "It doesn't matter; go prepare for bed. Go there behind that screen, and you must know you must not peek—be not a bad badaud."

"I had begun to fear what you have told me," she said, removing her mascara, "that you were not enchanted at all, but in your true form. And I will not be so dishonest as to claim that I nurse no tiny morsel of regret," she said, removing her left shoe with the three-inch heel. "But, at the same time," she said, taking off her wig, "it is foolish to expect too much of life," loosening her falsies, "and in the long run, if one cannot realize one's ideal, one must idealize one's real," rubbing the covermark from cheeks and neck, "and mutual adjustment is always necessary," she said, "and I think—nay, I am sure," with a quick motion of hand to mouth, "vat we will come to be very happy wif eatf ovver, and I'm ready to try my beft right now!"

3. The Cardinals' Tale. Riss was the youngest son of Mr. Mattock by his favorite wife. When he was of a certain age, his father took him out to the far pasture—the one furthest up the notch, where the Stream poured over a pretty little waterfall out of the Hills and began its leisurely journey through the meadow to the River—and introduced him to the sheep.

"Riss," said Mr. Mattock, "from now on the flock in this pasture is in your care, part of the time, while your half-older-brother Ross rests. And you must know each sheep by name, and never let them wander off, and chase away the wolf if he comes down out of the Hills, or call out for help if there are many wolves. Now heed me well, and learn their names and faces," he said. "This one is Ada; and this one is Chick; and here with the curls on her head is Doe; and this one with the black and white head is Vi; and this is Jen; and here is Nan; and Tray; and that big ram over there is Juan; and the middle-sized ram is Thor; and the littlest ram is Sven."

And Riss watched, and was confused.

"Now," continued his father, "I will point to each again and say the name again, and you will repeat the names after me. And then Ross will stay with you for a spell and help you learn them all, and show you how to use your shepherd's crook; and after that you must fend for yourself, for I have many other things to do and so does Ross." And, in his kindly stern way, typical of a father-son culture, he did; and Ross did, after a fashion. And in a few days Riss was on his own.

Mr. Mattock was a mighty shepherd. Even in the dark of night he could name any sheep of any of his flocks, by touch and sound. Now he, like everyone else in the valley, would have claimed, if asked, that their ancestors had been tending sheep since the beginning of the world. But in actual fact they had themselves come down out of the Hills only a few generations back and started to herd sheep, instead of hunting them as the wolves still did. It was a new sort of thing (though it seemed old), with twists and turns that they had not yet discovered.

And Riss was new too; moreover, if the truth be known, Mr. Mattock had not married Riss's mother for her brains. Riss found it terribly hard to keep the sheep apart, and got their names hopelessly mixed up. There was no one to whom he could turn for help, nor in whom he could confide his troubles, for the smallest boy in a large patriarchal household is less conspicuous than even the newest lamb. Forced to rely on his own dim-witted resources, and knowing all too well the fearful consequences of losing a sheep unnecessarily, he managed to work out a private way for keeping track of them. At first he placed little confidence in his trick. But the days went by and all was well, so he relaxed his vigilance slightly and started composing psalms.

One day this one came to him:

> I watch the sheep—
>> there's nothing else to do.
> I'd give a heap
>> if *I* were ram or ewe:
> then *I* could graze
>> and carefree go to sleep;
> another's gaze
>> the wolves would tum-ti-tum,
>> and watch above me keep.

As he was working away at the unfinished line, trying to get it to end with "-oo," or maybe with "-eep," he was so absorbed that he failed to notice the looming threat of a storm. Before he could make any preparations, it struck in all its fury.

Later, as the wind and rain abated, Mr. Mattock dispatched Ross to the far pasture to see how Riss had managed. Ross came up behind Riss without being seen. The sheep were all there. Riss, clothes torn and legs bloody and muddy, was pointing to them and naming them off—but in a most peculiar way. Ross was horrified, and ran silently back to report.

"He does not know the names of his sheep," said Ross to Mr. Mattock.

"Which were missing?" asked Mr. Mattock.

"They were all there; but Riss does not know their names," said Ross.

Somber, Mr. Mattock told Ross to go to the far pasture and take over, and to send his half-younger-brother to him for questioning.

"Riss," he said when the boy had arrived, "do you know the names of your sheep?"

Riss squirmed. "I have not lost any of them," he said.

"That is irrelevant, immaterial, incompetent, exterior to the evidence, and nonresponsive," said Mr. Mattock. "Answer my question. Do you know the names of your sheep?"

Riss was silent for a moment. "I know the names," he murmured, "but I cannot remember which is which."

Mr. Mattock sighed. "I was afraid this might happen." he said. "You do not know the names of the sheep. You can never be a great shepherd. And I fear you may never be the father of shepherds. If we lose sheep, we die. Go to your pallet and wait. I am sorry, Small Son, but the Council must hear of this."

The Witenagemot met, and listened to Ross's story, and gave Riss a chance to explain. "It is not the usual way," said Riss, "but I have lost no sheep."

"But you might," said the oldest old man. "Hear you now the history and the judgment. When the world began, we were taught how to keep track of our sheep, and that is the way it is done. If we lose sheep, we die. You have not learned. We will allow you to tend your small flock, for your father now, for your oldest brother later. But you may never be a master shepherd, and you must never be the father of shepherds." And he pronounced the sentence that Riss's father had feared, and that only the Council could pronounce, and Riss was castrated.

So Riss did not grow to manhood and seek his own pastures and build his own flocks and get his own wives and beget his own sons. He tended his own small flock, day after day. From time to time a ram or a lamb was taken for slaughter, but Riss would not permit this except just as a new lamb was born, and then he gave the new one the old one's name. When the first pain was over, Riss discarded his old psalm and tried to compose a new one:

> I guard these silly sheep,
>> for now that's all I fit for am.
> I'd really give a heap
>> if I were like that largest ram.
> Then I could screw
>> my courage really tight
> and every ewe
>> would fill me with delight.

He didn't like the last part of this, but was never able to figure out how it ought to go.

So Riss did not grow to manhood; but he grew; and in due time he was no longer the smallest boy in the valley, and the old men of the Council were gathered to their fathers, and the old age-old tradition was slowly replaced by a new age-old tradition. And Riss rarely lost a sheep—only when the wolves were too quick and help too slow, and that happened sometimes to anybody. And after while new young boys, through laziness or stupidity, came to him secretly to learn his trick for keeping track of his flock, and he freely taught them. And his way spread, since nothing succeeds like success. And when, at last, he died, the shepherds of the valley honored his name, giving him the posthumous title of Count, and erecting in his memory the finest and largest statue the valley had ever seen, made completely of sun-dried ram-turds.

For Riss Mattock had invented the art that has ever since borne his name. Even if he could not tell the sheep apart, he had memorized their names. Pointing to the sheep, and careful not to point to any again until he had pointed to all, he would recite the names, and if the pointing and the naming were finished at the same time then no sheep was missing. He had even composed a special Psalm to Help Remember:

> |: Juan, Doe, tickle my toe;
> Tray, Thor, what a bore;
> Vi, Chick, I feel sick;
> Sven, Ada; wolf's a raider;
> Nan, Jen; beyond my ken
> to go beyond; so start again. :|

4. We have, then, three examples of the creative process. Our hunter devised the sinew-backed bow. Beauty and the Beast developed (at least for themselves) innovative standards of physical attractiveness. Riss invented counting. The second account reminds us that an innovation need not be permanent to be important; indeed presumably no innovation lasts forevermore.

Throughout human evolution, man has been at once creative and conservative. The easiest way to do anything is ordinarily the way one has done it before, or has seen others do it. From time to time, circumstances preclude this mere repetition. If the doing is sufficiently important, one casts about, trial-and-error fashion, for another way of accomplishing the same purpose. Often no alternative way is found; the individual or community involved may even, as a consequence, become extinct. Sometimes a new way is found. Sometimes it turns out to be better than the old way. In retrospect, we call such successful changes of behavior "innovative" or "creative." The "survival of the fittest" is a tautology. Only those who survive are in position to proclaim themselves the fit.

Our folk culture is wise about all this, acknowledging the nature of creativity through many proverbs: "Make a virtue of necessity"; "Necessity [or Laziness] is the mother of invention"; "Yankee ingenuity"; and so on. Like all pat phrases, these are heard so often that we become deaf to them. They tinkle in our ears and cut inquiry short. They reflect our conservative streak by seeming to belittle the creator (most smart people tend to be a little surprised, perhaps a bit jealous, when someone else turns out to be clever too). They replace, instead of conveying, a vital half-truth, without which the search for the other half of the truth is not likely to be undertaken.

The attitude towards creativity of the more serious philosophical-religious tradition in the West is another matter. Early in the Christian era the Manichaeans, doubtless influenced by Zoroastrianism, taught that both God and the Devil are creative. This doctrine is sufficiently rich to be interesting, but by the time of Justinian it had been declared a heresy. The Church teaches that God alone is creative; the Devil can only imitate and deceive. The rejection of Manichaeism was a return to pure shamanism, since the official doctrine explains anything that actually happens, and thus explains nothing. Let a man create, and he is an instrument of the Lord; if he does not, that is God's inscrutable will. The monotheism of this terminology—for it is only that, not a theory—is Hebrew, but the ethics are Greek: if the creative individual is only a vessel, he has no grounds for hubris.[2]

Such major shifts as the Reformation and Counterreformation turned largely on other issues, leaving the official Christian teachings about creativity unchanged. Their flavor pervades nineteenth-century natural philosophy, but with such subtlety that it is perhaps almost indetectable except by a lapsed Unitarian (such as the writer). There are two aspects of this residual influence, of which the second is more important for our purposes than the first.

The first aspect is this. The scientist steers a perilous course between the Scylla of redundancy and the Charybdis of tautology. If the rejection of Manichaeism was a return to tautology, it was also a reduction of redundancy: an effort to get along positing as small as possible a number of independent factors. Just so, in the nineteenth century, caloric was

2. [∇ I now think Cauchemar had his argument here exactly backwards. Perhaps it depends on just how one interprets antique theological jargon. But it seems to me that the Manichaean doctrine had to be declared a heresy. It misconstrued the human tragedy as a melodrama, thus making all laughter hollow and turning all art to kitsch.]

thrown out and heat reduced to motion; the luminiferous aether was discarded when it proved to have no detectable properties; more recently, Einstein and certain of his successors have sought a generalized field theory; Hsu seeks to categorize all human cultures on the basis of certain major alternatively possible emphases in kinship behavior and their reflections and analogies in other social institutions. Science inherits Occam's Razor from the theologians.

The second aspect is this. The Newtonian and Hamiltonian mechanics which prevailed in physics until early in the present century proposed a deterministic clockworklike physical universe. Measure accurately six parameters for each particle of an isolated physical system, at a given point in time; one can then predict the state of the system at any later time and postdict its state at any earlier time. Now, a theory which implies the impossibility of its own formulation is obviously futile. If man, and his mind, are part of a clockwork universe, then there can be no creativity, for creativity requires free will, and free will and determinism are incompatible. But if the minds of men somehow stand outside the physical universe, as it were like isolated bits of Godstuff, there is no dilemma. Despite protestations to the contrary, most natural philosophers of the nineteenth century were at least cryptodualists—they had to be, if they were to have confidence both in their theories and in their power to theorize. In the German tradition, where everything had to be covered one way or another, it was inevitable that there would come to be both *Naturwissenchaft* and *Geisteswissenschaft*.

But physics has changed. Relativity and quantum theory propose a physical universe very different from that of Newton and Hamilton. It can be shown that *no physical system is determinate*. For, in order to be determinate, a physical system would have to be truly isolated from the rest of the universe, and would have to have no moving parts. If there are moving parts then there must be thermodynamic indeterminacy—random wear and tear, the effects of which are predictable only in a gross statistical way. And if the system is not isolated then there must be relativistic indeterminacy: the impingement of individually unforeseeable influences from outside, whose effects, again, are only statistically predictable. But the only physical system with no moving parts is an elementary particle (if, indeed, there is any such thing), which is not isolated; and the only system that is isolated is the whole physical universe, which contains moving parts. Q.E.D.

One might attempt to impeach this argument on the grounds that it rests on the assumption that observations are always made from a *place*: that is, from a limited neighborhood of the plenum. But it makes no sense to speak of observations made from nowhere, or from everywhere at once. Relativity, either Newtonian or Einsteinian, proposes the elimination of those factors that vary depending on the particular vantage point from which observations are made, but that is not at all the same thing. Some theologians will doubtless argue that God is omnipresent and omniscient (of which the second clearly requires the first), and that, to omniscience, the world must be determinate; this Judeo-Christian heresy is operational nonsense and can safely be ignored. We live in, and are part of, a physical universe in which causality is stochastic, not absolute. The past, of course, is determinate. That the future can sometimes be predicted is evidence for varying degrees of *stability* of different physical systems, not for predestination.

In such a world, creativity is possible and not mysterious. It is understandable without any (ultimately futile) resort to dualism. *Geisteswissenschaft* becomes, not a parallel to, but a part of, *Naturwissenschaft*.

Physics is not the only field that has changed. The major problem of psychology in the nineteenth century was: what are the lines of psychic causality along which a given human being is led to act and think in a certain way rather than in some other way? This question is not meaningful until we eliminate the epithet "psychic." But when psychology gives up the ghost, there isn't much left. The psychologists did not solve the problem. The answers have come from biology, with the discovery of genes, from anthropology, with the discovery of culture, and from linguistics, with the discovery of language. With these developments, which now date back at least a half century, psychology lost its raison d'être. But here again we see the power of human conservatism: academic psychology today is a walking corpse, lacking even enough good sense to die gracefully.[3]

5. Essentially, what we have said above amounts to asserting that *the physical universe is creative*. That sounds outlandish only because the juxtaposition of words is unfamiliar. But we can take it in small steps.

Absolute stability would imply determinacy. Indeterminacy goes with varying degrees of stability, which means also varying degrees of instability. Instability means noise. Without noise there can be no signal, for

---

3. Here I must file a demurrer. Though academic psychology has been in a state of chaos for a half century, Cauchemar overlooks the vital contributions of certain individuals and schools: surely Freud (not, true enough, an "academic" psychologist); also A. P. Weiss, an honest physicalist; doubtless others. My own top candidate for the intellectual scrapheap alongside alchemy and astrology would be not psychology but "political science," which has told us nothing of importance for at least a century and whose ossified intracultural point of view has worked incalculable harm in the world. —C.F.H.

signal and noise are the same sort of thing: the sorting out of the two by a particular receiver is a function of the design of the receiver. With noise, there can be signal, and signals can be noisy. That is, they can be received in a form different from that in which they were transmitted. Therefore error is possible. All creative acts are the result of error, though not all errors are creative. Any stable physical system is a *record*—that is, stored information. The information is about the event that made the record; but no record is ever complete. A signal is about the event that generated it; a signal is generated by rubbing two (or more) records together. An event is the rubbing together of two (or more) records. A signal is a record to a potential receiver whose world-line lies close and parallel to that of the signal. A record is a signal to a potential receiver with which it actually collides. There is no absolute difference between signals and records, except that a signal in the form of electromagnetic radiation, under relativity, cannot be a record to any possible transmitter or receiver.

Information is the inverse of entropy. Information is lost when entropy increases—which, by the second law of thermodynamics, it ultimately does in any sufficiently inclusive physical system. A loss of information is an *event*. Information is about events. Without the second law of thermodynamics, there would be no events, and therefore nothing for information to be about, and therefore no information. It follows that in order for information to exist, it is necessarily incomplete.

The storing of information, since it involves (or, indeed, consists of) a decrease in entropy, can be local (and temporary). In cosmology, matters of purely provincial import are intentionally ignored, that one may attempt to describe the gross geometry of the universe. Yet even in cosmological theory, only the very unpleasant (and probably incorrect) steady-state hypothesis does away altogether with macrocosmic events. All varieties of the Big Bang hypothesis posit a Big Bang, which—whatever may have preceded it (if anything)—was an event, and clearly a creative one.

6. Since the universe is creative (we can drop the epithet "physical" as otiose in the physicalist view), we have no right to be surprised that man, throughout his evolution, has been creative. Human creativity may be special in various ways, but we do not know what these ways are unless we first see what human creativity has in common with innovation in other contexts.

The various sorts of innovative changes possible in genes and gene pools are too familiar to require review. A mutation is a paradigmatic instance of the workings of noise: a stray bit of radiation replaces or eliminates a particular nucleotide in an RNA or DNA molecule, whereupon it performs differently from before. Most mutations, under most circumstances, are not creative (that is, the results are not viable). But some, under some circumstances, are. As we said, "all creative acts are the results of error [= noise], though not all errors are creative."

Ontogenetic and social adaptations in animal evolution show just the same properties. The behavior of the individual animal is purposive, because an organism, having feedback loops, is a teleological mechanism. So are most animal communities (otherwise we do not recognize them as "communities"). Adaptation of behavior to unusual circumstances is by trial and error, making do with whatever is available; evolutionists call this *opportunism*. It is reported that some decades ago the lions of parts of West Africa, facing new living circumstances because of the introduction of firearms, developed the custom of hunting in groups instead of individually. It would be nice to know whether this report is true or not; if it is, it is not surprising.

Romer gives two beautiful examples of the opportunism of evolution.[4] The fishlike ancestors of the land vertebrates did not grow strong fleshy fins "in order to" move around on the land instead of in the water. Some of the fish at the relevant epoch had relatively strong fleshy fins; others did not. The climate was such as to make for recurrent sudden recessions of the water level in inland and coastal streams and marshes. Those fish survived this climatic situation whose fins allowed them, when stranded, to *get back to the water*. When far later environmental developments of a very different sort made it useful to stay ashore more of the time, strong fins were at hand and could be (opportunistically) so used. The earliest prebirds did not develop wings in order to fly. More likely, they climbed trees to feed, under circumstances in which those whose forelimbs were more winglike were better able to flop and flutter (rather than climbing) safely back to the ground, their primary habitat. Leglike fins developed when they were advantageous for a *conservative* reason—to get back home to the water. Winglike forelimbs developed when they were advantageous for a *conservative* reason—to get back down to the ground. All this is in sharp contrast to the old teleological nonsense of "preadaptation."

Ascher and Hockett, in a forthcoming article, generalize this in what they call "Romer's Rule": *The initial survival value of an innovation is conservative, in that it makes possible the continuation of a traditional*

4. A. S. Romer, *The Vertebrate Story*. Chicago: University of Chicago Press, 1959.

way of life in the face of changed circumstances.[5] This has, perhaps, a certain erudite cuteheit, but really says nothing more than the homely aphorism we quoted earlier: Necessity is the mother of invention.

This much, then, human creativity shares with all innovative events.

7. But, as we asserted back in §4, the aphorisms reflect only a half-truth. The other half can also be expressed aphoristically: Fun is the father of invention.

I think the assignments of sex in the paired aphorisms is correct. Parthenogenesis is not unheard of, and probably many innovations, even in human history, have been instances of virgin birth; that the fun factor, unaided by necessity, would ever suffice seems unlikely.

By "fun" I mean *play*: trial-and-error behavior, always within certain rough constraints (that is, never really completely random), carried on not because there is a goal to be sought but because the activity itself is pleasurable. An inorganic physical system hardly seems capable of this. It requires an organism, with something approaching a nervous system so that something like "pleasure" can be a reality; furthermore, it requires organisms whose economy is such that the primary biological activities of feeding and reproducing do not fill all available time. There must be "play" in another (but related) sense: ranges of alternatives within which the actual choice makes little or no practical difference. We know that fun, thus delimited, is at least common to all land mammals. Probably it is more widespread than that, and older.

But fun is not a physical universal; and, if "necessity" also isn't, at least it is far more widespread than fun. The origin of fun was itself an evolutionary innovation, to which man, among others, is heir, brought about in a context of "necessities" at which we could only guess, and no doubt as opportunistic as all other evolutionary changes, eftsoons with remarkably important consequences for mammalian ways of life: the young can get valuable practice at certain adaptive behavioral patterns, in mocked-up circumstances in which temporary failure does not lead to instant extinction; adults, when sufficiently fetalized (as our species is), can play endless games of "let's pretend" and, in just the same way, build up a stock of possible responses to possible challenges a few of which in time actually materialize. The existence of the fun factor in turn leads to a new category of "necessity": the necessity of having fun. Thus, thank

---

5. Cauchemar is referring to the article later printed as "The Human Revolution," *Current Anthropology* 5.135–147 (1964).—C.F.H.

G——*ahem!*—thus we have, in the human way of life, the whole wonder-ful panoply of the arts, without which, frankly, life would not be much fun. And science is one of them.

(I admit that the last part of the above paragraph turns into tautology. It could be attacked by citing the old story of the man who didn't like cheese, and who was awfully glad he didn't like cheese because if he liked it he'd eat it and he hated the damned stuff. But the analog is itself a demonstra-tion of the fun factor.)

8. In my opinion, the above is all there is to be said about human creativity—except, obviously, for enormous numbers of details, which I shall leave to some German who is stuck with the ten-volume *Kurze Einleitung* complex.

There remains, however, the relatively immediate issue of the *nurtur-ing of creativity* in our own Western world. The habit of speaking of "creativity" rather than merely of excellence of craftsmanship seems to be a recent one, dating back perhaps a century and a half. Earlier on, excellence of craftsmanship was apparently enough. The whole modern inquiry into the nature of our universe, the nature of change, of innova-tion, of creativity, may be doing a disservice to the artisan, by placing in the forefront of his consciousness a factor that ought, at most, to dance at its edges. Johnny asked Grandpa one day at breakfast whether he slept with his beard under the covers or outside; the next morning Grandpa came downstairs with bleary eyes and a clean-shaven chin. We must believe that, in the long run, the Truth does not have such consequences; but we may have to take active steps to prevent them.

What I believe is the proper procedure runs counter to much modern educational theory and to the particular poetic genius of American adver-tising. Society needs all the brilliant people it can find. Our collective problems, in the complex modern world, constantly outstrip our collec-tive ability to tackle them. But undisciplined genius is a total waste. One cannot nurture a genius by urging him to be creative. One cannot really even identify a person as having unusual abilities unless he is, first of all, thoroughly trained in the specialized skills of a particular trade. The greatest rewards that most of us can hope to win require such grounding: the rewards of participation in a collective enterprise and of pride of artisanship—of being able to do competently and patiently something that only those with special training can do at all. In this setting, genius, to the extent that it is present, shows and is fruitful; in this setting it is its own reward. Without this setting, genius is autistically frittered away. Most

useful innovations are very small increments; most of the world's work is
done by . . .

In the tattered offprint Cauchemar gave me, the next sheet is missing.
Since the following pages contain nothing but bibliography, not much of
the text is lost to us. Still, it would be sort of nice to know what Cauchemar
had chosen for his peroration.—C.F.H.

H12. WHERE THE TONGUE SLIPS, THERE SLIP I

1958–1966. Reprinted from *To Honor Roman Jakobson* (The Hague; Mouton, 1967) 910–937, with the permission of Mouton and Company.

I remember how it was twenty-odd years ago in the then Division of Modern Languages at Cornell: at our staff luncheons we would mix business with shoptalk, crack wise, and catch one another in many a slip of the tongue, commenting in the approved popular pseudo-Freudian vein; then we would return to our offices and our diverse technical involvements, as though what we had just been doing had no bearing on linguistic theory or vice versa. (At least, that was the way it seemed to me; I really shouldn't speak for my colleagues.) Valid technical linguistics was marble-slab grammar!

The experiences that led to my change of view are outlined in the prefatory remarks to H6 (p. 107). Even while at the Center in Palo Alto I was beginning to register lapses more carefully; later I began writing them down. By 1958 or thereabouts, what with my long discussions with Drs. Pittenger and Danehy, I had assembled a talk on slips of the tongue, delivered to various audiences. It became clearer and clearer that post-Bloomfieldian atomic-morpheme two-stratum marble-slab grammar simply could not explain actual speech behavior; and, if it couldn't, it was defective. I issued a veiled warning to that effect at the end of "Linguistic Elements and their Relations" (1961a; written 1959–1960)—the very paper in which my own version of stratificational theory reached its fullest flower—and a broader hint at the end of "Grammar for the Hearer" (1960c).

But I offered no replacement for the old orientation until the present paper, which evolved slowly and with many interruptions from that talk of the late 1950s; and even this paper contains only a chrysalis of a "theory of speaking and hearing," which is what we need. Why did it take so long? Why couldn't I have left "Linguistic Elements and their Relations" unpublished and, instead, have polished this paper for earlier release?

The answer is threefold: inertia, computational linguistics, and Noam Chomsky. The older views involved some pretty toys that I couldn't discard without saying a fond farewell. I spent much time for two years on automatic language data processing before I realized that it was a game better left to others. And I had to examine Noam Chomsky's proposals with great care, as unappetizing as some of them struck me, to see what of value there might be in them. All three of these factors forced the preparation of "Language, Mathematics, and Linguistics" (1966b), a futile exercise in abstraction except for its chapter 4. My slow and painful discovery that, despite their remarkable popularity, there was not only not much of value in Chomsky's proposals but actually a good deal that was positively harmful, necessitated the writing of *The State of the Art* (1968a).

But I got back to this paper and its implications early enough to include something similar to the discussion in its §11 in the last chapter of the *The State of the Art,* and in my review of Lenneberg (1967e). There is a fuller but nontechnical treatment of language, in terms of the new orientation, in chapter 8 of *Man's Place in Nature* (1973a).

For this new appearance of this essay, I have deleted an introductory biblical quotation (James 3:6–10) and two allusions to it from the text.

0. The Problem and the Approach. At one point in his *Psychopathology of Everyday Life*, Sigmund Freud suggests that an understanding of the mechanisms involved in slips of the tongue may lead towards an elucidation of the "probable laws of formation of speech."[1] I propose here to take Freud's suggestion seriously. I am not aware that any linguist has yet done so, at least in the detailed way projected.[2]

There are two related aims. The linguistic tradition is richer now than it was in Freud's time. Thus, we may be in a position to offer a more searching interpretation of slips of the tongue, in some respects, than Freud did. Such an outcome would surely be of interest to our cousins in psychiatry. More important to us as linguists is that Freud's remarkable insights, properly supplemented and amplified, may tell us things about language that we have not known, and help us properly to evaluate the various incompatible theories and views of language design currently available.

We cannot hope to follow up the clues Freud has given us unless we are willing to do two things that are contrary to our usual professional custom.

(1) There is a difference between the generation of speech (or, as Freud's translator puts it, the "formation of speech") and the structure of sentences. Our customary angle of approach in descriptive linguistics has been in terms of the later. We have viewed sentences as stable wholes, and by comparing them have attempted to determine their content and organization. The structure of individual utterances thus revealed has been assumed to reflect, though perhaps only with great distortion, the abstract "set of habits," or "system," or "internalized grammar" (terminologies,

1. All references to this are via a paperback reprint (Mentor Book MD67, 6th printing 1958, New York, The New American Library) of A. A. Brill's translation and adaptation of the fourth German edition; the first German edition appeared in 1901.

2. Many studies, of course, may not have come to my attention. I do know of Rulon S. Wells, "Predicting Slips of the Tongue," *Yale Scientific Magazine* 26:3 (December 1951), 9 ff. Wells deals exclusively with the relative frequency (and, hence, relative probability) of slips of different sorts, as conditioned by phonological habits. Insofar as the results of my observations agree with his, his are incorporated into the present paper, especially into §1.

at least, differ) that constitutes the language. It is the language as a system or code or set of patterns ("langue"), rather than any particular utterance as a message ("parole"), that we have basically sought to characterize; observed sentences are simply a crucial part of the available evidence. But all of this, we have usually tacitly assumed, has little to do with the process by which a speaker builds an actual utterance.

However, it is also possible to think of a language as a system whose design is reflected not only by the utterances produced by its speakers but also by the process of production itself. To follow Freud's lead, we must be prepared to explore this possibility, even though it requires certain techniques of observation and interpretation at which none of us is particularly adept.

(2) The second and more radical requirement has to do with the difference between speech marred by blunders and what I shall simply call "smooth speech." Usual linguistic practice has ignored the problems connected with this difference by accepting, for further analytical examination, only "normalized" text from which slips of the tongue and the like have been deleted (sometimes by the informant, often enough by the analyst). In the field, at work on an undescribed language, there is justification for this: one's aim is to discover and describe the specificities of a particular language, rather than those phenomena and mechanisms that recur, seemingly, in most or all languages or speech communities. Besides, the fruitful exegesis of specific slips of the tongue requires rather far-reaching control of the particular language (and culture) in which they occur: this degree of control lies beyond that achieved in the average term of field work.

But a transfer of the usual field procedure, and of the attitude it implies, to our deeper investigation of more familiar languages, or to our search for the basic and universal features of language design, is not justified. The commonest view of speech defects and lapses, among linguists and laymen alike, from Freud's day to our own, has been that smooth speech reflects the internalized system (the language, "langue") more accurately, and that paralallies are pathologies external to the language, intrusions from some other realm or system, an annoyance to the users of a language because they disrupt communication and a bother to linguists because one must somehow work around and past them to get at what really counts. This was the view of Meringer and Mayer, criticized by Freud;[3] it is, with

---

3. R. Meringer and K. Mayer, *Versprechen und Verlesen* (Stuttgart: 1895); Freud also refers to W. Wundt.

considerable elaboration, Chomsky's view today.[4] Freud does not al-together reject it—after all, he classes slips of the tongue among the *pathologies* of everyday life—; nor should we, for there are specific instances in which a diagnosis of this sort is obviously correct. I once met a woman, a native speaker of English, whose speech contained brief silences where the rest of us have /s/. The etiology was known: she had learned to speak English as she heard it, but had a congenital hearing loss so that she *heard* silence where most of us hear /s/. The problem is, then: exactly what features of specific utterances (as historic events) are due to intrusive factors of this kind, and what features stem from the workings of the "language" itself? The solution is not given us by divine inspiration nor by intuition. It must be sought through hard analytical work on specific examples.

An initial example will show how lost we are, in confronting data of this sort, unless we modify our approach along the two lines described above. Here are two anecdotes. The first is true; the second is fictional but, I hope, realistic:

(1) A father, exasperated with his noisy children, said:

/⁴dòwnt + ⁴šél + sòw + lâwd¹#/   (E1)
Don't shell so loud!

(2) A wife was sitting in the kitchen, removing fresh peas from their pods and dropping the pods into a metal pail, while her husband was trying to carry on a telephone conversation. He called to her:

/⁴dòwnt + ⁴šél + sòw + lâwd¹#/   (E1′)
Don't shell so loud!

Each of these episodes involves an English utterance. The phonological structure of the utterances is given,[5] and is the same for both. We wish to determine and to describe, in a systematic way, everything else about the two utterances that might be relevant.

For obvious reasons, a linguistic theory that merely sets E1 aside is of no use to us. In much the same way, we must reject any doctrine that purports to preclude altogether the use of semantic criteria. If such a constraint were taken seriously, then grammatical analysis would have to

---

4. Or so I infer from Chomsky's publications. The point is discussed in greater detail in §11 below.

5. In the Trager-Smith phonemic notation. I am not convinced that the theory underlying this notation is correct in all detail, but regard the notation, at least, as vastly superior to any other so far proposed.

be based on a corpus of utterances in phonemic notation but free of glosses and annotations. In such a corpus, E1 and E1′ would not be distinguished.

The purer sort of item-and-arrangement (IA) theory holds that any sentence consists of an integral number of minimal elements (morphemes) in a hierarchically nested set of constructions. IA procedures would treat E1 and E1′ identically except for the element *shell* that appears (as a phonemic shape) in both. In E1′, this element is just a particular morpheme, belonging to such-and-such a form class. What about the *shell* of E1? To treat this, also, merely as a particular morpheme (not the same one as that of E1′) ignores all the special characteristics of E1 in its setting. Alternatively, we might regard it as a composite form: say, an element *sh-* that recurs in *shout*, plus an element *-ell* that recurs in *yell*. But then, of course, *shout* must be this *sh-* plus *-out*, and *yell* must be *y-* plus *-ell*. If someone happens to say / šáwm/ instead of *shout* or *scream*, then the *-out* already dissected from *shout* is in turn revealed as composite, the *-ou-* recurring in / šáwm/. The ultimate end of this process of proliferation and subdivision is to recognize as many morpheme-occurrences in any utterance as there are phoneme-occurrences, or more. In particular, the *shell* of E1′ will turn out to be composite too (a particular *sh-*, plus a particular *-e-*, plus a particular *-ll*, or something of the kind); the distinction between E1 and E1′ again becomes blurred.

Item-and-process (IP) models allow us to interpret some forms in a sentence as produced from other forms by the application of a specifiable operation, the domain of application of which may be ordered *n*-ads of underlying forms where $n \geqq 1$ (e.g., for $n = 1$, *boys* can be taken as underlying *boy* subjected to the operation "pluralization"; the *-s* does not have to be a form at all). As within the IA framework, E1 and E1′ will be treated identically except for *shell*. But IP allows us to treat the *shell* of E1 in a more realistic way. We may regard it as built from the underlying ordered pair of forms (*shout, yell*) by the application of a certain operation. Let this operation be *B*: then we can say that *B*(*shout, yell*) = *shell*. Similarly, *B*(*yard, lawn*) = *yawn*; *B*(*corn, beans*) = *keans*; *B*(*yell, shout*) = *yout*. Other dyadic operations of the "blending" sort would also have to be recognized, since the one we have illustrated would not act on (*pin down, get at*) to yield the attested phrase *pin at*, nor on (*Richard, William*) to yield Lewis Carroll's *Rilchiam*.[6] Our ultimate solution ought to incor-

6. In his preface to *The Hunting of the Snark*, Carroll undertakes to explain the "hard words" of the poem *Jabberwocky* as "portmanteaus" (= our "blends"), and gives *Rilchiam* as a further example. His exegesis is about as good as Freud's was a quarter of a century later; however, the invented blend *Rilchiam* seems about as improbable as any conceivable blend of *Richard* and *William*.

porate the desirable features of this treatment, but should at the same time eliminate what seems to be a defect: that this approach neglects the possible relevance of the phonemic identity of (ordinary) *shell* and of *shell* blended from *shout* and *yell.*

1. Blending; Phonology and Phonological Constraints. Let us forget, for the present, our various more or less formalized models of language design, and try to discern what factors may actually have led the father in the first episode to say what he did say.

The second word of E1 is a *blend* of the two words *shout* and *yell.* There is nothing new about this term used in a purely descriptive or classificatory sense: but we intend to go beyond that and make it part of a diagnosis. In the situation in which the speaker found himself, either of the two words *shout* and *yell* would have been appropriate. We may surmise that both words presented themselves to him as possibilities, but that their equal appropriateness precluded the rapid selection of one and rejection of the other, and that the pressure to keep speaking, rather than to delay in order to force a clear choice, led him to try to say both words at once.

Now the latter is impossible. A single individual's share of articulatory equipment is such that two words or phrases cannot be uttered simultaneously.[7] The attempt to do so can only result in the production of a string of sounds drawn partly from each of the two words or phrases. This actually uttered form is what we call a blend. A blend may occur as the result of conscious planning, in which case it may qualify as a witticism. Or it may be as much a surprise to the speaker who produces it as to anyone else; in this case it is a slip of the tongue, or lapse. Example E1 is known to have been a lapse, not a witticism.[8]

What we have so far said does not complete the explanation of E1, because *shell* is not the only possible blend of *shout* and *yell.* Other possibilities are /yáwt/, /yét/, /šáwl/, /šét/, and /yáwl/. We must do our best to account for the speaker's "choice" of the particular blend *shell* rather than any of these alternatives. If our evidence in the case is not sufficiently detailed for us to be absolutely sure of the answer, then we must not speak with absolute sureness; but we can still profit from making the best guess we can.

Of the six possible blends of *shout* and *yell* that we have listed above, two, /šél/ and /yáwt/, are apparently somewhat more probable than the

7. To this there is one exception, with which we shall deal in §8.
8. For the sake of impersonality, I prefer to keep anonymous the source of the majority of the lapses cited in this paper. I assure the reader, however, that when I supply unusually detailed information about the attendant circumstances, with no hedging, I speak with impeccable authority.

other four because of a feature of the phonetic habits of English. An English monosyllabic word seems to consist, in the first instance, of two immediate constituents: the consonantism (even if zero) at its beginning, and all that follows. Thus, *shout* is /š-/ and /-áwt/, rather than /šáw-/ and /-t/ or /š...t/ and /<áw>/. Similarly, *yell* is /y-/ and /-él/, not /yé-/ and /-l/ or /y...l/ and /<é>/.

Part of the evidence for this view of phonetic IC structure is, true enough, just the predominant tendencies in slips of the tongue: for example, a metathesis like /stǽnd+sòwn/ for *sandstone* seems somewhat commoner than one like /grǽs+rìyk/ for *grease rack*.[9] But the argument is not circular; there is other evidence. In English verse, rhyming monosyllables differ only as to initial consonantism: *June, moon, spoon, croon.* Alliterative assonance appears in various proverbs and riddles, reversing the convention of rhyme to involve words with the same initial consonantism: *"Let us flee," said the fly; "let us fly," said the flea; so they flew through a flaw in the flue.* In the juvenile secrecy-system known as Pig Latin, monosyllables are broken between initial consonantism and remainder for coding: /áwt+šèy/ for *shout*; /él+yèy/ for *yell*; /íg+pèy/ for *pig*; even, in some versions, /áwč+èy/ for *ouch*, showing zero initial consonantism treated as the first immediate constituent of the whole monosyllabic word.[10]

I propose that this IC structure of monosyllables is one of a multitude of features that, taken together, *constitute* what we ordinarily call the phonological system of English.

The phonological system of a language imposes a variety of constraints on what speakers of the language may say, by way of either smooth speech or lapses. The most general of these constraints is the one already mentioned: that two words or phrases cannot be uttered simultaneously. This constraint is inherent in the phonological system of every language. Otherwise, languages are highly varied and few cross-language generalizations are possible. In English, *cone* /kówn/ might be metathesized to /nówk/, or *corn* /kórn/ to /nórk/, but hardly *corn* to */rnók/ or *song* /sóŋ/ to */ŋós/, since English words just do not begin with the consonant combination /rn-/ nor with the single consonant /ŋ-/.[11] The habits of other

9. Mary Livingston pulled the second of these years ago on a Jack Benny radio program. The references to statistics, here and later, are to an informal count I myself made, in a sample that was as large as practicable but probably not large enough to satisfy a professional statistician. Yet I did do *some* counting—the judgments are not entirely impressionistic.

10. See Morris Halle, "Phonology in Generative Grammar," *Word* 18.54–72 (1962), for a brief discussion of Pig Latin from another angle. Halle should note the obvious audible difference between /íyts+trêy/, from *treats*, and /íyt+strêy/, from *street*.

11. Even here we have to do with relative probability, with no absolute barriers. One of

languages, and thus the constraints, are different: [rn-] occurs, for example, in Georgian, and [ŋ-] is very common.

However, phonological constraints are for the most part not absolute: they are made of rubber, not of steel. Thus it is not impossible for a blend of *shout* and *yell* to yield /yét/, /šáwl/, /šét/, or /yáwl/. Blending can yield a pronunciation with a phoneme (a simultaneous bundle of components) not present in either of the contributing forms: *bubbles* and *tough* yielding /bávɨlz/. Here the voicing of the /v/ is from the medial /b/ of *bubbles*, while its degree of aperture is from the final /f/ of *tough*. I have no doubt that blending can yield a pronunciation with constituent sounds that stand outside the "normal" phonological system of the language, as, by way of an invented example, *sugar sack* yielding [čúgɨr+sæ̀x] with the degree of aperture of the initial and final consonants interchanged. Observing instances of this sort is difficult: the hearer, we suppose, usually interprets the result as though it did not deviate, or else the speaker has gotten his speech organs so entangled that he backs up and starts over again. However, such deviant results are progressively rarer, hence progressively less probable. Since the actual blend in E1 was one of the two most probable, we may allow ourselves to limit further inquiry to the reasons behind the "choice" of *shell* rather than of the phonemically equally likely /yáwt/.

Since the blend *shell* begins with a piece drawn from *shout*, we might interpret the "choice" of *shell* rather than of /yáwt/ as signaling a slight imbalance between the speaker's tendency toward saying *shout* and his tendency toward saying *yell*, in favor of the former. Indeed, this is about as far as Freud's own diagnosis would carry us: he customarily assumes two tendencies, a stronger one that he calls the *disturbed tendency* and an interfering weaker one that he calls the *disturbing tendency*.[12] We cannot rule out this possibility, but we should not overlook an alternative or additional possibility: that the blend begins with the first part of *shout* and continues with the second part of *yell* just because this way of blending the two will yield the form *shell* rather than /yáwt/. The latter would be only a blend. The former is more than a blend: it is homophonous with an ordinary English word. Furthermore, this word is of apt, if marginal, connotations for the situation in which the blending occurred. The outer ear is shaped like a shell and is sometimes (poetically) called a *shell*. And it

---

my children, at one stage, regularly used the form /ŋówp/ for *comb*, metathesizing the manner, but not the position of articulation, of the initial and final consonants. Such instances are clear evidence for the objective reality of phonological components. Of course, a slip yielding an initial /ŋ/ would be much rarer in the speech of an adult speaker of English.

12. *Psychopathology of Everyday Life*, chap. 5, passim.

is the ears that are offended by the shrillness of children. Also, there are very noisy objects shot very noisily from guns, named by the word *shell*.

I suspect that certain readers will prefer to take their departure at this point. In wishing them bon voyage, I must warn all readers that in our discussion of subsequent examples I shall allow imagination to roam just as widely as it has in the preceding paragraph. There is little point in trying to learn anything about language from Freud's approach unless we are willing to do this. But it should be noted that our exposition of the causes of E1 is not presented as *true*, only as *plausible*. A factual exposition of everything involved in any single lapse (as a historic event) is impossible, since there is no way in which all relevant factors could have been recorded. But if we examine many such events, we see now clearer evidence for certain kinds of contributory factors, now clearer evidence for other kinds. There can be useful convergence in such a sequential examination only if we allow ourselves maximum freedom of guessing for each individual instance.

2. Editing. Describing his wife's unprecedented outdoor activity in trying to get the grounds around a new house to grow grass, a husband said:

She's so anxious to get a yawn?—yard in.   (E2)

Here the symbol "?" represents sharp glottal cutoff by the speaker, and the dash represents a slight pause. In subsequent examples, we shall supplement either orthography or phonemic notation, as convenient, by these symbols. E2 thus differs from E1 in that it includes relevant features of articulation that are not phonemic; such features have been called "paralinguistic."[13]

The speaker was conversing at the time in a casual way with people he did not know very well. *Yawn* is one of the two phonologically most likely blends of *yard* and *lawn*; the other is *lard*. As between *yard* and *lawn*, the latter really fits the overt context better: a yard (= British English *garden*) may have grass or not, but a grassless lawn is stretching things a bit. If E1 led us to suspect that the initial element of a blend points towards the more dominant of the two participating tendencies, then E2 should weaken our confidence in that notion. It seems more likely that the choice of the blend *yawn*, rather than *lard*, was due to the ordinary word of that shape: the

13. For a brief introductory survey, see George L. Trager, "Paralanguage: A First Approximation," *Studies in Linguistics* 13.1–12 (1958). For a fairly extended application, see Robert E. Pittenger, Charles F. Hockett, and John J. Danehy, *The First Five Minutes* (1960).

blend was a comment on the immediate situation, indicative of some minor degree of boredom on the speaker's part, or, perhaps more likely, of a fear on his part that his interlocutors would be bored by what he was saying.

In addition to blending, this example shows us a second phenomenon of importance: overt correction or *editing*. The uttering of *yawn* was a lapse, not a witticism. The speaker heard the lapse as it occurred, and immediately—indeed, hastily—offered a correction. The intention was that *yawn* be erased, as though it had never been uttered, and *yard* substituted. There are many reasons why we can validly speak of intention here. Suppose the speaker had been writing a letter. He would then have corrected the error by erasing *yawn*, or by lining it out so that it could not be deciphered, or even by beginning over again on a clean sheet of paper: and then the recipient of the letter would not know what error had been made, and might not even know that one had occurred.

In speaking, however, erasure is a physical impossibility, and its seeming social equivalent is only a polite convention that usually works only superficially. Nevertheless, all of us do try to cover up some of our lapses. In E2, the speaker was in such haste to cover up that the proffered replacement was the wrong one: *yard*, which does not literally make sense in the sentence, rather than *lawn*, which would have. Thus, we have two more things to account for if we can: the haste, and the choice of replacement.

The haste may have been due to the speaker's desire to hide the lapse before his interlocutors could interpret it, as we have above, as a somewhat derogatory comment on the conversational context. In order to entertain this theory, we must assume that the speaker himself registered (surely out of awareness) the possibility of this interpretation as he heard his lapse.

As to the choice of replacement, we may suspect that concern with the more superficial implications of the lapse—including some chagrin at having produced a lapse at all—lowered the threshold of any running censorship against double entendre of other sorts in the presence of a mixed audience of casual acquaintances. The sentence with *yawn* makes an obvious sexual allusion. If *yawn* is hastily replaced by *yard*, that allusion, far from being annulled, is reinforced. The sexual allusion may also have been in part responsible for the haste with which the correction was offered. If so, then there could hardly be a more appropriate train of events to which to apply the tired cliché "out of the frying pan into the fire."

Having noted the sexual allusion in the sentence as actually uttered, we must recognize that either unblended *lawn* or the alternative blend *lard* could also be twisted, with little difficulty, toward such an allusion. However, granting such potentialities—sexual allusions can be read into practically anything if we want to—let us note that in general it requires some concatenation of signals pointing more or less in the same direction to render an interpretation realistic. Had the speaker's utterance been smooth, *She's so anxious to get a lawn in* (or with *yard* instead of *lawn*), the congruence with the overt topic of discussion would probably have masked any such overtones pretty effectively. Had *lard* been involved in the lapse, the effect might well have been in part that which we have described, except that the overtones of commentary on the immediate social situation would have been missing.

3. Counterblends. Discussing the acquisition of something that would generally be regarded as a luxury, a speaker said:

We weren't sure we could avord?—affoid it.   (E3)
(/... əvórd ... əfóyd .../)

Avord was a lapse; a blend of *avoid* and *afford*. Either of the latter would have fit the sentence, though with directly opposite meanings, since if something cannot be avoided it is presumably done, while if something cannot be afforded it is presumably not done. However, the sentence specifies uncertainty, so that the one word would have been about as appropriate as the other. The speaker was clearly both boasting and apologizing. We might also guess that he was wondering whether he could afford to speak in this particular way to his audience, and also whether he could avoid doing so.

In any case, some of the immediate technical details are clear. The speaker heard his blending lapse, cut it off, and then offered a replacement (as in E2). But the replacement was neither of the original target words: instead, it was the other phonologically most likely blend of *avoid* and *afford*. The original blend, that is, was followed by a compensating *counterblend*. We infer that the speaker's tendency to say *both* target words, each with its array of implications, was overpoweringly strong.

The role of phonological patterning in E3 deserves special mention. As the transcription shows, *afford* and *avoid* have highly similar phonemic shapes (for this speaker): they differ only in /f/ versus /v/ (that is, only as to voicelessness versus voicing at this point), and as to /r/ versus /y/ after the vowel. This similarity can be understood by pointing out that, under conditions of a relatively small amount of ambient noise, either word could be misheard as the other. This degree of similarity in sound is much greater than that between *shout* and *yell*, or *lawn* and *yard*. When two words are not only this similar in sound but also akin in meaning, then we must assume that *any* occurrence of either may carry associative reverberations of the other.[14] The vocabulary of a language involves a vast and intricate tracery of such secondary associations among words: this is the stuff of which poetry and advertising are woven. A blend of *avoid* and *afford* is therefore an underscoring of an associative tie that is reasonably strong to begin with.

4. Assimilations and Haplologies; Reading Aloud. A TV master of ceremonies introduced a commercial as follows:

The question is, how can you tell one sil?—filter cigarette   (E4)
from another these days?

Here *sil-* is only the beginning of a blend. If it had been completed, one would expect *silter*, from *filter* and *cigarette*. But the speaker quickly heard what he was doing and made a correction. The cover-up was extremely smooth, but I suspect that the lapse was nevertheless registered, at least out of awareness, by many viewers.

Presumably the announcer was reading his lines from a teleprompter. We must therefore consider what is involved in reading aloud. When a child is first learning to read, he examines each written word in succession and pronounces it before going on to the next. The result is a highly artificial kind of speech, in which the successive words are not tied together into groups by variations of stress, by intonation, and by junctures, as are the successive words of ordinary talking. A written text can be regarded as a set of instructions telling a reader what to say (aloud or silently as the case may be). But the instructions are incomplete. There are no special marks to tell him how to distribute stresses, and only skimpy indications of intonation. The adult who is effective at reading aloud makes an appropriate selection of stresses and intonations to fit the

14. See Charles F. Hockett, *A Course in Modern Linguistics* (1958), chaps. 35 and 63, and the references cited; there is, of course, a vast literature on this subject, including stimulating contributions from Jakobson. I remember Jakobson discussing the *poetic* function of language—in a properly broad sense of "poetic": the specific denotations and connotations of a particular actual sentence, as over against the underlying patterns and regularities with which we are usually concerned. As a trivial example, consider *Peter Piper picked a peck of pickled peppers*. The recurrent /p/'s in this catchphrase are not a "morpheme" of any sort; yet a paraphrase or translation which ignores them (*Pierre le joueur de musette a cueilli une livre de poivrons marinés*) totally misses the point of the original. No theory of language that conceives of sentences as composed (at any level, shallow or "deep") of an arrangement of an integral number of occurrences of elementary units, and nothing more, can possibly provide for such experimental realities as are afforded by even this trite tongue-twister.

succession of words in their particular context. For him to do this, his eyes often have to scan ahead of the point which has been reached by his speech organs, since the proper stress and intonation for a given word often depends on what comes later. The eyes, and the "mind's ear," as it were, lead the speech organs.

What has just been said is not a guess, but necessarily true. A simple example will prove it. Suppose a written sentence begins

After John had started the car . . .   (E5)

If the continuation is

. . . Mary jumped in.   (E6)

then *car* will be read with primary stress and a following terminal contour (normally /|||/, conceivably /|/). But if the continuation is

. . . pulled up to the curb.   (E7)

then the terminal contour will be placed after *started*. Thus the stress and intonation of E5 depends on what follows; therefore the reader must know what follows before he can properly deliver the initial part of the sentence. A written comma after *car* if the continuation is E6, after *started* if it is E7, would change the situation; but commas are often omitted.

Reading aloud is a complicated task, requiring precise but variable timing. Only the slightest disruption is needed to introduce an error—here definable quite simply as a deviation from the written text. Anyone who has read aloud (say, to children) can vouch for the high incidence of such errors.

A common type of error in this setting is wrong phrasing, due to a failure to scan ahead properly. Thus, one might read the printed sequence E5-E6 as:

²Àfter Jôhn had ²stárted²|| ²the câr ³Máry jûmped în¹#   (E8)

—which makes no sense. Or the error might be detected almost anywhere after the wrongly placed /|||/, and a correction made.

Again, a moment's inattention may lead the reader to supply words on his own, on the basis of what he has read so far, more or less deviant from those that are printed:

Those of your advisors who wished to throw us into the Garden   (E9)
of Clinging Vines must twine?—must step within this circle of
light.

where the printed version lacks the first *must* and the *twine*. The reader's attention was caught by the phrase *Clinging Vines* as a name for some-thing that two pages earlier had been called *Twining Vines*. This also shows us the source of the supplied word *twine*.

Again, a bit of what the eyes have scanned may be omitted from delivery:

(printed:) aroused her from her sleep (E10)
(read:)   aroused her from sleep

(printed:) listened to Dorothy's story with attention (E11)
(read:)   listened to Dory?—to Dorothy's story with attention

(printed:) looked at one another in wonder (E12)
(read:)   looked at wonder?—at one another in wonder

In E10 there was no overt editing, since the reader recognized that there was no significant difference in meaning between the printed version and what he had actually said. E11 and E12, both with corrections, attest to a phenomenon that is apparently extremely common in such omissions: the part omitted and the next part begin phonemically in the same way. Thus *D(orothy's st)ory* or *Do(rothy's sto)ry*; (*one another in*) *wonder*. Presum-ably the eyes are just scanning the second occurrence of the recurrent phonemic shape (that is, of spellings that require that phonemic shape) as the speech organs are delivering the first occurrence. The result, of course, is what is ordinarily called *haplology*.

In a fourth type of lapse in reading aloud, the word that the eyes are scanning at a given moment is blended with the word that is scheduled for pronunciation at that moment:

(printed:) added a sort of glue to his soapsuds, which made his (E13)
            bubbles tough
(read:)   . . . buvvles tough

Sturtevant's example[15] of a distant assimilation, *the illoptical illusion*, may have arisen in the same way if it happened during reading (this we are not told).

In still a fifth type, one may suddenly wonder whether a word already scanned and read aloud was properly delivered, and in checking this (perhaps with the eyes, perhaps only in memory) the next word due for delivery may be blended with the one being checked:

(printed:) they will soon crush you and devour your bodies (E14)
(read:)   . . . devour your bardies

15. Edgar H. Sturtevant, *An Introduction to Linguistic Science* (1947), p. 86.

Here /bárdiyz/ for /bádiyz/ has an intrusive postvocalic /r/ from *devour*. This is the other type of lapse that Sturtevant classes as a distant assimilation. A rough count in available lists of attested lapses suggests that this type may be the rarest, in either reading or free speaking; but possibly it is merely the hardest type to observe and record.

We can now return to E4 for further explication. The announcer's eyes, we assume, were scanning written *cigarette* as he came to the point of uttering *filter*, and the beginning of *cigarette* was routed through to his articulatory apparatus too quickly, so that he said *sil-* before he could readjust. The lapse was thus of the type illustrated above by E13. However, we must still ask why the disruption and the lapse should have occurred just as they did. Although we can only guess, it seems reasonable to suppose that *sil-*, homophonous with the beginning of *silly*, was an expression of the TV performer's private attitude towards the commercials in which he is obliged to participate.

We saw in our discussion of E3 that overt editing is not always "successful": *affoid*, supplied to replace *avord*, was another lapse. One recalls an example of the same sort of persistence of error, on a larger time-scale, supplied (and perhaps invented) by Joan Rivière in her translation of Freud's *General Introduction to Psychoanalysis*:[16] A typographical error made a war-correspondent's account of an army general appear as *this battle-scared veteran*. The apology and "correction" the next day changed it to *the bottle-scarred veteran*.

From E4 we learn something else about overt editing. The presence and exact timing of overt editing may play an essential part in transmitting additional information, particularly of the sort not consciously intended for transmission by the speaker. In a sense, the correction of a lapse can constitute a "metalapse." If our TV performer had ignored his slip, simply saying *one silter cigarette from another*, there would have been no discernible hint at *silly*. There is a good chance that few would have observed the error at all. For /s-/ and /f-/ are acoustically similar; the relatively low fidelity of the audio circuits in most TV receivers diminishes the difference even more; and the audience would have done the rest, since one hears largely what one expects to hear. Or if the performer had delayed his correction a bit longer, saying *one silter?—filter cigarette from another*, the slip, though more noticeable, would hardly have suggested a hidden comment *silly*. These, however, would have been different events, not the one that actually occurred.

16. My copy is a paperback reprint (Permabooks M-5001, 6th printing 1957), of Rivière's authorized translation of the revised German edition; the first German edition appeared in 1916.

Reading aloud is superficially very different from extemporaneous monolog or free conversation. Yet the sorts of lapses that occur are very similar, if not identical. This suggests that ordinary speech may, at least at times, be more like reading aloud than we have thought: as though the speaker first constructed a "text" somewhere inside himself and then read it off, sometimes inaccurately.

5. Metatheses. A common—one might also say popular—type of lapse is one known technically as the *distant metathesis*, colloquially as a *Spoonerism* (from the Rev. A. W. Spooner of Oxford, famous for such slips).[17] All distant metatheses belong together in this respect: that what is actually said differs from what is "intended" by an interchange of two nonadjacent parts: *beery wenches* for *weary benches*, with the nonadjacent /w-/ and /b-/ interchanged; *tons of soil* for *sons of toil*; *half-warmed fish* for *half-formed wish*. But the underlying mechanisms require us to distinguish two subtypes: the *double-blend* metathesis and the *single-blend* metathesis.

I have no example of the first type for which the attendant circumstances were adequately recorded, so that our analysis must be confined to relatively obvious factors. Consider:

(intended:) I feel so foolish   (E15)
(spoken:)   I fool so feelish

This is like E3 in that it involves a blend followed by a compensating counterblend. But it also differs essentially from E3. In E3, the first blend is of two words either of which would be suitable in the setting, and the following counterblend is another blend of the same two words. The sentence would not make sense with *both* words, one after the other. In E15, on the other hand, the first blend is of the anticipatory kind illustrated in E13: a blend between a word due for pronunciation now and one due to be spoken a moment later; and the following compensating counterblend is of the type illustrated in E14: between a word due for pronunciation now and one already spoken a moment earlier. The blend *fool* is intended *feel* "contaminated" by *foolish*; the blend *feelish* is intended *foolish* "contaminated" by preceding *feel* (even though *feel* did not in fact, in the actually spoken form, precede). Both of the "target" words involved actually belong: if the forms are remetathesized, without any deletion, the result is smooth and normal. There is also a key difference in the deliveries of E3 and E15. After the first blend of E3, the speaker cuts his articulation

17. Sturtevant, op. cit., p. 37.

off sharply and pauses before continuing. There is no such interruption in E15. A proffered "correction" might follow the whole metathesis: *I fool so feelish?—(I mean I) feel so foolish.*

Apart from any deep "Freudian" motivations behind a lapse of this sort, one inevitably thinks of this: by following the original anticipatory blend by a compensating retrogressive blend, at least all the phonemic ingredients of the intended phrase have been uttered, even if in a distorted order. One reason to suspect the functioning of this factor is that in some instances we know that the second part of a distant metathesis is *consciously* planned and produced by the speaker after he has heard himself "accidentally" produce the first part. That is, the first blend is a lapse, the second a witticism. Here is an instance: the pause denoted by the dash was longer in this episode than in most earlier examples:

(intended:) according to Smith and Trager   (E16)
(spoken:)   according to Smayth?—and Trigger

During the pause, the speaker decided that it would be more fun to carry the lapse through as a metathesis than to make the obvious correction. Beyond this, it is clear that the production of distant metatheses is in our culture a sort of game: in a poorer version, *I can't be under the alfluence of incohol, I've only had tee martoonis*; more elegantly, in that the metathesized phrase is itself meaningful and apt, *Brittania waives the rules*; *Time wounds all heels*; *A willful group of little men*; a newspaper headline about a woman who foiled a purse-snatcher: *She conks to stupor*; name of a syndicated newspaper column: *The Sighs of Bridge*; a certain high-level diplomat described as wielding *a velvet hand in an iron glove*; name of a brand of sun-tan oil: *Tanfastic*; slogan: *Contraception is a sin, as any See can plainly fool.* Once one has heard both a common phrase and its metathesis, particularly if the latter is also obviously meaningful (like *beery wenches* for *weary benches*) and sharply different in connotation, one may have to take special care to avoid using the metathesized form rather than the original—or, indeed, when one wishes to quote the metathesized form, not to slip and use the original instead. Linguists speaking in public live in dread of improperly metathesizing *stress and pitch*.

A double-blend metathesis does not necessarily involve the distortion of any constituent words, since whole words may be interchanged. In addition to the examples of this in the preceding paragraph, we may cite:

We'll try to get it done without too much rubber pipe or lead (E17) hose.

On the other hand, the form involved need not be longer than a single word: *Tanfastic*, cited above, or the case of a TV interviewer talking with a woman missionary, who glanced at his notes and said:

Then what mativoted?—what motivated you to go to Spain?

(E17 *bis*)

When the woman hesitated, the interviewer continued, incidentally explaining his lapse to us: *Your husband had something to do with it, didn't he?*

A single-blend metathesis involves the confusion of two phrases which are only slightly different in meaning and which are composed of the same words in opposite orders—most often, probably, a phrase of the form *X and Y* and one of the form *Y and X*. Example E16, or something very much like it, might have come about as a single-blend metathesis. Anyone acquainted with the work of Trager and with that of Smith is familiar with two phrases: *Trager and Smith* and *Smith and Trager*. On the point of referring to these two collaborators, one might fail to choose cleanly between the two orderings of the names, and say *Smayth and Trigger* (or *Trith and Smayger*, or the like), not as one blend followed by another but as a single blend of the two whole phrases. We can often know that a metathesis must be of the double-blend type: example E15 must be, since the "target" phrase is not one of a pair of the sort required for a single-blend metathesis. On the other hand, we can rarely be certain that a metathesis is of the single-blend type. We gave E16 as an example of the double-blend type, but that is far from certain. The pause after *Smayth*, and the completion of the metathesized phrase as a witticism, are not decisive either way: the speaker may have been headed towards a single-blend metathesis, which he decided, after the pause, to carry through with, or he may simply have produced a blend which he decided to follow by the appropriate counterblend.

Freud gives the example *the Freuer-Breudian method*, uttered by someone perhaps equally familiar with the phrases *Freud and Breuer* and *Breuer and Freud*. He infers that the person guilty of the lapse was probably not favorably impressed by psychoanalysis.

A metathesis, probably of the single-blend type, occurring as a lapse, initiated the following sequence, said as the speaker was heading his car east over the San Francisco Bay Bridge:

This is how we go to Berkland and Oakeley?—Erkland and (E18) Boakeley?—no, Boakland and Erkeley?—darn it! Oakland and Berkeley!

Note the progression. The original target is *Oakland and Berkeley*, or the reverse. In the first try, the entire first syllables are interchanged. In the second try, the initial consonants of the first try are interchanged. In the third try, the entire first syllables of the second try are interchanged. In the fourth try, the initial consonants of the third try are interchanged, resulting in the proper form. However, after the initial lapse, the speaker became dimly aware of playing the permutations for effect, so that the episode could be described as a half-witticism.

But E18 is our first example of another very important phenomenon: some of the words actually spoken are comments on the rest. There is a standard typographical convention to indicate that a word or phrase is being mentioned rather than used; we put it in single quotes:

The word 'eradicate' is a verb.

In such a sentence, the words outside the quotation marks are about the word enclosed in them. Since what we have in E18 is the reverse of this, let us use the opposite typographical device, enclosing the inserted comments between quotation marks that curve the opposite way:

This how we go to Berkland and Oakeley?—Erkland and (E18′)
Boakeley?—'no,‘ Boakland and Erkeley?—'darn it!‘ Oakland
and Berkeley!

The words that we have enclosed in these reversed quotation marks (call them "dequotation marks") are part of the apparatus of overt editing. Conversational speech is full of this, and writers of fiction imitate it accurately; here is an example from fiction, in which I have merely modified the typography to use our new convention:

"Do gangsters marry their molls? 'Or is it‘ frails?"

Dequotation, like quotation, occurs in "smooth" speech as well as rough, and has found its way into logical and mathematical discourse—where its presence has unfortunately been hidden by the lack of any conventional punctuation. When a mathematician writes

$$x_1, x_2, \ldots$$

(or something of this sort), the three dots are an *etcetera symbol*: instructions to the reader to go on inventing similar items as long as he likes. Now, clearly, this etcetera symbol is a comment on what surrounds it, and, given our typographical convention, ought to be enclosed in dequotation marks:

$$x_1, x_2, ' \ldots \, ‘$$

This, given the conventional understandings shared by mathematicians, is now a *grammar-generating sentence* (in contrast to Chomsky's would-be "sentence-generating grammars"). All mathematical discussion of infinite sets, and much of the mathematical treatment of finite sets, turns on the appropriate manipulation of such sentences; logicians have encountered various dilemmas and anomalies that might disappear if dequotation were regularly marked.

6. Complex Examples. In the preceding sections we have seen how a wide variety of lapses, traditionally classed under a number of rubrics (assimilation, haplology, metathesis, etc.), can be handled in terms of two basic mechanisms: blending and editing. Here we shall examine two blunders too complicated to fall simply into any of the traditional classes, but still susceptible to analysis in terms of the same two basic mechanisms.

I'm going to buy a new broof?—broof keese today.   (E19)

Here the initial lapse is the first *broof*: a blend of intended *brief* and the preceding word *new* (/núw/, not /nyúw/, in this speaker's dialect). The speaker heard the lapse, cut off, and hesitated. Then he decided (more or less as in E16) not to correct, but to carry on what had begun, and to metathesize *brief case*. Of course, this decision was based on a faulty diagnosis of what he had already uttered, and the intent had to fail. The appropriate metathesis would be *brayf keese*. Instead of this, *broof keese* repeats the *broof* for which we have already accounted, and then adds *keese* as a parallel blend of intended *case* with the undistorted form of the preceding word. That is, just as *broof* was *brief* with the vowel of *new*, so *keese* was *case* with the vowel of *brief*.

This is not the whole story. The sequence /-uw- ... -iy-/ in *broof keese* is familiar from a very small set of commonplace nouns that have /-uw-/ in the singular and /-iy-/ in the plural: *tooth : teeth*; *goose : geese*. Also, *keese* sounds like *geese* except at the beginning, where the two differ only as to voicing. The speaker was acknowledging that in some respect—perhaps in his indulgence in rather silly word-play—he was making a goose of himself.

I drove down to the Brome Couty?—Broome Couty   (E20)
Airpoint?—(slower) Broome County Airport.

Here *Brome* was the wrong word: the speaker had known a man named *Brome* who took a job in the county named *Broome*, and his confusion of the two words had been persistent. In his instant concern with whether he had spoken the right name, he produced next what we may call an *antiblend* (ordinarily called a *dissimilation*): instead of replacing something in the target word *county* by something in another relevant word (here the immediately preceding one), something that is actually present in both the target word and the interfering word—the postvocalic nasal continuant—is deleted, yielding *couty*. Such an antiblend is presumably due to overcompensation in trying to avoid a blend. After *couty* the speaker broke off and tried a correction, properly replacing *Brome* by *Broome* but repeating the distorted *couty*. Noting that the /n/ had again been left out of this word, he sticks it into the next. The replacement of the /or/ of *port* by /oy/, before the intrusive /n/, is obscure save that the prejunctural cluster /-rnt/ does not occur in this speaker's dialect, and that the resulting *point* is homophonous with an actual word—and just such factors may be those involved in all cases of what is traditionally classed as *contamination*. Finally, with a longer pause and with more deliberate articulation, a complete correction is appended.

7. Malapropisms, Bright Sayings, and Trouble with Personal Names. There are a number of phenomena not usually classed as lapses that show a significant kinship thereto.

At a rather formal preliminary hearing, the Army officer in charge said:

We should be reminisce in our duty if we did not investigate.   (E21)

Here *reminisce in our duty* is a blend of the cliché *remiss in our duty* and the word *reminisce*: the former predominates, as is shown by the grammatical inappropriateness of the context for the word *reminisce*. If this were spoken by someone thoroughly familiar with both the phrase and the word, we should class it either as a lapse or as a witticism. However, in this instance observers were able to infer from the speaker's other speech and behavior that neither the phrase nor the word was part of his everyday active vocabulary. This leads to the classification of the event as a *malapropism* rather than as an ordinary lapse: a malapropism is a ridiculous misuse of a word, in place of one it resembles in sound, especially when the speaker is seeking a more elevated or technical style than is his wont and the blunder destroys the intended effect. The incongruity is heightened if the speaker himself gives no sign of awareness of the blunder—and this speaker did not.

The key difference lies in the speaker's degree of familiarity with the vocabulary he is using. If we unintentionally blend familiar expressions, we produce an ordinary lapse; if we unintentionally blend unfamiliar expressions, we may produce the special kind of lapse that is also a malapropism.

There is a third possibility. We may, with conscious intent, use an expression in just the form in which we learned it, and yet turn out to be wrong (as measured in terms of prevalent usage). Perhaps the speaker of E21, in his previous history, was first exposed to *reminisce* and later to *remiss in one's duty*; and perhaps, in the very process of adding the latter to his vocabulary, he blended it with *reminisce*. If so, then any occasion appropriate for the phrase *remiss in one's duty* would elicit from this speaker, not that phrase, but rather the phrase *reminisce in one's duty*— not as a lapse of the moment but as the presumably appropriate form. We should still call the usage a malapropism, of course: it turns out that some malapropisms are lapses and some are not, while some lapses are malapropisms and some are not.

In the moment-to-moment generation of speech, a correct recall of an incorrectly learned expression is obviously a different mechanism from the blurred or blended recall and use of correctly learned expressions. Let us call this new mechanism *idiolectal divergence*: the speaker is speaking in full accord with his own linguistic repertory, but on the particular point his idiolect differs from general usage. If blending is involved in idiolectal divergence (as perhaps it often is), it is a blending that occurred somewhere in the speaker's past history, not one occurring now.

We cannot always know which mechanism is responsible for a particular blunder, and perhaps in some cases both mechanisms play a part. Thus, a young woman who intended to express how hungry she was once said, in my presence: *I'm simply ravishing* (for *ravenous*). The confusion of the two words was a standing one, not an innovation of the moment. At the same time, even if she had only rarely had occasion to use either word, her familiarity with both was sufficient that we could properly draw inferences, from the blunder, as to her emotional state at the moment of speaking. Such inferences would not be valid in the case of pure idiolectal divergence, any more than we could accuse someone of obscenity if a word he used happened to sound like an obscene word in a language known to us but not to him.

Since anything that occurs in one person's speech can spread into more general usage, what begins as an idiolectal divergence due to noisy learning can cease to be a potential malapropism and become a new "standard" expression, often in competition with the older one of which it is a distortion. American English *Here we go gathering nuts in May* probably stems in this way from British *Here we go gathering nuts and may*: the plant-name *may* is generally unfamiliar in the United States. *Cut-and-dried* methods are very different from *cut-and-try* methods; I learned the former first, but suspect that it is a distortion of the latter. One speaks of instances of something being *few and far between*; I once heard a politician, in a TV address, say *far and few between*, which may have been a lapse but may also be a competing "standard" form with the sort of origin we have just described.

Malapropisms from idiolectal divergence show an unexpected kinship with two other phenomena: "bright sayings" of children, and certain misapplications of personal names (or of place names, as in E20).

All parents know that what a child says must stem from the child's experiences, and that that experience is limited in comparison with their own. When a remark from a child reveals a sharp idiolectal divergence, parents think it cute rather than ludicrous, and if (within their adult frame of reference) it is in some way particularly apropos they call it a "bright saying." The child is thus rewarded for linguistic experimentation; but typically the mentors of the child also try in some way to correct the divergence, so as to bring the child's linguistic habits more in line with those of adults. Yet some divergences may go uncorrected for years. The older the individual grows, the rarer become the circumstances in which it is culturally appropriate for anyone else to correct his speech. If that which during childhood would be merely a childish error, perhaps even a "bright saying," survives to adulthood, it is then a malapropism that one's friends are too kind or too embarrassed to mention. Sometimes a malapropism stemming from idiolectal divergence is mistakenly interpreted as a slip of the tongue or a witticism, and a correction is offered; the sequel is usually agonizing.

Part of the new linguistic material to which one is exposed day after day throughout life in a complex society[18] consists of the names of new acquaintances. Sometimes the name one must learn is one never encountered before—say, when one meets for the first time a Chinese named *Eng*. But even when the name is itself familiar—say, *Smith* or *Bill*—an addition to one's *language* habits is required. In part, this typical situation can be compared to that which pertains when one first learns of a *frog* in a railroad track, having previously known only of a *frog* in a swamp or of a *frog* in one's throat. In either case, the phonemic shape is familiar (*frog*; *Bill*) while the semantics are such that former uses of the word are of little

---

18. I do not believe we have any reports on the forgetting of personal names—or, indeed, on most of the kinds of phenomena we are here discussing—from small face-to-face communities in which everyone knows everyone else personally. Such information would be enormously valuable.

or no help in acquiring the new use. In another respect, this comparison breaks down, because of a unique property of arbitrariness about personal names: all the individual occurrences of frogs in railroad tracks, to which the word *frog* can apply, have obvious features in common not shared by anything to which the word does not apply; but there is no necessary uniquely shared feature about all the people one knows whose names are *Bill*, except, extrinsically, just the sharing of that name. When one learns a new ordinary word (or a new range of use of one already familiar), one has acquired a suitable label for any of an indefinitely large class of items or events. When one learns the name of a new acquaintance, one has acquired the proper label only for a single individual.[19]

In addition to this special property of personal names, it is a fact that the name of a person one has just met is, and for a while remains, a relatively rare item in one's vocabulary. This is why the forgetting or mixing-up of personal names is akin to malapropisms, rather than to lapses involving thoroughly familiar ordinary words and phrases.

8. Puns. All the lapses we have chosen as examples involve, in one way or another, the mechanism of blending. But not every obvious blend is a lapse: some are produced "on purpose" rather than as "accidents." Whether a *pun* is a lapse or not depends on the same thing. For the moment, let us set aside any consideration of the planning of speech in or out of awareness, and show the relationship between blending and punning.

A blend of words or phrases that have little phonemic similarity does not resemble a pun at all. Thus, in E1, *shell* in its context is reminiscent of *shout* and of *yell*, but no one would call it a pun.

A blend of words or phrases that are similar, but not identical, in phonemic shape is indistinguishable from an inexact pun. If, in the situation in which E3 was spoken, the speaker had merely said *We weren't sure we could avord it*, we should have an inexact pun. The judgment of inexactness is rendered because in order to make *afford* sound more like *avoid* than it normally does (or vice versa) the phonemic shape must be distorted. Here is another example:

The Mexican weather forecast: Chili today and hot tamale.   (E22)

The inexactness is obvious: although *chili* and *chilly* are phonemically

19. There is nothing new in this discussion of the difference between proper names and other kinds of words—what is said in the text has been known for a long time. This topic is another on which I owe a personal debt to Jakobson, without whose guidance I would not have known of the traditional treatment.

identical for most speakers of English, *tamale* and *tomorrow* are only similar. It is easy to describe E22 as a blend, say of the phrases *chilly today and hot tomorrow* and *chili and tamales*.

An *exact pun* is a stretch of speech of a determinate phonemic structure which is susceptible of two or more interpretations. In order for the pun to be noticeable, it is also necessary for at least two of the interpretations to be relevant in the context in which the pun occurs. Thus:

> A father called his cattle ranch "Focus" because it was where (E23) /²ðə+sânz+rêyz+³míyt¹#/

A *double entendre* is at least similar to, perhaps the same as, the exact pun:

> The French missionaries moved westwards through the wilder- (E24) ness, converting the Indians, mainly to dust.

Theoretically, the difference is as follows. In the exact pun, two distinct words or phrases (*sons raise meat, sun's rays meet*) happen to be phonemically identical, whereas in the double entendre a single word or phrase (*converting*) has two relevant ranges of meaning, both brought to the hearer's attention by context. This distinction is not always easy to make, and may be spurious. In the examples, perhaps most speakers of English would agree that *meat* and *meet* are different words that "just happen" to sound alike, and that *convert* "change the state of" and *convert* "render Christian" are the same word. But this agreement may stem from spelling habits.

If we insist that the essence of blending is that elements drawn from two phonemically different words or phrases must be present, then we cannot discern the mechanism of blending in exact puns. But it is more profitable to consider, as the essence of blending, the tendency to say more than one thing, with no participating tendency completely suppressed. When the words or phrases involved are quite dissimilar, the result is an unpunlike blend. When they are similar but not exactly the same, the result is an inexact pun. When they are phonemically identical, the result is an exact pun (or a double entendre, if there is any point in making the distinction), since, in this case, by exception, it *is* possible for the speaker to say two forms at the same time: neither expression requires any articulatory motions that conflict with those required for the other.

9. Stuttering. A certain connection between slips of the tongue and *stuttering* (or *stammering*) can be discerned in the following:

You made so much noise you worke Cor?—wore?—w?— (E25)
woke Corky up.

The first slip here is an anticipatory blend: *worke* /wôrk/ was intended *woke* with the *-or-* of *Corky*, due to come next. The speaker noticed the lapse after he had gotten part way through *Corky*, and broke off. The first effort at a correction was itself wrong: instead of saying *woke*, the speaker began to repeat the wrong form he had already uttered. Again detecting the error, he again broke off. The next effort at a correction was broken off even more quickly. We cannot tell whether at this point the speaker was aimed properly at *woke* or was about to come out with another repetition of the blend. Perhaps the speaker could not tell either, and perhaps this was why he broke off again. The hesitation after the lone *w-* was a bit longer, as the speaker marshaled his attention to guarantee that on the next trial things would come out right. This is the point at which, in some instances of this sort of stammering, the speaker inserts a whistle, seemingly a device to "untangle" the speech organs, but certainly also a conventional acknowledgment of the stammering and a would-be-humorous apology for it.

The most obvious affinity shown by this example is between stuttering and overt editing. After the first breaking-off, the speaker makes three successive tries at a replacement for the incorrect phrase, and is successful only on the third. The resemblance to stuttering would have been greater if the speaker had detected the initial error more quickly, and so had said *you worke?—wore?—w?—woke Corky up.* Or suppose he had detected that he was headed in the wrong direction—or that he had merely begun to fear that he was headed wrong—at the very beginning of the target word *woke*; he might then have said *you w?—w?—w?—woke Corky up.* In this version, all difference from stuttering has vanished.

A lapse is, in a sense, an indication of indecision: the speaker is operating under two (or more) conflicting tendencies and does not completely resolve them. Many a lapse is followed by a correction, but such overt editing can also involve lapses. No one's speech is completely free of lapses—the only way to avoid them altogether is to keep silent. Although many lapses are utterly trivial, nevertheless everyone would prefer to avoid certain lapses under certain conditions, and probably some people are permanently fearful of any lapse at all. Whenever, for whatever reason, a speaker feels some anxiety about a possible lapse, he will be led to focus attention more than normally on what he has just said and on what he is just about to say. These are ideal breeding grounds for stuttering. The stutter need not be preceded by an overt and obvious blend, as it is in E25: a word can be broken off virtually as it begins merely for fear that it will not come out right, and then indecision between one word and another, or between the right word and a threatening blend, can produce a series of attempted corrections, each in turn cut off, before the speaker gets back on the track—if, indeed, he does.

I propose the foregoing as a general diagnosis of the stuttering of ordinary people, but only as part of the diagnosis of the articulatory spasms of the pathological stutterer. Apart from possible gross neurophysiological factors, the latter differs from "everyday" stuttering at least in that stuttering has itself become both a habit and a source of anxiety.

10. Blending and Analogy. Jespersen[20] cites a report of a child who, stifled by the heat in a house in the tropics, said

It's three hot in here!   (E26)

One of my own children (at age about 5), having often been told *Don't interrup(t)*, chose an appropriate occasion to say to me:

Daddy, you're înterring úp!   (E27)

It does not matter whether we think of these as lapses, as "bright sayings," or merely as childish errors: in any case, they are peculiar. The classical explanation is in terms not of blending but of *analogy*. Thus, for the first we can sketch a frame of reference as follows:

I'd like two pieces	:	I'd like three pieces	::
We waited two minutes	:	We waited three minutes	::
Give me two hot ones	:	Give me three hot ones	::
. . .	:	. . .	::
It's too hot in here	:	*X*.	

All the listed sentences are supposed to be already familiar, as wholes, to the speaker; of course, lacking detailed records, we can only guess as to their actual identity. The dots represent any number of further pairs of familiar utterances. The members of each pair differ in sound only in that the second of the pair has /θrîy/ where the first has /tûw/; in meaning, they differ in that the second of the pair refers to something more or bigger than does the first. Solving for X is simple: this, it is supposed, is exactly what the child did when he uttered E26. For E27 a similar scheme can be guessed at; we have to suppose that ambient noise had masked out, for the

20. J. O. H. Jespersen, *Language* (1922), p. 122.

child in question, the final /t/ of *interrupt* and the absence of any /+/
between the /r/ and the last vowel, but that is quite realistic:

Don't wake up the baby	:	You're waking up the baby	::
Don't burn up that paper	:	You're burning up that paper	::
Don't sit up	:	You're sitting up	::
. . .	:	. . .	::
Don't interrup(t)	:	*X.*	

A transformation, of course, is an analogy:

John shot the tiger	:	The tiger was shot by John	::
Bill read the book	:	The book was read by Bill	::
The butcher weighed the meat	:	The meat was weighed by the butcher	::
. . .	:	. . .	::
The meat weighed ten pounds	:	*X.*	

Thus the solution for *X* might be said, as a lapse or as a witticism.

In the context of nineteenth-century historical linguistics, where matters such as blending and analogy were first discussed in detail, the
concern was with the mechanisms by which a language changes in time.
Analogy was proposed, on excellent empirical grounds, as one of the
three basic mechanisms of linguistic change, the other two being borrowing and sound change.[21] It was recognized, however, that there are also
some minor phenomena not clearly reducible to any of the major mechanisms, and yet felt in some obscure way to be more closely akin to analogy
than to the other two. Blending was regularly listed as one of these
subsidiary types, along with haplology, metathesis, progressive and re-
gressive assimilation, contamination, and so on.

Now, the relation of blending to analogy is perfectly straightforward.[22]
In many, perhaps most, speech situations, many different analogies are at
work, each with its own degree of "pressure." Some of them are incompatible, in the sense that following one precludes accurately following
another. If all incompatibilities are suppressed, the result is, at most, a
lapse like E26 or E27. If two (or, in theory, perhaps more) incompatible
analogies are followed—as best one can, considering the limitations of
one speaker's quota of articulatory equipment—then the result is a blend.
Hesitating between *sigh* : *sighed* :: *swim* : *X* and *sing* : *sang* :: *swim* : *X*, a
child or a tired adult may come out with *swammed*, where both analogies

---

21. Thus in all the standard basic works, from Paul through Bloomfield.
22. On this one point, my treatment in *A Course in Modern Linguistics* (1958), p. 433,
goes beyond its predecessors: the kinship of blending to analogy is overtly recognized.

are attested. All the examples of blends we have given in earlier sections illustrate the same point: the diagnoses given earlier are easily recast into terms of conflicting analogies.

But this means that there is no longer any mystery about the relation of haplology, metathesis, and the like to analogy. In the preceding sections, we have shown how all the *phenomena* classed under such labels can be accounted for in terms of two *mechanisms*: blending and editing. Given the relation of blending to analogy, which we have just reviewed, we can conclude that all the kinds of blunders and allied phenomena we have discussed in this paper can be explained in terms of just three fundamental mechanisms: analogy; blending (= unresolved conflict of analogies); and editing.

11. The Generation of Speech. Let us now turn to the consideration of all speech, smooth as well as blunderful.

Clearly the difference between smooth and blunderful speech is real, except that this simple pair of terms undercuts the facts. The difference is one of degree, not of kind, and there are more than one norm and more than one direction of possible deviation from each norm.

It is currently fashionable to assume that, underlying the actual more or less bumbling speech behavior of any human being, there is a subtle and complicated but determinate linguistic "competence": a sentence-generating device whose design can only be roughly guessed at by any techniques so far available to us. This point of view makes linguistics very hard and very erudite, so that anyone who actually does discover facts about underlying "competence" is entitled to considerable kudos.

Within this popular frame of reference, a theory of "performance"—of the "generation of speech"—must take more or less the following form. If a sentence is to be uttered aloud, or even thought silently to oneself, it must first be built by the internal "competence" of the speaker, the functioning of which is by definition such that the sentence will be legal ("grammatical") in every respect. But that is not enough; the sentence as thus constructed must then be *performed*, either overtly so that others may hear it, or covertly so that it is perceived only by the speaker himself. It is in this second step that blunders may appear. That which is generated by the speaker's internal "competence" is what the speaker "intends to say," and is the only real concern of linguistics; blunders in actually performed speech are intrusions from elsewhere. Just if there are no such intrusions is what is performed an instance of "smooth speech." [23]

23. This, or something very much like it, is the only interpretation I can make of what Chomsky says, particularly in his *Aspects of the Theory of Syntax* (1965), chap. 1.

I believe this view is unmitigated nonsense, unsupported by any empirical evidence of any sort. In its place, I propose the following.

All speech, smooth as well as blunderful, can be and must be accounted for essentially in terms of the three mechanisms we have listed: analogy, blending, and editing. An individual's language, at a given moment, is a set of habits—that is, of analogies; where different analogies are in conflict, one may appear as a constraint on the working of another. Speech actualizes habits—and changes the habits as it does so. Speech reflects awareness of norms; but norms are themselves entirely a matter of analogy (that is, of habit), not some different kind of thing.

If, in a particular speech situation, only one analogy plays any part in determining what is said, then what is said is an exact repetition of something the speaker has heard or said before. The situation I face this morning is similar, as our culture categorizes things, to one yesterday morning, in which my satisfactory response was *Good morning!*; analogously, that is my response in the current situation. If the current situation is partly like various earlier situations, then various analogies may come into play, and what is said will often be new; even if, in historical fact, it is something that has been said before, it may be being newly composed now, by just the mechanisms we have discussed. It is the mechanisms of analogy, blending, and editing that account for our constant coinage of novel sentences. No more subtle or mysterious factor need be sought.

Anything that is actually said—unless it is just too long and complicated—may be registered as a unit, and may then recur by mere recitation from memory. This happens so often that we can never be sure, when we hear something novel to us, whether it is being coined at the moment or recited from memory. This is an important fact about language, but alters in no way our acceptance of analogy, blending, and editing as the basic mechanisms of the generation of speech.

The act of speaking aloud is indeed, as the currently popular view holds, typically a two-stage process, but not in the strange sense proposed by that view. The "inner" stage I shall call *primary generation*. This goes on partly in and partly out of awareness. It is "thinking in words": the virtually unbroken inner flow of "heard" speech, from which we make certain selections to be spoken aloud (§4, end). On the psychiatrist's couch, one is supposed to read out this inner flow as accurately as one can, with no further editing or suppression. The inner flow is self-generating: it is carried along in trial-and-error fashion in response to changing external circumstances, the heard speech of others, and its own past history (especially its immediate past); it can be blunderful as well as smooth. Thus, I have observed "slips of the tongue" in my own inner flow, often caught and edited out before they could be mapped into overt speech by tongue and lips. The mechanisms of this inner flow are not something weirdly different from those observable in overt speech. They are, in fact, exactly the same mechanisms, internalized from shared public experience. In *short* perspective, that which goes on internally is causally prior to that which is spoken aloud. But in *long* perspective—that of the individual life-history—public events are causally prior to the private ones.

Editing in the internal flow is *covert editing.* The norms reflected in this editing must themselves be the result of internalization, since there is no other possible source; but they can function differently here precisely because some of the internal flow is not mapped into overt speech. We very often think of something, during a conversation, that we decide not to say: norms have not prevented our thinking of it—that is, have not prevented the internal flow from phrasing it, or beginning to—but lead us to decide to keep it to ourselves. In certain formal circumstances, covert editing is thorough, and overt speech is unusually smooth. Much more typically, what is actually said aloud includes various signs of *overt editing,* as discussed in preceding sections.

Beyond the design implied by the factors and mechanisms we have discussed, a language has no design. The search for an exact determinate formal system with which a language can be precisely characterized is a wild goose chase, because a language neither is nor reflects any such system. A language is not, as Saussure thought, a system "où tout se tient." Rather, the apt phrase is Sapir's "all grammars leak."

The mechanisms of the generation of speech are also the mechanisms of linguistic change, just as our predecessors of a century ago suspected, except that there are two factors in the latter which play only indirect parts in the former. What one person says aloud, another person may try to imitate: hence we have borrowing, including noisy borrowing (§7). And sound change, as a mass statistical phenomenon, plays no immediate role in controlling what one says, overtly or covertly, at a given moment.[24]

---

24. See Charles F. Hockett, "Sound Change," *Language* 41.185–204 (1965). However, honesty forces me to retract all the favorable remarks made about Chomsky and his proposals in connection with my discussion of the "Fourth Breakthrough," which I now believe would more accurately be characterized as a "breakdown."

H13. JOKES[1]

1960–1971. Reprinted from M. E. Smith, ed., *Studies in Linguistics in Honor of George L. Trager* (The Hague: Mouton, 1973) 153–178, with the permission of Mouton and Company.

Most of this paper dates from the very early 1960s (see the first footnote). It began as a light talk that could be repeated for diverse audiences; as implied by the second footnote, it really did begin as a byproduct of—perhaps as a relief by contrast with—the research that led to H12. Yet for a long time it did not seem to tie in to anything else, and that was the real reason for the delay in publication (the spoof in the first footnote is just part of the fun). Section 8, which ties it in, was not drafted until late 1966 or early 1967; it could not have been prepared earlier, since it derives from H9, H10, and H11.

0. Introduction: The Nature of Jokes. Language is not to be understood unless we realize that it serves as a means for the transmission of information in a human community. But that realization is not enough, because a language also uses its speakers in other ways: for example, to entertain them. In some cultures, including our own, one of the ways of having fun with language is to tell jokes.

Sometimes a person says something funny without consciously intending to. Not all blunders in speech are funny, but many are, at least under suitable circumstances.[2] Sometimes a person does something funny, such as slipping on a banana peel, without consciously planning to. Not all accidents, by any means, are laughable; but some are, at least for some observers. Lapses and pratfalls are akin: a lapse is a pratfall in speech; a pratfall is a lapse in nonspeech behavior.

Neither a lapse nor a pratfall is a joke, any more than a beautiful sunset is a work of art or an interesting event is a short story. In all three cases, what is lacking is the hand of the human artist. If a painter puts the sunset on canvas, this representation is art—good or bad as the case may be. If a

---

1. This is a revision of a lecture first delivered at the Canadian Summer School of Linguistics, Edmonton, Alberta, 27 July 1960. One reason for the long delay in publication was my fear that exposure of the reader to an explication of the nature of jokes might spoil his enjoyment of them. But I am now convinced, since jokes are clearly a form of literature, that there can be no such danger. We have the precedent of thousands of teachers in our schools and colleges, whose exegesis, as is well known, has never spoiled any student's literary appetite.

2. See the companion paper to this one, "Where the Tongue Slips, There Slip I" [∇ the present volume, pp. 226–256].

writer describes the interesting event, the result is a short story, unless the author is a nineteenth-century Russian, in which case it is a long novel. If someone observes the funny episode and then tells about it effectively, the recounting is a joke. In all these cases, of course, the artist may edit and embellish at will, or may produce a composite or analog drawn in part from many different actual experiences, sometimes achieving an effect more profoundly moving than any of the originals. If he does, we may then call him a great painter, or a great writer, or a great humorist. Thus does art, at its best, improve on nature.

Jokes are an art form; specifically, I shall argue, a genre of literature. Literature is apparently a human universal, and so is laughter. Jokes, which combine the two in a certain way, may not be; but that will not concern us, for we shall confine our investigation to our own culture. If we wish to study the literature of some community—be it Victorian England, Han Dynasty China, or the aboriginal Swampy Cree—we must first determine what the literature of that community is. That is, we must discover those discourses, short or long, that the members of the community themselves agree on evaluating positively and that they insist on having repeated from time to time in essentially unchanged form. This is Joos's operational definition.[3] In specific cases it can be dreadfully hard to apply, but it is the only approach known to me that enables the scholar to rise above his own personal preferences, as all scholars by definition wish to do. In just the same way, if we seek to study the jokes of a community, we must observe what sorts of narration the members of the community laugh at or tend to laugh at. Laughter is surely the sign of one sort of approbation (that is, one sort of positive evaluation); thus discourses that are laughed at, and that are repeated from time to time in essentially unchanged form, are one genre of literature. That jokes in our own culture are told repeatedly is so obvious as hardly to need mention.

Our concern with jokes is purely taxonomic: we shall look mainly at their structure, not much at their individual or collective origin or at their cultural role. Five restrictions are adopted as a matter of practical convenience. With a few marginal exceptions, the jokes we use as examples will be not only (1) from our own culture, as already mentioned, but also (2) monolingual, not even requiring dialect differences to achieve their effect, (3) independent of any specific props, gestures, pictures, or nonlinguistic sounds, (4) not more than one million words long, and (5) clean. Cleanliness we define quite literally in terms of the written shapes in which

---

3. I must have heard this definition from Joos as early as 1955. He did not himself put it into print until *The Five Clocks*, written in 1961 and now most readily available as Harbinger Book H 058 (New York: Harcourt, Brace and World, 1967).

the examples are presented. If the reader chooses to discover shady interpretations, that is his responsibility. Regrettably, these constraints force the omission of some prime examples. But nothing else is lost, since all the points to be made can be drawn from jokes that meet the requirements.

1. A Structural Classification. Two short jokes will serve us as point of departure.[4]

    "Tough luck," said the egg in the monastery, "out of the   (J1) frying pan into the friar."

    An irate man came into a drugstore. "Yesterday I came   (J2) in here for hair tonic," he complained, "but what you sold me was glue. This morning I tried to tip my hat, and lifted myself two inches off the sidewalk."

We shall comment first on the features common to these two, and then (§2) on the differences.

Both J1 and J2 are *complete* jokes, and both are of a subtype that we shall call *simple*. A simple joke, like a simple sentence in grammar, has a bipartite structure. In a simple sentence the two parts are a subject and a predicate. For the two constituents of a simple joke, some may wish to adopt the learnèd coinages *epithesis* and *paiesis*, but I shall content myself with the traditional terms *build-up* and *punch*. In J1, the build-up consists of everything but the last word, which is the punch. In J2 the boundary falls just before the word *lifted*.

Given a particular wording for a simple joke, there is an easy procedure for locating the boundary between build-up and punch. Starting at the end, one finds the shortest terminal sequence, the replacement of which by suitably chosen other words will transform the joke into a nonjoke. Thus, in J1, all we need do to ruin things is to replace *friar* by, say, *fire*; in J2, replace everything after the last *and* by, say, *almost tore off the brim*.

In grammar, the relative position of subject and predicate is not absolutely fixed; even in English the subject may precede (*John ran away*),

4. Unfortunately my records are incomplete. J2, J37, J38, J77, and two or three others are from E. Davis, *Laugh Yourself Well* (New York: Popular Library, 1959). J9, J14, and about three others are from the July 1960 issue of *Coronet*. J5 is from the 16 July 1960 issue of the *New Yorker Magazine*. J67 and J68 are from *Sélections du Reader's Digest*. J32 is from *Inner Wrappers*, *Dubble Bubble Gum*, series of 1957. I heard J16 from R. P. Baldini; J48 from R. L. Birdwhistell; J68 from B. Bloch; J31 from E. Cantor; J17 from B. Cowan; J19 and J30 from J M. Cowan; J3 and J18 from C. D. Ellis; J29 and J54 from J. N. Gair; J24, J78, and J90 from R. C. Hockett; J21 and J85 from R. L. Leed; J34 from T. Lehrer; J25 from G. Marx; J74–J76 from L. Rodabaugh; J83 from A. Shah; J89 from W. L. Stafford.

follow (*Away ran John*), or interrupt (*Away John ran*) the predicate. In jokes—in any language, I believe, that has them—there is no such freedom. The build-up invariably precedes the punch. If the order is reversed, either the joke is no longer a joke or else what was the build-up has become the punch and vice versa. Thus, we can transpose J1 into a rather poor riddle:

> Q. Who said "Out of the frying pan into the friar?"   (J1')
> A. An egg in a monastery.

In a *compound* complete joke, a single build-up is followed by two or more punches in succession:

> Mr. Wong, a Canadian of Chinese extraction, visited the   (J3)
> nursery in the maternity ward and then hastened, much per-
> turbed, to his wife's bedside. Said he: "Two Wongs do not make
> a White!" Said she: "I can assure you it was purely occidental."

In a *complex* complete joke, on the other hand, the build-up of the whole joke itself consists of, or includes, a simple joke with its own build-up and punch:

> Arriving mid-morning at the penitentiary, a new convict   (J4)
> was hastily processed and taken out to the rockpile. Regulations
> permitted no conversation; but as things grew grim one inmate
> called out "Thirty-two!" and all the others burst into laughter.
> The guards stirred and things quieted down. Later, another
> inmate broke the monotony with "Forty-seven!" and got the
> same response.
> Puzzled, the new inmate asked his cellmate that evening what
> it was all about. "We pass around the best jokes we know,
> through the grapevine," said his cellmate, "and we give each
> one a number. Then out on the rockpile where we can't talk,
> when things get too tough we just call out the number of the joke
> we have in mind."
> The next afternoon the new convict decided he would get in on
> the act. After several others had told their jokes, and after an
> appropriate lull, he called out "Seventy-three!"—and was met
> with dead silence.
> That evening, puzzled, he tried to find out from his cellmate
> what had gone wrong. "Don't you have a number seventy-
> three?" "Oh, sure we do." "Well, is it a poor joke?" "No; it's
> one of the funniest." "Well, then, what *was* wrong?" The

cellmate, a little embarrassed, said "Leave us face it, bud; there's guys that can put a joke over and guys that can't."

Shorter complex jokes appear commonly as column-fillers in The *New Yorker Magazine*: an amusing account is reprinted from a newspaper or other source, followed by an appropriate comment:

> A former Flossmoor resident, Mrs. H. Roy Gordon, has an   (J5)
> exhibition of water colors at the Esquire theatre, 58 East Oak
> Street, Chicago, until July 8. Never having studied painting in
> water colors, Mrs. Gordon has seven grandchildren.—Home-
> wood (Ill.) *Homewood-Flossmoor Star.*
> Next time she'll take a few lessons.

We have compared the structure of these jokes with that of complex sentences; but we could also think of certain kinds of plots in stories, where a climax is followed by an anticlimax.

When nothing intervenes between the two punches of a compound or complex joke, I am not sure that the distinction between compound and complex can be maintained; if it is valid, it may rest in some difference in response, rather than in the joke itself. In any case, it is quite clear that not all (complete) jokes are classifiable as simple, compound, or complex. Compound and complex jokes are built by iterating, with certain inclusion relations, the build-up-plus-punch pattern of the simple joke, and more complex iterations and inclusions are possible, with no clearly defined limit. For example:[5]

> Roosevelt proved that any man can be elected president   (J6)
> four times. Truman proved that any man can be elected presi-
> dent. Eisenhower proved that we don't need a president. Ken-
> nedy proved that it is dangerous to have one.

There are also narratives that pose as unitary jokes but that actually consist of strings of simple jokes. At the large end of the size scale, these longer or more complicated structures merge into the "routines" of the stand-up comedian, which can be said to bear the same relation to a single joke that allegory bears to metaphor.

2. Poetic and Prosaic. The partial classification of jokes given above is intersected by a second. Our examples J1 and J3 both turn on what we might call "accidents" in the design of English. Thus, J1 involves the

5. Repeated now, after the tragic events of November 1963, this joke may give offense. I apologize. However, if the reader feels such a reaction, he should ticket it "Exhibit A" and hold it for use as evidence in the discussion of §7.

presence in English of the idiom *out of the frying pan into the fire*, on the similarity in sound of *fire* and *fryer*, and on the identity in sound of *fryer* and *friar*. It is unlikely that any other language of the world shares just these features. Hence J1, and in a similar way J3, are untranslatable. J2 and J4, on the other hand, could easily be told in French, Chinese, or Cree. If the translation turned out not to be funny, that would be due to cultural differences as to what is humorous, rather than to any differences in the designs of the languages.

This distinction is reminiscent of that in more high-flown literature between poetry and prose. The reason it is reminiscent is that it is the same distinction. As has frequently been pointed out, any language presents the literary artist with a vast and intricate tracery of partial resemblances of words and phrases in sound and in meaning. Poetry is literary discourse in which the artist makes as much as he can of this unique machinery, as a means of reinforcing or modifying the obvious "literal" meanings of the words and constructions. The emergence in some traditions of rhythm, rhyme, assonance, and the like comes about as one formal means to the end; yet discourse can be poetic without any sterotyped use of these devices, as witness the works of Walt Whitman. Poems are thus specific to a language in a way in which prose literature is not, and much more difficult—often impossible—to translate.

We therefore class jokes as *poetic* and *prosaic*. Jokes such as J1 and J3, that turn on accidental resemblances between words in sound and in meaning, are the former; translatable jokes, like J2 and J4, are the latter.

Roughly speaking, and with no intention to derogate the creative artist who composes good jokes, we may say that prosaic jokes stem from pratfalls as poetic jokes stem from slips of the tongue.

3. Varieties of Poetic Jokes. The commonest variety of (simple) poetic joke turns on a *pun*.[6] A pun may be perfect or may show any degree of imperfection. J1 turns on a perfect pun (since *friar* and *fryer* are identical in sound), as well as on the imperfect pun of either *friar* or *fryer* and *fire*. The following examples all turn on perfect puns; and all are of a single type in another respect that we will point out in a moment:

6. Here the discussion in "Where the Tongue Slips . . ." is important. A *blend* is what a speaker produces, often by way of a slip of the tongue, if he tries to say two words or phrases at the same time. If the two just happen to be identical in phonological shape (as are *friar* and *fryer*), then the effort can succeed, and the blend is a *perfect pun*. Otherwise, what actually comes out can at most be composed of ingredients drawn from each of the two target words or phrases (Lewis Carroll's *Richard* and *William* yielding *Rilchiam*); but as long as the hearer can detect both of the targets it is still a pun, though an *imperfect* one. A great variety of contaminations, assimilations, and metatheses can be shown to be the result of blending, and all can occur, by intent rather than accident, in a wisecrack or joke.

The Department of Classics at Cornell used to be housed (J7)
in the dusty top floor of the oldest building on the campus.
Appropriately, they taught Attic Greek.

A father called his cattle ranch "Focus" because it was (J8)
where the sons raise meat.

Sign on a tie shop: "Come in and tie one on." (J9)

Another sign: "Cohen and Son, Tailor and Attorney. Let us (J10)
press your suit."

Teacher: "Johnny, I understand you're a magician. What's (J11)
your favorite trick?"
Johnny: "I like to saw a girl in two."
Teacher: "Wonderful! Tell me, are there any other children in
your family?"
Johnny: "Yes; I have two half-sisters."

A beloved old doctor had had neither time nor desire to amass (J12)
worldly goods, and when he died there still stood on the lawn of
his unprepossessing cottage an old and faded wooden shingle
bearing his name. Since he left no money for a noble tombstone,
and his grateful patients couldn't afford to buy one for him, they
detached the shingle and tenderly placed it on his grave. It read:

DR. JONES, UPSTAIRS.

On the other hand, J3 turns only on imperfect puns: *Wong* and *wrong*,
white and *right*, *occidental* and *accidental*. The speaker from whom I first
heard this joke pronounced *white* with /w-/, not with /hw-/; thus the
difference in pronunciation is the same in the first two pairs, a parallelism
of imperfection that gives the joke more substance than it would otherwise
have. Most of us have had some experience in allowing for this particular
sound-substitution: some children go through a phase of using [w] for
adult prevocalic /r/, and some adults have a rather [w]-like /r/.
Here are further examples of poetic jokes turning on imperfect puns:

The Mexican weather forecast: Chili today and hot tamale. (J13)

Sign on the gate of a nudist club in October: "Clothed (J14)
for the season."

(Children's riddle:) Q. Why should one go on tiptoe past (J15)
the medicine cabinet?
A. So as not to wake up the sleeping pills.

A dentist had the habit of leaving his office each after- (J16)
noon at five and going to a bar downstairs in the same building
for a quick drink before he went home. The bartender came to
know him, so that without being asked he would prepare the
dentist's favorite drink: a daiquiri with some shredded walnuts
on top. One afternoon the barkeep found no walnuts, and went
to the back room for some more. There were none there either,
so he found a substitute and served the drink to the dentist. The
dentist sipped at it and said, "That's good, but it's a little
different. What did you do?" The bartender responded, "That's
a hickory daiquiri, Doc."

The imperfect pun may involve a metathesis (J17), or a couple of them
(J18), or some even more complex permutation (J19):

Two neighbors were in status competition. One bought a (J17)
bread knife so big that at one whack he could cut through a
whole loaf. The other bought one that would cut through two
loaves at one stroke. The first went to a butchers' supply house
and bought a cleaver with which he could chop at one blow
through *three* loaves of bread. The other placed a special order
with a cutlery factory and got a four-loaf cleaver.

Mr. Chan, who ran an oriental art shop in a small town near (J18)
Vancouver, discovered several mornings in succession that
some of his teakwood objets d'art were missing. Resolved to
catch the thief, he hid himself behind a counter the next evening
and waited. After a long vigil, he saw a window slowly raised,
and a figure climb in. Jumping up, he turned his flashlight on the
figure: there was a large bear, his forelimbs clutched around
pieces of teakwood, and standing on his hind legs, that ended
with feet like those of a young man. Said Mr. Chan: "Aha! Now I
have you, boyfoot bear with teaks of Chan!"

During the Civil War, word reached a sleepy Maryland town (J19)
that the Union troops were winning battles not far away and
would soon be arriving. A drygoods merchant was disturbed at
this because he had in stock a large quantity of gray material. He
decided to take it up the street to an old friend of his who was a
dyer, and have it dyed blue, so that he would be able to sell it to
be made up into Union uniforms. Unfortunately, just after this
had been done, word came that the fortunes of war had changed
and that the town was shortly to be occupied, not by Union

troops, but by Confederates. The merchant packed up his freshly dyed cloth and carted it up the street again, not to be redyed, but with the hope that his friend could at least spread it out in the sun and let it fade enough to pass as gray. But meanwhile his friend had gone off to join the Union army. Which just goes to prove that old dyers never fade, they just soldier away.

The imperfection of puns of the sort illustrated by J15 is often overlooked. It does not appear in the printed form (on which most of the layman's awareness of language matters is based), because it does not reside in a difference in the pronunciation of the vowels and consonants of the two phrases, but on different distributions of stresses. Pills to induce sleep are *sléeping pìlls*, with the first word louder than the second; pills that were asleep would be *slêeping pílls* (compare *slêeping chíldren*), with the second word louder. That a pun with an imperfection of this type can nevertheless carry some effect is no more surprising than is the occasional effectiveness of other sorts of imperfect puns.

In keeping with the obvious kinship of punning and blending, we class as imperfect puns—of special subtypes—not only J17–J19 but also the following:

> During the Eisenhower administration, Democrats had a new   (J20)
> name for the White House: The Tomb of the Known Soldier.

Metathesizing jokes (J17–J19) make possible such nonpunning jokes as the following, told (sotto voce) in Russia:

> Q. What is the difference between Capitalism and Com-   (J21)
> munism?
> A. In Capitalism, man exploits man; in Communism, the
> other way around.

Whether a pun is perfect, and, if not, how imperfect it is, depends on dialect. If the pronunciation habits of teller and hearer are too divergent, the point of a joke may be lost. But the fact that most of us hear and accommodate to a fairly wide variety of dialects other than our own helps to make an imperfect pun effective—since, for the hearer, dialect noise and channel noise require to be dealt with in much the same way. The following joke incorporates what for me is an imperfect pun; for some readers it may be perfect:

> At an international congress on machine translation, it   (J22)
> was proposed to recommend that the editors of scientific jour-

nals in all countries print all articles in a special simplified style optimally adapted to the practical limitations of machine processing, a style to be called *MT-clear*. The authorities in each country would then be free to develop, for use for classified military documents and the like, a special style of the very opposite sort, to be called *MT-proof*. The participants agreed that there was no need to take any special action about still a third style, prevalent in the work of politicians and philosophers: the *MT-headed*.

There is an important difference between punning jokes in which the pun constitutes, or is in, the punch, and those in which it appears in the build-up. All our examples so far are of the former: we shall call them *end-puns*. When the pun is in the build-up, as in the following, the effect is quite different:

> The French missionaries moved westwards through the   (J23)
> North American wilderness, converting the Indians, mainly to
> dust.

> Two men were in a bar. Said one, glancing at a girl, "Say!   (J24)
> Isn't that Hortense?" Said the other, "She looks perfectly re-
> laxed to me."

> If you hit me I'll wax wroth, and then Roth will be all   (J25)
> slippery.

> A bachelor girl was asked the perennial question—why she   (J26)
> hadn't married. She replied, "I could marry anyone I please; but
> so far I haven't *found* anyone I please."

> A young man met a fascinating girl at a dance, and asked   (J27)
> if he could take her home. "Certainly," she replied; "where do
> you live?"

> Attorney, addressing an elderly New Englander on the wit-   (J28)
> ness stand: "Have you lived here all your life?" He replied:
> "Not yet."

> Confucius say, Woman who cooks carrots and peas in same   (J29)
> pot very unsanitary.

In all these, the hearer is led during the build-up to expect that the words he is hearing should be interpreted in one way. If the game is played fairly, then those words must be such that if the hearer were allowed time to examine them at leisure he would discover the ambiguities: thus, imperfect puns in a joke of this variety are a much more serious blemish than they are in end-puns. The adjective *wroth* and the surname *Roth* (in J25) are identical to the ear, so that, in time, one could realize that the sound of the phrase *wax wroth* is ambiguous. But the hearer is not given time to run through the possibilities. The context is so constructed as to force one of the actual possibilities into the hearer's awareness; the punch then reveals the ambiguity. We shall call punning jokes of this variety *garden-path jokes*.

That which in speech would be an imperfect pun may, in written representation, appear to be a perfect one. J15, of course, is an example. Allowing for this, the congregation of a small Ohio church were the victims of an unintentional garden-path joke when the text for the sermon was announced as a quote from Kipling: *And faith! We shall need it!* It turned out that the minister had read this interpreting *faith* as a noun, antecedent to the anaphoric pronoun *it*, so that he intoned the passage in this way:

$$^2\text{ànd }^4\text{fáith}^1 \#\ ^2\text{wè shall nêed }^4\text{it}^2||$$

Garden-path jokes highlight a structural feature that may be identifiable in all simple complete jokes, poetic and prosaic alike. The garden-path joke is not a joke at all unless the build-up includes a pun; this pun may be called the *pivot* of the build-up. Jokes of other sorts have pivots too, which are not necessarily coterminous with the whole build-up. In J1, an end-pun, the phrase *egg in the monastery* is a pivot: if the hearer misses this, or if, in repeating the joke from memory, one forgets this key phrase and substitutes something else, the point is lost. In J2, the pivot is perhaps more diffuse, but I think there is one. Evidence for pivots is the fact that, in retelling a joke, a great deal of the build-up can be recast in widely varying ways; but if the pivot is altered or omitted, even if the punch is delivered correctly, the joke is either no longer a joke or, if it is still funny, is a different joke.

There is still a third type of poetic joke that turns on a pun, although there is no overt pun in either build-up or punch. The hearer, however, cannot get the point of the joke unless he *infers* a pun from what he does hear. We may speak of the *implied pun*. I think the following is an example:

A small midwestern college was hard pressed for funds, and   (J30)
the board of trustees sent out some scouts to rustle up donations
from successful alumni. One returned with word of a wealthy
alumnus who was prepared to contribute three million dollars—
in exchange, however, for an honorary degree. That seemed not

unreasonable, until the scout added that the alumnus wanted the degree not for himself but for his favorite racehorse. However, after considerable discussion, the president recommended that the offer be accepted, saying that he thought he could handle the matter in an appropriate way.

On commencement day the following June the time for the awarding of honorary degrees arrived, and the president arose. "Ladies and gentlemen," said he, "we are about to bestow the degree of Doctor of Laws under conditions which are unique in the annals of American education. This will be the first time in history that any college has granted an honorary degree to a *whole* horse."

4. Varieties of Poetic Jokes: Nonpuns. Not all poetic jokes involve puns, overt or implied. The following, for example, does not:

At an Army post they put some one-armed bandits into the   (J31)
Officers' Club. The slot machines were in the Officers' Quarters,
and soon the officers' quarters were in the slot machines.

This is not a pun because in a pun the key word or phrase, susceptible to two or more interpretations, occurs just once. Here, on the other hand, *quarters* occurs twice, once for each meaning.

The next nonpunning example turns—fraudulently, as a matter of fact—on a subtle point of English grammar.

Pud: Hey, Joe, didya year what happened down at the zoo?   (J32)
Spike got arrested.
Joe: How come?
Pud: He was feeding the pigeons.
Joe: Gwan! There's no law against feeding the pigeons!
Pud: Yeah, but Spike was feeding the pigeons to the lions.

By stretching things we could view this as an imperfect pun, except that the imperfection does not lie in mere similarity (rather than identity) of pronunciation of two words or phrases. The fraud is in Pud's second line. We use the verb *to feed* with two objects (*feed X Y*, transformable to *feed Y to X*), or with just one; but when there is just one object it is the *X* of the schema just given, hardly ever the *Y*.

Another variety may be called the *nonpunning garden-path*. The dash represents either a noticeable pause or a noticeable prolongation of the syllable written immediately before it:

Definition of a politician: a man who approaches every   (J33)
question with an open— mouth.

She's beautiful, and a wonderful cook, and her coffee tastes   (J34)
like sham- — -poo.

Underneath that rugged exterior there beats a heart of—   (J35)
stone.

Flattery will get you— everywhere.   (J36)

The eye can skip ahead so quickly in reading that jokes of this sort are not very effective when presented in print—they need to be heard, and to be recited with a certain artistry. The structure is clear: the context in the build-up, and our familiarity with the common idioms and clichés of the language, lead us to expect one word or syllable at the end (e.g., *open mind, champagne*); then a different one actually comes out.

Still another type has only some verbal play, along the line of rhyme or assonance, in the punch. I cite an extremely poor example, because it will be of use later when we discuss the various techniques for ruining jokes:

Did you ever hear about the man who had an operation on   (J37)
Monday, married his nurse on Wednesday, and was sued for
divorce on Thursday? He got stitched, hitched, and ditched in
less than a week.

Finally, there are poetic jokes that turn on differing ways of phrasing, stressing, or intoning a sequence of words:

Motto at a dietetic food store: If you are thin, don't eat   (J38)
fast. If you are fat, don't eat; fast.

Just as he finished putting a question to his class, a pro-   (J39)
fessor noticed that one student was nearly asleep, so he quickly
added, "Jones, what do you think?" Jones jerked his eyes open
and responded, "I'm not sure, Professor; what do *you* think?"
The professor drew himself erect and said, "*I* don't *think*; I
know." Jones replied, "Well, I don't think I know either."

^{2}What do you do with a ^{3}stiff^1| ^{3}neck^3|| (J40)

^{2}What's that rolling down the ^{3}road^1| ^{2}a^{3}head^3|| (J41)

All our examples in §§3 and 4 have been simple. Of course, poetic jokes can be compound or complex or even more complicated; thus J3 is a compound (or complex?) end-pun, and the following is a complex garden-path pun:

Two deaf Englishmen were in a train compartment. As the (J42)
train slowed for a station, one looked out the window and said,
"I say, is this Wembley?" The other answered, "No; it's Thursday." To which the first responded, "So am I; let's get off and
have a drink."

The next is nonpunning; I do not know whether to class it as hyper-
complex or as hypercompound:

> Oh John, let's not park here! (J43)
> Oh John, let's not park!
> Oh John, let's not!
> Oh John, let's!
> Oh John!
> Oh!

To summarize our discussion so far: we have classed (simple complete)
poetic jokes into those that turn on puns and those that do not. The former
are end-puns, garden-paths, or implied puns. Possibly there are additional
varieties: thus, I see no reason why a joke should not have a pun in the
build-up and another in the punch, so that it would be both a garden-path
and an end-pun; but I have encountered no worthy example. Nonpunning
poetic jokes are harder to classify. We have taken note of the nonpunning
garden-path; otherwise, we have simply illustrated a few obvious types,
without any pretense at exhaustiveness.

The classification of prosaic jokes is another matter. In the sequel we
shall at times be tempted to treat a particular prosaic joke, for classificatory purposes, as though it were poetic, and at one point we shall yield to
this temptation, defining the prosaic garden-path. Beyond this, there
seems to be no useful overall classification of prosaic jokes other than a
topical one, the full elaboration of which would amount to a patterned
cataloguing of our entire culture—a sort of humorist's ethnography. This
should not be surprising. It merely reflects the fact that culture as a whole
is considerably more complex than language. Linguists have long known
this; it is why, in analyzing and describing a language, we work from form
to meaning rather than in the other direction.

5. Riddles, Games, and Verses. In a *riddle*, a problem is posed by one
person and the solution is to be sought by another. Thus, riddles have a
bipartite structure similar to that of the simple complete joke. No sharp
line of demarcation can be found between jokes and riddles, nor between
the latter and various more sober sorts of verbal puzzles. At one extreme,

one has the joke that is cast in riddle form: the build-up is the question and the punch is in the answer, but the person to whom the riddle is posed cannot normally guess the answer and is not really supposed to try; instead, he is supposed merely to serve as a straight man. If the respondent fools the poser and gives the punch, the poser is frustrated. At the other extreme, the solution to a "serious" problem is in no sense a punch, and yet, depending on taste, the solver may enjoy finding it and may even be amused by it.

Let us travel partway along this scale, starting with straight-man riddle-jokes such as J1, J15, and J21, and stopping when the humor seems to vanish (or, for safety, a little later than that). Here are two very old riddle-jokes that fail to be puns in the same way that J31 does:

> Q. How is a beehive like a bad potato? (J44)
> A. A beehive is a bee holder; a beholder is a spectator; and a specked 'tater is a bad potato.

> Q. How is a lazy dog like a sheet of writing paper? (J45)
> A. A lazy dog is a slow pup; a slope up is an inclined plane; and an ink-lined plane is a sheet of writing paper.

Here are three that turn on metatheses; they are true puns (imperfect, of course), in that a single actually spoken phrase, in the punch, has to do double duty for itself and its metathesized partner:

> Q. How is Cleopatra like the Panama Canal? (J46)
> A. The Panama Canal is a busy ditch.

> Q. How is a tiger like an English sentence? (J47)
> A. The tiger has claws at the end of its paws.

> Q. How is a middle-aged businessman at a backyard barbe- (J48)
> cue like a middle-aged businessman at a backyard barbecue?
> A. A middle-aged businessman at a backyard barbecue is a spit-turner.

We note that J44–J45 share a format, as do J46–J48. Many riddle-jokes come in prescribed formats and constitute games, in the sense that there are sessions at which people take turns telling them, each trying to recall or invent a better one of the particular format than any yet told at the session. The structure of J44–J45 is a little too complicated for such game use. That of J46–J48 is occasionally so used, especially by adolescents. Some games of this sort have names: for example, *Stinky-Pinky*. The build-up of a Stinky-Pinky establishes the specifications for a brief verse:

the first part of the build-up specifies the rhyme and rhythm scheme, and the second part sets forth the content or meaning to be conveyed:

Q. Stinky-Pinky for a moth in a closet.   (J49)
A. Garment varmint.

Q. Stink-linky-pink-jinky for a punch-drunk Scandinavian   (J50)
father.
A. Slap-happy Lapp pappy.

A game called *Beheading* is played mainly with young children, as a pleasant pedagogical device to build correct spelling and vocabulary. To behead a word is to remove the initial letter of its written form:

Q. Behead a wind instrument and get a string instrument.   (J51)
A. Flute; lute.

There are dozens or hundreds of such pedagogical games. Many of them, like the one we have illustrated, are of material help in transmitting to successive generations certain traditional values of our civilization: especially, the confusion between language and writing and the even more serious confusion between symbols and what they stand for. These confusions appear constantly in riddle-jokes (perhaps mainly those of or for children) that are not in some game format:

Q. What is the longest word in the English language?   (J52)
A. *Smiles*, because there is a mile between the first and last
letters.

Other riddle-joke games (mainly adolescent, perhaps, but not childish) are defined in terms of content or topic rather than format: elephant jokes, our second example of which is also a garden-path, merging, via examples we do not cite, into grape jokes:

Q. How do you get six elephants into a Volkswagen?   (J53)
A. Three in front, three in back.

Q. What's gray and comes in buckets?   (J54)
A. An elephant.

Q. Who was purple and conquered the East?   (J55)
A. Alexander the Grape.

We pass next to riddles to which the respondent is really supposed to seek the answer but in which there is some source of humor. The making of a riddle is often misdirection of some sort, which is also (in the manner of a garden-path joke) the source of humor:

A doctor and a lawyer were lunching together in an elegant   (J56)
downtown Chicago restaurant, when there was a crash outside.
They ran out to see what had happened. A car was overturned
and a woman was crumpled on the street, covered with blood.
The lawyer looked at her and cried, "My God! It's my wife!" At
this, the doctor took out a gun and shot the lawyer. Why?

When the answer to a problem-riddle is not guessed quickly, the original
question is often supplemented by one or more additional clues—
formally, extensions of the build-up. For J56, I offer only the following,
appropriate for my fellow linguists: it is in part poetic, in that it would be
easier to pose in Chinese than in English, and almost impossible to pose in
French. Here is a numerical problem with a somewhat similar touch:

A streetcar left the car barn one morning with just a   (J57)
motorman and a conductor aboard. At the first stop, three
passengers got on; at the next, four. At the next, five boarded
and one got off. At the next, eight got on and three got off. At the
next, no one got on but two got off. At the next, fourteen got on
and five got off. At the next, three got on and no one got off.
How many times did the streetcar stop?

This is reminiscent of a very old one:[7]

As I was going to St. Ives   (J58)
I met a man with seven wives.
Each wife had seven bags;
Each bag had seven cats;
Each cat had seven kits.
Kits, cats, bags, wives,
How many were going to St. Ives?

The answer is supposed to be *one*—on the grounds that in order for the
narrator to have *met* the people and things enumerated, all of them would
have had to be traveling in the opposite direction. The reader will probably
agree with me that this is a fraud, putting an unrealistically narrow
interpretation on the word *meet*.

The misdirection in a numerical problem may be only that the interlocutor is led to think of a hard way of getting the solution, and to overlook
an easy way:

7. In fact, what may be a prototype appears in the Rhind papyrus, from Egypt from
about 1650 B.C. See H. Eves, *An Introduction to the History of Mathematics* (New York:
Holt, Rinehart and Winston, 1964), pp. 42–43.

How much would one pay for one hundred and eighty-seven   (J59)
eggs if eggs were twelve cents per dozen?

Two trains are four hundred miles apart, moving towards   (J60)
each other on a straight track, one at 60 mph, one at 40 mph. A fly
leaves the nose of one locomotive, flies at 75 mph to the nose of
the other, then back again, and so on. How far has the fly flown
when it is crushed between the colliding locomotives?

The second of these was once put to John von Neumann, who, in addition
to his other and deeper mathematical talents, was a lightning calculator:

Q. Dr. von Neumann, here is a problem for you: [J60 is   (J61)
posed].
Von Neumann (instantly): 300 miles.
Q. Gee! I didn't catch you. You know most people miss the
easy solution and think the only way to get the answer is to set up
an infinite series and sum it.
Von Neumann: How else?!

For some people, punctuation puzzles have a vague similarity to
jokes. In both our examples, the problem is to supply punctuation (or,
equivalently—though it is harder to do—to read off with appropriate
stress and intonation) in such a way that the sequence of words makes
sense:

TIME FLIES YOU CANNOT THEY GO TOO FAST   (J62)

JOHN WHERE BILL HAD HAD HAD HAD HAD HAD HAD HAD   (J63)
HAD HAD HAD THE TEACHER'S APPROVAL

If there is nothing amusing about a problem except something catchy in
the way it is worded, then it is no joke, and we have traveled along the
scale described earlier as far as we need to:

If a hen and a half lay an egg and a half in a day and a   (J64)
half, how many eggs does one hen lay in one day?

In the foregoing, as we followed the trail from straight-man riddle-jokes
to straightforward verbal problems, we encountered instances of jokelike
games disguised as riddles. There are also many joke games not so
disguised. Some of these involve dialogue, portions of it fixed for all jokes
of the particular type. In our examples we print the fixed parts in roman,
the variable parts in italics. One game of this sort is *Knock-Knock*; another
is *I've-Got-a-New-Job*:

A. Knock knock. B. Who's there? A. *Sam and Janet.* B. *Sam*   (J65)
and Janet who? A. *Sam and Janet evening.*

A. I've got a new job. B. What do you do? A. *I'm an ele-*   (J66)
vator operator, in the Linguistics Building at the University of
Buffalo. B. How do you like it? A. *Too many stresses.*[8]

In our terms (§3), a Knock-Knock is an end-pun, and an I've-Got-a-New-
Job is a garden-path pun.

Other game-jokes, like ordinary jokes, are all recited by a single person.
One of these is the *Tom Swifty*:

"I'm a nurse," said she drily.   (J67)

One, for which I know no name, removes an unremovable negative prefix
(or an element that has the shape of one), or, in a related version, treats a
primary derivative as though it were secondary:

I must say you're looking very couth, kempt, and heveled   (J68)
today.

If it's feasible, let's fease it.   (J69)

Reversing the convention of J68, a friend of mine used to refer to the
Unravel String Quartet. Still another unnamed game pulls apart a frozen
phrase-derivative in *-er* or *-ed*:

Have you any threes you want bagged, fours you want   (J70)
flushed, or sixes you want shot?

Have you any eaves to drop or swashes to buckle?   (J71)

I have also heard *Have you any buckles to be swashed?* Syntactically, we
recall the boy who, the day after Thanksgiving, went to a music store in
search of a turkey drum; and everyone knows Lewis Carroll's mock
turtle.

A less formal and more sporadic game is the invention of appropriate
names for characters or institutions in a story. Depending on how it is
played, the description of the character can be the build-up and the name
the punch, or vice versa; in the former case we have an end-pun, in the
latter, a garden-path.[9]

---

8. The earlier and less specialized version of this lacks the explanatory phrase after
operator, and has the punch *Oh, it has its ups and downs.*

9. Some of these violate constraint number 2 of §0.

Description	*Name*	(J72)
The sweet heroine	Agnes Day	
The nasty girl nightclub singer	Swingster Annie	
The feeble old lady	Maud Eaton	
The nervous opera impresario	Mac Snell	
The clerk in the ladies'-wear store	Susan Shocks	
The aging gardener	Peter Mossout	
The barber	Daniel Druff	
The demolition company	Edifice Wrecks.	

Joking-games and their ilk go by fashion. Culturally, they are comparable to such crazes as flagpole-sitting, goldfish swallowing, telephone-booth-crowding-into, or antifluoridation-campaigning. And all these share the advantage, as over against chess or bridge, that anyone can play. No special talent is required.

A joke can be cast into verse form (J58), but that does not render it poetic unless it would be anyway—indeed, verse form is no guarantee of poetry in any genre of literature. The limerick seems to have become particularly appropriate for verse jokes in English, as shuttle-rhyme has in German. Clean examples are hard to find, but here are three. The first is prosaic, the second an imperfect end-pun, the third a garden-path pun:

> There was a young woman from Rio   (J73)
> Who played flute in a Beethoven trio.
> > Since her technique was scanty
> > She played it andanty
> Instead of allegro con brio.

> A city man, while on a hunt,   (J74)
> Saw what he thought a very cute stunt:
> > A pig, with raised brow,
> > While sucking a sow,
> Was heard to say "Oink nurture grunt."

> There was a young lady from Mass.   (J75)
> Who had an unusual ass:
> > Not chubby and pink,
> > As well you might think,
> But had hair, and long ears, and ate grass.

Limerick-reciting is also a sort of game, in the sense described earlier. The prescribed rhyme-and-rhythm pattern for limericks gives rise to another type of poetic joke, which requires, for its effect, the setting of a limerick-reciting session. The session is disrupted if one participant suddenly recites something like the following:

There was a young lady named Grete   (J76)
Who was so tremendously broad in the beam
    That when she stepped in the ocean
    She caused such a commotion
That Admiral Byrd finally decided to claim her for America.

One pseudolimerick of this sort (*There was a young bard from Japan . . .*) is now so generally known that it has lost its effect.

6. Balance; How to Blow a Joke; Incomplete Jokes. The punch of a simple complete joke, either poetic or prosaic, must be relatively short. Impressionistically, one is inclined to say that it must be at least as short as the build-up, typically shorter. A more extended punch either turns out to be a series of punches, yielding a compound or complex joke, or else becomes an explanation instead of a punch, so that the force is lost.

That tells us one way to blow a joke: we shall call it Way Ia, and shall number the other ways as we encounter them here, interspersed with our discussion of some other matters. Way Ia is to make the punch too long and diffuse. Compare the following two versions:

A man rushed into a drugstore and said to the clerk, "Quick,   (J77)
do you handle urine specimens?" The clerk said he did. "OK;
wash your hands and make me an egg-salad sandwich."

A man rushed into a drugstore and said to the clerk, "Quick,   (J77′)
do you handle urine specimens?" The clerk said he did. "OK
then; please go wash you hands before you serve me, because I
want you to make me an egg-salad sandwich."

A long and involved build-up, followed by a weak and soggy punch, makes the *shaggy-dog* story. J19, as we presented it, is too short to qualify, but an expert could easily pad the build-up out to several pages of detail, mostly irrelevant, and thus turn it into one. Edgar Wallace's novel *The Day of Uniting*[10] would be a book-length shaggy-dog except for one "fault": the plot is too clever—the pivot, for which the dénouement is the punch, is too well hidden.

Way II for a joke to be ineffective is for the build-up to be so constructed, or so narrated, that the hearer knows the punch in advance: as

10. London: Hodder and Stoughton, 1930; New York: Mystery League.

we say, the build-up *telegraphs* the punch. We hardly need an example. But the frequency of telegraphy gives rise to another special variety of joke: that in which an obvious punch is telegraphed but a different one is actually delivered. Here we can use an example; but it is extraordinarily difficult to be sure of one, since so much depends on the immediate context and on the state of mind of the audience. The following may do:

> A scientist was showing a visitor around a zoological experi-　(J78)
> ment station. "In this cage," said he, "we have a cross between
> a turkey and a chicken; we call it a turken. Here in the next cage
> is a cross between a swan and a goose; we call it a swoose. And
> here is our special pride and joy: the first successful cross
> between a pheasant and a duck. He lurches a little when he
> walks, so we call him Limpy."

More vaguely, the build-up, instead of telegraphing a specific punch, may merely suggest that the punch will be of a certain general sort, and then the actual punch be of some other sort. This description would fit J75. All jokes that do this, poetic or prosaic—all jokes in which part of the point is a startling contrast between telegraphy and delivery—can be called garden-paths.

Garden-path "misleaders" also occur as the sort of riddle we call a *catch-question*:

> Q. Let's see: when we have tales passed down by tradition,　(J79)
> but with no known single author, to whom do we ascribe them?
> A. You mean to the "folk"?
> Q. Yes. And what was the name of the President of the
> United States between Tyler and Taylor?
> A. Polk?
> Q. That's right. And what do we call the white of an egg?

The respondent is apt unthinkingly to say *yolk* instead of *albumen*. Again:

> Q. How do you pronounce M, A, C, (pause), M, I, L, L,　(J80)
> A, N?
> A. MacMillan.
> Q. How about M, A, C, (pause), H, E, N, R, Y?
> A. MacHenry.
> Q. And how about M, A, C, (pause), H, I, N, E, R, Y?

More simply:

> Q. What do we call those things they use in battle, that　(J81)
> go on caterpillar treads?

A. Tanks?

Q. You're welcome.

This brings us to the first type of *incomplete* joke (cf. §1): the *lone build-up* or *zero-punch* joke. That is what one has if, with or without telegraphy, there turns out to be no punch at all—not even an irrelevant one, but mere silence.[11] One is reminded of Mark Twain's account of trying to read a long German novel, in two volumes, and ending up knowing nothing of what it was all about because the last page of volume two had been torn out, and that page had contained all the verbs. Examples are the bits published in the *New Yorker Magazine* as column-fillers, under the heading "Most Fascinating News Story of the Week." When these items originally appear in various newspapers they are not jokes, but lapses. They become jokes only when picked up and cited.

The let-down of the zero-punch is akin to that felt if one is expecting a joke when, it turns out, none is intended by the narrator, as well as to that felt when the intended joke turns out to be of a very different sort (that is, some variety of garden-path). Today we expect a limerick to be a joke. This was not so in Edward Lear's day. In the midst of a round of limericks, if someone recites one of Lear's, the let-down is of the sort we mean:

> There was an old lady of France,   (J00)
> Who taught little ducklings to dance;
>> When she said "Tick-a-tack!"
>> They only said "Quack!"
> Which grieved that old lady of France.

Just this experience has been encapsulated in the following limerick-joke of zero-punch structure:

> Edward Lear, the Victorian poet,   (J82)
> Wrote lim'ricks, though not so's you'd know it.
>> His plots were so terse
>> As to need no fifth verse.

Way III to blow a joke is to omit or distort the pivot (§3, end). Imagine a child trying to tell J1 and saying:

"Tough luck," said the egg; "Out of the frying pan into the   (J1?) friar."

I once blundered on J29 by saying *Woman who cooks peas and carrots . . . .* Another fatal slip here is to say *Woman who cook* (instead of

11.

cooks); this is an easy error to fall into because of the mock Chinese-Pidgin-English of the fixed opening phrase *Confucius say* shared by all the Confucius jokes.

Way Ia to blow a joke is to dilute the punch; in general, Way I includes also any other sort of mangling or distortion of the punch. Having heard J33, a child of my acquaintance recounted it as follows:

> A politician is a man who approaches every question with his (J33')
> mouth open.

Ways I and III show us a formula for the construction of one type of complex joke: the build-up tells of some character who loves to try to tell jokes but doesn't know how, and who hears a particular joke (e.g., J33); the punch is then his distorted recounting of it (e.g., J33'). Thus:

> I once told a friend of mine about the two men who were (J83)
> walking down the street when one of them caught sight of a man
> standing on the corner holding something in his hands. He said
> to the other, "Say, isn't that a Greek urn?" The other said,
> "What's a Greek urn?" The first said, "Oh, about a dollar an
> hour." My friend laughed, and later I heard him repeating the
> joke to someone else: "There were two men walking down the
> street, when one of them saw a man holding something in his
> hands. He said, 'Say, isn't that a Greek urn?' The other looked
> at it and said, 'How much does a Greek earn?'"

Children in middle-class families in which telling jokes is part of the way of life seem, in many cases, to catch on at a very early age to the typical bipartite structure of the simple complete joke. Wanting to get in on the family act, such a child often invents a passage that fits the required structure in every way except the ways that count—no pivot, or an irrelevant punch, or both. We may call these "dull sayings of children." Having recited his piece, the child laughs: loudly, because he has learned that the proper aftermath of a joke is laughter; but often also hollowly, since he has still not learned what makes a joke funny. The child is hardly helped if the surrounding adults laugh too—as they often do, not at the "joke" but at its pointlessness.

Such children's would-be jokes are imitated in the *pseudojokes* of adults and adolescents, sometimes cruelly told to test the (doubted) perspicacity of the respondent:

> Q. Why does a mouse spin?   (J84)
> A. Because the higher the fewer.

A man went into the butcher shop of his small hometown and   (J85)
asked for a pound of hamburger. The butcher said to himself,
"He's not very bright; I'm going to play a trick on him." So he
ground up some prime sirloin and gave it to the customer instead
of hamburger. The next day the man came back and said to the
butcher, "Ha-ha! You thought you were fooling me yesterday,
but I knew all the time that what you sold me was ground prime
sirloin instead of hamburger."

Way IV—probably the most important way—of making a joke poor is
for the build-up to be contrived. J13 and J37 are examples, but there is a
difference: the former has at least the merit of being awful (like a completely useless hand at bridge—say, nothing above a five), whereas the
latter is just dull (like the just-below-average hand at bridge). J37 does not
telegraph its punch. But as one hears the build-up one realizes that the
jokester first thought of a punch and is dragging in oddments from all over
merely to set the stage for it. There is nothing wrong with far-fetched
events (J30), or even impossible ones (J2), in a joke. If the absurdity is in
the punch, as in J2, this may be part of what makes a prosaic joke funny.
But if the absurdity is in the build-up, as in J30, then care and artistry are
required to induce a willful suspension of disbelief in the respondent. The
contrived build-up is found in all but the very best and rarest end-puns. I
believe it is really this, rather than anything undignified or immoral about
punning itself, that has given end-puns the disrepute in which they are
generally held.

Indeed, the design of a good prosaic joke, and that of a good garden-
path joke whether prosaic or poetic, resembles that of the classical detective story. In the latter, the author binds himself to conceal from the reader
no clues that are available to the detective, and to throw no false scents in
the reader's path unless they emerge naturally, are also encountered by
the detective, and are in due time plausibly accounted for. It must be
possible for the reader to infer the identity of the murderer from the
evidence he is given, though only with ingenuity and hard work. The bad
detective story either telegraphs the identity of the criminal or cheats the
reader with irrelevancies, just as with the poor joke.

We have mentioned one type of incomplete joke: the lone build-up. Is a
second type possible —the free-floating punch, with no build-up? That is
in part a matter of definition. A *wisecrack* is a clever verbal response
quickly coined and used in a situation in which it is apropos; the situation
serves as, or in lieu of, a build-up. But the wisecrack in this sense is hardly

a joke, because it is not *told*; rather, it *happens*. More jokelike is the *latent wisecrack*: a lone punch held in reserve, as complete jokes often are, for circumstances to arise in which it will be relevant and witty. Many a latent wisecrack is born as we belatedly think of a clever comment on a situation to which, at the time, we reacted stupidly. We then sadly store away the "I-should've-said," hoping that opportune circumstances may again be encountered, and that we will recall it when they do. I have been waiting for years for a chance to use (as someone is pouring beer), *If you want to get ahead, young man, don't tilt the glass*, or (in I have no idea what context) *Sex is the most fun you can have without laughing*; but I am now ready to abandon hope, so here they are, free, and cheap at half the price. An ingenious person with a latent wisecrack on his hands may not merely wait for proper circumstances to arise. Instead, he maneuvers others into an appropriate situation, or—more easily—imagines proper circumstances, verbalizes them as a formal build-up, and thus has a complete joke.

I do not believe that, strictly speaking, an incomplete joke in the form of a free-floating punch is possible. The nearest approach would be a latent wisecrack for which the appropriate circumstances are so prevalent in our culture that merely hearing the punch is enough to conjure up a picture of such circumstances in the imagination of the hearer. But in that case—if it exists—the person who presents a latent wisecrack is not quite telling a joke in our sense. Rather, he is saying to his audience, "Here is a punch; build your own joke with it." Try these: *Here's champagne to our real friends and real pain to our sham friends*; *The leisure of the theory class*; *As clear as a coast*; *Forego the whole hog*.

7. Laughter and the Sacred; Sick Jokes. Granting that laughter is an emotional reaction, we must point out that it is compatible with a wide variety of other emotions. Novelists know this: they have their characters laugh angrily, or in triumph, cruelly, bitterly, with childish delight, with frustration, with puzzlement, and so on. The common denominator of jokes is, by definition, their purpose of eliciting laughter; they differ widely as to the other emotions that are elicited at the same time. In current commercialized humor there is a strong tendency to link laughter to the more hostile and aggressive emotions. That is by no means inevitable. J12 links laughter and love.

We perhaps do not yet understand very well the nature of laughter, nor what makes a funny joke funny. But we do know something of what prevents some people from enjoying some jokes. Jokes are told in our culture about anything and everything. Yet each of us has, as part of his personal excerpt of our culture, certain areas that are not to be joked about. Indeed, just this gives us an operational definition of the *sacred*: that about which we will not laugh. This is the exception to the general compatibility of laughter with other emotions. When a joke touches on what we regard as sacred, then any possibly humorous reaction is swamped by reactions of other sorts—resentment, anger, embarrassment, as the case may be. Democrats used to laugh freely at the quip *the velvet hand in the iron glove* aimed at John Foster Dulles when he was Secretary of State; Republicans were less inclined to, and now that Dulles is dead many will feel that the joke is in bad taste—joking, apparently, is too much like speaking evil. Once, in about 1956, I was criticized for telling J20 on just these grounds: that is, the grounds that one should not joke about the dead. The Scots rarely enjoy Scotch jokes—understandably, since such jokes are always at their expense. Some people resent a "dirty" joke regardless of mood and circumstances. Many more, we may suspect, are disturbed only if the joke is told in a social setting they regard as inappropriate.

For it is not alone the respondent's own personal sense of the sacred that governs his reaction to a joke, but also his respect for what are, or may be, the sacrednesses of others. One who would enjoy a particular joke in privacy may refrain from laughter in public if he feels that laughing would be offensive to some of those present. Since, in a complex society, we can rarely be sure just what is sacred to other people, it can thus happen that a joke that is potentially funny for every member of an audience will nevertheless evoke no laughter. Here, in a nutshell, we have the distinction between the truly sacred and mere *propriety*. The proprieties of our culture—perhaps of any—have to do with what we are publicly and overtly *expected* to regard as sacred. Proprieties change with the times. Jokes that turn on the ways (real or imagined) of an ethnic minority are viable if that minority has a stable social status, no matter how low. If insecurity and social unrest develop, most of us set aside the jokes, regardless of their intrinsic merit. A bold man can fairly well sort out and classify the guests at an informal gathering, say a cocktail party, by telling a few jokes that are marginal as to the proprieties of the moment.

The *sick joke* exploits these habits of sacredness and propriety. Interestingly, jokes of this variety are almost always prosaic—there is already enough to deal with in such a joke, and adding word-play would be too much. The sick joke invades areas regarded as truly sacred by most members of our society, and does so in such a flagrant and violent manner that our defenses are broken down: we laugh despite ourselves, at least for a moment, before revulsion gets the upper hand:

Johnny: Mrs. Jones, can Billy come out and play baseball   (J86)
with us?
Mrs. Jones: But Johnny, you know Billy has no arms or legs!
Johnny: Yeah, but we want to use him as first base.

Apart from that, Mrs. Lincoln, how did you enjoy the play?   (J87)

8. The Joke Work. The simpler creative arts are *two-participant* arts: for example, a painter paints a picture, and his audience contemplates it. Most varieties of literature today are like that. The writer writes; the reader reads. Publisher and printer facilitate the transaction, often with worthy craftsmanship, but they are technological rather than artistic middlemen. Other arts are *three-participant* arts. In our literate society it is possible to read a play instead of going to the theater, but that is not the ideal; in principle, drama requires the playwright, the troupe, and the spectators. Music is an even clearer case. Some composers are performers, and some performers improvise, but the basic pattern is composer, performer, and audience.

In any three-participant art, a great deal depends on the relative prestige in which the first two participants are held. When the audience has at least as much respect for the first participant as for the second, and admires the second in proportion to his skill in interpreting the intentions of the first, one has what many people regard as the only "true" art. When the first participant comes to be viewed merely as a supplier, often anonymous, of raw material for the second, "true" art has given way to "mere" entertainment. The same thing can happen in two-participant arts: in literature, the technological middleman (say, a magazine publisher) becomes the boss, the writer the hired hack. These remarks are meant in the first instance as classificatory, not necessarily as evaluative. And it should be noted that we have described only the two extremes. All sorts of intermediate balances are also possible.

Jokes are a three-participant art; for the participants I shall use the terms *composer*, *poser*, and *respondent*. It is true that every composer is also a poser, and perhaps almost every poser, at least occasionally, is a composer; but anyone who tells jokes tells dozens he has heard from others for each one of his own devising, so that the two roles must be kept apart. Joke composers are largely anonymous. If this is like the anonymity of the kitsch-artist who supplies popular entertainers with their "material," it is also like the traditional anonymity of the original creators of folktales and folk-songs.

What I have called the *joke work* in the title of this section consists of two portions: the poser's work and the respondent's work. Both find their analogs in other arts. For example, it is obvious that the musical performer has to work; and anyone who thinks that music can truly be enjoyed just by lazily bathing in the sound is marked, by that opinion, as a thoroughly unmusical person. (He probably can't dance either.) Here we find another difference between true art and mere entertainment. Kitsch is simple. It makes the audience think itself clever without really trying. Like alcohol, it poses as a stimulant but is in fact a tranquilizer. That is why we call the boob tube a boob tube.

In jokes, the respondent's responsibility is to see the point, and the poser's responsibility is to see that there is a point to see. The work of each is the work he must do to discharge his responsibility.

Every joke—by no means only the true riddle—demands that the respondent infer something that is not overtly said, or interpret in more than one way that which is overtly said, or both. The words must run around inside the respondent's head for reparsing; the scenes that the words evoke must be scanned as carefully as one examines a cartoon. Even the pseudojoke (§6) must be processed in this way in order to see the point that there is no point. If the respondent can get more out of a joke than the poser thinks he put into it, that is all to the good. There is nothing wrong with building better than we know.

Different jokes require different kinds of respondent work. We shall not try to classify them all; the reader can reexamine our examples and do that for himself. I do want to underscore, however, how very generally a joke requires the respondent to call on his ability to *analogize*. This is perhaps the most basic of all human abilities, though perhaps it is not exclusively human except when it takes place in purely verbal form. That we do analogize is shown by the following:

> A student newly arrived from India was having lunch with   (J88)
> a Canadian student he had just met. He ordered tea, and when
> the materials were served he carefully tore open the teabag and
> poured the tea leaves into his cup. The Canadian explained that
> that was not necessary—that one could simply immerse the
> whole bag, and the water would filter right through the paper.
> Grateful for the guidance, the Indian student took two packets of
> sugar and dropped them into his cup with the tea.

Analogizing with things, rather than with words, is demanded of the respondent by the following:

> Two octogenarians decided to go their separate ways for a   (J89)
> year, seeking their fortunes, and then to meet again and ex-

change experiences. When the year had passed, the first reported: "I went to New York and started going to night clubs. I met a lovely dancer and married her, and just last week she presented me with a bouncing baby boy." Said the other: "Much the same thing happened to me. I went to Africa to hunt big game. For several days we found none at all. I got disgusted and set out one morning without my gun, just for a walk. Suddenly a lion jumped out from behind a tree. I didn't know what to do, so I pointed my finger at it and said 'Boom!' The lion keeled over, dead. Then I turned around, and there behind me was a native with a smoking gun."

Analogizing with words, rather than with things, is demanded by various of our earlier examples; for instance, by J78–J80—and by J59! J68–J71 are *built* by analogy, and that fact must be discerned by the respondent. The basis for analogy given the respondent by the build-up does not necessarily lead directly to the punch or "answer"; but, even when it does not (as in certain garden-paths), the analogy has to be followed out in order to know this.

A good deal of what we dignify by calling it "logic" or "reason" is, I believe, not really much more than a bit of analogizing, perhaps with both words and things. Perhaps the reader will agree at least in the case of the respondent work required by the following:

A farmer bought a prize bull to freshen his herd; after (J90) performing excellently for several days, the bull lost all interest. Worried, the farmer went into town and consulted the vet, who reassured him and supplied some medication: large pills, to be given to the bull one each day. In a week, all was again well.

Later the farmer was talking with a neighbor, and told him the whole story. "Gee, that's wonderful," said the neighbor; "I wonder what's in those pills!" "I don't know exactly," said the farmer, "though they taste like peppermint."

In any human community, there are some pairs of things or situations that have nothing directly to do with each other but that may be brought into juxtaposition indirectly, in the awareness of members of the community, by the language—merely because words that mean the things are similar or identical in sound. Poetic jokes rest on this. The fact that such jokes are told is evidence against any extreme version of the Whorf hypothesis, any proposal that language habits *determine* behavior. In this connection we can be sensible about our own culture and at the same time awfully silly about others. I once heard an otherwise intelligent but echt-monolingual American propose that one thing wrong with the Russians is that, since an important newspaper is called *The Truth* (*Pravda*), they assume that what they read in that newspaper must be the truth. It would be just the same thing to suggest that one may find out what time it is in New York City by consulting *The New York Times*, or that a *friar* must necessarily have something to do with *frying*. But if we were that easily victimized by our language (except perhaps for fleeting moments), jokes like J1 would not be funny. And, in fact, when no one is around for whom such matters are sacred, Russians joke about their two newspapers, *The Truth* and *The News* (*Izvestia*), by saying "*The Truth* gives no news and *The News* gives no truth."

The respondent work required by a poetic joke is that of recognizing the absurdity—at best, a culturally or situationally relevant absurdity—of juxtaposing things merely via the sounds that mean them. This, also, can be expounded in terms of analogy. The joke proposes that, as word or phrase X is to word or phrase Y, so that meant by X is to that meant by Y. The analogy yields a hypothesis. If the joke does not completely formulate the hypothesis, the respondent completes it, and then rejects it as false. The relation of champagne to shampoo (J34) is not, in fact, anything like the relation of the word *champagne* to the word *shampoo*. But the context in this particular joke renders the absurdity culturally apropos.

Next we turn to the poser's work. Let us consider some other sorts of oral discourse, to see how joke-telling fits in.

A man rises in church to recite the Apostle's Creed in chorus with the rest of the congregation. What he is to say is totally prescribed in advance. Even the phrasing and intonation are ritualized. He can do it if he has memorized what he is to do, in its exact linguistic form; otherwise he cannot. And, if he has, then he needs no help from Stanislavsky in order to achieve an acceptable performance. Now consider a witness to an accident who has been asked to dictate an account of what he saw to a police stenographer. What the witness dictates has not been stored inside his head in a fixed verbal form, ready to be "read off" to the stenographer. If he has memorized anything—and, if he has not, he is valueless as a witness—it is the sequence of sights, sounds, and smells at the accident. He calls these into awareness, scans them, and describes them in words. It does not in the slightest matter what words he uses, as long as they convey the right information.

It is a fact that a human being has both nonverbal and verbal memory, both nonverbal and verbal imagination, and that when one speaks one may be either reading stored words and phrases or putting words together to describe something stored or imagined in nonverbal form. If it is true that one's memory of an event or fact can sometimes be stored more securely by working out a verbal description of it and memorizing the description, it is also true that one may rely on remembered or imagined events to help remember words or phrases. We know little of the phylogeny or physiology of these abilities, but we know we have them. No normal person would deny it—the ordinary intelligent person can be surprised that we should consider it necessary to state what is so obvious. But some of us who have been led, by a special concern with the role of language in human affairs, to become linguists, psychologists, or philosophers, have been induced by our unnatural perspective to formulate all manner of weird alternative theories, most of which violate the first law of science in that they deny the possibility of, rather than trying to account for, things that everyday social experience endorses as realities. It is hard to avoid that trap, but we ought to try.

Remembering and posing a joke requires both of these typical human skills. I suppose that if someone were particularly anxious to be able to tell a certain joke well, he might memorize a specific wording of it the way one memorizes a poem. But I think that is rarely done, even (or perhaps especially not) by the professional comedian. On the other hand, even the prosiest of prosaic jokes cannot be remembered and posed effectively if one relies entirely on memory of what the joke is about. What is actually done, I believe, is as follows. The poser memorizes the exact wording of certain key parts of the joke: namely, its pivot and its punch. For a sufficiently short joke this may be tantamount to memorizing the whole joke, but for most jokes it is not. The poser memorizes, in nonverbal form, some skeleton sequence of the events covered in the joke. He makes no effort to memorize the rest of the material he has heard in any one telling of the joke. Instead, when he is about to tell it himself, he takes off from the part memorized verbally and the skeleton memorized nonverbally, and fleshes out the rest to fit. Evidence for this is the frequency with which someone will say, "Hey, I heard a good joke yesterday. But let me think it through for a minute so I'll get it straight." There ensues a moment or so of silent internal editing before the overt posing begins. The stored essence is being recalled, and suitable padding is being devised by newly creative trial and error.

The claim that jokes are a genre of literature is supported when we compare the joke work with the kind of thing done by the participants in what Joos calls consultative-style speech.[12] Consultation exchanges information and seeks a collective decision; it is the manifestation, in language, of community homeostasis. As Valéry[13] points out, the primary characteristic of ordinary language (that is, of speech in consultative style) is that as soon as it is understood it vanishes. All that counts and is retained is the new distribution of information and intent. In contrast, then, any discourse that does not thus disappear, that is stored away for more or less accurate repetition—that, as Joos says, becomes frozen *as discourse*—is thereby staking some literary claim.

Yet jokes are simpler and less demanding than are the kinds of discourse we more commonly dignify by calling them literary. The respondent's work for the most complicated joke is trivial as compared with the work demanded of a reader of Milton or Joyce; the poser's work, and the composer's, are the sort that most human beings can do, not a kind reserved for a thin scattering of geniuses. In their relative simplicity, jokes resemble kitsch, except that good jokes (there are plenty of kitschy ones) are a stimulant, albeit a mild one, rather than a sedative. The social importance of jokes lies in their simplicity. Jokes are propaedeutic for the young, rehearsing them for the much more complex respondent's work that will be demanded of them by the great literature and other great art works of their culture. And jokes are restorative catharsis for the adult, between successive bouts with his artistic heritage.

12. Op. cit. (in fn. 3 above).
13. I am quoting from S. R. Levin, *Linguistic Structures in Poetry* (The Hague: Mouton, 1962), who in turn quotes from P. Valéry, *The Art of Poetry*, D. Folliot, trans. (New York: 1958).

H14. INFORMATION, ENTROPY, AND THE EPISTEMOLOGY OF HISTORY

1964?–1974; never before published.

I don't remember just when I got the key notions, but I was talking about at least one of them as early as 1953 (see H4 and its prefatory remarks). The passage on local indeterminacy in H6 (written 1958) is another foreshadowing. In the fall of 1961 I began the necessary systematic reading in thermodynamics, relativity theory, and related aspects of physics. By 1964 some sort of draft had been completed, and I delivered its substance to several audiences in the next few years, first of all on 11 May 1966 to the Research Club of Cornell University. Section 4 of Cauchemar's "Innovation and Creativity" (H11) contains a paragraph on indeterminacy stolen from the draft. In the fall of 1966 I submitted the latest revision to the editors of *American Scientist*. They rejected it because (among other things) it was too long, so I revised it again and made it longer. In the fall of 1968 I sent a slightly retailored version to Sol Tax for *Current Anthropology*, but thought better of that and withdrew it before any editorial review.

Between then and now it has been subject to further sporadic tinkering. The reason for the repeated postponement of publication is that the essay raises certain problems that I have not been able to solve to my own satisfaction—in particular, I remain very unsure about what is said in §8. But I also believe that the paper includes some vitally important notions, especially about the nature of information storage. In any case, I can hold the tiger by the tail no longer; so here it is, and I hope it will be read by some theoretical physicists.

1

The comparative method of linguistics, one of the triumphs of nineteenth-century science, enables us to collate data from a set of related languages in such a way as to reconstruct a portrayal, often surprisingly detailed, of the earlier single language from which they are all descended.[1] Table 1 gives a fragmentary illustration. The headings of the first four columns are the names of four present-day languages of the Romance family. Each row gives a set of words, one from each of the languages,

1. For a full description of the method, see Bloomfield 1933 pp. 197ff or C. F. Hockett 1958 pp. 485ff.

which are similar in sound and in meaning. The fifth entry in each row represents the reconstructed archetype: the word in the parent language ("Proto Romance") of which the word in each daughter language is the direct descendant by unbroken tradition.

	FRENCH	SPANISH	ITALIAN	RUMANIAN	PROTO ROMANCE	MEANING
1.	nœv	nuéba	nuóva	nówə	*nóva	'new' (fem.)
2.	šãte	kantár	kantáre	kyntá	*kantáre	'to sing'
3.	bjẽ	bién	bɛ́ne	bíne	*bɛ́ne	'well'
4.	mẽ	máno	máno	mýne	*máno-	'hand'

The linguist must work with pronunciations, not with written forms. Hence the words are here given in a phonemic transcription rather than in traditional spelling. The four sets listed are representative of thousands.

Table 1

We know that in any community speech forms change in course of time. If a single community, speaking a single language, splits into two or more daughter communities which come to be out of touch with one another, then the changes in speech habits in the different daughter communities are largely independent. This explains the diversity of the forms in any one row of Table 1. Without this diversity, reflecting independent development, the comparative method is helpless. For example, we could not recover Old English from its sole descendant, Modern English. Even with diversity, the method would offer us nothing if we did not know a bit about the more and the less likely kinds and "directions" of linguistic change.

In a few crucial cases, of which Romance is one, the results of the comparative method can be checked against surviving documentary evidence of the parent language. It is because agreement is so close in these cases that we have confidence in the method also where documents are lacking. The forms in the fifth column of Table 1 look like Latin. They are, for Proto Romance and Latin are essentially the same. But the forms were not lifted from some ancient manuscript. Instead, they were reconstructed by the method we have just outlined. This fact is emphasized in the table by the appearance of an asterisk before each form. For over a century it has been standard practice to mark with an asterisk any form not directly attested in documents or from the lips of living speakers; thus, obviously, all reconstructions must be so marked.

Everyone who uses the comparative method uses it in much the same way. Most arguments have to do with fine details of interpretation. However, there is one long-standing dispute. The point at issue is the "significance of starred forms"—of forms reconstructed by the comparative method and therefore customarily marked with an asterisk. One's views on this characterize one as a member of the "realistic" school or of the "formulaic" school.[2]

The realists propose that the comparative method yields information about a real human language, actually spoken at a certain time and place (though both may be known only vaguely) by real human beings who were the linguistic, if not the genetic, ancestors of the speakers of the daughter languages. Accordingly, they believe also that a fair proportion of any set of starred forms represents words that actually on occasion passed the lips of the speakers of the parent language. They propose this as a truth and as an ideal: that is, reconstruction should be as realistic as possible, where realism is defined by the kinds of things we find in languages susceptible to direct observation or known through written records.

The formulaists hold that such realism, desirable or not, is unattainable. They assert that a starred form is merely a conveniently abbreviated *summary of correspondences*, giving no information not present in the set of directly attested words on which the starred form is based. Table 2 shows what they mean by this. As can be seen, each successive symbol in a reconstruction represents a particular correspondence of sounds from daughter language to daughter language, where each correspondence recurs also in other sets of words. Since that is all a starred form can do, say the formulaists, there is no reason to try to make it look "pronounceable": any set of arbitrary symbols could be used.

So much sense and so much nonsense have been presented on both sides of this dispute that it is difficult to be either partisan or wisely eclectic.

In its most vulgar form, the disagreement has to do merely with the relative reliability of written records and of the diverse testimony of the various lineal descendants of a single earlier language. In this version the debate is too parochial to interest us here.

But what are the implications if we move the dispute to a larger stage? The comparative method of linguistics is, after all, only one of divers methods used in historical research. All these methods have certain

2. Buck 1926 is a good discussion.

The first set of words in Table 1 shows the following correspondences from language to language; the starred symbols on the right can be viewed as summarizing them:

	FRENCH	SPANISH	ITALIAN	RUMANIAN	PROTO ROMANCE
C1.	n-	n-	n-	n-	*n-
C2.	-œ-	-ué-	-uɔ-	-ó-	*-ó-
C3.	-v	-b-	-v-	-w-	*-v-

Correspondence C1 recurs in many other sets, such as:

5.	nɔ̃	nómbre	nóme	núme	*nóme, *nómine	'name'
6.	nwar	négro	néro	négru	*nígru	'black'

Correspondence C2 recurs, for example, in:

7.	mœr(t)	muére	muɔre	mwáre	*móret	'he dies'

Correspondence C3 recurs in part in each of these:

8.	viv	bíba	víva	—	*víva	'alive' (fem.)
9.	—	niébe	néve	néwə	*níve	'snow'.

Table 2

features in common. What happens if we lift the dispute out of historical linguistics and consider it in history as a whole?

2

For our purposes we define *history* as that branch of science devoted to the inferring of past events from present evidence. Under this definition the historian, of course, need not belong to a department of history; he may instead be an ethnologist, a linguist, an archaeologist, an evolutionary biologist, a palaeontologist, a geologist, an astrophysicist, a police detective, or doubtless something else. In any case, he summarizes the evidence he has examined in the form of an *assertion* about the past. The question we ask is: what is the relation of such an assertion to what it asserts? How can we know whether it is true?

Consider the following two statements:

(1) The Declaration of Independence was signed in Philadelphia on 4 July 1776.

(2) You'll find a gas station right beyond that next hill.

If we are about to run out of gas and someone says (2) to us, we need merely drive over the hill. We find a gas station or don't, and conclude that (2) was true or false. The statement was a *prediction*, and has been verified or not. But we cannot drive to 4 July 1776, because there are no time machines. Therefore the empirical test of the validity of (1) must be of a different sort.

Whatever the test, it is clear that different historical propositions carry differing degrees of reliability. But that is equally true of predictions. So there is in this regard no obvious way of distinguishing between the status of a historical statement and that of a prediction.

To insist on the difference, some investigators distinguish between *likelihood* and *probability*.[3] Suppose an unconscious derelict is taken to a hospital. The doctors may make a guess as to his age—say, "about forty-five." In effect, this is a guess as to when he was born. Formally, the guess is (or implies) a likelihood estimate, since it is assumed that the patient was actually born on a perfectly determinate date. The uncertainty of likelihood pertains only to the statement, not to the event. In predicting the future—say, which team will win tomorrow's football game—the same sort of estimate can be offered, but in this case it is called a probability estimate. The uncertainty of probability pertains not only to the statement but also to the event itself.

Now, all this is valid if and only if the following is a basic fact about the universe: that, as observed from any single neighborhood, the past is determinate and the future is indeterminate. That which has not yet been may never come to pass, and it is physically impossible for us to collect enough relevant information to be sure—until, of course, the event in question either happens or does not happen, thus becoming part of the determinate past instead of the indeterminate future. But that which *has* been *will forever have been*.

The assertions just made are utterly in conflict with the spirit of nineteenth-century mechanics, and are thus counterintuitive for those whose intuition is an internalization of Laplaceanism. Laplaceanism is a useful experimental working principle in some contexts, but it is no obligatory basic tenet of science. Indeed, in origin it is not scientific at all, but a thinly disguised theological principle, traceable to the doctrine of

3. Feller 1957 pp. 43–44.

predestination of medieval north European Protestantism, or to the kismet of Islam, or both. The physicists of a century ago assumed that if one measured everything about the state of a closed mechanical system—to wit, six parameters for each particle—at a given time t_0, one could then compute the state of the system at any earlier *or later* time. To be sure, for many a system the measurements were unfeasible, but the difficulties were viewed as purely practical, not essential. The past and the future were thus symmetrical around the present—or around any other arbitrarily chosen point of time—as an axis of symmetry.

Twentieth-century physicists have found reason to explore a different view, one which is in some ways much more similar to the realities of everyday life than was the earlier view, and within which it can be shown that *no physical system has a determinate future.* If a physical system were determinate, then its entire future could be predicted from its present state. Now although it is, not merely practically but *in principle*, impossible to observe *everything* about the momentary state of any physical system, we shall learn more if we ignore this and set forth certain other facts from which this one follows as a corollary:

The entire future of a physical system could be predicted from its present state only if the system had no moving parts and was completely isolated from the rest of the universe. For, if there are moving parts, then there is "thermodynamic" indeterminacy: individually unpredictable motions of the parts, whose effects on the whole can be taken into account only statistically, not absolutely. And, if it is not isolated, then there is relativistic indeterminacy: individually unpredictable influences from elsewhere, whose effects, again, can be dealt with only statistically. But the only system with no moving parts is an elementary particle (if there is any such thing), which is not isolated. And the only system that is isolated is the universe (if there is any such thing), which has moving parts. Thus, unless thermodynamics and relativity are both wrong, the assertion is proved.[4]

Viewed thus, the world turns out to have an essential and permanent *asymmetry* as between past and future. I said earlier that the past is determinate, the future indeterminate. The remark posed as a characterization, but perhaps we should take it instead as a *definition* of past and future.

Neither our everyday language nor the special mathematical jargon of modern physics is really well adapted for talking about the world in this

---

4. The observational indeterminacies of quantum mechanics are not mentioned separately here because they seem to be subsumed under the two sources of indeterminacy itemized.

way. The time of the physicist is the time of "earlier" and "later" and of quantified durations, and any moment can arbitrarily be chosen as t_0; the present moment is not a singular point. Relativity changes some things, but not that.

The physicist's traditional frame of reference needs supplementation, not replacement. Wiener noticed this,[5] and was led to speak of "Newtonian and Bergsonian time." I have found a supplementary frame of reference elsewhere, and shall now describe "Hopi-Whorf time," so called because it is a way of viewing time and events that Whorf ascribes to the Hopi Indians.[6]

Hopi verbs are said to have three formally marked tenses. The *nomic* is used in assertions of "permanent" truths: "Pike's Peak is high." The other two appear in assertions about specific states or events. The *reportive* refers to events from which information has been directly or indirectly received: "I went into town yesterday"; "The rabbit you were trying to shoot has just disappeared over that hilltop." The *expective* refers to events which, or the consequences of which, one may encounter, and for which one may need to prepare: "I'm going into town tomorrow"; "Bill is on his way home; he should be coming over that hill any moment now." (We are not interested in the fact that any of the tenses can be used in a mistaken assertion or an outright lie; in that respect all languages are alike.)

Circumstances which would lead a speaker of English to say "John is in that house over there" might induce a speaker of Hopi to use either the reportive or the expective, with a difference of emphasis for which English does not systematically provide, though of course we can paraphrase it. The reportive would imply that the speaker speaks on the basis of direct or indirect observation, perhaps having just come from the house in question, where he saw John. The expective would emphasize that the assertion may be verified, perhaps shortly by John leaving the house and emerging into view.

This system is really quite different from the formal tense system of any European language. All the latter, for example, have some sort of a *present* tense form—used, to be sure, in various ways; but these uses must be distributed in Hopi among the nomic, the reportive, and the expective, depending on circumstances of a sort that speakers of European languages mostly ignore. Accordingly, for a person who handles the world in terms of Hopi-Whorf time there is no such special thing as the

5. Wiener 1948 chap. 1.
6. Whorf 1938. (I have replaced Whorf's unusual term "assertion" by the more familiar and traditional "tense.")

"present," which is merely the cutting edge of the determinate, the becoming-determinate of the indeterminate.

European languages, and some others, handle time like space. So our physicists (and, for that matter, our historians) freely draw diagrams on paper or blackboard in which one of the spatial dimensions represents time. Furthermore, in European languages we think of the future as "ahead," the past as "behind." Experience is like a train ride, the train moving out of the past and into the future, using that line on the blackboard as a track. Hence the common politician's cliché "let us move together bravely into the future"—as though we had any choice in the matter except perhaps as to the bravery. By a reversal of perspective, we can also think of the train as stationary and the scenery as sliding by. It is spatial images of this sort that gave rise to the remarkably banal phrase "the flow of time," which physicists have been using at least since Newton.

Non-European languages that agree in treating time like space need not agree in all detail. In Fijian the train is running backwards, or else we are sitting in it facing the rear: the past is "ahead," where it can be clearly seen (until it blurs with distance), while the future constantly sneaks up from "behind."[7]

If we *must* have a spatial metaphor, the Fijian is more realistic than our own. But Hopi shows that we need none. In Hopi one cannot "move into the future"—frontwards or backwards or sidewise—because the future is not a *place*; and representing time by a line on a blackboard would be an absurdity.

So Hopi-Whorf time is the additional frame of reference we need.

The realm for which the expective tense is appropriate is that of the indeterminate, the unresolved, the anticipated, the hoped-for or dreaded, the planned-for: that part of the world about which uncertainty is a matter of inherent objective indeterminacy. The realm for which the reportive tense is appropriate is that of the determinate, the accomplished: that part of the world about which we have information and about which uncertainty, at bottom the product of noise, is properly characterized in terms of likelihood. For these two realms I shall henceforth use our familiar words "future" and "past"; and I shall try not to use them in any other way. When I speak of the future or the past relative to a particular date and place, say relative to 4 July 1776 in Philadelphia, the place and date designate a neighborhood in space-time in the traditional frame of reference of physics, while "future" or "past" refers to Hopi-Whorf time. It is

7. Observed 1960–1961 in Fiji by F. M. Cammack, A. Schütz, and me.

easy to see, with this terminology, that the future for Philadelphia as of 4 July 1776 is not in any way to be identified with some segment of our own past as of here-and-now. The former is, or was, the probabilities of the date and place in question; the latter is our own here-and-now certainties.

The reportive, then, defines the province of history in the broad sense we have assigned that term. Using two other familiar words in equally broad senses, we may say that the expective defines engineering, and that the nomic defines physics.

3

The proposal that information and entropy bear an intimate and (perhaps) simple relation was first given wide publicity by Norbert Wiener.[8] Let us consider this notion.

There is no consensus as to just what happens to the laws of thermodynamics when one attempts to lift them out of their original context of phenomenological heat theory and promote them to the status of general laws of nature. If one accepts the approach of statistical mechanics as it is usually interpreted, then there is no point in such an effort. Statistical mechanics attempts the very opposite: to account for heat, especially for the empirical irreversibilities in the behavior of heat systems, by a reduction to the reversible laws of classical mechanics. Even the mathematical doctrine of probability used in statistical mechanics (the "frequency" theory of probability, on which the less commonly espoused "personal probability" is no marked improvement) is rooted in Laplacean determinism. This approach is excellently presented by Bergmann.[9] It is interesting to note that even when one views the matter in this way one finds it necessary to speak of information: the temperature or entropy of a (real) system is dependent on inadequacies in our information about it, and if our information were complete those purely statistical measures would become meaningless.

I think all that is backwards. I think statistical mechanics must be read in the opposite direction, so that reversible systems appear as special limiting—and perhaps asymptotic or even nonexistent—cases of irreversible ones, and so that incompleteness of information comes to be the *result* of such matters as temperature and entropy, rather than their cause.

The original formulation of the laws of thermodynamics speaks of heat,

8. Wiener 1948 passim.
9. Bergmann 1951, especially pp. 126ff.

pressure, temperature, entropy, and enthalpy. To generalize, we must speak of energy in all and any forms rather than just of heat. In the general case we don't need both temperature and pressure, both entropy and enthalpy. It is somewhat surprising to discover that, although the first of each of these pairs of terms is the one used, the generalized meanings stem rather from the second terms. "Temperature" in the generalized case means *energy density*: the average amount of energy per unit volume (like thermodynamic pressure, rather than per unit mass, like thermodynamic temperature) within a physical system. "Entropy" in the generalized case means the degree to which the actual distribution of energy in a system approximates uniform distribution.

The first law now states that, in a closed physical system, the amount of energy does not change with time. As has often been remarked, this is merely the law of conservation of energy (in its most general form, subsuming such bylaws as those of conservation of momentum, of angular momentum, of mass). A closed physical system would be one whose boundary cannot be crossed: energy inside the system therefore stays in, and energy outside the system stays out. Hence the first law has sometimes been thought of as a tautology or a truism. It is neither. It is not a tautology, because there is an alternative: the proposal that energy may appear from nowhere or may vanish without trace. The assumption that these things do not happen has been enormously productive in uncovering previously unknown forms of energy and previously unrecognized modes of energy transmission. It is not a truism, because it may not even be true: the Steady State hypothesis proposed that it was in fact false, though so nearly true that we were entitled to assume it for almost all purposes. However, if the first law is neither tautologous nor truistic, its acceptance does mean that the mere existence of energy ceases to be of any particular interest. Instead, we can profitably concern ourselves only with its distribution and migrations. Hence the importance of the other laws.

The second law asserts that, in a closed physical system, entropy is more apt to increase than to decrease, until it reaches a maximum for the particular system, after which it is apt to remain nearly constant. That is the whole of the law, but a little comment is necessary. The steady maximum for a particular system may be quite low, and it may require only a slight triggering input of energy from outside to send the system towards some higher maximum of entropy. As an example, think of a stone rolling down a hillside and lodging against an obstruction; a slight nudge can free it to roll the rest of the way to the bottom—or to another obstruction. As another example, consider that an atom, even of U^{235}, is reasonably stable despite the fact that most of its energy is concentrated in the nucleus; an invading neutron may scatter this energy into a somewhat more nearly equitable spatial distribution.

Nernst's Heat Theorem, sometimes called the "third law," asserts that, other factors being held constant, lower temperature means lower entropy; at absolute zero, entropy would also be zero.

These three laws extrapolate beyond all actual or possible observation in two ways. There is no such thing as a closed physical system, unless the universe as a whole be one, a proposition of doubtful meaningfulness. The nearest to it that can be achieved is a system only weakly coupled to anything outside; if the observer is not part of the system, then one of the weak couplings must be a peephole. Also, there is no such thing as absolute zero. The Kelvin scale is erratically antilogarithmic. That should not surprise us, when we remember that mass is a form of energy. That is, in order to remove all the energy from a physical system we should have to remove not only all the kinetic energy and all the radiation, but also all the matter, so that there would be no physical system left. Under general relativity even that would not be enough, for the hole in space left by the removal of the things we have mentioned would still not be completely devoid of flux (gravitational, at least) as long as there were any matter anywhere in the universe. Therefore to remove all the energy from a physical system one would have to reduce all its dimensions to zero. It turns out that absolute zero is the temperature of nothing.

That the three laws of thermodynamics are idealizations does not diminish their power. However, it is worthy of note that they achieve their elegant simplicity by ignoring relativistic effects.

4

In the foregoing, the term "entropy" has proved particularly puzzling—and not only to the layman. Popularizing explanations (invented, if not read, by experts) often resort to the analogy of shuffling a deck of cards. We break open a fresh deck, remove the jokers, and shuffle, say ten times. Although it is not impossible that we will find the deck once again in factory sequence, it is highly improbable. Our expectation is that the longer we shuffle the greater will be the deviation from factory sequence, until some maximum randomness has been achieved. This "increase of disorder" is supposed to be like the "increase of entropy" in a physical system, proposed by the second law. Thus, entropy is supposed to be something like disorder.

It is surprising that the patent fraud in this analogy has never been pointed out. Why should we claim that the factory sequence is any more "orderly" than any of the other 52! possible sequences for the cards of a deck? The probability that *any* of these sequences, once it has occurred, will recur after ten shuffles is equally small. To judge that certain sequences are more "orderly" than others says nothing about the cards; it says something about us. We play card games, and have learned from experience that any of a certain relatively small number of sequences of the cards in a deck will yield fascinatingly interesting good hands, any of another relatively small number of sequences will yield interestingly bad hands, while any of an enormously large number of sequences will yield hands of monotonous mediocrity. We class all the dull sequences together and refuse to distinguish among them. It is this factor of human *interest* that supplies our statistics, not any inherent property of the cards.[10]

Now, is this part of the intended analogy? Are we to infer that in dealing, say, with gasses, entropy is purely a function of human interest? Obviously, that is not what we meant—though it is suspiciously similar to Bergmann's proposal that entropy (like temperature) is a measure of the experimenter's ignorance of the system he is observing.[11] In confusion, we retire to dream up a better analogy.

But we shouldn't. There is something important to be learned from card-shuffling. Once again, let us break open a deck and shuffle it ten times. Now, before looking at the faces of the cards, let us ask the following two utterly ridiculous questions. First: why do we have to look at the faces of the cards in order to know what sequence they are now in? Why don't we already know? Second: when we do note the new sequence, how will we be able to know whether it is the same as, or different from, the sequence before the shuffling?

The answer to the second question is that we can know whether the sequence has been changed *only if we have retained a record of the original sequence*. In starting from factory sequence, we may keep this record in our heads, and thus forget that we are keeping it. But the experiment is really the same if we pull a used deck out of a drawer, note its sequence, and then shuffle; in this case we might try to memorize the preshuffle sequence, but are more apt to play it safe by writing it down. In one way or another, however, we must have a record. If we do not, then we have no way of knowing whether the sequence after the shuffling is the same one or a different one.

The answer to the first question is that we do not know the new

10. Weaver 1948.
11. Loc. cit.

sequence until we look at the faces of the cards *because we have kept no record of what happened during the shuffling*. One could imagine focusing a high-speed camera from a strategic angle, filming the shuffle, and then developing and studying the film. If this were carefully done, we would be able to know the new sequence without looking at the faces of the cards after the shuffling. But we could no longer call the operation "shuffling"! If a card sharp pulls anything like this as he is ostensibly shuffling the deck, we accuse him of cheating. For by "shuffling" we mean, quite precisely, a manipulation that *renders information obsolete*.

One connection of information with entropy is now clear. The second law proposes that, in any closed physical system, a shuffling over which we can ultimately have no control goes on constantly, in a way that, in the long run, renders obsolete any information we may have gathered about the internal structure of the system.

5

There is another connection between information and entropy, or another manifestation of the same connection, that we can get at by considering the nature of records.

We usually think of a record as stored information, to which a user can have access repeatedly rather than just once. For our purposes it is convenient to omit the requirement of more than one access, but to insist that the user of the record has some latitude as to just when he will read it. So defined, every mode of transmission or storage of information, except one, qualifies as a record. The one exception is a radiation signal. The receiver of a message, or reader of a record, must surely be a material body of some sort, not a pattern of radiation. Thus, no matter how a receiver is itself moving relative to some transmitter, a signal in the form of modulated electromagnetic radiation whizzes by just once, and is either read on that one occasion or is gone forever. In a practical way, for human beings, much the same is true of a sound signal; but in principle, of course, it is not. One can imagine shouting something very loudly, then rushing faster than the speed of sound to a point at the head of the wave train, then slowing down to the speed of sound and staying ahead of the wave train until ready to stop and read the signal. The required accelerations might be tough to take, but no laws of physics would be violated.[12]

Accepting this broad definition of a record, we find that there is an axiom about the storage of information that can best be set forth first in a

---

12. One recalls the jet pilot who, about 1960, shot down his own plane.

way that is not quite correct: *the recording of information requires the establishment of a stable spatial array of matter.* To be sure, stability is a matter of degree; all that we are requiring is that the array endure long enough to give the user some choice as to when he will read it. The stability need hold only within certain limits of size-level. For example, I have before me a sheet of paper with ink marks on it. I can move the whole sheet around, even put it in an envelope and mail it to Timbuctoo, without destroying the record. Also, the component molecules of the paper and ink are jiggling around, each within certain rough bounds. But within these two limiting size-levels the array of paper and ink is stable enough to count as a pretty good record. Unless it is torn up, burned, or lost irretrievably, I shall be able to read it again tomorrow. Everything that we ordinarily think of as a record meets the specifications we have given.

Indeed, we can turn our original phrasing around, and achieve a somewhat closer approximation to the axiom towards which we are heading: *any stable spatial array of matter is a record, attesting to the event or events that wrote it.*

Now, whether a record can be read or not depends on two things. In the first place, a great many records (particularly of certain sorts produced by human action) are the transductions, by one or another arbitrary code, of information that was originally in some other form; and we may not know the code. A record of this kind, like any record, is about the events that "wrote" it; but it is also, indirectly and often more interestingly, about whatever the original information was about. If I were walking through the woods and found some nāgarī characters carved in a tree trunk, I should be able to infer that someone had carved them, and might be able to estimate how long ago the carving was done, perhaps even something about the size and shape of the carving tool. But I would not know what the inscription "means," as we ordinarily understand that term, because I do not know nāgarī, nor the conventions for its use for any of the languages of India and nearby that are written with it, nor, indeed, do I know any of those languages.

In the second place, records deteriorate as time passes—some of them quickly, as when one traces a word with one's toe in the sand of a beach, some of them slowly, as when cuneiform symbols are pressed into clay tablets that are then dried and kept in a hot desert climate. Here, again, we see the second law at work. If a record has become too noisy, the remaining information may be highly ambiguous. An old, weathered book, even if printed in a language we know, may be virtually impossible to read. When archaeologists disagree about the proper interpretation of a find, or geologists dispute the history of a particular rock formation, it would seem to be this second factor that is responsible, rather than the workings of an unknown arbitrary code.

Familiar records of any durability are typically arrangements of crystalline matter, or of supercooled liquids, or of colloids in the gel state, or of mixtures of materials such as these—*hard* things rather than soft things. It is difficult to store information other than very briefly in a fluid. When we think we have done so, it often turns out that the information is not really in the fluid but in some rigid exoskeleton or endoskeleton, or both, that does the main job of "remembering" the gross arrangement in which the fluid is supposed to remain. It is the water that carves the river bed, but it is the river bed that guides the water to the sea. It is the skeleton and the flexible but tough skin of a vertebrate that remember the proper shape of the whole animal. Bones (or their three-dimensional imprint in stone) are valuable finds for the palaeontologist because they can do for him just what they did for their original owners, and this is also exactly why they are more apt to survive for subsequent discovery than are an animal's soft parts. Sometimes an endoskeleton, with no skin, is enough, but the only good example I can think of is a planet such as Earth, whose lithosphere, by virtue of gravity, is an endoskeleton for the hydrosphere and atmosphere. That matter in the crystalline state is not really essential is shown by the stability of an amoeba. Here the droplet of liquid is so small, relative to surface tension, that the outer layer serves as a sort of exoskeleton. Of course, if we consider an extremely small record, such as an RNA molecule or a helium atom, or an extremely large one, such as a galaxy, then such terms as "crystalline" and "liquid" cease to have any relevance; but the same basic principles apply.

Let us consider a record in the form of a configuration of crystalline matter. For fun, we shall suppose that the proprietor of a saloon at Point Barrow has carved the word "LIQUOR" on the face of a block of ice and has placed it in front of his door. The matter in this ice block might be changed to the liquid or gaseous state, but it is clear that melting or sublimating it would destroy a lot of the information stored in it—certainly, all the information coded into the carved letters. Now, by the third law, any given assemblage of matter has lower entropy at lower temperature. To melt or sublimate a solid one must add heat, raising the temperature, increasing the entropy—and decreasing the information.

Suppose that the ice sign is carved and put in place when the ambient temperature is −20 C, and that the temperature then rises to −10 C. The inscribed word is still legible. Can we say that information has been lost? Or suppose the temperature falls to −30 C. Can we say that information has increased? The ordinary solid citizen, interested in his drink, would say no, because he can still read the sign in the first case and cannot read it any better in the second. But it is possible, I believe necessary, to insist on an affirmative answer in both cases. We must remember that arbitrary codings, such as that of the English language and that of English orthography, are typically characterized by *redundancy*: that is, by an under-exploitation of the full range of physical possibilities, so that within certain limits noise is not apt to destroy intelligibility.[13] There is more information in the ice sign at -30 than at -10 because the coding is more redundant at the lower temperature than at the higher. By suitable choice of code, one could store more coded information in the ice (keeping the redundancy constant) at the lower temperature than at the higher. But that really means exactly the same as to say that, to raise the sign from -30 to, say, 0, one must add more heat, hence more entropy—and, hence, more noise—than is needed to raise it from -10 to 0.

As remarked earlier, we usually think of a record as something that can be read more than once. But when that is so it is only because the information in which we are interested has been coded redundantly. Suppose we consider our ice sign during the arctic night, when it is so dark that anyone who wishes to read it must use a flashlight. Each time it is read, the light adds a little energy to the sign. This energy may then dissipate, if the surrounding air is cold enough, thus restoring the amount of information in the sign; but the new information is no longer about the same thing. A few molecules of the sign have been knocked about in a way that is random and unpredictable relative to the arrangement that constitutes the carved letters; with the lowering of temperature after the flashlight is turned off, the new information is not about what is available in the saloon, but is about the event that knocked the molecules about and then lowered the temperature again—that is, about the flashing of the light. Thus, it is as though the information coded by the carving were present in a very large number of copies. Each reading removes a copy. Even if there were no other interactions between sign and surroundings, a sufficiently large number of readings would remove all copies.

Clearly, the reading of a record always has some impact on the state of the record, but the seriousness of this depends on the reading apparatus—or, we may say, on the reader. The ambient of a transfer RNA molecule, in a yeast cell nucleus, is able to read the information in that molecule very delicately indeed: a single molecule of the type is enough to get the job done. If human experimenters want to read the same information, they are forced to use apparatus and methods so gross that only the

13. See Shannon 1949.

existence of vast numbers of duplicates of the RNA molecule makes the task possible. Robert Holley estimates that in the seven-year determination by him and his colleagues of the chemical (not yet fully the stereochemical) structure of one type of transfer RNA molecule, they were required to manipulate approximately 2×10^{19} copies.[14]

Let us consider the limiting case, in which what holds our interest in a record is not some message coded into it in a particular arbitrary way, but just *all* the information in it. In this case there is no redundancy. And in this case there can exist no reading apparatus sufficiently delicate to make even a single *complete* reading possible. Unless there is some redundancy, then some of the information is bound to disappear before we can get around to it.

Every observable physical system must, by definition, contain *some* information. For if there be some material system in which entropy has actually reached a steady maximum—not the stone lodged part way down the hill, but the stone that has rolled to the very bottom—, so that it contains no information at all, then we have no way of knowing of its existence. For all intents and purposes, such a system would form a universe of its own, separate from ours.[15]

However, there are systems that contain dreadfully little information, usually because they are very small. In order to read what little information there is in an electron, we must interact with the electron in such a way that what we learn is ancient history (on the electron's time scale) by the time we have learned it. There is so very little information in the electron that we cannot read both its position and its momentum, but must settle for less accuracy about one of these if we want more accuracy about the other. An electron cannot even identify itself. One can distinguish an electron from some other kind of particle, or one electron from two electrons, but not one electron from another. Nor can additional information be stored in an electron—we cannot label one in such a way that we can recognize it for sure if we encounter it again. It is also a brute empirical fact that we cannot guarantee that we will observe a particular electron a second time by storing it apart from others. This is the method the priest uses in order to know which wine has been consecrated and which has not; if he forgets which is which, no chemist can help him. But electron-tight containers are physically impossible.

We have been aiming towards an axiom, which can now be stated in

14. See Apgar and others 1966, and earlier reports referred to in that one. The quantitative estimate was supplied by Holley at my request.

15. A black hole, matter contracted to within the Schwarzschild radius, is *not* an example: it is detectable through its gravitational field.

correct form: *the recording of information consists in the lowering of the entropy of a quantity of matter.* This is now perfectly general. The record need not be in crystalline matter, but can be in a solid, a single molecule, a galaxy, or anything else.

We can underscore these connections of entropy and information by presenting a beautiful conceptual experiment originally devised by von Neumann.[16] He does not mess around with playing cards, but deals directly with a gas system. If the principles of thermodynamics are correct, he says, then they must apply even in the limiting case of a one-molecule gas. Let us enclose such a gas in a rigid cylinder, connected to a heat reservoir so that pressure and temperature can be kept constant, and then insulate the cylinder, the heat reservoir, and ourselves as observers from the rest of the universe. At a given moment, we should like to know whether the one molecule is in the left-hand half or the right-hand half of the container. To find out, we insert a very thin rigid partition in the middle of the cylinder, perpendicular to its axis, in such a way that it is then free to slide along the axis to either end. If the partition in fact slides to the left, we know that the gas was in the right-hand half of the container at the moment the partition was inserted; correspondingly if the partition in fact slides to the right. The terminal position of the partition is our record of the location of the molecule. Or we can make some other record, and then remove the partition for reuse. Either way, the record that is kept involves a local lowering of entropy. On the other hand, in performing the mechanical work of moving the partition, the subsystem consisting of the gas and the heat reservoir has undergone an increase in entropy; as von Neumann says, we "trade entropy for information."

It should further be noted in this experiment that the very act of obtaining the desired information renders it obsolete. We know, at the end of the experiment, where the one-molecule gas *was.* But we do not know where it is *now*, because, by pushing the partition to one end of the cylinder, the gas has regained access to the cylinder's entire interior.

There are thus two inferences to be made. One: *the transmission of information entails an entropy increase at the transmitter.* Two: *information is always about the past.*

Before closing this part of our discussion we must make it clear that all we have said verges on tautology. That is not an apology; one proper aim of science is to unearth hidden tautologies. To say that information is always about the past is tautologous because, as was pointed out in §2, we are operationally forced to define the past exactly as that segment of the

16. von Neumann, J. 1955 pp. 399ff.

universe about which we have information. And all that we have said about the tie between information and entropy follows from the laws of thermodynamics if we merely define information as the inverse of entropy, as that which decreases when entropy increases and vice versa. We could even restate the second and third laws using information instead of entropy as the variable; in a sense, that would leave us just where we were before.

6

We have said that any stable spatial array of matter is a record. But that means that transducers (including the kinds we class as "transmitters" and "receivers") are just as much records as are the messages, other than those in the form of modulated radiation, that they handle. A phonograph disc is a record; so is the phonograph on which we play it. Yet there is clearly a difference. What is it?

Once upon a time there was a wealthy and eccentric music-lover who wanted to have ready access to all his favorite compositions, but who insisted on being different about how he did this. The ordinary way is to have a single phonograph, on which one may play any disc one chooses, and a different disc for each composition. Our millionaire decided to have just a single disc, and a different phonograph for each composition.

But when his highly paid engineers had finished the job according to specifications, he discovered that he didn't really need the disc to make things go. All it did was to turn on the particular phonograph on whose turntable it was placed. So he exchanged the disc for a central control panel on which was a single switch, with as many settings as he had phonographs. To choose a particular composition, he merely turned the switch to the proper setting. Next, he noticed that all the phonographs had certain circuits exactly in duplicate: for example, each had its own loudspeakers. That seemed wasteful, so he sold all but one set of speakers and wired what was left of all the phonographs to the single remaining set of speakers. When he had finished eliminating all duplications of circuitry and gadgetry, he discovered that everything that still remained in the individual phonographs, different from one to another, was stored information of the sort that could be more conveniently repackaged on vinylite discs. So, in the end, he had after all a single phonograph and many discs.

My inclination is to say that the phonograph disc is *reportive* while the phonograph is *nomic*. The disc remembers a particular performance, by a particular orchestra at a particular past time. The phonograph stores information of a vaguer sort, about the common features of a whole large class of specific events in the past, and makes equally vague predictions. The boundaries around the class of events of which the phonograph has knowledge can be explored by testing it with some unusual inputs. Given a disc on which the wiggles are too high or low in frequency, or too low in amplitude, the phonograph does not respond no matter how high the gain be set. Given one on which they are too high in amplitude, the circuits are overloaded and the performance distorted.

Two different phonographs, say one high-fi and one antique, will react to the same disc in different ways; and a still different sort of information is read from the disc if, instead of putting it on a turntable, we break off bits of it and put them into a series of test tubes with different reagents. In one sense, the information in a record is an absolute matter. In another, it is relative to the particular transducer that reads it. A signal is what is produced when two records collide, but the signal depends not only on the structure of the records but also on the exact geometry of the collision. That is perfectly obvious. What may not be so obvious is that we have already made this point twice, in other ways. We made it in §5 when we spoke of the recording or transmission of information by an arbitrary code; such information is then recoverable if and only if it was recorded or transmitted by a nonsingular transducer T and is read or received by a transducer T^{-1} which is the inverse of T. And we made essentially the same point when we spoke of our *interest* in one or another of the kinds of information present in some record. Entropy is not a function of interest, as is suggested by the traditional card-shuffling analogy (§4); but interest is a function of entropy. The only possible definition of the interest of a transducer, inorganic or organic, is simply its response characteristics: that is, the class of inputs about which it "has knowledge." That the response characteristics of some transducers change rapidly, those of others only slowly, is true and important, but at the moment irrelevant.

Another part of the same point is that there is no reason whatever why one and the same signal should convey the same amount of information to different receivers. A simple example using Shannon's measure of information in the discrete case suffices to show this. We have a transmitter T and two receivers R_1 and R_2. T is a person or mechanism that will pull a billiard ball at random out of an urn full of balls, each either white or black. The signal is the observed color of the ball. R_1 knows, in advance, that the urn contains the same number of white and black balls. R_2, on the other hand, knows in advance that there are three times as many white balls as black ones. This state of affairs can pertain because R_1 or R_2 is misinformed. It can also pertain because of different response characteristics: for example, let the balls actually range through various shades of gray, and let the effective cut-off shade between the judgment "white" and the judgment "black" be a lighter shade for R_2 than for R_1. Now a signal is transmitted—a ball is drawn and displayed. R_1 receives 1 binit of information. R_2 receives only 0.81128 binits.

In asserting that transducers are nomic, I am of course proposing that *all* so-called "general" information is in fact *vague*. The nomic is a generalizing bridge between the realm of the reportive and that of the expective; its vagueness is required by the noisiness of reports and the probabilistic indeterminacy of the future. All oracles, from Delphi to the present, have known that the vaguer prognostication is the safer one. Quantum theory asserts that this is inherent in nature, not just the consequence of some parochial defect in that small segment of nature constituted by human experimenters and their apparatus. Because an experiment can tell us fairly accurately where an electron or a photon *was*, we are led to speak of both in terms of particle mechanics. But if we want to predict where an electron or photon *will be*, our best tool is wave mechanics. It is too bad that de Broglie used the sober expression "théorie ondulatoire." Had he been a bit jazzier, we could now correctly assert that la théorie des vagues est nécessairement une théorie vague.

If our proposal about the nature of the nomic is correct, then it ought to hold of all nomic assertions. Here we must be careful. Not all nonreportive and nonexpective assertions are necessarily truly nomic—even in Hopi. "Mountains are high" is none of the three; it is a definition or a tautology, conveying information, at most, about a word (and thus serving, at most, to intercalibrate transducers). But "Pike's Peak is high" is nomic. Is it vague?

In the frame of reference of everyday life we find nothing imprecise or misleading about it; the reader who disagrees may replace the statement by "Pike's Peak stretches to an altitude of 4300 meters above sea level" without materially affecting our argument. Let us note that there are an enormous number of imaginable states for the totality of matter that we call "Pike's Peak" which, if observed, would be summarized by calling it high (just as there are, proportionately, a lot of possible bridge hands we would lump together as mediocre). Even if we group these states into sets within each of which the differences would be indistinguishable to ordinary human perception, the number of sets is still very great. The nomic assertion summarizes an indefinitely large number of past observations each of which found the matter in one of these states, but tells us nothing about *which* state was actually observed on any particular occasion. The nomic assertion also predicts that observations in the (geologically near) future are far more apt to register one of these states than one of an even vaster number that would yield a judgment other than "high."

The nomic, then, rests on stabilities, and hence also on a certain degree of vagueness. In turn, it is the nomic that establishes for us what has been called the *specious present*.

In classical mechanics, the assignment to a particle of an *instantaneous* momentum (or position) was actually a sort of anthropomorphizing: the instantaneous property was an artifact imposed on the particle by the old-fashioned methods of the infinitesimal calculus, in which infinitesimals were quantities smaller than any finite quantity yet greater than zero.[17] It is as though there could exist, for the particle, a very brief "specious present" during which nothing happens. But that does not make operational sense. Momentum and position are both time-dependent. Instantaneous observation is impossible. Any report on the state of a physical system must be based on some sort of averaging over an *interval* during which the observation took place, and that interval necessarily lies wholly in the past, in the realm of the reportive. In the frame of reference of Hopi-Whorf time, no one would ever have thought otherwise, since there simply *is* no present other than the specious present defined by the nomic.

Of course, the specious present so defined is a perfectly good kind of present. But it can be a reality only for a physical system both complex and stable enough that it can ignore—that is, can afford to be vague about—differences or changes below certain thresholds. The absolute threshold is defined by quanta. But this necessary minimum is far from sufficient: even in a cryotron, the lower bound for the miniaturization of components is set by thermal noise, not by quantum indeterminacies. A sufficient minimum would seem to be enough complexity to permit the internal shunting-around of information, combatting vagaries in the environment by homeostatic feedback. This we find in organs, in organisms, in some communities of organisms, and in some inorganic assemblages made by man; I do not know whether it occurs elsewhere in nature.[18]

For human beings, the specious present has a certain texture, that I should like to believe is necessarily the texture for any physical system complex and stable enough for the specious present to be a reality, though at the moment I do not know how that could be demonstrated. The

---

17. Such infinitesimals have once again been rendered mathematically respectable by the methods of so-called "nonstandard analysis." But that does not alter the physical judgment we pass on them in this paragraph.

18. Compare Schrödinger 1944.

boundary of the specious present is fuzzy, and its "size" and complexity change. Things or events within the specious present, however, do not have to be separated *spatially* in order to be distinguished. That is an error we would fall into only if we confused the specious present with the wholly fictive "instantaneous" present suggested by the traditional time of the physicists. Yet, clearly, the annoying itch and the relieving scratch are distinct, though the one is not above, to the left of, or behind the other. The specious present has four dimensions, not three. Were that not so, such an art as music would be impossible.[19]

7

As remarked at the end of §3, thermodynamics achieves its elegant simplicity of formulation by ignoring relativistic effects. The converse is also true: relativity theory achieves its grace and power by ignoring thermodynamics. That is clearly so, since the theory is set forth in terms of absolutely rigid rods and absolutely exact clocks, none of which can exist. Given this complementation, we cannot close our inquiry until we have made a reasonable effort to take both relativity and thermodynamics into account. But to do that we must first set thermodynamics aside temporarily and consider just relativity.

Historians tell us that the Battle of New Orleans was fought on 8 January 1815, fifteen days after the signing of the Treaty of Ghent on 24 December 1814. On 9 January 1815, in New Orleans, the survivors of the battle knew that the battle had been fought, but did not yet know about the signing of the treaty. For those survivors, at that date and place, did the treaty-signing lie in the past or in the future?

To ask such a question is to propose the following:

The epistemological status of an assertion about an event depends not only on the time but also on the *place* of the asserting, relative to the time *and the place* of the event. Operationally, what we have so far been calling the past and the future (in Hopi-Whorf time) must always be understood as the *local* past and future, relative to the site where observations and assertions are made. There is an operational link between the local future and the *spatially remote*. Uncertainty as to what is now happening elsewhere is on a par with uncertainty about what is going to happen next here. Our evidence for what is now happening elsewhere can only be some kind of message from elsewhere, and the transmission of messages requires time. Thus, if a message from elsewhere is on its way towards us now, its arrival here is a matter of the local future. The spatially remote

19. See a discussion elsewhere in this volume (p. 207).

becomes part of our local past only when (and if) the message arrives.

We must complicate our terminology slightly. From here on, instead of speaking simply of "past" and "future" we shall contrast the past with the *nonpast*, and the future with the *nonfuture*; the epithet "local" is always to be understood. The relevant distinctions and connections will become clear as we proceed.

Let us think of information transmitted over enormous distances at the fastest possible rate, the velocity of light in a vacuum. Let us imagine that we have established a colony on New Ghent, a planet of Alpha Centauri. There is an interstellar war, brought to an official close by the signing of a treaty in Orléans, on Earth. News of the treaty-signing is immediately dispatched via laser beam towards Alpha Centauri. But it takes 4.3 years to get there. Two weeks before the news arrives, there is a battle on New Ghent. Now, for the survivors, we must surely say that the Battle of New Ghent lies in the (local) past but that the signing of the Treaty of Orléans lies in the (local) nonpast until news of its signing has in fact arrived.

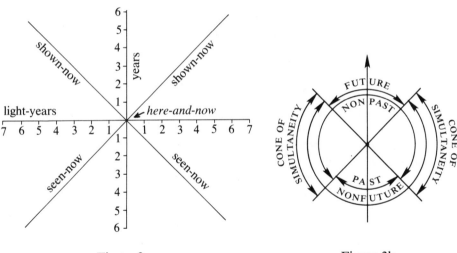

Figure 3a   Figure 3b

Still thinking of events taking place very far apart, let us look at Figure 3a. Here a single dimension of the page (left-and-right) is made to do duty for the three dimensions of space. The ordinate is time, marked off in years. The origin is the point marked "here-and-now." The abscissa, marked off in light-years, represents our everyday sort of imagined "universal now," which in fact turns out to be operationally meaningless but which is useful as a momentary prop. The lines running downwards from "here-and-now" at angles of 45° represent the here-and-now-observed. Eddington called these the "seen-now" lines.[20] But since space is three-dimensional, the two lines on the page really stand for one nappe of a hypercone with here-and-now at the vertex; so let us speak instead of the "seen-now-nappe." Relative to any given here-and-now, the seen-now nappe is the boundary between the past and the nonpast (Figure 3b). The rest of the hypercone, represented in the figure by the two lines angling upwards at 45° from the origin, can be called the "shown-now" nappe. Relative to any given here-and-now, the shown-now nappe is the boundary between the nonfuture and the future.

At merely earthly distances, the divergence between the seen-now nappe and the imaginary "universal now" is very slight. That would be obvious if we tried to redraw Figure 3 marking off the coordinates in units of everyday human relevance, say seconds and kilometers. Indeed, just that is the source of the imaginary "universal now": just as human beings are very much larger than elementary particles, so they are very much slower than light—and perhaps *must* be so, for reasons comparable to those discussed towards the end of §6—so that the man on the street, and even the physicist until the end of the nineteenth century, is led to assume that information can under some conditions be transmitted instantaneously.

However, the velocity of light, which affords the basis for the construction of the seen-now and shown-now nappes, is only an upper bound to the range of rates at which messages can travel. For a given neighborhood, the seen-now nappe is the boundary between the past and the nonpast only if in actual fact all messages from elsewhere are arriving with the velocity of light. But that is rarely the case. There are other (slower) channels, such as a messenger on horseback, and there are all sorts of delays in transmission, such as the messenger stopping to eat or rest.

In the interstellar case, the significance of the seen-now nappe is that it is an excellent approximation to the *received-now* nappe for information transmitted over interstellar distances. There is little indeterminacy about the nappe, since few messages are transmitted over such distances except via radiation (perhaps there is an occasional meteor of extrasolar origin), since the velocity of radiation in a vacuum can be taken as a constant, and since interstellar space is virtually a vacuum.

But the rate of transmission of messages in other channels is not a constant. For earthly affairs, the simple seen-now (and received-now) nappe of Figure 3 must be replaced by a jagged hypersurface whose

20. Eddington 1929 pp. 42ff.

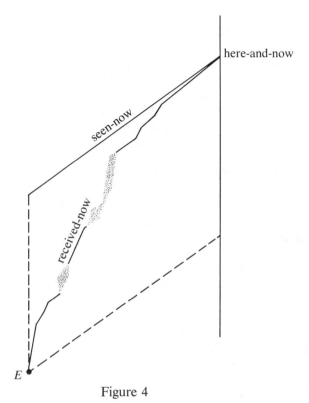

Figure 4

If, here-and-now, we receive a dated message from *E*, all we can know is that its trajectory towards us lies somewhere within the parallelogram and that no part of that trajectory has a slope less that 45°, that of the seen-now line. If the message is brought by a courier who records his route, his speed, and his stops, then we can reconstruct the "received-now" line in more detail, as shown (with fuzzy patches where the record is not explicit).

segments have various slopes, none of which are less than that of the seen-now nappe. Furthermore, for any chosen here-and-now, this jagged hypersurface may be incompletely known, as I have tried to show in Figure 4. That is because we can know the rate at which an incoming message traveled during a particular portion of its journey towards us only if we also receive information about that rate. Typically that additional information is incomplete or wanting.

In the earthly case, then, for any selected neighborhood, it is the jagged and fuzzy received-now hypersurface that constitutes the operationally relevant boundary between the local past and the local nonpast.

For just that reason, the interstellar war described above is an exact parallel of the actual events towards the end of the War of 1812. Ten years after the interstellar war, a wise historian would not say that the Treaty of Orléans was signed before the Battle of New Ghent was fought, nor vice versa. Rather, he would say that the two events were *simultaneous*— which is to say that each event lay in the "cone of simultaneity" of the other (Figure 5). Now, in the actual case, it does not matter that untold quintillions of neutrinos passed through the earth from Ghent to New Orleans, at nearly the speed of light, as the treaty was being signed, nor that radio waves bounced from the former city to the latter between the surface of the earth and the Heaviside layer during the same interval, because these transits in fact carried no information from those who were signing the treaty to those who fought the battle. Relative to the rates at which relevant information *actually traveled* from one human community to another in 1814 and 1815, the treaty-signing and the battle were simultaneous.[21] So Figure 5 can depict Ghent and New Orleans as validly as Orléans and New Ghent.

An event lies in our past if we have received information from it. It lies in our nonpast otherwise. An event lies in our future if we lie in its past. It lies in our nonfuture otherwise. Thus the local future lies wholly within the local nonpast, and the local past wholly within the local nonfuture; but the local nonpast and the local nonfuture intersect, as that region which constitutes our "cone of simultaneity" (Figure 3b).

When two events, A and B, both lie in our past, then there are three possible judgments we may pass as to their position relative to each other. If A lies in the local past of B, we say that A occurred before B. If B lies in the local past of A, we say that A occurred after B. If neither lies in the local past of the other, we say that they were simultaneous.[22]

When two events, A and B, lie respectively in our local past and our local nonpast, a judgment that "A is before B" has a different meaning. This is a different "before," only a homonym of the one defined in the preceding paragraph. We are predicting. We are speaking in the expective tense, not the reportive, and are saying that, when certain indeterminacies

21. "Simultaneous" (referring to the "cone of simultaneity") is the relativistic physicist's term. Historians and anthropologists usually speak, instead, of *independent* events: for example, the invention of writing among the Mayas neither influenced nor was influenced by the invention of writing in the Old World. But the meaning is the same.

22. A fourth alternative, that each of A and B lies in the local past of the other, is precluded by all solutions so far found for Einstein's equations of general relativity, except for a very queer solution worked out by Gödel that is so counterintuitive that I shall ignore it (see Bonnor 1964 pp. 144–156).

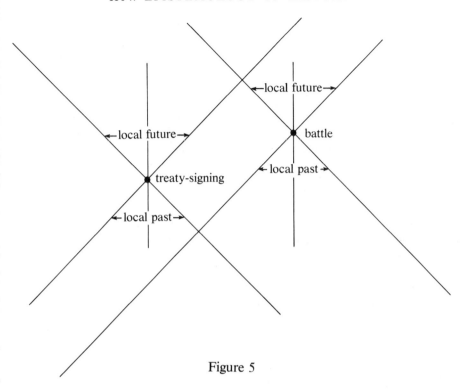

Figure 5

have been resolved so that both *A* and *B* are in our past, it will turn out that *A* was before *B* in the reportive sense. Like any other expectation, this one can turn out to have been wrong.

There is still a third legitimate use of "before"—actually, the commonest one, but to be clearly distinguished from both of the above. In 1814 and 1815, as still today, local events all over the European-American world were being timed and recorded by a single calendrical system, with frequent recalibration from one locality to another. Such practices succeed in spreading a quasi-absolute time-scale to all points within a limited region of space. Thus, when we note that the treaty was signed on 24 December 1814 and that the battle was fought on 8 January 1815, of course we are entitled to assert that the treaty was signed "before" the battle— but only in this limited *calendrical* sense of "before," drawing no inferences as though the word could here have one of its other senses.

General relativity tells us that such synchronization of clocks or calendars in different places cannot be exact, and that the achievable approximation to exactness diminishes with the distance between the places.[23] It turns out that this is irrelevant to our argument; but we must see why. Indeed, suppose that it actually *were* possible, through some complicated combination of light signals and of shipments of clocks and accelerometers, to spread a uniform time-scale as far as from here to Alpha Centauri, and suppose that that had been done before the interstellar war. The logic of the hypothesized events would in no way be changed. As long as there is a *finite speed limit for the transmission of information*, the boundary between the local past and the local nonpast must be the "received-now" nappe.

8

When we try to take both relativity and thermodynamics into account at the same time, we encounter two sorts of difficulty.

First: relativity treats material things, which are in fact (as thermodynamics shows) world-tubes, as though they were world-lines, and it treats events, which are in fact regions of the plenum, as though they were points. That is harmless when the events are far apart as compared with their internal extension, as in the case of the treaty and the battle either of the War of 1812 or of our imagined interstellar war. It breaks down when one event, such as the making of a report, an observation, a prediction, or a decision, is smaller than and embedded within another.

Second: thermodynamics does not tell us how to interpret the situation when information leaves one event by two or more channels, traveling at different rates and thus arriving at some other place at different times.

Here is a problem that involves both of these difficulties.

Standing on a hilltop, we dispatch a delegate into the valley to negotiate with a representative from a neighboring tribe. We watch them confer, but cannot hear their words. They wave goodbye and we see our delegate start back up the hill. The parley itself now lies in the past, for our delegate and for us. How about the *substance* of the parley?—what was said, what agreement (if any) was reached? This, also, lies in the past for our delegate: any uncertainty about it for him is due to some sort of noise, say a poor memory. For us on the hilltop, as we await our delegate's report, is uncertainty about the substance of the parley a matter of likelihood or of probability?

As the question has just been phrased, the correct answer is: *both*. With

23. The effects of gravitational and accelerational fields do not have to be mentioned separately, since they can be taken into account by the geometry within which distance is measured.

a slight change of orientation, however, one gets a different but equally correct answer: *neither*.

(1) *Both*. It is clear that both the parley and its substance lie in the local nonfuture for us on the hilltop: that is, we cannot influence either. The fact of the parley lies in our past as soon as we see that it is over. Its substance lies then in our nonpast, and hence in our cone of simultaneity. Before the parley began, our uncertainty about the substance was a matter of probability. After our delegate has reached us and reported, any uncertainty will be a matter of likelihood. But while he is climbing back up the hill our uncertainty involves probability because his report lies in our future, and likelihood because when we do receive his report noise may have introduced discrepancies between what he tells us and what actually went on during the parley.

That is the answer we get by focusing on the group of us at the top of the hill.

(2) *Neither*. Instead of that, let us regard our delegate, ourselves waiting on the hilltop, and the rest of our tribe as parts of a single homeostatic system. Then it is only relative to the whole system that we can legitimately speak of past, nonpast, and the like. The uphill climb of our delegate is an episode in the internal shunting-around of information by virtue of which the system is homeostatic and has a specious present (§6). Since the uphill climb is taking place within the specious present of the system, neither likelihood nor probability is relevant.

So it depends on the size and nature of the system at the focus of attention. The parts of a big homeostatic system can themselves be homeostatic systems, so that events which are internal to the more inclusive one are external to an included one.

9

What, then, of the epistemology of history?

We have learned that the historian, like the engineer or the physicist, must itself be a reasonably large, complex, and stable physical system, in order that there may exist for it a specious present. Surely an amoeba is complex enough to have some sense of history, but a very feeble sense compared with our own; a pebble, I suppose, or an electron, has none at all. At the same time, the system must be reasonably compact, so that the local past can be virtually the same everywhere within it. A spherical historian with the radius of a light-year would be able to deal only with the relatively remote past, as we judge such things, only with relatively ponderous events, and only rather ponderously. Fortunately, all the historians of immediate concern to us fall well within these rough limits—even such a massive historian as, say, the Mississippi Valley Historical Association.

The realm of the historian is the realm of the reportive. His data—his only possible data—are records. These records exist in his specious present: they can be copied, shuffled, collated, compared. They contain information, but they are also noisy. The noise is of two sorts. "Absolute" noise is the result of increasing entropy, and in the long run nothing can be done about it. The historian may curse it, but we shall see in a moment that he would be quite helpless without it. "Relative" noise is ultimately the same, but in the first instance is quite different: it is what Shannon was referring to when he pointed out that noise can be regarded as "unwanted signal."[24] A signal or record that carries certain information by one arbitrary code may at the same time carry other information by other codes; if we happen to be interested in the first, then the rest can be an annoyance. Snow on the television screen is noise for the viewer who wants to watch the show, but signal for a repairman if it tells him which part of the circuitry to test first.

The task of the historian is so to collate and arrange his data as to minimize the effects of noise. This is what the academic historian means by the "critical method."[25] The limits within which he is forced to work are set by the redundancy with which the information has been recorded (and has survived). Since the historian and his data exist in the specious present, we may say in the first instance that the historian's shuffling of the data merely attempts to set it out in the clearest array, within the dimensionality afforded by the specious present.

Now we see why it is so important to recognize that the specious present itself has four dimensions, not merely three (§6, end). If a historian tries a purely spatial array, he can find no arrangement that makes sense. He is forced to introduce a fourth coordinate supplied by the texture of the specious present; and he is forced to stretch it far beyond the maximum limits within the specious present. Of course, he calls this fourth axis "time." We must understand that this backwards-stretched "time," devised by the historian, is part of the necessary geometry of the local past, and that in the Hopi-Whorf frame of reference it has nothing directly to do with the expective: it is not, or not yet, the "time" of the physicist.

The historian can do nothing without evidence; he can do nothing *with* evidence unless he has some guiding principle by which to organize it. It

24. Op. cit.
25. See, for example, H. C. Hockett 1955, especially pp. 3–82.

turns out that this principle is exactly the second law of thermodynamics, in any of innumerable manifestations, which tells the historian which of two nonsimultaneous states of affairs must have come first. In general, the lower rock stratum is the older; that is the second law at work. King George the First was not called that until there was a second, so that a coin bearing the inscription "Georgivs I Rex" must be spurious, a later counterfeit; that is the second law at work. When sound change leads to the coalescence of two phonemes of a language, the chance that the state of affairs before the coalescence can be reestablished is vanishingly small; that is the second law at work. Entropy, which destroys historical evidence, also serves to order it. It is a law of nature that historical evidence must be incomplete; for, if it were complete, there would have been no increase in entropy, hence no *events*—and hence no historians!

It is the historian's discovery that the reportive requires four dimensions, not three, that underlies the physicist's usual frame of reference for the whole plenum. By a remarkable act of faith, the physicist decides that he can talk about *all* events, future as well as past, with a four-dimensional framework constructed on the analogy of that of the historian.

Sometimes a historian tries a sort of experiment. He considers only some of the available data, and attempts to arrange them in such a way that the proper location for the data temporarily set aside will be obvious. The linguist does this if he first reconstructs Proto Romance without using the evidence of, say, Portuguese, and then examines that evidence; he does this if he first uses the evidence of all the daughter languages and only then consults our surviving written records of Latin. This is like the procedure of a communications engineer in testing the capacity of a particular channel. The only way he can test the channel is by comparing what it delivers with the same information transmitted by other channels. When he has thus compared the transmission of *all* channels, there is simply nothing else he can do. Similarly, when the historian has actually taken into account *all* the evidence bearing on a particular region of the past, he is done. Yet his exegesis of a particular region of the past is never definitive, for nature constantly forces on him the very same experiment that he sometimes performs intentionally. No matter how thoroughly one has searched for evidence bearing on a particular past state or event, it is always possible that new evidence will turn up; that is, some information may have been transmitted from the state or event by slow channels, so that it has not yet reached the historian, so that some aspects of the state or event are still in the historian's cone of simultaneity.

And so, at long last, we may return to the methodological dispute in historical linguistics with which we began our inquiry.

Let us recall that this dispute has a narrow interpretation (merely about the relative reliability of written records and of the diverse descendant forms of a single earlier language) which can hardly interest anyone but a specialist. Our aim was to see whether there is a broader and more generally significant interpretation of the same dispute.

But if we transfer the comparative method into the whole realm of history, in which one is committed to using *all* available evidence, that method simply becomes the sole method by which any historian can proceed. Further, on this broadest possible stage, the recommendations of the realists and those of the formulaists become indistinguishable. Thus, if the debate is not trivial, it is vacuous.

REFERENCES

Apgar, J., G. A. Everett, and R. Holley. 1966. "Analyses of large nucleotide fragments obtained from a yeast alanine transfer ribonucleic acid by partial digestion with ribonuclease T1." *Journal of Biological Chemistry* 241.1206–1211.

Bergmann, P. G. 1951. *Basic theories of physics: Heat and quanta.* New York: Prentice-Hall.

Bloomfield, L. 1933. *Language.* New York: Holt.

Bonnor, W. 1964. *The mystery of the expanding universe.* New York and London: Macmillan.

Buck, C. D. 1926. "Some questions of practice in the notation of reconstructed IE forms." *Language* 2.99–107.

Eddington, A. S. 1929. *The nature of the physical world.* Cambridge: The University Press and New York: Macmillan.

Feller, W. 1957. *An introduction to probability theory and its applications.* 2nd ed. New York: Wiley.

Hockett, C. F. 1958. *A course in modern linguistics.* New York: Macmillan.

Hockett, H. C. 1955. *The critical method in historical research and writing.* New York: Macmillan.

Schrödinger, E. 1944. *What is life?* Cambridge: The University Press.

Shannon, C. E. 1949. "The mathematical theory of communication." In C. E. Shannon and W. Weaver, [same title]. Urbana: University of Illinois Press.

von Neumann, J. 1955. *Mathematical foundations of quantum mechanics.* Princeton: Princeton University Press. (Translated from the German original of 1932).

Weaver, W. 1948. "Probability, rarity, interest, and surprise." *Scientific Monthly* 670.390–392.

Whorf, B. L. 1938. "Some verbal categories of Hopi." *Language* 14.275–286.

Wiener, N. 1948. *Cybernetics.* New York: Wiley.

BIBLIOGRAPHY, 1939–1976

ABBREVIATIONS

AA   *American Anthropologist.*
IJAL *International Journal of American Linguistics.*
Lg   *Language, Journal of the Linguistic Society of America.*
PT   V. B. Makkai, ed., *Phonological Theory: Evolution and Current Practice* (New York: Holt, 1972).
RiL   M. Joos, ed., *Readings in Linguistics* (Washington, D.C.: American Council of Learned Societies, 1957).
SiL   *Studies in Linguistics.*

(1) 1939. Potawatomi syntax. *Lg* 15.235–248.
(2) 1940. Review of: F. Boas, ed., *Handbook of American Indian Languages, Part 3. Lg* 16.54–57.
(3) 1942a. A system of descriptive phonology. *Lg* 18.3–21. Reprinted in *RiL* 97–108; in *PT* 99–112.
(4) 1942b. English verb inflection. *SiL* 1:1.
(5) 1942c. Review of: M. Haas, *Tunica* (extract from *Handbook of American Indian Languages, Part 4*). *AA* 44.489.
(6) 1943. The position of Potawatomi in Central Algonkian. *Papers of the Michigan Academy of Science, Arts, and Letters* 28.537–542.
(7) 1944a. (With C. Fang) *Spoken Chinese: Basic Course.* Military edition published (without authors' names) as a War Department Education Manual. Civilian edition, New York: Holt.
(8) 1944b. Review of: E. A. Nida, *Linguistic Interludes* and *Morphology: The Descriptive Analysis of Words* (preliminary edition). *Lg.* 20.252–255.
(9) 1945a. (With C. Fang) *Guide's Manual* for *Spoken Chinese.* Military edition published (without authors' names) as a War Department Education Manual. Civilian edition, New York: Holt.
(10) 1945b. (Coeditor, with C. Fang) *Dictionary of Spoken Chinese.* Military edition only, published (without editors' names) as War Department Technical Manual 30–933. Authorized revision prepared under the supervision of R. A. Miller by the staff of the Institute of Far Eastern Languages, Yale University (New Haven: Yale University Press, 1966); nowhere in this version is credit given explicitly to the editors or other workers on the original military edition.
(11) 1946. Sapir on Arapaho. *IJAL* 12.243–245.
(12) 1947a. Peiping phonology. *Journal of the American Oriental Society* 67.253–267. Reprinted in *RiL* 217–228.

(13) 1947b. Componential analysis of Sierra Popoluca. *IJAL* 13.258–267.

(14) 1947c. Review of: E. A. Nida, *Morphology: The Descriptive Analysis of Words* (first edition). *Lg* 23.273–285.

(15) 1947d. Problems of morphemic analysis. *Lg* 23.321–343. Reprinted in *RiL* 229–242.

(16) 1948a. Potawatomi [in four installments:] I, II, III, IV. *IJAL* 14.1–10, 63–73, 139–149, 213–225.

(17) 1948b. Implications of Bloomfield's Algonquian studies. *Lg* 24.117–131. Reprinted in *RiL* 281–289; in D. Hymes, ed., *Language in Culture and Society* (New York: Harper and Row, 1964), 599–609, and, with a few emendations of wording by the author, in *A Leonard Bloomfield Anthology* (Bloomington: Indiana University Press, 1970), 495–511.

(18) 1948c. Review of: H. Hoijer, ed., *Linguistic Structures of Native America* (Viking Fund Publications in Anthropology, No. 6). *Lg* 24.183–188.

(19) 1948d. Review of: M. Swadesh, *Chinese in Your Pocket. SiL* 6.49–50.

(20) 1948e. A note on "structure." *IJAL* 14.269–271. Reprinted in *RiL* 279–280.

(21) 1948f. Biophysics, linguistics, and the unity of science. *American Scientist* 36.558–572. Reprinted in *ETC.: A Review of General Semantics* 6.218–232 (1949), as A-115 in the Bobbs-Merrill Reprint Series (1962), and in the present collection.

(22) 1949a. Two fundamental problems in phonemics. *SiL* 7.29–51. Reprinted in *PT* 200–210.

(23) 1949b. Review of: Y. R. Chao, *Mandarin Primer. Lg* 25.210–215.

(24) 1950a. Peiping morphophonemics. *Lg* 26.63–85. Reprinted in *RiL* 315–348.

(25) 1950b. Language "and" culture: A protest. *AA* 52.113.

(26) 1950c. The conjunct modes in Ojibwa and Potawatomi. *Lg* 26.118–121.

(27) 1950d. Which approach in linguistics is "scientific"? *SiL* 8.53–57.

(28) 1950e. Reactions to Indian place names. *American Speech* 25.118–121.

(29) 1950f. Age-grading and linguistic continuity. *Lg* 26.449–457. Reprinted (without author's permission) without the footnotes and under the shortened title "Linguistic continuity" in S. Rogers, ed., *Children and Language: Readings in Early Language and Socialization* (London: Oxford University Press, 1975) 66–77.

(30) 1950g. Learning pronunciation. *The Modern Language Journal* 34.261–269. Rewritten from the Introduction of item 31.

(31) 1951a. *Progressive Exercises in Chinese Pronunciation*. Mirror Series, Yale University Institute of Far Eastern Languages.

(32) 1951b. Review of: A. Rappoport, *Science and the Goals of Man*. In *ETC.: A Review of General Semantics* 8.132–141.

(33) 1951c. Review of: A. Martinet, *Phonology as Functional Phonetics. Lg* 27.333–342. Reprinted in *PT* 310–317.

(34) 1951d. Review of: J. de Francis, *Nationalism and Language Reform in China. Lg* 27.439–445.

(35) 1951e. (With W. G. Moulton) Germanic and Algonquian: A modern myth. *American-Scandinavian Review* 39.314–318.

(36) 1952a. (With W. E. Welmers and others) *Structural Notes and Corpus: A Basis for the Preparation of Materials to Teach English as a Foreign Language*. Washington, D.C.: American Council of Learned Societies. The names of the participants do not appear.

(37) 1952b. An approach to the quantification of semantic noise. *Philosophy of Science* 19.257–260.

(38) 1952c. A formal statement of morphemic analysis. *SiL* 10.27–39.

(39) 1952d. A new study of fundamentals [review of: Z. S. Harris, *Methods in Structural Linguistics*]. *American Speech* 27.117–121.

(40) 1952e. Review of: *Recherches Structurales (Travaux du Cercle Linguistique de Copenhague*, vol. 5). *IJAL* 18.86–99.

(41) 1952f. Speech and writing. *Report of the Third Annual Round Table Meeting on Linguistics and Language Teaching* (Institute of Languages and Linguistics, Georgetown University, Monograph Series no. 2) 67–76.

(42) 1953a. Review of: C. L. Shannon and W. Weaver, *The Mathematical Theory of Communication*. *Lg* 29.69–93. Reprinted in S. Saporta, ed., *Psycholinguistics: A Book of Readings* (New York: Holt, 1961) 44–67, and in the present collection. Polish translation: Recenzja Książki C. L. Shannona i W. Weavera *Matematyczna Teoria Komunikacji*, in *Z Zagadnień Językoznawstwa Współczesnego, Gramatyka transformacyjna, Teoria informacji* (Warszawa: Państwowe Wydawnictwa Naukowe, 1966) 123–158.

(43) 1953b. Errata in Bloomfield's Algonquian Sketch. *IJAL* 19.78.

(44) 1953c. Introduction. In W. W. Gage and H. M. Jackson, *Verb Constructions in Vietnamese* (Cornell University Southeast Asia Program Data Paper no. 9, July) ii–iii.

(45) 1953d. Linguistic time-perspective and its anthropological uses. *IJAL* 19.146–152.

(46) 1953e. Short and long syllable nuclei, with examples from Algonquian, Siouan, and Indo-European. *IJAL* 19.165–171.

(47) 1954a. [Untitled note objecting to remarks in a review of P. L. Garvin.] *Lg* 30.195.

(48) 1954b. Two models of grammatical description. *Word* 10.210–234. Reprinted in *RiL* 386–399.

(49) 1954c. Chinese versus English: An investigation of the Whorfian theses. In H. Hoijer, ed., *Language in Culture* (Memoir 79 of the American Anthropological Association, supplement to *AA* 56:6), 106–123. Reprinted in M. Fried, *Readings in Anthropology* (1st ed.; New York: Crowell, 1959) 1.232–248, and in the present collection.

(50) 1954d. Translation via immediate constituents. *IJAL* 20.313–315.

(51) 1955a. *A Manual of Phonology*. Indiana University Publications in Anthropology and Linguistics, Memoir 11.

(52) 1955b. Attribution and apposition. *American Speech* 30.99–102.

(53) 1955c. How to learn Martian. *Astounding Science Fiction* 55.97–106 (May). Reprinted in M. Greenberg, ed., *Coming Attractions* (New York: Gnome Press, 1957) 38–51, in E. Z. Friedenberg and others, eds., *The Cosmos*

Reader (New York: Harcourt Brace Jovanovich, 1971) 147–155, and in the present collection.

(54) 1955d. Review of: E. Otto, *Stand und Aufgabe der allgemeinen Sprachwissenschaft. Lg* 31.92–93.

(55) 1956a. Central Algonquian /t/ and /c/. *IJAL* 22.202–207.

(56) 1956b. Idiom formation. In M. Halle and others, eds., *For Roman Jakobson* (The Hague: Mouton) 222–229. Adapted from a preliminary version of a chapter in item 61. Italian translation: T. Bolelli, ed., *Linguistica Generale, Strutturalismo, Linguistica Storica* (Pisa: Nistri-Lischi, 1971) 404–418.

(57) 1956c. Review of: W. La Barre, *The Human Animal*; C. S. Coon, *The Story of Man*; V. G. Childe, *Man Makes Himself*; G. G. Simpson, *The Meaning of Evolution. Lg* 32.460–469.

(58) 1956d. Review of: S. E. Martin, *Korean Morphophonemics. Lg* 32.814–819.

(59) 1957a. Central Algonquian vocabulary: Stems in /k-/. *IJAL* 23.247–268.

(60) 1957b. The terminology of historical linguistics. *SiL* 12.57–73.

(61) 1958a. *A Course in Modern Linguistics*. New York: Macmillan. Polish translation: *Kurs Językoznawstwa Współczesnego* (Warszawa: Państwowe Wydawnictwa Naukowe, 1969). India edition: New Delhi: Oxford and IBH, 1970. Spanish adaptation by E. Gregores and J. A. Suárez, *Curso de lingüística moderna* (Buenos Aires: Eudeba, 1971).

(62) 1958b. English stress and juncture. *Language Learning*, special issue for June, 57–67.

(63) 1958c. (Editor for posthumous publication of:) L. Bloomfield, *Eastern Ojibwa: Grammar, Texts, and Word Lists*. Ann Arbor: University of Michigan Press.

(64) 1959a. Animal "languages" and human language. *Human Biology* 31.32–39 (February). Whole issue reprinted as J. N. Spuhler, ed., *The Evolution of Man's Capacity for Culture* (Detroit: Wayne University Press, 1959).

(65) 1959b. On the format of phonemic reports, with restatement of Ocaina. *IJAL* 25.59–62.

(66) 1959c. The stressed syllabics of Old English. *Lg* 35.575–597.

(67) 1959d. Review of: S. Ullman, *The Principles of Semantics. AA* 61.158.

(68) 1959e. Review of: R. Brown, *Words and Things. American Sociological Review* 24.729–730.

(69) 1959f. Objectives and processes of language instruction. *California Schools* 30.456–460 (November). Reprinted in Australia in *New Australians*, and in a comparable service journal in India sponsored by the British Council, New Delhi.

(70) 1959g. Language study and cultural attitudes. *The Linguistics Reporter* 1:5. 1,4–6. Reprinted in *California Schools* 31.112–116 (February 1960) under a different title: Relationships between development of language skills and cultural attitudes.

(71) 1960a. (With R. E. Pittenger as senior author, and J. J. Danehy) *The First Five Minutes: An Example of Microscopic Interview Analysis*. Ithaca, N.Y.: Paul Martineau. The chapter on "Findings" reprinted, with minor

emendations, in J. A. DeVito, *Communication: Concepts and Processes*, revised and enlarged edition (New York: Prentice-Hall, 1976) 82–97.

(72) 1960b. Ethnolinguistic implications of studies in linguistics and psychiatry. *Report of the Ninth Annual Round Table Meeting on Linguistics and Language Study* [held 1958] (Institute of Languages and Linguistics of Georgetown University, Monograph Series no. 11) 175–193. Reprinted in the present collection.

(73) 1960c. Grammar for the hearer. In R. Jakobson, ed., *The Structure of Language in its Mathematical Aspects* (American Mathematical Society Proceedings of Symposia in Applied Mathematics, vol. 12) 220–236. Russian translation: *Novoe v Lingvistike* 4.139–166 (Moscow, 1965).

(74) 1960d. Logical considerations in the study of animal communication. In W. E. Lanyon and W. N. Tavolga, eds., *Animal Sounds and Communication* (Washington, D.C.: American Institute of Biological Sciences Symposium Series, no. 7) 392–430. Reprinted in the present collection.

(75) 1960e. The origin of speech. *Scientific American* 203.3 (September). Available from W. H. Freeman as an offprint, and included in two volumes of offprints from *Scientific American* published by W. H. Freeman: *Human Variations and Origins* (about 1968); *Physiological Psychology* (about 1972). German translation: Der Ursprung der Sprache, in I. Schwidetzky, ed., *Über die Evolution der Sprache* (Frankfort am Main: S. Fischer Verlag, 1973) 135–150.

(76) 1961a. Linguistic elements and their relations. *Lg* 37.29–53.

(77) 1961b. Review of: L. Kaiser, ed., *Manual of Phonetics*. *Lg* 37.266–269.

(78) 1961c. European struggles with [the] Fijian [language]. Suva, Fiji: *Fiji Times*, 20 and 21 July.

(79) 1962. (Editor for posthumous publication of:) L. Bloomfield, *The Menomini Language*. William Dwight Whitney Linguistic Series of Yale University. New Haven: Yale University Press.

(80) 1963a. The problem of universals in language. In J. H. Greenberg, ed., *Universals of Language* 1–22; 2nd ed. (1966) 1–29 (Cambridge, Mass.: MIT Press). Reprinted in the present collection.

(81) 1963b. Review of: J. C. Lilly, *Man and Dolphin*. *AA* 65.176.

(82) 1963c. Comment on: A. L. Bryan, The essential morphological basis for human culture. *Current Anthropology* 4.303–304.

(83) 1963d. (With N. Brooks and E. V. O'Rourke) *Language Instruction: Perspective and Prospectus*. Bulletin of the California State Department of Education 32:4.

(84) 1964a. Scheduling. In F. S. C. Northrop and H. H. Livingston, eds., *Cross-Cultural Understanding: Epistemology in Anthropology* (New York: Harper and Row) 125–144. Reprinted in the present collection.

(85) 1965b. The Proto Central Algonquian kinship system. In W. Goodenough, ed., *Explorations in Cultural Anthropology: Essays in Honor of George Peter Murdock* (New York: McGraw-Hill) 239–258.

(86) 1964c. (With R. Ascher) The human revolution. *American Scientist* 52.70–

92 and *Current Anthropology* 5.135–168. The version in *American Scientist* is slightly shorter but has one paragraph not included in the other; the version in *Current Anthropology* has full critical apparatus and comments from 26 colleagues. Reprinted as A-306 in the Bobbs-Merrill Reprint Series (1966). Also reprinted (in full or with cuts) in a number of books, including the following: M. F. Ashley Montagu, ed., *Culture: Man's Adaptive Dimension* (New York: Oxford University Press, 1968). Y. A. Cohen, ed., *Man in Adaptation: The Biosocial Background* (Chicago: Aldine, 1968; 2nd ed., 1974). P. Shepard and D. McKinley, eds., *The Subversive Science: Essays towards an Ecology of Man* (Boston: Houghton Mifflin, 1969). J. D. Jennings and E. A. Hoebel, *Readings in Anthropology,* 3rd ed. (New York: McGraw-Hill, 1972). M. H. Fried, ed., *Readings in Anthropology*, 2nd ed. (New York: Crowell, 1968).

(87) 1965a. Sound change. [Presidential address to the Linguistic Society of America, 28 December 1964, New York City.] *Lg* 41.185–204.

(88) 1965b. On race and language. In C. S. Coon, *The Living Races of Man* (New York: Knopf) 40–42.

(89) 1966a. What Algonquian is really like. *IJAL* 32.59–73.

(90) 1966b. Language, mathematics, and linguistics. In T. A. Sebeok, ed., *Current Trends in Linguistics Volume 3: Theoretical Foundations* (The Hague: Mouton) 155–304. Also issued separately, in slightly revised form with a crucially important new preface, in 1967, as number 60 in Mouton's *Janua Linguarum, series minor*.

(91) 1966c. Reply to: Some comments concerning Hockett and Ascher's contribution on the human revolution (*Current Anthropology* 7.197–203, 1966). *Current Anthropology* 7.203–204.

(92) 1967a. Review of: G. Milner, *Samoan Dictionary. AA* 69.257.

(93) 1967b. The quantification of functional load. *Word* 23.300–320.

(94) 1967c. The Yawelmani basic verb. *Lg* 43.208–222.

(95) 1967d. Where the tongue slips, there slip I. In *To Honor Roman Jakobson* (The Hague: Mouton) 910–936. Reprinted in V. A. Fromkin, ed., *Speech Errors as Linguistic Evidence* (The Hague: Mouton, 1973) 93–119, and in the present collection.

(96) 1967e. Review of: E. H. Lenneberg, *Biological Foundations of Language. Scientific American* 217.141–144 (November).

(97) 1968a. *The State of the Art.* The Hague: Mouton (*Janua Linguarum, series minor* number 73). Italian translation by G. R. Cardona, *La linguistica americana contemporanea* (Roma: Editori Laterza, 1970).

(98) 1968b. Leonard Bloomfield. *International Encyclopaedia of the Social Sciences* 2.95–99.

(99) 1968c. [Untitled note correcting a prevalent misinterpretation of Two models of grammatical description (1954b in the present list).] *Lg* 44.212

(100) 1968d. (With S. A. Altmann) A note on design features. In T. A. Sebeok, ed., *Animal Communication* (Bloomington: Indiana University Press) 61–72.

(101) 1968e. Reply [to M. Haas's comments on Bloomfield's *The Menomini Language*]. *AA* 70.569.

(102) 1968f. (Participation in) CA* book review of T. A. Sebeok, ed., *Current Trends in Linguistics Volume 3: Theoretical Foundations. Current Anthropology* 9.125–179 (specifically 128, 171–174).

(103) 1968g. Review of: S. M. Lamb, *Outline of Stratificational Grammar. IJAL* 34.145–153.

(104) 1968h. Comment on: F. B. Livingstone, Genetics, biology, and the origins of incest and exogamy. *Current Anthropology* 10.51–52.

(105) 1970. (Editor:) *A Leonard Bloomfield Anthology.* Bloomington: Indiana University Press.

(106) 1972a. (With I. Goddard and K. V. Teeter) Some errata in Bloomfield's *Menomini. IJAL* 38.1–5.

(107) 1972b. Completing the allegory [of *The Wizard of Oz*]. *The Baum Bugle,* Spring 23–24.

(108) 1973a. *Man's Place in Nature.* New York: McGraw-Hill.

(109) 1973b. (With S. Bryan) *Instructor's Manual for Man's Place in Nature.* New York: McGraw-Hill.

(110) 1973c. Jokes. In M. E. Smith, ed., *Studies in Linguistics in Honor of George L. Trager* (The Hague: Mouton) 153–178. Reprinted in the present collection.

(111) 1973d. Erwin Allen Esper [obituary and appreciation]. In E. A. Esper, *Analogy and Association in Linguistics and Psychology* (Athens: University of Georgia Press) v–xxvii.

(112) 1973e. Yokuts as testing-ground for linguistic methods. *IJAL* 39.63–79.

(113) 1973f. The reconstruction of Proto Fijian-Polynesian. [60 pages; xeroxed and distributed to about 100 Austronesian specialists.]

(114) 1974. Leonard Bloomfield. *Dictionary of American Biography, Supplement Four: 1946–1950,* 89–91.

(115) 1975a. (Editor for posthumous publication of:) L. Bloomfield, *Menominee Lexicon.* Milwaukee Public Museum Publications in Anthropology and History, No. 3.

(116) 1975b. If you slice it thin enough it's not baloney. *American Speech* 47.233–255 (belatedly published issue for Fall-Winter 1972).

(117) 1976. A new point d'appui for phonology. In P. A. Reich, ed., *The Second Lacus Forum, 1975,* 67–90.

German translations of numbers (3), (20), and (48) appear in E. Bense, P. Eisenberg, and H. Haberland, eds., *Beschreibungsmethoden des amerikanischen Strukturalismus* (München: Max Hueber Verlag, 1976).

Number (96) is reprinted in a volume of offprints from *Scientific American* published by W. H. Freeman under the title *Biological Anthropology* (about 1975).

INDEX